ISBN: 9781314384758

Published by:
HardPress Publishing
8345 NW 66TH ST #2561
MIAMI FL 33166-2626

Email: info@hardpress.net
Web: http://www.hardpress.net

GENEALOGY COLLECTION

SHAKERS OF OHIO

Fugitive Papers Concerning the Shakers of
Ohio, With Unpublished Manuscripts

BY

J. P. MacLean, Ph. D.

Life Member Gaelic Society of Glasgow, and Clan MacLean Association of
Glasgow; Corresponding Member Davenport Academy of Sciences, and
Western Reserve Historical Society; Author of History of Clan
MacLean, Scotch Highlanders in America, Antiquity of
Man, The Mound Builders, Mastodon, Mammoth and
Man, Norse Discovery of America, Fingal's
Cave, Introduction Study St. John's
Gospel, Jewish Nature Worship,
Life of Richard McNemar,
Bibliography of Shaker
Literature, Etc.

ILLUSTRATED

COLUMBUS, O.
The F. J. Heer Printing Co.
1907

THE SHAKERS.

- -

BY RICHARD MCNEMAR.

Go search the whole creation, and trace the world around,
See if in any nation, a people can be found,
Whose doctrine and behavior is honest, just and true,
Who live like Christ the Savior; who are the faithful few.

To draw the perfect likeness of God's beloved few,
With justice and exactness, is more than I can do:
But give me leave to mention those virtues which excel,
Which grace the new creation, where God delights to dwell.

Upright in all their dealing, and just in ev'ry case —
A friendly, tender feeling for all the human race:
They follow Christ's example with all their heart and mind,
Like children mild and simple, long suff'ring, meek and kind.

In love they are united — They serve the Lord with zeal:
While others are invited to share the bliss they feel:
Their love cannot be mixed with that which leads to sin,
Nor is it solely fixed on self's beloved kin.

An int'rest they inherit, that strangers do not find,
A watchful pray'rful spirit, a peaceful humble mind:
A thankful heart possessing, to crosses reconcil'd,
And this ensures a blessing to ev'ry gospel child.

These are the heirs of heaven, and thither they are bound:
The likeness here is given, the people can be found;
With Christ they are partakers, tho' form'd of flesh and blood,
And you may call them Shakers, these people are of God.

(3)

PREFACE.

The publication of the collected papers on Shakerism in Ohio, contained in this volume, is due partly to the assistance of The Ohio State Archaeological and Historical Society, in the volumes of which some of the papers previously appeared. The Society not only willingly consented to the reprinting of these papers but also contributed to the expense of the same in recognition of the past services of the author to the Society. The author is also indebted in large measure to the enterprise of Mr. Fred J. Heer, one of the leading publishers in Ohio. The suggestion of this publication came from him. The author has no financial or other interest in the issuing of this volume, save only for the success of this undertaking and the hope that the information herein contained may add to the preservation of Ohio history and the correct understanding of the sect thus described.

The articles were written, the one independent of the other, just as the matter fell into the author's hands or the subject favorably impressed him. In all things he has tried to be just, and in no sense wrote with the idea of trying to please. It is a matter of pride, here to record, that his efforts for the most part, have met with the approval of the Shakers. Elder Daniel Offord, of the North Family, Mt. Lebanon, New York, stated, that of all who had written about the Shakers, the author had been the fairest, and the only one who had a thorough knowledge of the subject. Coming from such a source, it can but make these pages of value. To this might be added the fact that the writer has been made a member of four different communities.

This is not a history of Shakerism, for the purpose has been to confine the attention to Ohio, though necessarily touching on other communities outside this commonwealth. The Shakers, during their history, have changed very much, adapting themselves to conditions. In all probability this effort will be the last I shall put forth on the subject.

CONTENTS.

(7)

LIST OF ILLUSTRATIONS.

(8)

INTRODUCTION.

The first paper I prepared on Shakerism related to the extinct community once located near Cleveland, Ohio. I had no thought of pursuing my investigations any farther, until after I had accidentally come across a small pamphlet relating to the mob, which in 1810, assembled at Union Village, Ohio. Having written the accounts concerning Union village, the Mob of 1810, the Mission to the Shawnee Indians, and Spiritualism at Union Village, I abandoned all idea of writing anything further concerning the subject. Even after the MS. journals of Issachar Bates and Samuel P. McClelland were placed in my hands, I had no intention of pursuing the subject. An examination of the two last named MSS. aroused me to the fact that if anything was done pertaining to the history of Shakerism in Ohio, now was the time. The Shakers were few in number; many of their MSS. had been lost or destroyed; I had gained the confidence of those in authority, and what was to be done should no longer be delayed. As soon as possible I wrote a sketch of the life of Issachar Bates, an account of the extinct Society at West Union, Indiana, and the history of the Whitewater communiy, near Harrison, Ohio. The Church Record of the Watervleit Society had been mislaid; and was not recovered until March, 1905, though in the meantime, I wrote out a sketch of the society from such material as I could command. On the recovery of said record I proceeded to rewrite the account.

The "Life of Richard McNemar" and the "Bibliography of Shaker Literature," though intimately connected with Shakerism in Ohio, were published in separate form. To have included the same in this volume would have made the book too bulky.

In the composition of the various papers I have written, I have studiously avoided the discussion of doctrinal theories, because it would have been superfluous and no tangible results would have been derived therefrom. However, I take this occasion to correct a prevalent error. The Shakers do not and never did worship Ann Lee. They call her "Mother Ann" purely as a matter of veneration and respect for her memory. The same title was bestowed on Lucy Wright, Ruth Farrington and others. At the present time the belief is that Ann Lee was a highly gifted, spiritually minded woman, and by revelation the second appearing of Christ was manifested through her; but she was not so exalted in the spiritual realm as to be beyond the attainment of others.

Those desiring to enter into the dogmas of Shakerism will best promote their intentions by communicating directly with Believers, or else consulting their standard publications.

RISE OF SHAKERISM.

There were three religious upheavals that assisted in the promotion of the growth of Shakerism. The first of these was in 1779, or five years after the arrival of Ann Lee in America, which broke out at New Lebanon, Columbia County, New York. Of the origin and nature of this occurrence I am so little informed as not to pretend to give an intelligent answer. I do know, however, basing my judgment on Shaker documents, that out of it came a host of converts to Ann Lee.

The second upheaval was the Kentucky Revival of 1799-1805, of which I have treated at some length.

The last commotion was the Miller excitement of 1846, which rapidly increased the number of Shakers. All these upheavals had much of the millennium,* or second appearing of

---

* The doctrine of the Millenium, or visible reign of the Messiah, originated in the Messianic expectation of the Jews, and even more remotely in the Zoroastrian doctrine of the final triumph of Ormuzd over Ahriman, and by the Christians connected with Christ's second coming. This reign was to be preceded by great calamities. It was a wide spread belief during the first century; the fourth century saw the same doctrine, and in the fifth there were certain fanatics that indulged in the hope; but every now and then the doctrine made its appearance in the most sudden and obstinate manner; and by many the year 1000 A. D. was thought to be the Last Day. The Reformation gave a partial revival, and the pope became Anti-christ.—a belief still adhered to by many. The "Fifth Monarchy Men," of Cromwell's time were

Christ. As the millennium did not follow in the wake of the revival, the converts saw they had been duped. The Shakers appeared on the scene, and pointed out that the desired event had already appeared. It came as a healing balm to many a wound.

So long as the world looks forward to a millennial reign, so long will there be prophecies of its consummation being near at hand. Before speculating on the subject it would be well to listen to what Jesus himself declared on the subject: "There be some standing here, which shall not taste of death, till they see the Son of Man coming in his kingdom," Matt. xvi, 28. There is a class, who, seeing the force of this and other passages of Scripture, maintain a third appearing.

IMPEDIMENTS TO SHAKERISM.

The Shakers admit that during the past fifty years their Communities have been on the decline. In September, 1805, there were 126 Believers in Ohio. On April 30, 1811, at Union Village there were 300 members. At the present writing (1903), there are in Ohio, all told, 90, in the two existing communities. Some of the reasons for this decline may here be pointed out: The existence of all communistic societies depends on leadership. This leadership requires a peculiar combination of faculties. Of all those placed in the lead, at Union Village, David Darrow alone possessed the requisite qualifications. The supreme pontiff of Shakerism is an autocrat. To choose proper persons for lead is a rare gift, and the pontiff himself has not always been wise in making his selections. Nor is this all, nor the worst part, for the selection of a supreme pontiff has not always been a wise choice. The placing of the wrong man at the head of affairs, in the very nature of things, had a tendency to drive out strong men, and to keep strong men out. The early Shakers frowned upon a broad education, although there were some learned men

---

millenarians of an exaggerated type. The Thirty Years' War caused the doctrine to flourish. There have been many attempts to fix the date of the beginning of the millenium. Bengel fixed it at 1836, which became popular, especially in Germany. Swedenborg held that the judgment took place in 1757. Cumming fixed the time at 1866 or 1867.

in the ranks. Newspapers were not allowed to be generally circulated, and, for the most part, only Shaker books were read. This did cause trouble at Union Village, as the records amply testify. The younger Shakers saw the neighboring youth reaping advantages to which they were denied, which caused them to become unsettled and discontented. Social intercourse with those of other sects was not permitted, which could only breed irritations. The rules or government were unnecessarily severe, in so much so that only certain temperaments could submit to them.

In the closing chapter of "Shakerism: Its Meaning and Message," Eldress Anna White gives a masterly presentation of some of the difficulties with which the sect has been beset. She also sets forth the progressive nature of the aims or designs.

There has, however, been a marked reformation in the order, and many a fiction has been laid aside, so that, at the present time, there is no more discipline exerted than is found to be absolutely necessary. Still, existence, to a greater or less extent, depends upon the leader. When that leader is gifted, the spirit of liberty abounds, and an uplifting influence reigns.

THE SHAKERS AS A PEOPLE.

If the Shakers are not a happy people, it certainly is their own fault: for they are surrounded by all the comforts of life, and no restraint is placed on their opinions. They have no creed and the widest latitude is given for religious belief. Mr. Moore S. Mason, a Believer, volunteered to conduct me through all the buildings at Union Village. From garret to cellar, I was all through the dwellings. Everywhere there was cleanliness and order. The cellar was filled with useful stores. The gardens surpassed all those I had ever entered before. So far as I could see the members were happy and contented. By invitation of Eldress Clymena Miner I sat down with the family to a bountiful repast. No conversation, save that which was necessary, was indulged in. Each retired quietly when sufficed, without any ceremony. On retiring I asked my guide: "Do you live that well all the time?" He replied, "That is a sample of our usual meals." When I see the distress and hardship endured by so

...any deserving people who are and have been unfortunate, I can but wonder why they do not seek a retreat that presents so many advantages as afforded by the Shakers. Do not think the Shakers always wear somber faces. I have heard them roar with laughter, and I have engaged in the most lively conversation with them. They are of the same flesh and blood as other people, — only their discipline is of a different stamp. Nor must it be surmised that communism keeps down all ambition, or dwarfs the intellect. The Shakers have published quite a list of inventions made by their membership. Among these Elder John Martin, of Union Village, in 1847, invented a machine to knead dough. Of the invention of Daniel Baird I have mentioned in the article on North Union. The journal, under various names, published from 1871 to 1899, shows the Shakers of Ohio to have been possessed of literary taste and a poetic genius of no mean ability.

SHAKER HOMES.

Of the homes of the Shakers much has been written. Their buildings are large and strong, — constructed with a view to permanency. All resident houses in Ohio and Kentucky are built solid, and mostly of brick, and in the form of the letter T. Such houses in the Eastern States are of barn-like structure, save in a few instances. The Western houses have large hallways, with stairsteps on either side, — the one side for the sisters and the other for the brethren. Formerly the sexes were divided in respect to the side of the home occupied, but this is no longer observed.

The buildings show most excellent workmanship. The lands, orchards, and gardens, and all kinds of chattels exhibit thrift, plenty, and care. Of all the farms I have ever seen those of the Shakers are pre-eminent.

Of the management of the homes, the people had devised the most complete system. Every department had its head or lead. The elder and eldress presided over the family; the trustees looked after the finances of the estate; the deaconesses provided the provisions; there was a deacon for the yard, another for the orchard, etc., etc., so that everything received the utmost care. A system so complete kept everything in the highest pos-

sible state. The same spirit still continues, though lacking in
numbers prevents the glory of the ancient order.

The early leaders in the West were sent out from Mt. Lebanon, with a few from the Watervleit Society near Albany, in
New York. The parent society (Mount Lebanon) encouraged
the Western missions financially, as well as in actual members
sent. In a letter from Alonzo G. Hollister to Elder Andrew
Barrett, dated May 31, 1903, I find that in 1805, the first three
delegations of Shakers to the West, set out with $5,467; in 1812
the sum of $750 was contributed; in 1814, $1,335, and $150 in
1818. This does not cover the entire amount, for the archives
of the Mt. Lebanon Ministry exhibit that the Mt. Lebanon community contributed $18,793; Hancock, Mass., and Enfield,
Conn., $3,009; Canterbury, N. H., $3,750, and Enfield, N. H.,
$1,375, or a total of $26,927. A large percentage of this amount
helped defray the personal expenses of the first missionaries and
the rovings of the Central or Mt. Lebanon Ministry. Of the
$5,467, sent in 1805, $1,640 was used to purchase land, or what
was termed the Ministry's Lot, at Union Village; and as there
were sixteen sent in the three companies, that would leave on an
average of $238, which would be a moderate sum for traveling
expenses and first year's support. None of this money was
wasted, for the early Shakers were frugal and every investment
made judicious. All this money was afterwards returned to Mt.
Lebanon. The $1,640, used to purchase the Ministry's Lot, was
the last refunded, which was in 1841 or 1842. At that time
Ithamar Johnson was one of the trustees, and he refused permission to build the present residence (completed in 1844) until
the debt was paid. When Benjamin Seth Youngs was recalled
in 1835, South Union, Ky., sent $500 by him to cancel an old
donation.

It is more than probable that persecutions and legal obstruc-
tions helped to swell the ranks of early Believers. The legisla-
tures of New Hampshire, New York and Kentucky caused much

perplexity and vexation to such societies as were under their respective jurisdictions. It remained, however, to the legislature of Ohio to enact a law, sufficient to make the state a hissing and a by-word through all time. This oppressive law was enacted January 11, 1811.* When William Henry Harrison became a

---

* "An act providing for the relief and support of women who may be abandoned by their husbands, and for other purposes.

"WHEREAS, it is represented to the general assembly, that a sect of people in this state, called and known by the name of Shakers, inculcate and enjoin upon all who become attached to them, that they must lead a life of *celibacy*, in consequence of which women have been abandoned by their husbands, robbed of their children, and left destitute of the means of support. — Therefore

"Sect. 1. *Be it enacted by the General Assembly of the State of Ohio,* That, if any man being joined in marriage relation, shall renounce the marriage covenant, or refuse to live with his wife in the conjugal relation, by joining himself to any sect, whose rules and doctrines require a renunciation of the marriage covenant, or forbid a man and woman to dwell and cohabit together in the conjugal relation, according to the true interest and meaning of the institution of marriage, it shall and may be lawful for the wife in such case, to file her petition in the office of the clerk of the court, at least two months before the time of the sitting of said court, and shall also serve the adverse party with a copy of said petition, within one month from the time of filing the same, which petition shall state the true cause of complaint. And in case he shall not reside in her county, she shall publish such notice in some newspaper published in said county, or in next adjacent county in which a newspaper is published.

"Sect. 2. *Be it further enacted,* That it shall be the duty of the clerk of such court, where the petition is filed, to issue a summons requiring the person complained of, to appear before the said court to answer the allegation of said petition; and, if the party complained of shall not appear, or appearing shall deny the facts stated in the petition, the court shall proceed to hear and determine the same.

"Sect. 3. *Be it further enacted,* That if it shall appear to the said court, that the woman complaining has been lawfully married to the man of whom complaint is made, and that he hath renounced or violated the marriage covenant by joining such sect as above described, the court shall take such measures as to them shall seem right, to ascertain the amount of the property real and personal of such husband, and shall decree such part thereof to the woman as shall appear just and equitable.

"Sect. 4. *Be it further enacted,* That if the said husband and wife shall have a child or children (yet being in a state of minority), the husband so violating the marriage covenant shall be considered as having

member of the legislature, in 1821, he caused an enactment to be made relieving the Shakers from militia† duty, by working out an equivalent on the public highway, a remedy meeting their approval.

If trouble does not manifest itself along one line, it is very likely to present itself in another. Unfortunately some men had been placed in authority who were deficient in financial ability. Sharks have taken advantage of this and have not scrupled to plunge societies into debt. Once lawyers looked upon the Shakers as beings who were sincere and doing the work of the Lord.

---

renounced and divested himself of all the authority he could have otherwise exercised over his children, and the court shall decree such part (or the whole) of the remainder of his property, real and personal, as to them shall seem right, to the use and support of the child or children aforesaid; and such child or children shall be, and remain under the care and direction of the mother: — *Provided,* that the court shall have power, if they shall deem it necessary, to appoint a guardian or guardians for such child or children, agreeably to the provisions of the thirty-fourth and thirty-fifth sections of the act, entitled "an act for the proving and recording wills and codicils, defining the duties of executors and administrators, the appointment of guardians, and the distribution of insolvent estates, passed February tenth, one thousand eight hundred and ten: *And provided, also,* that if the court shall deem it necessary, they may direct such child or children to be bound to apprenticeship, agreeably to the sixth section of the act, entitled 'an act for the relief of the poor,' passed February nineteenth, one thousand eight hundred and ten.

"Sect. 5. *Be it further enacted,* That all gifts, grants, or devises of money or property, real or personal, which may be made by any man as aforesaid, violating the marriage covenant, to such sect as before described, or any members of such sect, which may tend to deprive his wife or children of that support to which they are entitled, according to the true intent and meaning of this act, shall be utterly void; and all money or property so given, granted or devised, may be recovered at the suit of the party injured.

"Sect. 6. *And be it further enacted,* That if any person shall, with an intent of causing any married man or woman, to renounce the marriage covenant, or abandon their wives, husbands, or children, entice or persuade such person to join any sect, or denomination of persons whatever, whose principles and practice inculcate a renunciation of the matrimonial contract, or the abandonment of wives and children, or either of them, contrary to the true intent and meaning of the marriage institution, shall, on conviction thereof be fined in any sum not exceeding five hundred dollars, at the discretion of the court having by law j:;risdiction; and that all fines incurred under this section, shall be paid into the treasury of the proper county for the use of the same: *Provided,* that nothing in this section contained shall be construed or understood to extend to any person for delivery any public sermon, exhortation or address.*

"This act shall take effect and be in force from the passage thereof.

Edward Tiffin,
Speaker of the House of Representatives.

Thos. Kirker,
Speaker of the Senate."

Janary 11, 1811.
Laws of Ohio, Vol. IX, pp. 13-16, 1811.

To-day they look upon the Shakers as legal prey, whatever might be the nature of their distress. It might be well to notice that this people were fleeced out of $12,000 in defense of North Union; another case for legal services was $5,000 and afterwards $5,000 more; but a strong case was that of an Eastern sister having been invited by a lawyer to spend an evenng at his home. During the conversation, at his residence, she asked him, for the sake of information, some questions pertaining to law. Soon after he sent to the society a bill of $250 for legal advice.

It might be well to note that a former merchant prince of Chicago, whose name has been often mentioned in terms of great praise, through one of his agents, mulcted the Shakers of Union.

---

† I fail to find the enactment in the Laws of Ohio for 1821. The Shakers later were persecuted for military fines.

On January 27, 1818, the Ohio Legislature, among other militia laws, passed the following:

"Be it further enacted, That in collecting all fines, assessed by the provisions of this act, all stewards, managers, agents, trustees or elders of any connected or associated society, whose property is all vested in common stock, shall be bound for each and every member thereof, who is liable to do military duty, and the common stock, goods, chattels, lands and tenements, of all or any body or bodies so connected or associated, shall be held liable and bound for the payment of any fines assessed by the provisions of this act." This act is not found with the regular session laws, but with the militia laws, which was published separately in a pamphlet of 76 pages. The above clause may be found on page 12.

It was the above clause that caused the Shakers to issue their address "to the civil rulers and citizens of the state of Ohio, and all whom it may concern," in a pamphlet of 24 pages.

2

Village, out of $40,000 in cash. The money was a part of the proceeds of the sale of the North Union property.

SHAKER CONSCIOUSNESS.

The Shakers are not and have not been a boastful people. Their mode of life practically forbids them from being aggressive. They are and have been unobtrusive, being devoted to the cause of religion and practicing the Christian graces. In their vicinage they have left an impress for good. From their communities thousands have gone forth schooled in the purest morals and an implicit faith in the Divine Being. Whatever the world may think, yet the simple fact remains that Shakerism has been an active example of the quiet life and simplicity of habits as well as an intelligent view of the Creator.

THE KENTUCKY REVIVAL AND ITS INFLUENCE ON THE MIAMI VALLEY.

The Miami Valley properly embraces all the country north of the Ohio that is drained by the Great and Little Miami rivers and their tributaries. In this paper it is used to designate the southwestern quarter of the State of Ohio, or that territory lying west of a line drawn due south from Columbus to the Ohio river and south of another line drawn due west from Columbus to the State of Indiana. This district was greatly excited and stirred up by the "Great Kentucky Revival," and its camp-meetings lasted for a period of over fifty years.

Owing to the rapidity of the increase in population and the advent of foreigners with their variant sectaries, it is difficult to measure the depth of the influence of the enthusiasm resultant from the religious upheaval of 1801. However diverse may have been the elements to be operated upon, there was sufficient time and opportunity to carry out the work of the reformers.

The year 1800 showed Ohio with a population of about 45,-000 and Cincinnati with about 500. In 1810 the city had increased to 2,540 and the entire state to 230,760. The population was principally made up of emigrants from the older states. Kentucky, with a population of 73,677 in 1790, had increased to 220,959 in 1800 and 406,511 in 1810. These figures show both states to have been sparsely settled, when considered with the present population. The settlements were almost wholly communities of farmers. Books and newspapers were but sparingly supplied to them, and religion was their chief intellectual food. Without the advantages enjoyed by their descendants, scattered, though naturally gregarious, a religious revival would hold out its allurements to all alike.

STATE OF SOCIETY.

The early settlers of both Ohio and Kentucky, for the most part, were Christians by profession. Different denominations of religionists were early in the field, employing their zeal in making proselytes and propagating their respective tenets. The great majority ranked among the Presbyterians, Baptists and Methodists. The first church organized in Ohio was the Baptist church at Columbia, near Cincinnati, in 1790, and the build-

[Columbia Baptist Church, constituted by Dr. Stephen Gano, in 1790.]

ing erected in 1793, which stood until 1835. In 1797, besides the Presbyterian church at Cincinnati, there were preaching points at Clear Creek (a short distance south of Franklin), Turtle Creek (now Union Village, west of Lebanon), Bethany (two miles east of Lebanon) and Big Prairie (at the mouth of Dick's Creek in Butler county, afterwards called Orangedale). Of these country congregations the largest and most influential was Turtle Creek.

The various sects, acknowledging one another as of the same parent stock, "stood entirely separate as to any communion or fellowship, and treated each other with the highest marks of hostility; wounding, captivating and bickering another, until their attention was called off by the appearance of" deism. As early as 1796 a religious apathy appears to have pervaded the pulpit. One writes, "the dead state of religion is truly discouraging here, as well as elsewhere;" another says ,"I have this winter past preached with difficulty, my heart but little enjoyed," and still another, "I see but little prospect of encouragement."* However dark the picture may be painted, the despondent were soon awakened to what they deemed a season of refreshment.

THE KENTUCKY REVIVAL.

During the year 1799, on the Gasper, in Logan County, Ky., on land now owned and occupied by the Shakers, of South Union, there began a religious revival, which was the precursor of the most wonderful upheaval ever experienced in Christian work. The excitement commenced under the labors of John Rankin. Where this awakening commenced a church still stands, some three miles from church founded at South Union, owned by the Cumberland Presbyterians. Almost immediately James McGready, also a Presbyterian clergyman, was seized with this same spirit as possessed by Rankin. He has been described as a homely man, with sandy hair and rugged features, and was so terrific in holding forth the terrors of hell that he was called a son of thunder. He pictured out "the furnace of hell with its red-hot coals of God's wrath as large as mountains;" he would open to the sinner's view "the burning lake of hell, to see its fiery billows rolling, and to hear the yells and groans of the damned ghosts roaring under the burning wrath of an angry God." Under his preaching the people would fall down with a loud cry and lie powerless, or else groaning, praying, or crying to God for mercy. The news of the excitement spread not only over Kentucky, but also

---

* McNemar's "Kentucky Revival," p. 13.

into Ohio and Tennessee, and people rushed to the Gasper to witness the scenes and returned to their homes carrying a measure of the enthusiasm with them. Among those drawn to the spot was Barton W Stone, afterwards the head of a new sect. Early in the spring of 1801 he repaired to the scene of excitement, which was now carried on by several Presbyterian ministers, headed by James McGready. "There, on the edge of a prairie in Logan County, Kentucky, the multitudes came together, and continued a number of days and nights encamped on the ground; during which time worship was carried on in some part of the encampment. The scene to me was new and passing strange. It baffled description. Many, very many, fell down, as men slain in battle, and continued for hours together in an apparently breathless and motionless state—sometimes for a few moments reviving, and exhibiting symptoms of life by a deep groan, or piercing shriek, or by a prayer for mercy most fervently uttered."* At this time Stone was preaching at Cane Ridge and Concord, in Bourbon county, under the Presbytery of Transylvania. He returned home, believing that he had "witnessed the work of God." Multitudes awaited his return at Cane Ridge; and he effected the congregation "with awful solemnity, and many returned home weeping." That night he preached at Concord where "two little girls were struck down under the preaching of the word, and in every respect were exercised as those were in the south of Kentucky. Their addresses made deep impressions on the congregation. On the next day I returned to Cane Ridge, and attended my appointment at William Maxwell's. I soon heard of the good effects of the meeting on the Sunday before. Many were solemnly engaged in seeking salvation, and some had found the Lord, and were rejoicing in Him. Among these last was my particular friend Nathaniel Rogers, a man of first respectability and influence in the neighborhood. Just as I arrived at the gate, my friend Rogers and his lady came up; as soon as he saw me, he shouted aloud the praises of God. We hurried into each other's embrace, he still praising the Lord aloud. The crowd left the house, and hurried to this novel scene. In less than twenty

---

* "Biography of Stone," p. 34.

minutes, scores had fallen to the ground—paleness, trembling,. and anxiety appeared in all—some attempted to fly from the scene panic stricken, but they either fell, or returned immediately to the crowd, as unable to get away."*

The revival became a veritable contagion. Its operations flew abroad and stirred up the curious, the sincere and the indifferent. Multitudes poured into the various meetings and the strange exercises increasing, no respect for stated hours was observed, and then it was deemed expedient to encamp on the ground, and continue the meeting day and night. To the various encampments they flocked in hundreds and thousands; on foot, on horseback, and in various vehicles.

By January 30, 1801, the excitement had reached Nashville, Barren, Muddy, Knoxville and other places. Owing to the multitudes attending the meetings, the encampments took the name of "Camp Meetings." The camp-meeting once so popular had its origin in Kentucky, in 1801. It grew out of a necessity, but was prolonged until its usefulness had not only departed, but became a stench, a byword, a demoralizing power and a blighting curse.

As camp meetings became the order of the day, the first of note began at Cabin Creek, Lewis County, Kentucky, May 22, 1801, and continued four days and three nights. Attending this meeting were persons from Cane Ridge and Concord, and also Eagle Creek, in Ohio. The next general camp-meeting, was at Concord, in Bourbon county in May and June, same year. There were about 4,000 people present, among whom were seven Presbyterian clergymen. Of these, four spoke against the work until noon of the fourth day, when they professed to be convinced that "it was the work of God." This meeting continued five days and four nights. The next was held at Eagle Creek, Adams County, Ohio, beginning June 5th, and continuing four days and three nights. The country being new, the outpouring was not so great. Following this was the one at Pleasant Point, Kentucky, which equalled, or even surpassed any of the previous mentioned. This meeting spread the work extensively through Bourbon, Fayette

* *Ibid*, p. 36.

and adjoining counties. The meeting at Indian Creek, Harrison county, began July 24th, and continued nearly a week. Next came the great meeting at Cane Ridge, seven miles from Paris, beginning August 6th. The number of people on the ground at one time was supposed to have numbered 20,000. The encampment consisted of one hundred and thirty-five wheel-carriages, and tents proportioned to the people. Rev. James Crawford, who kept as accurate account as he could on that occasion, computed there were 3,000 that fell on that occasion, or an average of 500 a day.

The people among whom the revival began were generally Calvinists, and all the principal leaders were clergymen of the Presbyterian church; yet other sects were rapidly swept into the maelstrom. Generally the first affected were children, and from them the contagion spread. "A boy, from appearance about twelve years old, retired from the stand in time of preaching, under a very extraordinary impression; and having mounted a log, at some distance, and raising his voice, in a very affecting manner, he attracted the main body of the people in a few minutes. With tears streaming from his eyes, he cried aloud to the wicked, warning them of their danger, denouncing their certain doom, if they persisted in their sins; expressing his love to their souls, and desire that they would turn to the Lord and be saved. He was held up by two men, and spoke for about an hour with that convincing eloquence that could be inspired only from above. When his strength seemed quite exhausted and language failed to describe the feelings of his soul, he raised his hand, and dropping his handkerchief, wet with sweat from his little face, cried out, 'Thus, O sinner! shall you drop into hell, unless you forsake your sins and turn to the Lord.' At that moment some fell, like those who are shot in battle, and the work spread in a manner which human language cannot describe." *

One of the affecting speakers was Vincy McNemar, daughter of Richard, nine years of age. Her father held her on his arm while she addressed the multitude.†

---

* McNemar's "Kentucky Revival," p. 25.
† Vincy afterwards became a prominent Shaker. I have a kerchief owned by her, presented to me by Eldress Clymena Miner.

PHYSICAL PHENOMENA.

The strange manifestations appertained to all the camp meetings. What would be a description of one would be the same recital in all, perhaps, varying only in excess. These excesses have thus been described by Barton W. Stone: "The bodily agitations or exercises, attending the excitement in the beginning of this century, were various, and called by various names: —as the falling exercise—the jerks—the dancing exercise—the barking exercise—the laughing and singing exercise, etc.—The falling exercise was very common among all classes, the saints and sinners of every age and of every grade, from the philosopher to the clown. The subject of this exercise would, generally, with a piercing scream, fall like a log on the floor, earth, or mud, and appear as dead. * * * I have seen very many pious persons fall in the same way, from a sense of the danger of their unconverted children, brothers, or sisters—from a sense of the danger of their neighbors, and of the sinful world. I have heard them agonizing in tears and strong crying for mercy to be shown to sinners, and speaking like angels to all around.

The jerks cannot be so easily described. Sometimes the subject of the jerks would be affected in some one member of the body, and sometimes in the whole system. When the head alone was affected, it would be jerked backward and forward, or from side to side, so quickly that the features of the face could not be distinguished. When the whole system was affected, I have seen the person stand in one place, and jerk backward and forward in quick succession, their heads nearly touching the floor behind and before. All classes, saints and sinners, the strong as well as the weak, were thus affected. I have inquired of those thus affected. They could not account for it; but some have told me that those were among the happiest seasons of their lives. I have seen some wicked persons thus affected, and all the time cursing the jerks, while they were thrown to the earth with violence. Though so awful to behold, I do not remember that any one of the thousands I have seen ever sustained an injury in body. This was as strange as the exercise itself.

The dancing exercise. This generally began with the jerks, and was peculiar to professors of religion. The subject, after jerking awhile, began to dance, and then the jerks would cease. Such dancing was indeed heavenly to the spectators; there was nothing in it like levity, nor calculated to excite levity in the beholders. The saints of heaven shone on the countenance of the subject, and assimilated to angels appeared the whole person. Sometimes the motion was. quick and sometimes slow. Thus they continued to move forward and backward in the same track or alley till nature seemed exhausted, and they would fall prostrate on the floor or earth, unless caught by those standing by. While thus exercised, I have heard their solemn praises and prayers ascending to God.

The barking exercise (as opponents contemptuously called it), was nothing but the jerks. A person affected with the jerks, especially in his head, would often make a grunt, or bark, if you please, from the suddenness of the jerk. This name of barking seems to have had its origin from an old Presbyterian preacher of East Tennessee. He had gone into the woods for private devotion, and was seized with the jerks. Standing near a sapling, he caught hold of it, to prevent his falling, and as his head jerked back, he uttered a grunt or kind of noise similar to a bark, his face being turned upwards. Some wag discovered him in this position, and reported that he found him barking up a tree.

The laughing exercise was frequent, confined solely with the religious. It was a loud, hearty laughter, but one *sui generis;* it excited laughter in none else. The subject appeared rapturously solemn, and his thoughts excited solemnity in saints and sinners. It is truly indescribable.

The running exercise was nothing more than, that persons feeling something of these bodily agitations, through fear, attempted to run away, and thus escape from them; but it commonly happened that they ran not far, before they fell, or became so greatly agitated that they could proceed no farther.
* * *

I shall close this chapter with the singing exercise. This is more unaccountable than anything else I ever saw. The subject in a very happy state of mind would sing most melodiously, not from the mouth or nose, but entirely in the breast, the sounds issuing thence. Such music silenced everything, and attracted the attention of all. It was most heavenly. None could ever be tired of hearing it."*

Richard McNemar, who wrote the most complete history of the Kentucky Revival, applies the above exercises to the Schismatics, or New Lights, or Christians, as they called themselves, but also supplies another, which he called "The rolling exercise." "This consisted in being cast down in a violent manner, doubled with the head and feet together, and rolled over and over like a wheel, or stretched in a prostrate manner, turned swiftly over and over like a log. This was considered very debasing and mortifying, especially if the person was taken in this manner through the mud and sullied therewith from head to foot." (Page 64.)

PERSONNEL OF THE REVIVAL.

While the revival was distinctively a Presbyterian one, yet, the Methodist Church was drawn almost bodily into it. While individuals from other sects participated in the meetings and came under the influence of the mesmeric current, yet the respective denominations of these latter were not thereby materially affected. Nor is it to be presumed that every individual who witnessed this carnival of folly were deluded into the conviction that "it was the work of the Lord." Stone admitted† that "in the wonderful things that appeared in the great excitement," "that there were many eccentricities, and much fanaticism," which "was acknowledged by its warmest advocates." The people were gathered into an atmosphere pregnant with animal excitement, mesmeric force and religious zeal which would readily operate on the sensitives, the impulsives, the excitables, the ignorant and the weak. The character of the leaders, however, is a guarantee of their honesty. Even in later campmeetings which had a blighting influence on community, it must be admitted that the intent was for the public weal.

---

* *Biography of B. W. Stone,* p. 39.

† Biography, p. 42.

It would be impossible, even to call by name all the active participants in the great revival. However there are characters that stand out conspicuously in every movement supported by influence and numbers. To Richard McNemar has been assigned the post of first importance. He regarded the phenomena as a miraculous work. He was tall and gaunt, commanding in appearance, with piercing, restless eyes, ever in motion, with a very expressive countenance. His manner of preaching was fervent and exciting, full of animation and vociferation, which gave him great power over his audiences. With all this he was a classical scholar and read Latin, Greek and Hebrew with ease.

Probably next in importance was Barton W. Stone, who has been described as a man of great independence of mind, and of firmness and decision of character. As an orator he was gifted with the power of swaying his audience. John Dunlavy possessed a clear, penetrating mind, was scholarly in his habits, but not very aggressive. He inclined to studious habits. David Purviance possessed energy, clear perceptions, honesty of purpose, and disinterested motives. Malcolm Worley, possessing much ability, was excitable and somewhat eccentric, but never at a loss to act when convinced of his duties. Robert Marshall was conservative, lenient, and somewhat vacillating.

DISCORD AND DISUNION.

Whatever zeal may have been felt or displayed in the revival, there were elements of discord that had their origin anterior to the awakening. Heresy had been implanted in the hearts of certain of the Presbyterian ministers even before the year 1800. Just what influence had been exerted by the Methodist doctrine of free grace, might be difficult to fathom at this late date; but as is well known, the doctrinally tutored, though illiterate pioneer Methodist preachers did herculean service in storming the citadel of ultra-Calvinism. In the year 1793 Barton W. Stone was a candiate for admission into Orange Presbytery in North Carolina. Previously he had been a teacher in a

Methodist school in Washington, Georgia. In 1797, we find he was in the Presbyterian churches at Cane Ridge and Concord, in Kentucky, but did not receive "the call" until 1798. "Knowing that at my ordination I should be required to adopt the Confession of Faith, as the system of doctrines taught in the Bible, I determined to give it a careful examination once more. This was to me almost the beginning of sorrows. I stumbled at the doctrine of Trinity as taught in the Confession; I labored to believe it, but could not conscientiously subscribe to it. Doubts, too, arose in my mind on the doctrines of election, reprobation, and predestination as there taught. I had before this time learned from my superiors the way of divesting those doctrines of their hard, repulsive features, and admitted them as true, yet unfathomable mysteries."* When the day of ordination came, Stone frankly informed Doctor James Blythe and Robert Marshall, the state of his doubts. In vain they labored to remove his difficulties and objections; but when Stone informed them that he was willing to receive the Confession as far as it was "consistent with the word of God," upon that admission the Presbytery of Transylvania ordained him. By the year 1801 he had cordially abandoned Calvinism, though still retaining his charge at Cane Ridge and Concord.

The minutes of the Presbytery of Washington, at its session at Springfield (Springdale, Ohio) on November 11, 1801, show the decision respecting charges that had been made against Richard McNemar, respecting certain doctrines advocated by him.

It should be specially noted that at the commencement of the "revival, preachers in general, who were truly engaged in it, omitted the doctrines of election and reprobation, as explained in the Confession of Faith, and proclaimed a free salvation to all men, through the blood of the Lamb. They held forth the promises of the gospel in their purity and simplicity, without the contradictory explanations, and double meaning, which scholastic divines have put upon them, to make them agree with the doctrines of the Confession. This omission caused their preaching

---

* *Ibid,* p. 29.

to appear somewhat different from what had been common among Presbyterians; and although no direct attack was made on these doctrines, as formerly explained; yet a murmuring arose because they were neglected in the daily ministration. This murmuring was heard in different parts of the country; but, notwithstanding, preachers and people treated with each other with toleration and forbearance, until a direct opposition to the new mode of preaching took place in the congregation of Cabin Creek."* These complaints, as previously noted, were formulated against Richard McNemar.

As the campmeetings were places where clergymen resorted as well as the multitude, it is but natural to assume that kindred spirits were attracted together, and thus were enabled to exchange opinions and advise with one another. The tendency of such communications, when free and unrestricted, would, sooner or later, constitute dissimilar aggregations. Hence it is not singular that other sects should be formed. Out of the Kentucky revival there originated three sects, or religious denominations entirely new to the western country. The first to notice is the

CUMBERLAND PRESBYTERIANS.

The Cumberland Presbyterian Church takes its name from the Cumberland Presbytery, which was a part of the Synod of Kentucky. This presbytery was not constituted until 1802, which then was struck off from Transylvania. Cumberland Presbytery was greatly divided on the subject of the great revival then in the full force of its existence. The great tide of immigration into the Cumberland Presbytery and the interest awakened by the revival, showed a dearth of preachers and religious teachers. Under the advice of Rev. David Rice, then the oldest Presbyterian minister in Kentucky, a number of men were licensed to preach who did not possess a classical education. Against this procedure a protest was entered by those not in sympathy with the revival. In the new Presbytery the majority favored the revival work and the licensing of probationers without a classical education.

_____

* *Ibid.* p. 148.

During the controversy about the revival, the Cumberland Presbytery licensed and ordained a number who took exceptions to the idea of "Fatality" as expressed in the doctrines of Decrees and Election in chapter 3 of the Confession. The Synod of 1804 cited all the members of Cumberland Presbytery to appear at its next meeting. The citation was disobeyed on the grounds of want of authority. Owing to the action of the Synod, in other matters, a new Presbytery was proclaimed and met March 20, 1810. This Presbytery accepted the Confession of Faith, excepting the idea of fatality; but in 1813 when the first Synod was formed, a brief doctrinal statement was adopted, which gave the points of difference from the Westminster Confession. The points expressed against the idea of "Fatality" are "(1) There are no eternal reprobates. (2) Christ died not for a part only, but for all mankind. (3) That all infants dying in infancy are saved through Christ and the sanctification of the Spirit. (4) The Spirit of God operates on the world; or, as coextensively as Christ has made the Atonement in such a manner as to leave all men inexcusable."

This young denomination did not stretch its arm into the Miami country until long after the ground was preoccupied. The first church was established at Lebanon, in Warren county, in 1835. At the present time there are twelve churches, seven of which sustain preaching all the time. Their buildings represent a value of $40,000. What influence this church has exerted in the Miami could not be told, or wherein it has prepared the way for other thought. Sometimes church literature is more potent than the congregation. Of the literature of this demonination I am absolutely ignorant, not even knowing the title of a single volume. Hence I must rest this part of the discussion with the facts above enumerated derived from sources without the Church, excepting the statistics.

THE CHRISTIAN CHURCH.

The sect, or new denomination, growing out of the Kentucky revival, which has exerted most power over the Miami, is generally called "New Lights," and sometimes "Schismatics." The sect repudiates both these names, and styles itself "The Christian

Church." According to Levi Purviance it assumed the name Christian in 1804.* The origin of this sect in the West may be said to date its birth at the time charges were preferred against Richard McNemar, although the actual separation did not take place until the month of May, 1803. For some unaccountable reason Richard McNemar passes over his trial, but says that a particular account of the separation "is published in a pamphlet, entitled, *An apology for renouncing the jurisdiction of the Synod of Kentucky,* printed in Lexington (K.), 1804." This *apology* is published in full in the "Biography of B. W. Stone," covering one hundred pages. The historical part, with which we are concerned, embraces forty-four pages, written by Robert Marshall. The second part pertains to dogma, written by Stone, and part three by John Thompson discusses the Westminster Confession of Faith.

The trial of McNemar brought prominently out the fact that similar views were entertained by John Thompson, John Dunlavy, Robert Marshall and B. W. Stone. To these must be added David Purviance, then a licentiate. Soon after Matthew Houston was added to the list. At the time of the final separation, McNemar, Dunlavy and Thompson were in Ohio and Stone, Marshall, Houston and Purviance in Kentucky. As the *Apology* is entirely too long to quote in this connection, an epitome of the first part must suffice:

On November 3, 1801, three elders of Cabin-creek Presbyterian church, made formal charges to the Washington Presbytery, against their pastor, Richard McNemar, which charges are thus stated:

"1. He reprobated the idea of sinners attempting to pray, or being exhorted thereto, before they were believers in Christ.

2. He has condemned those who urge that convictions are necessary, or that prayer is proper in the sinner.

3. He has expressly declared, at several times, that Christ has purchased salvation for all the human race, without distinction.

4. He has expressly declared that a sinner has power to believe in Christ at any time.

---

* *Biography of David Purviance,* p. 49.

5. That a sinner has as much power to act faith, as to act unbelief; and reprobated every idea in contradiction thereto, held by persons of a contrary opinion.

6. He has expressly said, that faith consisted in the creature's persuading himself assuredly, that Christ died for him in particular; that doubting and examining into evidences of faith, were inconsistent with, and contrary to the nature of faith; and in order to establish these sentiments, he explained away these words — *Faith is the gift of God,* by saying it was Christ Jesus, the object of faith there meant, and not faith itself; and also, these words, "No man can come to me, except the Father who hath sent me draw him," by saying that the drawing there meant, was Christ offered in the Gospel; and that the Father knew no other drawing or higher power, than holding up his Son in the Gospel."

At the meeting of the Presbytery. McNemar made the following explanation of his ideas:

Upon the first charge, he observed, that faith was the first thing God required of the sinner; and that he had no idea of him praying but in faith.

On the second, that the question in debate was, whether any other considerations are necessary to authorize the soul to believe than those which arise from the testimony of God, in his word.

On the third, that Christ is by office the Savior of all men.

On the fourth, that the sinner is capable of receiving the testimony of God at any time he heard it.

Upon the fifth, that the sinner is as capable of believing as disbelieving, according to the evidence presented to the view of his mind.

The first part of the sixth charge was groundless.

On the second, which respects doubting and self-examination, his ideas were, that doubting the veracity of God, and looking into ourselves for evidence, as the foundation of our faith, is contrary to Scripture.

On the third part, viz., explaining away those Scriptures, he replied, if that was explaining them away, he had done it.

As no person present purposed to substantiate the charges, the same was dismissed as irregular. This action of the Presbytery quenched the flame of opposition, and all parties became reconciled.

In 1802 McNemar took charge of the Turtlecreek church (near Lebanon, Ohio), where his labors met with abundant success. At the meeting of Presbytery in Cincinnati, October 6, 1802, an elder of Rev. James Kemper's congregation (Cincinnati), entered a verbal complaint against McNemar, as a propagator of false doctrine. The accused insisted the question was out of order, for charges must be made in writing. Nevertheless Presbytery proceeded to examine him "on the fundamental doc-

CINCINNATI IN 1802.

trines of the sacred Scriptures," which were election, human depravity, the atonement, etc. The finding was that McNemar held these doctrines in a sense different from that in which Calvinists generally believe them, and that his sentiments were "hostile to the interests of all true religion." Notwithstanding this condemnation he was appointed one-half his time at Turtle-creek, until the next stated session: two Sabbaths at Orangeville; two at Clear-creek; two at Beulah; one at the forks of Mad river; and the rest at discretion.

At the next session at Springfield* in April, 1803, a petition from a number of persons, in the congregations of Beulah, Turtle-creek, Clear-creek, Bethany, Hopewell, Dicks-creek, and Cincinnati, was presented praying for a re-examination of McNemar,

---

* Springdale, some eleven miles north of Cincinnati.

and that Rev. John Thompson undergo a like examination. The Presbytery refused, to acquiesce. A petition, signed by sixty persons of the Turtle-creek congregation, asked for the whole of McNemar's time, which was granted. Kemper, Wallace, Reader, and Wheeler protested against the action of the Presbytery. The sentiment of the majority of Presbytery had changed and was now in sympathy with the accused.

In the interval between the meeting of Presbytery and that of Synod, no pains were taken by the disaffected members to bring about an accommodation. Through the committee of overtures the matter was brought before the Synod, held at Lexington, September, 1803. The Synod sustained the action of the Presbytery at Cincinnati, except that part which assigned appointments to McNemar, and condemned the action at Springfield. The Synod further voted to enter upon an examination of both McNemar and Thompson. While the Synod was deliberating upon the last proposition (September 10), Messrs. Marshall, Dunlavy, McNemar, Stone and Thompson, entered the meeting and formally protested against its action. The protest was read, and its advocates retired. Synod then appointed a committee consisting of David Rice, Matthew Houston, James Welsh and Joseph Howe to confer with the aggrieved, which latter offered to answer any questions proposed by Synod, provided all questions and answers should be in writing; that they should be constituted into one Presbytery, and that all charges of doctrine against them should be according to the book of discipline. On a motion to accede to these proposals the following voted in the affirmative: M. Houston, J. Welsh, J. Howe, and W. Robinson, ministers; J. Henderson, J. Wardlow and C. McPheeters, elders; those opposed, A. Cameron, P. Tull, J. Blythe, J. Lyle, R. Stewart, S. Rannels, J. Kemper, J. Campbell, S. Finley, ministers; J. Moore, John Henderson and T. Bennington, elders. 1359790

Immediately, after the action of the Synod, Robert Marshall, John Dunlavy, Richard McNemar, Barton W. Stone and John Thompson, withdrew from the jurisdiction of the Synod of Kentucky, and formally constituted the Presbytery of Springfield, and formulated a circular letter addressed to the congregations under their care. Late in the evening a resolution was received from the Synod which had appointed a committee to inquire into such objections as they might have to the Confession of Faith. Before the answer was received Synod suspended the protesting members, and declared their parishes without ministers. The Springfield Presbytery was dissolved at Cane Ridge, Bourbon county, Ky., June 28, 1804, by Marshall, Dunlavy, McNemar, Stone, Thompson and David Purviance.

McNemar has been described to have been a mild and unassuming man up to the time of charges of heresy being made against him. His trials appear to have awakened all the resources of his strong nature. With enthusiasm he began his work at Turtle Creek, and in summer his congregations were so large that the meetings were held in the grove near his church. The strange physical phenomena of the revival attended his ministrations in Warren county, Ohio. At Turtle Creek almost all the adult persons in a large congregation would fall in a short time and lie unconscious, with hardly a sign of breathing or beating of the pulse.

The dissolution of the Springfield Presbytery launched a new denomination in the West. The preachers carried their churches with them. Every Presbyterian church in southwestern Ohio was swept into this new organization except those at Duck Creek and Round Bottom; and even the church at Cincinnati was fairly tainted with the new doctrines and methods. The Turtle Creek church, with uplifted hands, was constituted a schismatic church. The influence of Richard McNemar was irresistible. Before the close of the year 1804, Turtle Creek, Eagle Creek, Springfield (Springdale), Orangedale, Clear Creek, Beaver Creek and Salem had joined the new movement. A demand for more preachers went up. Malcolm Worley became active, and Andrew Ireland, John Purviance, David Kirkpatrick and William Caldwell, were sent out two and two as traveling evangelists. Afterwards Nathan Worley became a tower of strength. Camp meetings were still popular and were used to extend the general influence. The custom of giving the right hand of fellowship was introduced, and the name of "brother" and "sister" applied to church members. The spirit of the Kentucky revival, especially in camp meetings, was kept aflame. "Praying, shouting, jerking, barking, or rolling; dreaming, prophesying, and looking as through a glass, at the infinite glories of Mount Zion, just about to break open upon the world." "They practiced a mode of prayer, which was as singular, as the situation in which they stood, and the faith by which they were actuated. According to their proper name of distinction, they stood *separate* and *divided*, each one for one; and in this capacity, they offered up each their separate cries to God, in one united harmony of sound; by which the doubtful footsteps of those who were in search of the meeting, might be directed, sometimes to the distance of miles." *

The year 1805 opened most favorably to the new sect: Ohio, Kentucky and Tennessee were in its grasp. It appeared to be an irresistible force opposed to the older and better organized sects. The name of the sect (Christian) was most charming to the ear. It carried the believer back to Apostolic times. Then there was the pleasing pronouncement that the Bible alone was its creed. Man-made statements and creeds must be trampled under foot. Little did they realize that a creed was a creed just the same whether written or spoken. There was a consensus of opinion, and to this unwritten and unsigned creed they were just as devoted as was the Presbyterian to his Confession of Faith. I have heard, myself, just as strong doctrinal points discussed from the Christian (New Light) pulpit as I ever listened to from those reputed to be most conservative in theology. Moreover, an old friend of mine, as firm a believer in Christianity as it was possible to believe, was expelled for heresy, from one of the very churches that was wrenched from Calvinism and brought under the new order.

But the year 1805 awoke the revivalists, or schismatics, or New Lights, or Christians, to a sense of their danger. The rude awakening was sudden, powerful and disastrous. It has been sung that

> "Five preachers formed a body, in eighteen hundred three,
> From Anti-christ's false systems to set the people free;
> His doctrine and his worship in pieces they did tear —
> But ere the scene was ended these men became a snare;"

* *Kentucky Revival,* p. 73.

but it was doomed that only one of this number should continue
with the new order of things. In 1805, both Richard McNemar
and John Dunlavy joined the Shakers, and within a few years
Robert Marshall and John Thompson returned to the Presbyterian fold. Barton W. Stone — of all the prophets — was left
to encourage the saints. The defection placed him at the head of
the organization, and he was soon after known as "Father Stone."
Nor was the disaster to rest here, for calamity after calamity was
in the track of the Shaker propaganda, for church after church,
and too the very strongest, were swallowed up by the disciples of
Mother Ann Lee. This alarmed several of the preachers and converts "who fled from us and joined the different sects around us.
The sects triumphed at our distress, and watched for our fall.'
"Never did I exert myself more than at this time to save the
people from this vortex of ruin. I yielded to no discouragement,
but labored night and day, far and near, among the churches
where the Shakers went. By this means their influence was happily checked in many places. I labored so hard and constantly
that a profuse spitting of blood ensued. Our broken ranks were
once more rallied under the standard of heaven, and were soon
led on once more to victory." *

The Shaker trial was "a fiery one" to Stone and his remaining coadjutors. Five years later (1810), the defection of Marshall and Thompson added to the sorrows. They issued a pamphlet entitled, "A brief historical account of sundry things in the
doctrines and state of the Christian, or as it is commonly called,
the New Light Church. — By R. Marshall and J. Thompson,
Ministers of the Gospel and members of said church, containing
their testimony against several doctrines, held in that church, and
its disorganized state. Together with some reasons, why these
two brethren purpose to seek for a more pure and orderly connection." This pamphlet induced several young men who had engaged in the ministry also to follow into the Presbyterian ranks.
The pamphlet brought out a reply from David Purviance.

During all the troubles that rapidly accumulated upon the
infant sect David Purviance and Barton W. Stone stood together
and defended their citadel from the repeated assaults and rebuilt

---

* *Memoirs of Stone*, p. 62.

the ramparts as rapidly as they were thrown down. Neither was a leader of great ability. Their success was due more from the momentum created by the revival than any special management on their part. It is, however, probably true the bark would have sunk beneath the waves had they not piloted it through the storm. The success of this church, during its entire history, is unique; for never has it presented a leader of marked ability. Even its literature is mediocre. The formal existence has covered a period of a hundred years, and yet the literature of the entire organization, East, West, North and South, according to the "Christian Annual for 1903," embraces but two books and two pamphlets in the historical group; in the biographical, twenty; theological and doctrinal, thirty, and miscellaneous, thirty-three.

The present condition of the Christian church, as given by the same Annual is thus related:

Miami conference — embracing parts of Hamilton, Preble, Darke, Shelby, Miami, Montgomery, Warren, Green, Clark and Champaign counties. Ordained preachers 56; licentiates 5; churches 55, of which 25 are country. Only 11 have preaching full time. Membership 7,062. Value church property $164,650.

Ohio Central Conference — comprising churches in Champaign, Clark, Clinton, Delaware, Fayette, Franklin, Hardin, Madison, Ross, Union, Marion, Morrow and Pickaway counties. Ordained ministers 21; licentiates 1; 33 churches of which 21 are country; preaching full time, 3; valuation church property, $51,750; membership, 2,160. Ohio Conference — covering Jackson, Vinton, Pike, Scioto, Ross, Fayette and Gallia counties. Ordained ministers 32; licentiates 1; churches 32; membership 1,900. To this array must be added Antioch college, which under Horace Mann attained unto great renown, but since his death has undergone a checkered career.

So far as the personnel of the ministry is concerned—speaking wholly from personal observation—it has been composed of earnest, devoted and self-sacrificing men. Of the intellectual caliber it has been equal to the average, with here and there one far above the general. In point of scholarship, especially in oriental lore, America has not produced a greater than Austin Craig.

Notwithstanding the fact that the Christian church started with established churches and possessed with unbounded enthusiasm, yet the leaders were not equal to the occasion. The early preachers inveighed against a hireling ministry, which forced into the ranks many whose minds were diverted to the question of sufficient support; there was a want of organization, and a wise administration of government. The power of other churches forced them into intellectual lines, which, they have not been slow, in these later years, to take advantage. Within the last dozen years there has been quite a hegira into the ranks of the ministry of other denominations, especially the Congregational. Some six years ago a conference between the Congregationalists and Christians was held at Piqua, but with no perceptible results.

The Miami country owes much to the Christian church, and the showing of that church, contrasted with other sects, will compare favorably. A Presbyterian may not regard the coloring as of the brightest hues; for, in all probability, had it not been for the "Kentucky Revival," Presbyterianism in Kentucky and Southwestern Ohio, would be relatively as strong as it is to-day in Western Pennsylvania.

THE SHAKER CHURCH.

The Kentucky revival paved the way for the establishing of Shakerism in the West. The official title of this sect is "The United Society of Believers in Christ's Second Appearing." The name Shaker is universally applied to them and generally used by the members. So it is no longer regarded as a term of reproach, for it is used in their literature to designate them.

From the year 1801 to 1805, the newspapers of the Eastern States gave wonderful accounts of the extraordinary revival in Kentucky, Tennessee and Ohio. This was a theme of frequent discussion among the then established Shaker communities. The Shaker authorities gave the western movement their most careful reflection. During the month of December, 1804, it was decided to send, without further delay, a propaganda into Kentucky, with ample powers to take such action as would be beneficial to their advancement. The men selected were John Meacham, Benjamin Seth Youngs and Issachar Bates. They were eminently qualified for their mission. They were pre-possessing in their appearance, neat and plain in their dress, grave and unassuming in their manners, very intelligent and ready in the Scriptures, and of great boldness in their faith. The power of Bates as a missionary, may be gained from the statement[*] that from 1801 to 1811, as a Shaker missionary he traveled, mostly on foot, 38,000 miles and received the first confession of about 1,100 converts. Benjamin S. Youngs was scholarly and indefatigable in his labors. Of John Meacham, I know but little. From a poem I learn that he set out for New Lebanon, August 19, 1806. He afterwards became first in the ministry at Pleasant Hill, Ky., but recalled to the East in 1818. He was born in 1770 and died at Mount Lebanon, N. Y., December 26, 1854.

At three o'clock on the morning of January 1st, 1805, the three missionaries set out on their mission. The first 62 miles they were carried in a sleigh. From that on they were afoot, with one horse to carry their baggage. They went by the way of Philadelphia, Baltimore and Washington. Arriving in Kentucky they passed through Lexington, Abingdon and Hawley; there turning their course they crossed the Holston into Green County, Tennessee; recrossed the Holston, they passed over Clinch mountain; went through Crab Orchard, and about the first of March arrived at Paint Lick, where Matthew Houston was then stationed. From there they went to Cane Ridge, and were hospitably entertained by Barton W. Stone. Whether Stone directed their course into Ohio or not, there appears to be no existing evidence. On the 19th of March the propaganda crossed the Ohio; thence to Springdale, where John Thompson was preaching, and on March 22d, arrived at Turtle Creek, and directed their steps to the house of Malcolm Worley, having traveled 1,233 miles.

On the first advent of the Shaker missionaries, Barton Stone's conduct was all that could be desired. "We had much conversation with him and a number more; they sucked in our light as greedily as ever an ox drank water, and all wondered where they had been that they had not seen these things before.

---

[*] MS. Autobiography of Issachar Bates, in author's possession.

Barton said that he had been expecting that it would come about so in the end they were all filled with joy; this is what we have been praying for and now it is come."* Stone requested that they should attend the next camp-meeting soon to begin at Cane Ridge.

Malcolm Worley received the trio as divine messengers, and on March 27, became formally a Shaker. Malcolm declared "that his heavenly Father had promised to send help from Zion and I am glad, said he, that you are come."*

Richard McNemar had fully imbibed the idea that the Bible alone should he the resort for religious instructions. On the next day (March 23) the Shaker propaganda visited him. He "observed that he had never undertaken to build a church and if we had come for that purpose he would not stand in the way, his people were all free for us to labor with and he would go to the Gentiles. We stayed that night with Richard and the next day which was Sabbath, we went to meeting with him. He preached much to our satisfaction. After he got through I asked liberty to speak a few words which was granted. I spoke but short after which Benjamin came forward and spoke and read the letter† which was sent from the church."

On March 27, Bates started on foot to attend the camp-meeting at Cane Ridge, according to request. It was at this meeting where the first hostility was shown against the Shakers, by the new sect of Christians. It is thus told by Bates in his MS. Autobiography:

*"I arrived at Barton Stone's on Saturday night and found many of the preachers there and a number of others. I was received with outward kindness and a number of the people felt very friendly but the preachers were struck with great fear and concluded that if I was permitted to preach that it would throw the people into confusion, and to prevent it they would counteract their former liberality and shut out all other sects from preaching at that meeting and that would shut me out. All this they did by themselves without the knowledge of the people, and the people, expecting that I would preach Sabbath morning, after much

---

* *Ibid.* †See *Quarterly,* Jan., 1902, p. 253.

conversation with the people, we took breakfast and went onto
the camping ground. Marshall and Stone preached first and
preached the people back into Egypt. Stone told them to let no
man deceive them about the coming of Christ, for they would
all know when He came, for every eye would. see him in the
clouds and they would see the graves opening and the bones
rising and the saints would rise and meet the Lord in the air
whose names are written in the Lamb's book of life (which is
this little book that I hold in my hand) the Bible, and Marshall
went on much in the same track. He warned the people not to
follow man. Keep your Bibles in your homes and in your pocket
for in them you have eternal life. Don't believe what man says;
don't believe me for I have told lies. Thus they went on till
they were covered with death and even the woods around us appeared to be in mourning. A great number paid but little attention to it, but were encircling me round, asking me questions
and testifying. at every answer that is eternal truth, that is the
everlasting gospel and many other expressions of joy for the
truth. At length Matthew Houston took his turn of preaching,
and he took this text: Let us go up and possess the land for we
are fully able. And he had them across the Red sea in short
order you may be sure; the woods began to clap their hands,
the people skipping and jerking and giving thanks, and a great
part of them interceded with the preachers to have me preach,
but were put off for that day. After the exercises of the day was
over I returned to Stone's again and stayed all night and had
much conversation with a number of people. The next day I
went on the ground again. There were some preaching and a
little of everything that amounted to nothing. The people insisted on my preaching. At last eight men went to the stand
and said I should preach, so to pacify them they told they would
dismiss the meeting at 12 o'clock, and then I might preach, and
they did so. Then I mounted a large log in front of the stand
and began to speak, and altho the preachers and many others
went to their horses to get out of the way of hearing, yet when I
began to speak they all returned and all paid good attention. I
spoke about one hour. The subject I was upon was to show the
difference between the spirit and the letter, and when I got

through and dismissed them they began the controversy; one
cried spirit, spirit, all spirit, and another cried I bless God for the
spirit, for it is all that will do us any good, and so the multitude
were completely divided, so I left."

STANDING OF LEADING CONVERTS.

Owing to the spirit displayed towards those schismatics that
afterwards became Shakers, the following may be given to show
the estimation in which they were held previous to their final
change in belief.

Under date of Cane Ride, April 2, 1805, Stone wrote to
Richard McNemar as follows:

"MY DEAR BROTHER RICHARD: — I never longed to see any person so
much. If I was not confined in this clay tabernacle, I should be in your
embraces in less than an hour. The floods of earth and hell are let loose
against us, but me in particular. I am seriously threatened with impris-
onment and stripes, I expect to receive for the testimony of Jesus. Kentucky is turning upside down. The truth pervades in spite of man —
Cumberland is sharing the same fate — the young preachers, some of
them, will preach Jesus without the covering put on him by the fathers —
the scribes, the disputers of this world are gnashing upon us — Brother
Matthew Houston has clean escaped the pollutions of this world — and
he and his people are going on to perfect holiness in the fear of God —
a few more will soon follow — come over and help us, is the cry made
to us from every part.— Brother Purviance is gone to Carolina, to preach
the Gospel there, by the request of some there. In a few weeks I start
to fulfill a long daily string of appointments to Cumberland — by request
I go — I have appointed two commissioners among many Christians, on
the heads of Little and Big Barrens — Brother Dooley is among the Cher-
okees again — his last route there was successful — some poor Indians
received the Gospel — he was solicited to return — he is truly an apostle
of the Gentiles — some few are getting religion amongst us. The churches
thus quid dicam? Nescio: *What shall I say? I know not, my heart
grieves within me. Certain men from afar whom you know, inject ter-
ror and doubt into many; and now religion begins to lament in the dust
among us. Some as I suppose will cast away the ordinances of Baptism,
the Lord's Supper, etc , but not many as yet. Most dear Brother, inform
me what you think of these men among us and you, from a distant region. Thank God, he gave me his word.**

---

* The italics were originally in Latin, unquestionably to prevent Bates
from understanding the same.

Letters show the substance and faith eats it. We all want to meet with you shortly. But by reason of my absence to Cumberland — Brother Purviance to N. Carolina, Brother Houston in Madison, we cannot meet on Turtle Creek, nor sooner than third Sabbath June, and that in Kentucky. Brothers Marshall and Houston parted from us yesterday. We administered the Lord's Supper at Cane Ridge the day before — many communicants — much exercise — I am pushed for time to write to you — We have five students of the Bible, all but one know the language, full of faith, and of the Holy Ghost — just ready to preach. They all fled from the Presbyterians, to their grief, pain and hurt. Brother Stockwell exceeds expectation and is beloved and useful. Our Apology is yet living and working, and tearing down Babylon in Virginia. It was reprinted there to the great injury of Presbyterianism. It is also reprinted in Georgia. We are just publishing a short tract on Atonement — I will send you one soon. This truth has unhinged the brazen gates already.— I am hurried — pray for me — farewell.

B. W. STONE.

By Friend Bates."*

As to the estimation in which Malcolm Worley was held, witness the following, dated Springfield (Springdale, near Cincinnati), March, 1804:

"Forasmuch as our brother, Malcolm Worley, has made known to us the exercises of his mind for some time past, expressive of a Divine call to labor in word and doctrine; and we being satisfied, from a long and intimate acquaintance with him, of his talents, both natural and acquired, being such as, through the grace of God, may render him useful; and considering that the way of God is above our ways, it therefore seemed good to us, with one accord to encourage our brother to the work, whereunto we trust the Holy Ghost is calling him; and we do hereby recommend him to the churches scattered abroad, to be forwarded to his calling, according to the manifestation of the Spirit given to him to profit withal. Signed in behalf of the Presbytery, B. W. Stone, Clk."†

PERSECUTING THE SHAKERS.

It is foreign to our purpose to follow the Shaker missionaries' peregrinations. Their success was phenomenal. In rapid succession they swept into their fold the churches at Turtle Creek,.

---

* *Kentucky Revival,"* p. 85.   † *Ibid,* p. 46.

Eagle Creek, Straight Creek, Shawnee Run, Cabin Creek, etc., besides converts at various points. They made it a point to follow up the camp-meetings, where they invariably made accessions to their number. Richard McNemar joined the Shakers April 24; to the camp meeting at Eagle Creek, Adams County, Ohio, held the first Sunday in August, 1805, repaired both Benjamin S. Youngs and Issachar Bates; they converted many; among whom was Rev. John Dunlavy; followed by Matthew Houston in February, 1806. Nearly every member of the Turtle Creek church followed McNemar into Shakerism. This gave them a solid foundation as well as numbers. Their landed interest became large. To this they added the estate of Timothy Sewell at a cost of $1,640.

So long as the inroads were made upon the domain of the Christian Church, the discomfiture was greatly enjoyed by the other denominations. The Christians were grieved, chagrined, exasperated and early became aggressive, and took every measure to withstand the storm that presaged ruin to their cause. When the Shakers began to make visible success in other folds, then all united to put them down. Methods of the most questionable kind were resorted to. In the very year of their beginning at Turtle Creek (now Union Village, Warren Co., Ohio), the Shakers had their windows broken, their orchards cut down, their fences cast over, and their buildings burned. Four days after his conversion (April 28), Richard McNemar undertook to hold a camp meeting at Turtle Creek. On that day "a great body of blazing hot Newlights with John Thompson (then stationed at Springdale) a preacher at their head determined to break down all before them. Thompson mounted the stand and began his preachment and undertook to show how they had been imposed on by deceivers and how much he had borne with one Worley and now these Eastern men had come to tell us that Christ had made his second appearance, (pause), but they are liars, they are liars, they are liars. Now I will venture to say that the tumult at Ephesus was no greater than was at this place, for about half an hour it was one steady cry glory to Jesus, glory to Jesus, glory to Jesus and almost every other noise; this must be the cause of their giving so much glory to Jesus this poor suffering witnesses were proved

·out to be liars that they might have the privilege of enjoying the pleasures of their fleshly lusts for a season. I stood on a log hard by alone, for Elder John nor Benjamin was not there, at that time I was ordered back to hell from whence I came and called all the bad names that they could think of, after the noise began to cease I stepped off the log and passed through the multitude and as I passed they cried out, see how his conscience is seared as with a hot iron, he does not regard it all."*

It will not be necessary to follow this dark picture any farther. There was that to rouse the passions of such as cared more for an *ism* than for the spirit of Jesus Christ. But after years have rolled away and all incentives to malice obliterated, it is to be expected that the vision should no longer be obfuscated. Years after Barton Stone did not hesitate to libel them: "John Dunlavy, who had left us and joined them, was a man of a penetrative mind, wrote and published much for them, and was one of their elders in high repute by them. He died in Indiana, raving in desperation for his folly in forsaking the truth for an old woman's fables. Richard MeNemar was, before his death, excluded by the Shakers from their society, in a miserable, penniless condition, as I was informed by good authority. The reason of his exclusion I never heard particularly; but from what was heard, it appears that he had become convinced of his error. The Shakers had a revelation given them to remove him from their village, and take him to Lebanon, in Ohio, and to set him down in the streets, and leave him there in his old age, without friends or money."†

I called the attention of the Shakers of Union Village to the above citation. They had never heard of the charges before. Eldress Jane Cowan, of South Union, Ky., probably the best informed historian in their order in the West, was exceedingly indignant. Richard McNemar was ever a trusted man among them and died, full in the faith, at Union Village, September 15, 1839. The old church record says of him in noticing his death: "One of the most zealous and loyal believers who ever embraced the gospel in this western land, altogether more than ordinary intelligent." For more complete particulars see MacLean's "Life of McNemar."

* MS. *Autobiography of Bates.*
† *Biography of B. W. Stone, p.* 63.

John Dunlavy was long the preacher for the Shaker community at Pleasant Hill, Ky. On June 3, 1826, he arrived at the Shaker community of West Union in Knox county, Indiana,. on a visit. On September 8th he was taken sick with biliousfever and died on the 16th. On the 17th David Price was dispatched to Union Village as a bearer of the sorrowful news, and on the 18th William Redmond started on the same mission to Pleasant Hill. His death was greatly lamented by the various communities. Summerbell, in his "History of the Christians A. M. 4004—A. D. 1870, Cincinnati 1873," seizes the libel of Stone and gives it a fresh start (p. 533), although living less than twenty-five miles from Union Village at the time he copied the statements from Stone, and by next letter could have informed himself. He further calls Shakerism "Only Romish monkery broken loose from popery." Notwithstanding the estimation in which the Shakers were held — as quoted above — Summerbell thinks it best to slur them and others — "Those who went to the Shakers were too much inclined to fanaticism; and had they remained would have caused trouble, while Thompson and those who returned to the sects would not have followed the word of truth in baptism (Summerbell was an immersionist), a duty in which they would soon have been tested." David Purviance ("Biography of David Purviance," p. 146), speaks of Richard McNemar as being vain or "lifted up," after the separation in 1804. "I also discovered some of the same detestable pride in John Dunlavy. They were not content to abide in the simplicity of the truth. They became fanatics, and were prepared for an overthrow, when the Shakers entered in among us and swept them off with others who were led into wild enthusiasm." "I have thought there might be something providential in the coming of the Shakers, although some honest and precious souls were seduced and ruined by their means; yet a growing fanaticism was drawn out of the church, which threatened the most deleterious effects" (p. 148).

SHAKER ELEMENTS OF SUCCESS.

When all the facts are confronted it is not singular that Shakerism should have been so successful in the West. There

were certain regnant elements in operation among the revivalists that were congenial to the believers in Ann Lee. Dancing
was introduced among the revivalists in 1804; the Church in
general taught that the second coming of Christ was yet in the
future; a community of goods could be derived from the New
Testament; religious fanaticism was the order of the day; a
high sense of morals and implicit faith were specially taught.
The Shakers danced in their religious exercises; they taught that
Adam and Eve were the father and mother of the natural man
while Jesus and Ann Lee were the father and mother of the
spiritual family; they held all goods in common; the early Shakers were given to fanaticism; they practiced strictly the highest morals and were devout in their worship. If they taught that
God was dual,* that was not a greater credulity than the doctrine of a triune God. The simplicity of their manners would
impress favorably those who opposed prevailing fanaticism.

SHAKER INFLUENCE.

The early Shakers of the West possessed members representing all the various professions and trades. There were
scholars and theologians among them. It would be no exaggeration to say that it possessed the flower of the Western Presbyterian Church, one of whom wrote a book, which has ever remained a standard of authority among them. I refer to John
Dunlavy's "Manifesto;" written in 1815, published in 1818, at
Pleasant Hill, and republished in 1847 in New York. It is a
royal octavo of 486 pp. The great standard work of the Shakers
— "Christ's First and Second Appearing" — is a western production, and first published at Lebanon, O., in 1808; the second
edition at Albany, in 1810; the third at Cincinnati, in 1823, and
the fourth in Albany, in 1856. It is a royal octavo of 631 pp.,
and was principally written by Benjamin S. Youngs. It was
originally published under the sanction of David Darrow, John

---

* Theodore Parker prayed to "Our Father and Mother in Heaven."
I heard the same utterance in the Universalist church, Galesburg, Ills.,
many years ago.

4

Meacham and Benjamin S. Youngs.*   The publications of the western Shakers have been quite extensive. A bibliography of Shaker literature is appended to Axon's "Biographical Notices of Ann Lee," but this I have never seen. The books I possess, written by Shakers, number 30 bound volumes and 50 pamphlets, most of which were presented to me by Eldress Clymena Miner, who stands second in the ministry in the Sisters' lot, of the Western Societies.

While the Shakers own great possessions yet their number is greatly reduced, and their days appear to be numbered. No efforts are now made either to increase their membership or extend their literature. They have most thoroughly demonstrated that men and women can live together as a band of brothers and sisters.

The western ministry is appointed by that at Mount Lebanon in New York. It has not always been wise. The making of Elder Slingerland both first in the ministry and trustee was most disastrous. The particulars are too painful to narrate. It was a case of imbecility on the one side and sharpers on the other. Suffice it to say that of the $316,000 obtained for the North Union property, every dollar of it was lost. Nearly $200,000 more went into wild cat speculation. The leaders of Union Village prayed the Eastern ministry for redress, but in vain. As a last recourse the law was appealed to, and finally a new ministry was appointed, which has all the appearance of an intelligent conservatism. Through the stubbornness of Harvey L. Eads, formerly chief in authority at South Union, $80,000 was lost at one time. The finances of Pleasant Hill are not in good condition.

A candid study of the Shakers evokes one's sympathy and admiration. I confess it would be a pleasure to me to realize that the halls of the Shaker villages teemed with human life as they did at the time of my earliest recollection. Thousands have gone forth from these communities schooled in the purest morals and implicit faith in the Divine Being. Shakerism has been productive of good. As such it must receive the enconiums of the just.

---

* Thomas Jefferson pronounced it the best ecclesiastical history he had every read.

OTHER SECTS.

The revivalists to a greater or less extent were fanatical, but time mellowed the trenchant words, and a deeper spiritual outlook was observed. In religious thought the various conferences differ—that known as the Miami is reputed to contain the broadest minds. The religious paper—published at Dayton —"Herald of Gospel Liberty," is rather conservative in its tone. While the church, as a body, rejects the doctrine of the trinity, yet nowhere has it paved the way for the Unitarian denomination. In the whole state of Ohio there are but three churches, viz., Cincinnati, Cleveland and Marietta, none of which-has more than a local force. The handing over of Antioch college proved to be a failure, owing to the want of a constituency. Yet the measure of this church is most potent. Backed by Harvard college and with the impetus of an unrivaled ministry in education and intellect, its advocates have gained renown in all departments of knowledge. Its literature stands almost alone. It keeps abreast with human thought. All clergymen, west of the Alleghenies, may receive, gratis, an installment of their books, which has been largely accepted. What influence this may have could not even be approximated.

UNIVERSALISM.

Although there is a large per cent. of the clergymen of the Christian sect that accepts the doctrine of universal salvation, yet it has nowhere paved the way for the Universalist church. In short, there has always been an antagonism between the two. The Universalist church in Ohio, like the Unitarian, has been practically a failure, although tremendous efforts have been put forth to gain and maintain a footing. The first preacher in the state was Timothy Bigelow, who removed to Palmyra in 1814. The first organized church was in Marietta, in 1816, now merged into the Unitarian. The first conference in the Miami country was at Jacksonsburg, Butler county, in November, 1826, at which were James Alfred, Jonathan Kidwell and Daniel St. John. The "Register" for 1903, gives for the state 42 ministers and 80 churches, 34 of the latter being in the Miami country. The efforts to maintain a religious periodical have all been failures, as the following list demonstrates: "The Lamp of Liberty," Cincinnati, 1827; "The Star in the West," Cincinnati, 1827-1880; "The Glad Tidings," Columbus and Akron, 1836-1840; "The Universalist Preacher," Dayton, 1839-1841; "Ohio Universalist," Cleveland, 1845-1846; "The Youth's Friend," Cincinnati, 1846-1860; "The Universalist Advocate," Centreburg, 1849; "Western Olive Branch," Cincinnati, 1849-1850; "The Guiding Star," Cincinnati, 1871-1880. Nor has the denomination generally been much more successful. The Rev. Dr. Richard Eddy, in his "Modern History of Universalism," appends a list of periodicals, showing that out of 181 journals only four are still in existence, viz., two family, one juvenile, and one Sunday school. Eddy's bibliography, for and against the doctrine of universal salvation, compiled in 1886, enumerates 2,096 titles. This does not embrace the literature in other departments. What that bibliography may be I am unable to ascertain.

While it has been foreign to my intention to comment on the subject of doctrine, for that must require some temerity, because it is treading on delicate ground, I will here, however, transgress the rule for this reason: The Universalist church boasts it stands for that phase of Christianity that represents all who believes in the ultimate salvation of all. If their boasts be true, then they should either have no written creed, or else one which would cover all believers in the Bible who accept the salvation of all. This church is the only one of the liberal sects that has a written creed. In the year 1803, the following creed was adopted, known as the Winchester Profession:

ARTICLE 1. We believe that the Holy Scriptures of the Old and New Testaments contain a revelation of the character of God and of the duty, interest and final destination of mankind.

ARTICLE II. We believe that there is one God, whose nature is Love, revealed in one Lord Jesus Christ, by one Holy Spirit of Grace, who will finally restore the whole family of mankind to holiness and happiness.

ARTICLE III. We believe that holiness and true happiness are inseperably connected, and that believers ought to be careful to maintain order and practice good works; for these things are good and profitable unto men.

Considering the purport of the Universalist church no reasonable man could take exceptions to the above, unless it is the grammatical error in the first article. Yet for twenty years the ministers wrangled over the word "restore," when all controversy was throttled and the following theological monstrosity was adopted at Boston in 1899:

II. The conditions of fellowship shall be as follows:
1. The acceptance of the essential principles of the Universalist Faith, to-wit: 1. The Universal Fatherhood of God; 2. The Spiritual authority and leadership of His Son, Jesus Christ; 3. The trustworthiness of the Bible as containing a revelation from God; 4. The certainty of just retribution for sin; 5. The final harmony of all souls with God.

The Winchester Profession is commended as containing these principles, but neither this nor any other precise form of words is required as a condition of fellowship, provided always that the principles above stated be professed.
2. The acknowledgment of the authority of the General Convention and assent to its laws.

Only a slight examination of these conditions of fellowship exhibits that it is:

I. Anti-Christian, for it teaches that God is without mercy, pity and compassion; it teaches the doctrine of retaliation.

II. It teaches post mortem punishment, a doctrine in which Universalists have always been divided.

III. It is materialistic.

IV. It is fatalistic.

V. The word "Universal" is all-reaching, unlimited in its signification. Then this creed places man on a level with the brute and inanimate creation. Doubtless it was intended to mean that "God is the father of all mankind," but the words do not say nor mean that.

VI. It contains a gross falsehood. It states that the "Winchester profession is commended as containing these principles," when the utmost stretch of the imagination cannot make it teach "the certainty of just retribution for sin."

VII. One of the cardinal principles of Christianity is forgiveness, but here we have "the *certainty* of retribution."

The adoption of such a conglomeration is evidence that the Universalist church has no humorist in it, and that such theologians as it may contain have their vision obscured.

PRESENT RELIGIOUS STATUS.

The religious, moral and intellectual status of the Miami country will compare favorably with any other part of the State of Ohio. Whatever may be deleterious in that region may also be found elsewhere. If other districts are progressive, likewise the same elements are here at work. To speak of any particular phase would only be to rehearse what may be known elsewhere.

So far as the Kentucky revival is concerned it has passed into history never again to repeat itself. It has been observed that when one species of animals died out it can never be reclaimed, because the cònditions are against it. Likewise the Kentucky revival can never be repeated. The conditions have changed. Society is not the same. The standards have been raised. In order to have a revival the minds of the people must be concentrated on that one point. The daily newspaper distracts the attention by its variety and sensational publications. The free schools direct the minds of youth into various channels and pursuits become innumerable.

BIOGRAPHICAL.

In previous issues of the *Quarterly* I have given sketches of all the prominent men hereunto mentioned, save Barton Warren Stone. He was born near Port Tobacco, Maryland, Dec. 24, 1772; in 1779 the family moved near the Dan river in what was then the backwoods of Virginia; in 1790 he commenced the study of Latin at Guilford (N. C.) Academy; active and a leader in the Kentucky revival, during which time he was settled at Cane Ridge; first married in 1801 and again in 1811; taught school; commenced publishing the "Christian Messenger" in 1826, and through his efforts the New Lights in Kentucky were turned over to the Campbellites in 1832; removed to Illinois in 1834; wrote his autobiography in 1843; died at the residence of his daughter, in Hannibal, Mo., November 9, 1844. Besides writing part two of the "Apology," in 1805 he published his "Letters on the Atonement," and "Address to the Christian Churches," and in 1822 appeared his "Letters to Dr. James Blythe." His autobiography was edited by John Rogers and published in Cincinnati in 1847. The editor closes the volume with a lengthy and wholesome chapter upon the bodily phenomena produced during the great revival. Among other things he observes: "While it is granted that genuine Christians have been, in many instances, subjects of these strange agitations, this cannot be admitted as

ELDER BARTON W. STONE.

proof, that they are the offspring of proper influences: for no such cases occurred under the preaching of Christ, and His Apostles. And we cannot doubt that under their ministry, all proper influences were brought to bear upon their hearers. The conclusion therefore cannot be avoided, that the gospel, preached as it should be, never produces such results." "Where these exercises were encouraged, and regarded as tokens of the divine presence there they greatly prevailed. But where they were looked upon as manifestations of enthusiasm, and fanaticism, and therefore, opposed, they did not prevail" (p. 371).

CONCLUSION.

Spasmodic efforts in behalf of mankind are not to be looked upon with the eye of censure. While there may be much chaff,

yet it is out of the chaff that the grain of wheat is rescued.
Sometimes the cloud of dust obscures even the brightness of the
sun, yet when that dust is settled the road way may be more
passable. Thoughts are often quickened, and experience is a
tell-tale for future good. I have not condemned the Kentucky
revival. Good did flow from it. When all the circumstances are
considered it was an effort greatly demanded, however wild
was the revel, and grotesque the carnival. Persecutions of all
descriptions must be condemned. The history of man proves that
in every instance the persecuted have been nearer the Kingdom
than the persecutors.

May 19, 1903.   J. P. MacLean.

NOTE. On May 27th, I received from Eldress Jane Cowan,
the principal leader of the Shaker community at South Union, Logan county, Ky., the church records of that society. Prefacing
these records is an autobiographical sketch of Rev. John Rankin
written in 1845. As this throws light on the Kentucky revival,
and what has never been published before, I herewith transcribe a
portion of it:

"In August, 1799, a sacrament was appointed at Gasper River, old
meeting house five miles below South Union. The preachers attended,
gifts were given to men, their language was clothed with power which
pervaded the congregation, many were convicted, some called on ther
neighbors to pray for them, one under view of his exposure to justice,
asked in consternation of soul: "Is there no hand to stay the justice of
God?" Some few could rejoice in hopes of mercy and promise of·God,
et cetera. This same summer or early fall, at a sacrament held at Big
Muddy River Meeting House: a work of similar nature made its appearance in a very striking manner; my text on this occasion was Acts 40
and 41. Beware therefore, lest that come upon you which was spoken
of in the Prophets; Behold ye despisers and wonder and perish; for I
work a work in your days, a work which you shall in no wise believe,
though a man declare it unto you: Due attendance, serious attention to
preaching, and solemn inquiry, what they should do to be saved appeared
to agitate the minds of the congregations throughout the following winter
and spring. In the mean time, the members of this society (Gasper) were
cordially engaged in building a meeting-house for their future accommodation.

"Sometime in the month of June in the year 1800, the principal members of the three awakened congregations met together at the Red River
Meeting house, with a large accession of citizens of every description, and

also two zealous preachers from the state of Tennessee, in whom we could confide, came to see the strange work, and take part in the labors of the day. Believing them to be men of the same spirit with ourselves, we made them more than welcome to participate on the occasion; and rejoiced in hope that they might be instruments, destined to transfer the same light and power to their respective neighborhoods, which was the result. All our gifts and ministerial efforts were united and tended to the same end; the conviction, conversion and salvation of souls.; The surrounding multitudes sat and heard with reverence and awe, with increasing solemnity depicted in their countenances through the meeting; at the conclusion of which, a part of the people went out of the house, in order to return to their places of residence. A large part remaining on their seats in contemplative silence. But wonderful to be seen and heard; on a sudden, an alarming cry burst from the midst of the deepest silence; some were thrown into wonderful and strange contortions of features, body and limbs, frightful to the beholder — others had singular gestures, with words and actions quite inconsistent with Presbyterial order and usage — all was alarm and confusion for the moment. One of the preachers, a thorough Presbyterian, being in the house beckoned me to one side, and said, in evident perturbation of mind: What shall we do? What shall we do? He intimated some corrective to quell the confusion. I replied: We can do nothing at present. We are strangers to such an operation. We have hitherto never seen the like; but we may observe, their cry, and the burden of their prayers to God is for mercy and the salvation of their souls. This prayer is both scriptural and rational, and therefore it is most safe to let it work; lest in attempting to root out the tares, we should root out the wheat also. Let the disorder stand to the account of human imperfection. At this instant the other preacher from Tennessee, a son of thunder, came forward and without hesitation, entered on the most heart stirring exhortation, encouraging the wounded of the day never to cease striving, or give up their pursuit, until they obtained peace to their souls. On seeing and feeling his confidence, that it was the work of God, and a mighty effusion of his spirit, and having heard that he was acquainted with such scenes in another country, we acquiesced and stood in astonishment, admiring the wonderful works of God. When this alarming occurrence subsided in outward show, the united congregations returned to their respective abodes, in contemplation of what they had seen, heard and felt on this most oppressive occasion.

The next large meeting was held on Friday week after the beforementioned meeting on Red River, being an appointment for a sacramental meeting at Gasper River, at the new meeting house one mile and a half below South Union in the month of July, 1800.

In the intervening two weeks, the news of the strange operations which had transpired at the previous meeting had run throughout the county in every direction, carrying a high degree of excitement to the minds of almost every character. The curious came to gratify their curiosity. The seriously convicted, presented themselves that they might receive some special and salutary benefit to their souls, and promote the cause of God, at home and abroad. The honorable (?) but sentimental exemplary and strictly formal Presbyterians attended to scrutinize the work, and judge whether it was of God and consistent with their sentiments, feelings and order, or whether it was a delusive spirit emanating from the Prince of darkness, of which they were very apprehensive. * * * On Friday morning at an early hour, the people began to assemble in large numbers from every quarter, and by the usual hour for preaching to commence, there was a multitude collected, unprecedented in this or any other new country of so sparse a population. The rising ground to the south and west of the meeting house, was literally lined with covered wagons and other appendages — each one furnished with provisions and accommodations, suitable to make them comfortable on the ground during the solemnity. When I came in view of this vast assemblage I was astonished." On the evening of the following Monday "inquirers began to fall prostrate on all sides, and their cries became piercing and incessant. Heavy groans were heard, and trembling and shaking began to appear throughout the house; and again in a little time, cries of penitential and confessional prayer sounded through the assembly. Toward the approach of night, the floor of the meeting house was literally covered with the prostrate bodies of penitents, so that it became necessary to carry a number out of doors and lay them on the grass or garments, if they had them."

Rev. John Rankin was born November 27, 1757, in North Carolina. He took charge of the Presbyterian church on the Gasper (now South Union), in December 1798. Similar to the other revivalists, his views were not in harmony with those of his co-religionists. On October 28, 1807, he avowed his belief in Shakerism and confessed to Issachar Bates, Richard McNemar and Matthew Houston. He was the preacher at South Union until his death, which occurred July 12, 1850.

THE SHAKER COMMUNITY OF WARREN COUNTY.

ITS ORIGIN, RISE, PROGRESS AND DECLINE.

INTRODUCTION.

Located three miles west of Lebanon, Ohio, is the seat of the bishopric of the Shaker communities west of the Allegheny Mountains. The tract of land possessed by them is irregular in its boundaries, and embraces 4,500 acres of as rich soil as may be found in the state. Its location meets the approval of the most critical eye. The postoffice is known as Union Village, but to the surrounding country it is known as Shakertown. The people who own this tract of territory are honored and respected by their neighbors. The land has been brought under a high state of cultivation, and the buildings are commodious, well constructed with all modern improvements. The Shakers number about forty-five souls, who take life quietly, and enjoy all the luxuries they desire. The office, where resides the ministry, is one of the finest executive buildings in America, and furnished more luxuriously than any business office in the state. Notwithstanding the fact that here we may find nearly every desire that an upright mind might demand, yet the community is growing less, and apparently its days are numbered.

On Monday, May 20, 1901, I called upon Dr. Joseph R. Slingerland, first in the ministry, who had both special and general charge of all the western communities of Shakers, for the purpose of obtaining all the facts relative to the transactions of the mob of 1810, and further to see if I could secure the privilege of examining the archives of the recently extinct community at Watervliet, near Dayton. During the conversation I was informed that there was a MS. history of the Union Village community. Requesting the loan of the MS., it was placed in my hands, with liberty to make such use of its contents as I might deem advisable.

SHAKER MS. HISTORY.

The MS. history of the Shaker community of Union Village is. type-written and covers 221 pages of foolscap, and the product of one who was a member for eighty years. It is entitled, "A history of the principal events of the Society of Believers, at Union Village, commencing in the month of March, 1805, containing a tolerably explicit account of most of the scenes of the said society onward. Compiled both from memory and the several journals kept in the society from the beginning. By O. C. Hampton, who was a member of said society since 1822." The MS. can hardly be said to be a history. It is simply an epitome of each year's transactions as viewed by the compiler, Oliver C. Hampton, born April 2, 1817, died March 29, 1901, becoming a Shaker through the conversion of his father in 1822, having held important positions ever since his early life, not the least of which was that of schoolmaster, and second in the ministry until a short time before his decease, possessed all the information relating to the community he loved so well. However, he did not possess the ordinary instincts so essential in an historian. His MS. is disappointing in many respects. The manners, customs, costumes, etc., we only learn when said expressions were ordered discontinued. Besides this, there is often a want of clearness which not only confuses the reader, but leaves the account so broken as to make it unintelligible to the uninformed reader. The account that follows is based on the Hampton MS.

OLIVER C. HAMPTON.

ORIGIN OF THE SHAKERS OF UNION VILLAGE.

The wild carnival of religion of 1800, 1801, but better known as the "Great Kentucky Revival," thoroughly shook and even prostrated the Presbyterian and Methodist churches that came under its influence. The effect was felt in the valley of the Great Miami; and although one hundred years have elapsed, still the Presbyterian church within the last named region has not recovered from the stroke. After the revival had spent its force we find the Rev. Richard McNemar, who had been a prominent figure in the movement, preaching at Turtle Creek church, at Bedle's Station, now Union Village. The noise of the revival reached the Shakers at New Lebanon, New York, who, in consequence of which, sent three missionaries—John Meacham, Benjamin S. Youngs and Issachar Bates—to the southwest as a propaganda. On March 22, 1805, having traveled the whole distance on foot, they reached the Turtle Creek church, and first went to the house of Malcolm Worley, a wealthy and influential man, and on the following day visited Rev. Richard McNemar. The first convert was Malcolm Worley and Richard McNemar soon after.

On the ensuing Sunday, after the arrival of the missionaries, Benjamin S. Young and Issachar Bates attended the public meeting of the Revivalists, or Newlights, as they were later called, and by permission read the following letter:

"The Church of Christ unto a people in Kentucky and the adjacent states, sendeth greeting: We have heard of a work of God among you; Who worketh in divers operations of His power, for which we feel thankful, as we have an ardent desire that God would carry on His work according to His own purpose. We know that God's work as it respects the salvation and redemption of souls, is a strange work which He hath promised to bring to pass in the latter days. We also know that the servants of God have been under sackcloth and darkness since the falling away of the Apostolic Order which from the time of Christ's ministry continued about four hundred years; since that time Anti-Christ has had power to reign in Christ's stead, and hath 'set up the abomination that maketh desolate,' spoken of by Daniel the prophet, and which, according to the Scriptures, Christ was to consume with the spirit of His mouth, and destroy with the brightness of His coming. But not to tarry on those things we will come to matters in the present day. The time being nearly finished, according to the Scriptures, that Anti-Christ should reign, and time fully come for Christ to make His second appearance, God, out of His everlasting goodness and mercy to His creatures, in the fulness of His promises, raised up to Himself witnesses and gave unto them the same gifts of the Holy Spirit that were given to the Apostles in the day of Christ's first appearing. The light and power and gifts of the Holy Spirit were so convincing, especially in the First Pillar, attended with the word of prophecy in so marvelous a manner, that every heart was searched and every rein of those that heard was tried. The loss of man and the way and work of salvation by Christ in the present witnesses appearing so unspeakably great, that although we had been a people that were greatly wrought upon by the spirit of God, and were looking for the coming of Christ, yet the light manifested in the witnesses showed us that we were unspeakably short of salvation, and had never travelled one step in the Regeneration towards the New Birth. For it showed us that it was impossible for those who lived in the works of natural generation, copulating in the works of the flesh, to travel in the great work of regeneration and the new birth. And as these witnesses had received the revelation in this last display of grace of God to a lost world they taught and opened unto us the way of God which is a way out of all sin in the manner following: First. To believe in the manifestations of Christ in this display of the grace of God to a lost world. Secondly. To confess all our sins; and thirdly, to take up our cross against the flesh, the world, and all evil; which (counsel) we, by receiving and obeying, from the heart, have received the gift of God which has separated us from the course of this world and all sin in our knowledge, for twenty years past and upward.

We, therefore, as servants of Christ and children of the resurrection, testify to all people that Christ hath made his second appearing here on earth, and the poor lost children of men know it not. We know there are many among the wise and prudent of this generation who are looking for the coming of Christ in this latter day, who entirely overlook the work of God as the ancient Jews did, in the day of Christ's first appearing; for Christ has come and it is hid from their eyes and we marvel not at it, for Christ said, 'I thank Thee, O Father, Lord of heaven and earth, that Thou hast hid these things from the wise and prudent, and revealed them unto babes.' But as the work of God which has wrought mightily in us to purify us from the nature of sin, has been progressive from step to step, as we were able to hear, from one degree to another, we cannot write particularly in this letter. We hope and trust you will be so far informed as will be necessary for your salvation. We feel union with the work of God that is among you as we have heard, and have a desire to communicate something to you that will be for your good. The light of God in the Gospel has taught us the straight and narrow way that leadeth to life, and not only so, but I as given us to see the devices of Satan that from ages past down to this day when God hath given His Holy Spirit to enlighten and convert the children of men, of sin, Satan would also work to heal their wounds slightly and to lead them into by and forbidden paths, if possible, to dishonor and destroy the work of God, even in them that God ·had enlightened and called to be his witnesses. We have had a great desire that some of you might have visited us before now, and we have been waiting for some time to know the mind of God in relation to you. We now, out of duty to God and our fellow creatures, have sent three of our brethren unto you, viz., John Meacham, Benjamin S. Youngs, and Issachar Bates, who, we trust, will be able to declare things more particularly, and to open unto you the way of life which is a way out of all sin — a way that the vulture's eye never saw and the fierce lion never passed. Receive them, therefor, as messengers of Christ and friends to your salvation.

Written in the church at New Lebanon, in the Township of Canaan, County of Columbia, and State of New York, December 30, 1804.

Signed in behalf of the Church,

DAVID MEACHAM,
AMOS HAMMOND,
EBENEZER COOLY."

The second convert was Anna Middleton, a slave, who was received just as cordially as though she had been white and free. Richard McNemar, wife and children were received on the 24th of the following April. On May 23 the first meeting of the Believers was held on the farm of David Hill, about a mile southwest of Union Village. During the year 1805, or shortly thereafter about sixty families had united, together with many unmarried persons of both sexes and all ages, making a total of about 370 persons.

On June 29, Elder David Darrow, Daniel Mosely and Solomon King arrived at the home of Malcolm Worley, the first named having been ordained and sent by the leading authority of the parent church at New Lebanon, to take charge of the newly forming communities in the West.

REIGN OF DAVID DARROW, 1805-1825.

The history of the Shakers of Union Village is essentially the history of the one who was first in the ministry, which office is practically that of a bishop. The selection of the ministry has always been made by the ministry of New Lebanon, and afterwards confirmed by vote at Union Village.

For a period of 20 years David Darrow was the head of the western ministry, and most faithfully bore the burdens of his calling, with an upright and conscientious integrity. He possessed that desirable combination of qualities of firmness, justice, and unswerving righteousness, blended with charity and tenderness, which added to his wisdom or foresight, made him just such a leader as the infant colony required. The success or failure of the entire movement rested upon the shoulders of this man. He became a father to his people, and in his hands were placed their temporal, spiritual, moral and intellectual welfare. The people had been brought out of the Calvinism of Knox, and now entered into a different faith, and different manners and customs. Elder Darrow must direct the new ship amidst breakers and other dangers until he safely brings it into a haven of stability. The country was comparatively new, the people lived in log houses, and the state of society was somewhat primitive. The herculean task was undertaken, and the work fully accomplished. While it was necessary for Elder David to begin at the very foundation and build carefully and substantially, yet it was absolutely necessary that his hands should be strengthened. To this fact the New Lebanon ministry was fully alive. To his assistance they sent Eldress Ruth Farrington, Prudence Farrington, Lucy Smith, Martha Sanford, Molly Goodrich, Ruth Darrow (David's daughter), Peter Pease, Samuel Turner, Constant Mosely and John Wright, all of whom arrived at the residence of Malcolm Worley on May 31, 1806. All of these remained in the West except John Wright, who returned in the following August. Eldress Ruth Farrington, before leaving New Lebanon, was appointed as the First in care on the Sisters' side and to stand in the lot with Elder Darrow. On the 5th of the following June all the brethren and sisters who had come from the East, removed from Worley's house, which had been the headquarters, to their own premises, which they had purchased of Timothy Sewell, which had some log cabins on it. This now was called the Elders' Family. However, they soon erected a frame building and moved into it at what was termed the South House. On December 6 following Peter Pease, Issachar Bates and others purchased a farm owned by Abraham

La Rue, which was afterwards turned over to the Trustees of the Society.

It would be difficult to picture the trials endured by the early Shakers, and the constancy of their leader. Many heavy sacrifices had to be made, and much physical as well as mental and moral trials were endured. But little of their land was cleared and the living poor, and some years must elapse before the comforts of life could be secured. The church cheerfully faced all these trials, economized what they had and patiently endured privations in victuals and clothing,—too often exposed to severe and inclement weather. Everything of a mechanical nature was scarce, and in many instances must be created on the ground. Even these must be postponed until mills could be built in order that machinery could be constructed for the manufacture of many things of immediate necessity. All this took time, patience and hard labor, as well as suffering. Through this formative period their zeal in their faith did not abate nor their love towards one another grow cold. Under the guidance of David Darrow, within a few years, they were in advance of the neighboring vicinity, and from the superiority of their productions they received the highest prices in the markets. Any article manufactured by the Shakers was to be relied on. The prestige thus gained carried a ready sale to them for anything from a basket to a fine carriage. Their uprightness in this temporal line, in time, forced a due regard for their religious convictions. All this cannot be ascribed to their own unaided zeal, for there was more or less of an influx from the mother church. It is related that "on August 15, 1807, Elder Constant Mosely returned from Wheeling whither he had gone to meet the following persons from the East, viz: Nathan Kendal, Archibald Meacham, Anna Cole, Lucy Bacon, and Rachel Johnson." Joseph Allen, a good mechanic, arrived on December 4, from Tyringham, Mass. "On May 26, 1809, Constant Mosely returned from New Lebanon, and with him Hortense Goodrich, Comstock Betts, Mercy Picket and Hopewell Curtis."

The genius and inspiration of David Darrow and his coadjutors may in part be realized, when it is considered that the colony passed through rapid changes in many ways. From log huts to

5

frame buildings, and thence to substantial brick buildings for dwellings, with all other necessary improvements. A minute of the gigantic undertaking shows a saw mill in 1807, and a new one in 1808; a new church in 1809, with its successor in 1818; the West frame dwelling in 1813; the East house in 1816; the large brick dwelling, a few rods north of the church, in 1820. In short, all the families, East, West, North, South and Center were established under Elder Darrow. In 1819 the population had increased to about 600 souls, among whom were blacksmiths, masons, stone-cutters, carpenters, tanners, fullers, clothiers, cabinet-makers, tailors, weavers, carders, spinners, etc., etc., all of whom were employed in their favorite vocation. All the clothing, boots, shoes, etc., used by the community were made by its own members. Besides all this, their land produced nearly all their living, animal, vegetable and fruits. Tea and coffee were not then used, and the beverages consisted of spice brush, sassafras root, sage, etc., all grown on their lands. The sugar was produced from the maple tree, and some years 5,000 pounds were manufactured. The fields produced large crops of corn, flax, wheat, rye, etc. Such was the organization that the society may be said to have lived within itself.

Upon first view it might be inferred that a people so peaceable, and who lived so much within themselves, would be left to work out their own destiny. But it was not so. Religious rancor and hatred are the most intolerable. Although persecution was bitter enough, but not carried to the same extent as experienced by the eastern communities. Mobs assembled at Union Village in 1810, 1812, 1813, and 1817; but as these will form a special paper, this reference must here suffice. The saintly Eldress Ruth Farrington and Eldress Martha Sanford received blows fom a cowhide in the hands of one John Davis.

Discouragements arose from various sources, among which were the accidental burning of buildings containing crops, the work of incendiaries, and the perfidy of members. The most notable instance of the last was the case of John Wallace, one of the trustees, who in 1818 left home avowedly going to Columbus, under pretext of a business engagement, but turned his course to Cincinnati, borrowed $3,000 of the United States bank, signed the note

"Wallace and Sharp," leaving the society to pay the debt,—a large burden for that period. Wallace annoyed the community as late as 1832, for in that year, with a company of his fellow apostates, he took possession of the grist mill, but was dislodged, and then tried to have the brethren indicted by the grand jury.

One of the misfortunes that the Shakers have been heir to, during the period of their whole history, is that of lawsuits, although they have ever tried to avoid the same. As early as 1811, one Robert Wilson, an apostate, commenced suit against Elder Darrow for $250, which was decided in favor of the latter by the Supreme Court. In 1816 a case in Chancery was brought by one Jonathan Davis, which was decided in favor of the Shakers. Lawsuits also grew out of the mob of 1817.

The Shakers have always been opposed to war, but notwithstanding have been forced to suffer. About the 8th of September, 1813, Elder Samuel Rollins, Elder David Spinning, Robert Baxter, William Davis, Jr., Adam Gallaher and Samuel McClelland (the last two from Busrow), were drafted into the army, — the country then being at war with England. They were required to join the detachment under Major Frye at Lebanon, but on the 11th were furlowed. On the 18th they were marched under guard to Dayton. On the 22nd they returned home, but on October 1 they were taken to Lebanon under pretense of having deserted, and on the 3rd were marched to Xenia; thence to Franklinton, and then to Sandusky. No amount of authority or coercion could force them to shoulder arms, so on November 24 they were discharged, and returned home where they were received with great rejoicing.

While the worldly interests of the community were looked after with consummate care, yet the special feature announced and looked after was the moral and spiritual. The church was the sole object of the organization. It was not until 1812 that attention towards gathering the Society into "Church Order," according to the pattern of the mother church at New Lebanon, was carefully considered, and acted upon. We find that in this year, the ministry, consisting of David Darrow, Solomon King, Ruth Farrington and Hortense Goodrich, occupied the upper part of the church building, and on the 15th of January the first covenant of the church was signed by all the members who were considered eligible to such a privilege.   In brief, this covenant required every signer to surrender totally, together with all possessions, and an absolute consecration to the church, in obedience to the ministry and deacons of the Society, and to practice strict celibacy.   Then arose the Children's Order, the Youths' Order, and the Gathering Order, as well as the church proper.   Among the rules early adopted was, that, just before Christmas, in every year, all hard feelings and all disunion must be put away and reconciliation completely established.   Then, thus united, Christmas was celebrated by singing, dancing, feasting and giving of presents.

The missionary spirit was fully exercised, but appears to have practically died out on the demise of Elder Darrow.   All movements are most energetic in their infancy, but appear to crystallize on gaining a firm foothold.   As early as 1807 a report reached the Believers that a religious revival had broken out among the Shawnee Indians, located at Greenville.   Immediately (March 17), Elder David Darrow, Benjamin S. Youngs and Richard McNemar set out to visit the tribe, and endeavor to persuade them to receive the testimony.   During the following month of August the tribe was visited by Issachar Bates and Richard McNemar.   During the two visits the Shakers gave the Indians $10 in money, and loaded 20 horses with the necessaries of life which they delivered. But no Indians were gathered.   Missionary work was prosecuted during 1807, wherever an opening was offered.   In 1808 the missions extended to Straight Creek, Ohio, into Kentucky and Indiana, where Societies were formed—the last named having a great trial, especially from the soldiers and Indians.   North Union near Cleveland, was established in 1822, in Watervliet, near Dayton, in 1810, and Whitewater, near Harrison, in 1824. The Societies at Straight Creek, and Eagle Creek, were short-lived.   In 1824, a mission was sent to Zoar, in order to interest that colony, who then practiced celibacy.

The Shakers were subjected to experiences of revivals.   During the month of February, 1815, an extraordinary revival pervaded the church.   It received the name of "War-time."   The worship was attended with many displays of muscular exercise, such as stamping, shaking, vociferating and shouting, besides the usual exercises of dancing, marching, singing, etc. It continued for many months, and was ascribed to the manifestation of war between Michael and his angels, and the Dragon and his angels, spoken of in Revelations. On May 9, 1824, a very large concourse marched along the principal street singing and praising God and manifesting great joy and thanksgiving. On the 12th of the following September there was another joyful march and demonstration.

The first school for the education of the youth was opened November 10, 1808, with John Woods for instructor of the boys, and Malinda Watts for the girls. The teaching of the sexes separately was thought to be more in keeping their mode of life and discipline, but after many years this plan was abandoned. But very few books were in their possession, and in 1816 those in use were the New Testament, Webster's spelling book, and the branches taught were the elementary principles of grammar, arithmetic, spelling, reading and writing.

On June 15, 1808, John McLean, of Lebanon, Ohio, commenced, for the Shakers, a book, entitled "Christ's Second Appearing." The object of this book was to inform the public, as well as novitiates, of the faith, doctrines and discipline of the church. In 1823 this book was republished at Union Village.

The Hampton MS. makes no mention of the fact that in 1819, there was published a 16 mo. of 175 pages, a book entitled "The Other Side of the Question. A Vindication of the Mother and the Elders. By order of the United Society at Union Village, Ohio." It is possible that forgotten tracts were also published. Under date "Miami Country, State of Ohio, August 31, 1810," Benjamin Seth Youngs published his "Transactions of the Ohio Mob, called in the public papers 'an expedition against the Shakers.'" This also escaped Elder Hampton's attention. He must have been aware of the fact that Richard McNemar, in 1807, at Union Village, then called Turtle Creek, wrote his history of "The Kentucky Revival," a work of unusual interest, even to those who do not espouse the Shaker faith.

On October 28, 1821, the Society sustained a great loss in the death of Ruth Farrington. As first in the ministry on the sisters' lot, she had so won the hearts of the people that they called her by the endearing name of Mother. She died of dropsy, which caused her great suffering, but was borne with patience and Christian rectitude.

Rachel Johnson, who was standing second in the ministry, was elevated to the place made vacant by the demise of Eldress Ruth, and on October 30 Eunice Serring was promoted to the second place.

David Darrow had won the confidence and esteem of his people, who called him, even to this day, "Father David." His faithful years of labor told upon his frame. After failing in health for some time, he departed this life June 27, 1825, aged 75 years and 6 days. His loss was irreparable. His funeral was largely attended on the 28th, and was a very solemn and weighty occasion. Richard McNemar composed a poem of fifty-six lines in commemoration.

INTERREGNUM 1825-1829.

Experience has taught governments that an interregnum is a period of uncertainty if not of danger. It proved both to the Society of United Believers. The death of Father David left a membership of about 500 souls. His arm had been strong and his heart warm with love. He had kept the believers in subjection. His presence no longer felt, the smouldering embers burst forth into a flame. There was both a revolt and a dangerous schism which marked the period.

Among the first Shakers were men of education, but these were few in number. The intellectual status of the church was not of a high discriminating order. Consequently there was a pronounced antagonism to every kind of literary, scientific or other intellectual attainment. The first members generally brought in their families. The children on reaching maturity, although able to read and write, now demanded greater attainments than had been allowed. The number of books and periodicals permitted by the Trustees was extremely limited. But few books, outside their own publications, could be found among them, and only one or two periodicals, for the entire community. A demand not only for greater facilities, but also for a paper published among them for the use and entertainment of the Society at

large.   The newspaper was allowed and issued in manuscript.
The revolt of the younger members, also culminated in the withdrawal from the Society of many an ambitious person.   Many of
the children of the pioneers sought homes among strangers.   This
has been followed more or less ever since, and defections came to
be looked upon as a probable occurrence.

The history of the Christian church has demonstrated that
schism is the most disastrous of all the dangers that lurk within
her folds.   The first schism at Union Village broke out in 1828,
which was projected by Abijah Alley.   Having become unrecon-
ciled to the condition of things as administered, he openly opposed
the existing authority.   He was borne with, and attempts made
to reconcile him, but all efforts failing, he was suspended.   He
persisted in his efforts and persuaded quite a large number to take
sides with him.   With some of his followers he withdrew and
attempted to found a similar institution with broader views.   Not
having the means nor the capacity for such an undertaking his
enterprise collapsed.

The Shakers have been prone to prophecies and revelations.
In 1827 there came among them from Canada Daniel Merton and
Jason Shepherd.   The former, in that year, after fasting for three
days, made the following prediction: "At the present time the
church is in great peace and prosperity, and it seems as if nothing
could arise to disturb her tranquility.   But a change will come
over her, and many will prove unfaithful and drop out from her
ranks.   Sorrow and adversity will visit her and desolation and
defection will be such that even the most faithful and devoted
among you will begin to forbode the entire annihilation of the
church.   But this destruction will not take place, but after she has
reached the lowest level of her adversity, she will arise and move
to a higher culmination of glory than at any previous period, and
to the highest reachable in that day."

In 1827 the Society at West Union, Indiana, was broken up,
owing to the malarious district in which it was located.   The
members were distributed — as each one elected — among the
societies at Union Village, Watervliet, Whitewater, in Ohio, and
South Union and Pleasant Hill in Kentucky.

Owing to the prevalent idea that changes in residence should be effected, the order went forth in 1828 that the South Family should break up and be dispersed among the other families of the church, and their building to be occupied by the West Frame Family, which in turn was to be occupied by a family selected from among the younger Believers. The East Family, or Gathering Order, to be removed to the North Lot building, and from there many to be removed to the West Frame. The East Family to be occupied mostly by children, but furnished with a regular elders' order and care-takers.

The monotony of Shaker life was relieved on July 16, 1825, by a visit from Henry Clay, which was repeated on the 18th by another visit, accompanied by a number of persons from Lebanon. On the 22nd a visit was made by Gov. Geo. Clinton, of New York; Gov. Morrow, of Ohio; General Harrison and others, who had been attending the celebration of the opening of the Miami Canal at Middletown. On May 2, 1826, the Duke of Saxony paid a visit with his retinue.

REIGN OF SOLOMON KING, 1829-1835.

On the 3rd of November, 1829, the ministry and elders held a meeting to fill the vacancies caused by the death of Elder David Darrow and the removal of Eldress Eunice Serring to Whitewater. It was decided to appoint Joseph Worley to live in second care, with Elder Solomon King, and Nancy McNemar to fill the second place in the ministry with Eldress Rachel Johnson. The announcement was made to the full church a few days later, and was fully endorsed by said church.

In 1830 the order of the ministry, elders, trustees, and family deacons was as follows:

Ministry—Solomon King, Joshua Worley, Rachel Johnson, Nancy McNemar.

Elders—CENTER HOUSE: Daniel Serring, Andrew C. Houston, Eliza Sharp, Molly Kitchel.

Elders—BRICK HOUSE: William Sharp, James McNemar, Anna Boyd, Caty Rubert.

Elders—NORTH HOUSE: Abner Bedelle, Joseph C. Worley, Charlotte Morrell, Betsy Dunlavy.

Elders—SOUTH HOUSE: Stephen Spinning, Daniel Davis,. Elizabeth Sharp, Nancy Milligan.

Elders—WEST BRICK HOUSE: Eli Houston, John Gee, Jr., Caty Boyd, Charity Slater.

Elders—SQUARE HOUSE: Nathaniel Taylor, Clark Valentine, Malinda Watts, Martha Houston.

Elders—EAST HOUSE: James Smith, Jacob Holloway, Anna Bromfield, Peggy Knox.

·*Trustees, or Office Deacons*: Nathan Sharp, Henry Valentine, Ithamar Johnson, Polly Thomas, Betsy Dickson.

Family Deacons: Thomas Hunt, William Davis, Amos Valentine, Daniel Miller, William Runyon, Samuel Holloway, Jesse Legier, Betsy Wait, Betsy Patterson, Rachel Duncan, Susannah Miller, Jenny Slater, Janna Woodruff, Esther Davis.

The above arrangement has reference only to the church proper. At that time there were three other families, viz: the North Lot, the West Lot, and the Grist Mill. The last named, although belonging to the church proper, was not supplied with a regular order of elders, but were under the spiritual care of the Center House elders. Also a family formerly lived on the south side of the Lebanon road, about a quarter of a mile from the cross road. It was a school or children's order, and broken up in 1828. The population at this time (1830) consisted of 238 males (two of which were colored), and 264 females (six being colored). The beginning of the year 1831 showed the Society composed of 11 families, named as follows: Center, Brick, North, South, East House, West Brick, West Frame, West Lot, North Lot, Square House, and Grist Mill. The first four of these was considered the church proper; but the two Mill families—Square House and Grist Mill—were under the care of the church, and worshipped with them. The three next may be termed, intermediate families, although they were under the temporal care and control of the Trustees. The North Lot and West Lot were novitiates, or as called in that day, Gathering Orders. Additions, from time to time, were being made, but it was observed that they were not of the same substantial material as the older stock. The year 1831 saw a greater decimation of numbers than heretofore experienced, the causes being assigned as follows: First, the gradual wearing off of former inspiring testimony of the Word; second, the reception of unsteady characters.

Most of the houses of the Society were now built, and many of the conveniences known in that day, for a pleasant and easy life, were enjoyed by the community, even to many of its luxuries. Yet all this worldly inducement was insufficient to attract adherents to the fold.

The church had always been a temperance institution. In 1820 Richard McNemar composed a poem on the question. In 1832, in order to save medicinal expense, the younger members of

MEETING HOUSE (LOOKING NORTH).

the Society proposed to use their peppermint and other oil mills for the purpose of distilling apple brandy. The older and more experienced of the members looked with serious apprehension upon the matter. It was abandoned. Cider was a common beverage, but afterwards was rejected.

On June 30, 1835, Nathan Sharp, the principal trustee, withdrew from the Society, taking with him a valuable horse and equipage; also an unknown amount of money, papers, etc. This defection was a heavy shock to many of the novitiates and younger portion of the community, producing more or less of a want of confidence in the stability of the institution. On the 14th of September, the ministry and elders being convened in council, for the purpose of inquiring into the affairs of the office, relative to Nathan Sharp, who had absconded, united in declaring that he was divested of all his power, and that all his transactions, after his departure, relating to transactions concerning the Society or its property are unauthorized and void, and that William Runyon has been placed in the office of trustee of the temporalities of the church.

The Hampton MS. practically leaves the reader in the dark relative to the method of conducting the affairs of faith and the constitution of the church, until the year 1829, when the full text is submitted. A history of the Shakers is of no special value without a sample of their logic and the transcript of their constitution. A circular letter with a new edition of their constitution, from the ministry of New Lebanon, was read on the 27th of December, 1829, and submitted to the consideration of the church, and on the 31st the church covenant was signed by the church members. The whole is here transcribed:

" The Covenant or Constitution of the United Society of Believers commonly called Shakers * * * ' Come let us join ourselves to the Lord in a perpetual Covenant that shall not be forgotten.' Jeremiah."

A brief illustration of the principles on which the Covenant of the United Society is founded. When man by transgression lost his primitive rectitude, he then lost the unity of his true interest both to God and his fellow creatures. Hence he became selfish and partial in all his views and pursuits. Instead of feeling it his interest and happiness to honor and build up the cause of God, and benefit his fellow creatures, his feelings were turned to exalt and build up himself at the expense of the happiness and peace of his own species, and the loss of his union to his Creator. The object and design of the Covenanted interest of the Church and the covenant relation of this institution by which it is maintained; are, to regain the unity of that relation to God and that social order and connection with each other which mankind lost at the beginning; and to place it upon that solid foundation which cannot be overthrown; so that its blessings, and effects may be felt and enjoyed by all who are willing to build on that foundation as an ever-living Institution. It is a matter of importance that those who are admitted into this Institution, should not be ignorant of the nature of such an understanding; — that they should know for themselves the principles and practice of the Institution, and learn by their own experience what are the requirements of the Gospel. In a Church relation founded on true Christian principles, one faith must govern all the members. Their interests must be one, and all their plans and pursuits must be regulated by one head or leading influence, and tend to one general end and purpose, according to that unity of faith manifested in their written covenant. For as a body without a head possesses neither life nor power; so a Church without a head or leading power, cannot support its existence, much less maintain the life and power of the Gospel. In the first associations of Believers, in America, their first object was to locate themselves near together, for the benefit of religious worship and protection. And having determined to submit to the government of Christ, according to His revealed will to them, and to devote themselves to the service of God, and the mutual benefit of each other, they found it most convenient for their purpose, and more conformable to the example of the primitive Christians, to bring their property together and unite it in one consecrated interest for the mutual benefit of the Institution.

Agreeably to this plan, the idea of a united interest was introduced, and the property was entrusted to managers in whom they had full confidence, and who were considered faithful, capable and trusty. A Gospel government in things spiritual and temporal was then established upon its proper foundation. It is proper to remark here, that the foundation of the real estate of the Church was laid, and a large portion of it was made upon property which was devoted and consecrated by persons who have since left the world. And it was the special object and desire of these persons, as expressed in their *last wills and testaments* that it should forever remain a consecrated interest, devoted to the sacred purposes for which it was given, and which are expressed in the covenant. Another portion of this united interest has been made up of the consecrated property and labors of those who are still living and faithful in the sacred cause. Hence it is obvious that the Society can never appropriate this consecrated property to any other uses without violating the sacred *wills* and defeating the pious interest of the consecrators.

The government of Christ in His Church is a Divine government, and all who justly expect to be benefitted by it, must come within the bounds of its protection, acknowledge its authority and approve and yield obedience to its requirements; for it is a truth confirmed by the experience of all ages, that a government whether human or Divine, cannot be beneficial to those who will not acknowledge its authority and come under its protection. Every Divine Institution emanating from God, who is the God of Order, is necessarily formed according to some consistent principle. The Church of Christ must therefore be established upon a foundation which cannot admit of a precarious or uncertain tenure. Divine Providence for wise purposes, has permitted all earthly governments, in some way or manner, to emanate from the people:—but whenever Infinite Wisdom has seen fit to establish a spiritual or religious government for the benefit of His covenant people, it has necessarily originated from Divine appointment; and its continuance has been signally blessed by an overruling Providence. This is clear from the records of the Scripture. God appointed Moses, and established him a leader of the tribe of Israel, and by Divine Revelation Moses appointed Joshua to succeed him. Altho' these things were done under the law, they evidently pointed to a Gospel government, which was more clearly manifested under the ministration of Jesus Christ, and confirmed by His Word and works. 'Ye have not chosen me, but I have chosen you and ordained you. As my Father has sent me, so send I you.' Jesus Christ appointed His Apostles as the visible head and leaders of His Church; and the Apostles appointed their successors, 'and ordained Elders in every Church.' And while the government of the Church was kept on this foundation its purity was preserved; but when thro' the influence of human wisdom, the rulers of the Church come to be elected by vote then were produced those unhappy diversions by which the true union of the Church was broken, its orders destroyed 'and the power of the Holy people scattered.' But when the second manifestation of the Spirit of Christ came forth in the revival of the true faith and precepts of the Gospel for the restoration and establishment of the true nature and order of the Church, then the same Divine Order of spiritual government was again revised. Hence the Ministerial Institution must be considered as originating from Divine authority: — Of course the appointment of the Ministry is, in reality, a Divine appointment, given through the preceding Ministry and confirmed and established in the Society by the general union and approbation of the Church; and when duly established, the first visible authority, together with the necessary powers of government are confided to them. Hence to this authority, all final appeals must be submitted for decision. As regulation and good order are the strength and support of every Institution, so they are essentially in all concerns of the Society. Hence arises the necessity of Elders, Deacons and Trustees, to conduct the various concerns of the Church and Society, which fall under their respective jurisdiction.

It is the province of the Elders to assist in the spiritual administration and government of their respective families or departments. The Superintending Deacons or Acting Trustees, are the constitutional depositories of the temporal property which forms the united and consecrated interest of the Church, and the official agents for the transaction of temporal business with those without. And as the governing power is vested in the Ministry, and supported by the general union of the Society, it is therefore very important that the Elders, Deacons and Trustees in all their concerns should maintain a proper union and understanding with the Ministry and with each other. The present Order of the Church was first established at New Lebanon in the year 1792, under the ministration of Joseph Meacham and Lucy Wright, who were considered as the founders and spiritual leaders of Church Order in this day of

Christ's Second Appearing. Under their ministration Ministers and Elders
were appointed, to whom were entrusted the more immediate charge and
protection of Believers in the different Societies. Deacons were also appointed to officiate as acting Trustees of the temporal concerns of the Believers who were then collecting into families, and getting into the order
of the Gospel. In this appointment David Meacham and Jonathan Walker
were the first in temporal trust and took the charge of superintending
and regulating the consecrated interest and property of the Church; and
by their labors and union, its temporal affairs were brought into order.

As a preliminary to the establishment of Gospel order in the Church,
the members thereof entered into a solemn Covenant with each other to
stand as a Community, and keep the way of God, in Church relation
for the mutual support and protection of each other, in their Christian
travel, both in things spiritual and temporal. In this Covenant they freely
gave themselves and services, together with all their temporal interest to
the service of God, for the support and benefit of each other and for such
other pious and charitable uses as the Gospel might require. As the light
of the Gospel increased, in the Church, and the necessity of further improvements opened to view, it was found expedient to renew the Covenant, in order to renew its written form.

Though we consider the law of Christ planted in our souls, as more
valid and more binding upon us, than written laws, creeds or covenants
because on our obedience to this law, depend all our hopes and happiness
— here and hereafter; — yet while our temporal prosperity remains under
the influence of human laws, written instruments may serve to protect
it against all unjust and unlawful claims from those without, and against
any infringement from the lawless invaders of our just and equitable
rights and privileges. The written Covenant however, is but a transcript
of the internal principles and law of Christ which govern and protect
this Society.

It is worthy of remark that the first Covenant into which the members of the Church unanimously entered, was verbal: — yet it was made
in good faith; and being considered by them as a sacred contract which
was religiously binding upon them, it was conscientiously kept. In 1795
it was committted to writing and signed by all the members. In 1801 it
was renewed with the addition of some amendments that were found by
experience to be essential. In March, 1814, it was again renewed with
further amendments, and its written form considerably improved. But
in all its amendments and improvements the original and main object
of the Covenant has always been kept in view, and the substance of it
preserved entire.

It is now more than sixteen years since the last Covenant was executed. During this period the Church has passed through many trying
scenes, gained much valuable experience in things spiritual and temporal.
Hence some further amendments are found necessary, to make the written

Covenant more complete in its provisions, and better calculated in its form for a general Covenant applicable to all the branches of the Society, where Gospel order is established: to protect the Church and its members in their religious and consecrated rights and privileges, and to give all concerned a more clear and explicit view of its nature and principles.

It is therefore agreed that the Covenant of 1814, be renewed, and its written form revised and improved as in the following Articles.

NEW LEBANON, April 30, 1830."

" The undersigned, Ministry of the United Society at New Lebanon, having duly examined the following Covenant which has been recommended to the Society, and agreed to: — and regularly signed and sealed by the members of the Church, do hereby approve of and recommend the same as a general Constitution for the Church at New Lebanon and Watervliet, and also for the United Society in all its branches, wherever and whenever they may be prepared to adopt it.

New Lebanon, April 30, 1830. Ebenezer Bishop, Rufus Bishop, Mary A. Landon, Asenath Clark."

COVENANT OR CONSTITUTION.

PREAMBLE.

We, the Brethren and Sisters of the United Society of Believers (called Shakers,) residing in the County of Warren, and State of Ohio, being connected together as a religious and social Community, distinguished by the name and title of — The Church of the United Society at Union Village, which for many years has been established, and in successful operation under the charge and protection of the Ministry and Eldership thereof: — feeling the importance of not only renewing and confirming our spiritual covenant with God and each other, but also of renewing and improving our social compact, and amending the written form thereof: — do make, ordain and declare the following Articles of agreement as a summary of the principles, rules and regulations established in the Church of said United Society which are to be kept and maintained by us, both in our collective and individual capacities, as a Covenant, or Constitution, which shall stand as a lawful testimony of our religious Association before all men, and in all cases of question in law, relating to the possession and improvement of our united and consecrated interest, property and estate.

ARTICLE I. OF THE GOSPEL MINISTRY.

We solemnly declare to each other and to all whom it may concern, that we have received, and do hereby acknowledge as the foundation of our faith, Order and government, the testimony or Gospel of

Christ, in His first and second appearing; and we do hereby solemnly
agree to support and maintain the same as administered by the Founders
of this Society, and kept and conveyed through a regular Order of Ministration down to the present day; And although (as a religious Society)
we are variously associated, with respect to the local situations of our
respective Communities; we are known and distinguished as a peculiar
people, and consider and acknowledge ourselves members of our general
Community, possessing one faith, and subject to the administration of
one united and parental government, which has been regulaily supported
from the first foundation pillars of the Institution, and which continues
to operate for the support, protection and strength of every part of the
Community.

SECTION 2.   THEIR ORDER AND OFFICE.

We further acknowledge and declare, that for the purpose of pro-
moting and maintaining union, order and harmony throughout the various
branches of this Community, the Primary authority of the Institution
has been settled in the first established Ministry at New Lebanon, there
to rest and remain as the general center of union by all who stand in
Gospel relation and communion with this society. The established order
of this Ministry includes four persons, two of each sex.

SECTION 3.   PERPETUITY OF THEIR OFFICE AND HOW SUPPLIED.

We further acknowledge and declare, that the aforesaid primary
authority has been, and is to be perpetuated as follows, namely, that
the first in that office and calling possess the right, by the sanction of
Divine Authority, given through the first Founder of the Society, to
appoint their successors, and to prescribe or direct any regulation or appointment which they may judge most proper and necessary respecting
the Ministry, or any other important matter which may concern the welfare of the Church or Society subsequent to their decease.

But in case no such appointment or regulation be so prescribed or
directed, then the right to direct and authorize such appointment and
regulations devolves upon the surviving members of the Ministry in
Counsel with the Elders of the Church, and others, as the nature of
the case, in their judgment may require. Such appointments being officially communicated to all concerned, and receiving the general approbation of the Church, are confirmed and supported in the Society.

SECTION 4.   OF THE MINISTERIAL OFFICE IN THE SEVERAL SOCIETIES
OR COMMUNITIES.

We further acknowledge and declare, covenant and agree that the
Ministerial Office and authority in any Society or Community of our
faith, which has emanated or may emanate, in a regular line of order,

from the center of union aforesaid, is, and shall be acknowledged, owned and respected as the Spiritual and primary authority, of such Society or Community, in all matters pertaining to the Ministerial Office. And in case of the decease or removal of any individual of said Ministry, in any such Society, his or her lot and place shall be filled by agreement of the surviving Ministers, in counsel with the Elders of the Church and others, as the nature of the case may require, together with the knowledge and approbation of the Ministerial authority at New Lebanon aforesaid.

Section 5. Powers and Duties of the Ministry.

We further acknowledge and declare, that the Ministry being appointed and established as aforesaid, are vested with the primary authority of the Church and its various branches; hence it becomes their special duty to guide and superintend the spiritual concerns of the Society, as a body of people under their care and government; and in connection with the Elders in their respective families and departments, who shall act in union with them, to give and establish such orders, rules and regulations as may be found necessary for the government and protection of the Church and Society within the limits of their jurisdiction; and also to correct, advise and judge in all matters of importance, whether spiritual or temporal. The said Ministry are also invested with authority, in connection with the Elders aforesaid, to nominate and appoint to office Ministers, Elders, Trustees and Deacons, and to assign offices of care and trust to such brethren and sisters, as they, the said Ministry and Elders shall judge to be best qualified for the several offices to which they may be appointed; — And we hereby covenant and agree that such nominations and appointments being made and officially communicated to those concerned, and receiving the general approbation of the Church as aforesaid, or the families concerned, shall thenceforth be confirmed and supported until altered or revoked by the authority aforesaid.

ARTICLE II. INSTITUTION OF THE CHURCH.

Section 1. The Object and Design of Church Relation.

We further acknowledge and agree, that the great object, purpose and design of our uniting together as a Church or body of people in social and religious compact, is, faithfully and honestly to occupy and improve the various gifts and talents, both of a spiritual and temporal nature, with which Divine Wisdom has blest us, for the service of God, for the honor of the Gospel, and for the mutual protection, support, and happiness of each other, as Brethren and Sisters in the Gospel, and for such other pious and charitable purposes as the Gospel may require.

6

SECTION 2. WHO ARE NOT ADMISSABLE INTO CHURCH RELATION.·

As the *unity, purity* and *stability* of the Church, essentially depend on the character and qualifications of its members; and as it is a matter of importance that it should not be encumbered with persons not duly qualified for that distinguished relation: — therefore, we agree, that no member of any company or association ·in business or civil concern; no copartner in trade; no person under any legal involvement or obligations ·of service; no slave nor slave-holder, shall be deemed qualified for admission into the covenant relation and communion of the Church.

SECTION 3. PREPARATION FOR ADMISSION INTO THE CHURCH.

In order that Believers may be prepared for entering into the sacred privilege of Church relation, it is of primary importance that sufficient opportunity and privilege should be afforded under the ministry of the Gospel, for them to acquire suitable instruction in the genuine principles of righteousness, honesty, justice and holiness; and also that they should prove their faith and Christian morality by their practical obedience to the precept of the Gospel, according to their instructions. It is also indispensably necessary for them to receive the *uniting Spirit of Christ*, and to be so far of one heart and mind, that they are willing to sacrifice all other relations for this sacred one. Another essential step is, to settle all just and equitable claims of creditors and filial heirs; so that whatever property they possess may be justly their own. When this is done, and they feel themselves sufficiently prepared to make a deliberate and final choice to devote themselves wholly, to the service of God, without reserve, and it shall be deemed proper by the leading authority of Church, after examination and due consideration, to allow them to associate together in the capacity of a Church, or a branch thereof in Gospel order; they may then consecrate themselves, and all they possess, to the service of God forever and confirm the same by signing a written Covenant, predicated upon the principles herein contained, and by fulfilling on their part, all its obligations.

SECTION 4. ADMISSION OF NEW MEMBERS.

As the door must be kept open for the admission of new members into the Church, when duly prepared, it is agreed that each and every person who shall at any time after the date and execution of the Church Covenant, in any branch of the Community, be admitted into the Church, as a member thereof, shall previously have a first opportunity to ·obtain a full, clear and explicit understanding of the object and design of the Church Covenant, and of the obligations it enjoins on its members. For this purpose he or she shall, in the presence of two of the deacons, or acting Trustees of the Church, read said

Covenant, or hear the same distinctly read; so as to be able, freely, to acknowledge his full approbation and acceptance thereof, in all its parts. Then he, she, or they, as the case may be, shall be at liberty to sign the same, and having signed and sealed it, shall thenceforth be entitled to all the benefits and privileges thereof, and be subject to all the obligations required of the original signers: And the signature or signatures thus added, shall be certified by the said Deacons or Trustees, with the date thereof.

Section 5. Concerning Youth and Children.

Youth and children, being minors, cannot be received as members of the Church, in its Covenant relation; yet it is agreed that they may be received under the immediate care and government of the Church, at the desire or consent of such person or persons as have a lawful right to, or control of, such minors, together with their own desire or consent but no minor under the care of the Church can be employed therein for wages of any kind.

ARTICLE III. OF THE TRUSTEESHIP.

Section 1. Appointment, Qualifications and Powers of the Trustees.

In the establishment of orders in the various branches of the Society, it has been found necessary that superintending Deacons or agents should be appointed and authorized to act as Trustees of the temporalities of the Church. Deaconesses are also associated with them to superintend the concerns of the female department. They must be recommended by their honesty and integrity, their fidelity and trust, and their capacity for business. Of these qualifications the Ministry and Elders must be the judges. These Trustees are generally known among us by the title of Office Deacons, and being appointed by the authority aforesaid, and supported by the general approbation of the Church, they are vested with power to take the general charge and oversight of all the property, estate, and interest, dedicated, devolved, consecrated and given up for the benefit of the Church; to hold, in trust, the fee of all lands belonging to the Church; together with all the gifts, grants and donations, which have been, or may be hereafter dedicated, devoted, consecrated and given up as aforesaid; and the said property, estate, interest, gifts, grants and donations, shall constitute the united and consecrated interest of the Church shall be held in trust by said Deacons as acting Trustees — in their official capacity, and by their successors in said office and trust forever.

SECTION 2. DUTIES OF THE TRUSTEES.

It is and shall be the duty of the said Deacons or acting Trustees to improve, use and appropriate the said united interest for the benefit of the Church in all its departments, and for such other religious and charitable purposes as the Gospel may require; and also to make all just and equitable defence in law, for the protection and security of the consecrated and united interest, rights and privileges of the Church and Society jointly and severally, as an associated Community, as far as circumstances, and the nature of the case may require. Provided nevertheless, that all the transactions of the said Trustees; in the use, management, protection, defence and disposal of the aforesaid interest, shall be for the benefit and privilege, and in behalf of the Church or of the Society as aforesaid, and not for any private interest, object, or purpose whatever.

SECTION 3. TRUSTEES TO GIVE INFORMATION AND BE RESPONSIBLE TO MINISTRY AND ELDERS.

It shall also be the duty of the said Trustees to give information to the Ministry and Elders of the Church, concerning the general state of the temporal concerns of the Church and Society committed to their charge; and to report to said authority all losses sustained in the united interest thereof, which shall come under their cognizance; and no disposal of the real estate of the Church, nor any important interest, involving the association in any manner, shall be made without the previous knowledge and approbation of the Ministry aforesaid; to whom the said Deacons or Trustees are, and shall at all times be held responsible in all their transactions.

SECTION 4. ACCOUNT BOOKS AND BOOKS OF RECORD TO BE KEPT.

It is, and shall be the duty of the said Trustees or Official Deacons to keep, or cause to be kept, regular books of account, in which shall be entered the debit and credit accounts of all mercantile operations and business transactions between the Church and others; all receipts and expenditures, bonds, notes, and ·bills of account, and all matters pertaining to the united interest of the Church; so that its financial concerns may be readily seen and known whenever called for by the proper authority; — and also, a book or books of record, in which shall be recorded a true and correct copy of this Covenant; also all appointments, removals and changes in office of Ministers, Elders, Deacons and Trustees; all admissions, removals, decease and departure of members; together with all other matters and transactions of a public nature which are necessary to be recorded for the benefit of the Church, and for the preservation

and security of the documents, papers and written instruments pertaining
to the united interest and concerns of the Church, committed to their
charge.   And the said records shall, at all times, be open to the inspection of the leading authority of the Church, who shall appoint an
auditor or auditors to examine and correct any errors that may, at any
time be found in the accounts, and whose signature and date of inspection
shall be deemed sufficient authority for the correctness and validity of the
facts and matters therein recorded.

Section 5.   Trustees to Execute a Declaration of Trust.

For the better security of the united and consecrated interest of
the Church to the proper uses and purposes stipulated in the Covenant,
it shall be the duty of the Trustees who may be vested with the lawful title or claim to the real estate of the Church, to make and execute
a Declaration of Trust, in due form of law, embracing all and singular,
the lands, tenements and hereditaments, with every matter of interest
pertaining to the Church, which, at the time being, may be vested in him
or them or that may in future come under his or their charge, during his
or their Trusteeship.   The said Declaration shall state expressly, that such
Trustee or Trustees hold such lands, tenements, hereditaments and all
personal property of every description, belonging to the Church or Society, *in Trust*, for the uses and purposes expressed in, and subject to
the rules, regulations and conditions prescribed *By* the Covenant or Constitution of the said Church, or any amendments thereto which may
hereafter be adopted by the general approbation of the Church, and in
conformity to the primitive facts and acknowledged principles of the Society; and the said declaration shall be in writing, duly executed under
the hand and seal of such Trustee or Trustees, and shall be recorded in
the Book of Records, provided for in the preceding section.

Section 6.   Vacancies in Certain Cases How Supplied.

We further covenant and agree, that in case it should at any time
happen that the office of Trustee should become vacant, by the death or
defection of all of the Trustees in whom may be vested the fee of the lands
or real estate belonging to said Church or Society, then, and in that case,
a successor or successors shall be appointed by the constitutional authority
recognized in the covenant, according to the rules and regulations prescribed by the same; — and the said appointment, being duly recorded
in the Book of Records provided for in this *Article*, shall be deemed,
and is hereby declared to vest in such successors, all the right, interest
and Authority of his or their predecessors in respect to all such lands,
property or estate belonging to the church or Society aforesaid.

ARTICLE IV. OF THE ELDERSHIP.

Section 1. Choice and Appointment of Elders.

The united interests and objects of Believers established in Gospel order, requires that Elders should be chosen and appointed for the spiritual protection of families, who are to take the lead in their several departments, in the care and government of the concerns of the Church, and of the several families pertaining to the Society. Their number and order should correspond with that of the Ministry. They are required to be persons of good understanding, of approved faithfulness and integrity, and gifted in spiritual administration. They must be selected and appointed by the Ministry, who are to judge of their qualifications.

Section 2. Duties of the Elders.

As faithful Watchmen on the walls of Zion, it becomes the duty of the Elders to watch over their respective families, to instruct the members in their respective duties; — to counsel, encourage, admonish, exhort and reprove, as occasion may require; to lead the worship; to be examples to the members of obedience to the principles and orders of the Gospel, and to see that orders, rules and regulations pertaining to their respective families or departments are properly kept.

ARTICLE V. OF FAMILY DEACONS AND DEACONESSES.

The office of family Deacons and Deaconesses has long been established in the Church, and is essentially necessary for the care, management and direction of the domestic concerns in each family, order or branch of the Church. They are required to be persons of correct and well grounded faith in the established principles of the Gospel; honest and faithful in duty, closely united to their Elders, and of sufficient capacity for business. Of these qualifications the Ministry and Elders, by whom they are chosen and appointed are to be the judges. Their numbers in each family is generally two of each sex, but may be more or less, according to the size of the family and the extent of their various duties.

Section 2. Their Duties and Obligations.

The Deacons and Deaconesses of families are entrusted with the care and oversight of the domestic concerns of their respective families. It is their duty to make proper arrangements in business; to maintain good order; to watch over and counsel and direct the members in their various occupations, as occasion may require; to make application to the Office Deacons for whatever supplies are needed in the several departments of the family; to maintain union, harmony and good understanding with the said Office Deacons and Deaconesses; and to report to their Elders, the state of matters which fall under their cognizance and observation. But their power is restricted to the domestic concerns of their respective families or departments, and does not extend to any immediate or direct correspondence or intercourse with those without the bounds of the Church: They have no immediate concern with trade and commerce; it is not their business to buy and sell, nor in any way to dispose of the property under their care, except with the union and approbation of the Trustees.

ARTICLE VI. PRIVILEGES AND OBLIGATIONS OF MEMBERS.

SECTION 1. BENEFITS AND PRIVILEGES OF MEMBERS IN CHURCH RELATION.

The united interest of the Church having been formed by the free-will offerings and pious donations of the members respectively, for the objects and purposes already stated, it cannot be considered either as a joint tenancy or a tenancy in common, but a consecrated whole, designed for, and devoted to the uses and purposes of the Gospel forever, agreeable to the established principles of the Church; —

Therefore, it shall be held, possessed and enjoyed by the Church, in this united capacity, as a sacred covenant right; that is to say, all, and every member thereof, while standing in Gospel union, and maintaining the principles of the Covenant, shall enjoy equal rights, benefits, and privileges, in the use of all things pertaining to the Church, according to their several needs and circumstances; and no difference shall be made on account of what any one has contributed and devoted, or may hereafter contribute and devote, to the support and benefit of the Institution.

SECTION 2. PROVISO.

It is nevertheless PROVIDED, STIPULATED AND AGREED, that in case any one, having signed this Covenant, shall afterward forfeit his or her claim to membership, by renouncing the principles of the Society, or by wilfully and obstinately violating the rules and regulations thereof, then, and in that case, his or her claims to all the aforesaid benefits, privileges and enjoyments, shall be equally forfeited.

SECTION 3. OBLIGATIONS OF MEMBERS.

As subordination and obedience are the life and soul of every well regulated community; so, our strength and protection, our happiness and prosperity, in our capacity of Church members, must depend on our faithful obedience to the rules and orders of the Church, and to the instruction, counsel and advice of its leaders: Therefore, we do hereby covenant and agree, that we will receive and acknowledge our Elders in the Gospel, those members of the Church, who are, or shall be chosen and appointed

for the time being, to that office and calling, by the authority aforesaid;
and also, that we will, as faithful Brethren and Sisters in Christ, conform
and subject to the known and established principles of our Community,
and to the counsel and direction of the Elders, who shall act in union as
aforesaid and also to all the orders, rules and regulations which, now are,
or which may be given and established in the Church, according to the
principles, and by the authority aforesaid.

SECTION 4.   DUTIES OF THE MEMBERS.

The faithful improvement of our time and talents in doing good, is
a duty which God requires of mankind as rational and accountable beings,
and more especially as members of the Church of Christ — therefore
it is, and will be required of all and every member of this Institution,
unitedly and individually, to occupy and improve their time and talents
to support and maintain the interest of the same, to promote the objects
of this Covenant, and discharge their duty to God and each other, according to their several abilities and callings, as members in union with one
common lead; so that the various gifts and talents of *All* may be improved
for the benefit of *Each* and all concerned.

SECTION 5.   NO SPECIAL CLAIMS IN CASE OF REMOVAL.

As we esteem the mutual possession and enjoyment of the consecrated
interest and principles of the Church, a consideration fully adequate
to any amount of personal interest, labor or service, or any other contri-
bution made, devoted or consecrated by any individual; — so we consider
that no ground of action can lie, either in law or equity, for the recovery
of any property, or service, devoted, or consecrated as aforesaid. And
we further agree, that in case of the removal of any member or members
from one family, society or branch of the Church to another, his, her,
or their previous signature or signatures to the Church or family *Covenant*
from whence he, she, or they, shall have removed, shall forever bar all
claims which are incompatible with the true intent and meaning of this
Covenant, in the same manner as if such removal had not taken place; yet,
all who shall so remove in union, and with the approbation of their Elders
shall be entitled to all the benefits and privileges of the family or order
in which they shall be placed, as they shall conform to the rules and regulations of the same.

ARTICLE VII.   DEDICATION AND RELEASE.

SECTION 1.   DEDICATION OF PERSONS, SERVICES AND PROPERTY.

According to the faith of the Gospel which we have received, and
agreeable to the uniform practice of the Church of Christ from its first establishment in the Society, WE COVENANT AND AGREE to dedicate, devote

and consecrate and give up, and by this Covenant WE DO SOLEMNLY AND CONSCIENTIOUSLY dedicate, devote, consecrate and give up ourselves and our services, together with all our temporal interest, to the service of God and the support and benefit of the Church of Christ in this Community, and to such other pious and charitable purposes as the Gospel may require, to be under the care and direction of the proper constituted authorities of the said Church, according to the true meaning and intent of the Covenant, and the established rules and practice of the Church.

SECTION 2.   DECLARATION AND RELEASE OF PRIVATE CLAIM.

Whereas, in pursuance of the requirements of the Gospel, and in the full exercise of our faith, reason and understanding, we have freely and voluntarily sacrificed all self-interest, and have devoted our persons, services and our property as aforesaid, to the pious and benevolent purposes of the Gospel; — Therefore, we do hereby solemnly, and conscientiously, unitedly and individually, for ourselves, our heirs and assigns, release and quit-claim to the Deacons, or those who, for the time being, are the acting Trustees of the Church, for the uses and purposes aforesaid, ALL our private personal right, title, interest, claim and demand, of, in and to the estate, interest, property and appurtenances so consecrated, devoted, and given up: And we hereby jointly and severally promise and declare, in the presence of God and before witnesses that we will never hereafter, neither directly nor indirectly, under any circumstances whatever, contrary to the stipulations of this Covenant, make nor require any account of any interest, property, labor or service, nor any division thereof, which is, has been or may be devoted by us, or any of us, to the uses and purposes aforesaid, nor bring any charge of debt or damage, nor hold any claim, nor demand whatever, against the said Deacons or Trustees, nor against the Church or Society, nor against any member thereof, on account of any property or service given, rendered, devoted or consecrated to the aforesaid sacred charitable purposes. And we also ratify and confirm hereby, every act and deed which we, or any of us, have acted or done agreeable to the true intent and meaning of the Covenant.

In confirmation of all the aforesaid statements, covenants, promises and articles of agreement, we have hereunto subscribed our names and affixed our seals, on and after this twenty-seventh day of April, in the year of our Lord and Savior — one thousand eight hundred and forty-one."

The above Constitution was the result of experience, owing to the fact that undesirable members had been added from time to time and who had made trouble on the score of property rights. This Constitution is practically the same as that adopted in 1829 and no material change has been made since.

Agreeable to the Constitution of 1829, on March 18, 1830, all
the deeds and conveyances of land belonging to the Church (containing at that time 3,642 acres), were collected for the purpose
of making out declarations of trust, which was accordingly done
and duly executed by all the Trustees.

The year 1830 was disastrous to both the Communities at
North Union and Whitewater, for a special record is made of
donations sent from Union Village. The year was marked by
some desertions from the ranks.

The years 1831 and 1832 were successful in the product of
corn, yielding 10,000 bushels for each year, but a disaster happened in the burning of the flax barn, the work of an incendiary.

The population in 1834 was 331. The year 1835 was one of
disaster and changes. Caterpillars denuded the forest trees of
every leaf and killed many. On the 9th of June the village was
visited by the most unparalleled freshet ever known. The water
fell to a depth of nine inches. All the mill-dams were swept away
or broken through. One-half the clothing, fulling and coloring
shops were swept away, and the oil mill shared a similar fate.
The tail-race of the great mill was filled with gravel and stones.
Much timber was carried off and the lands of the Big Bottom
were overflowed to a depth that would support a steamboat. The
leather in the tanyard floated out of the vats. The damage was
estimated at $25,000.

There were internal disorders that greatly afflicted the more
sedate and conservative. There was a manifest tendency to
looseness of discipline and consequent disregard for good order
among the more giddy and thoughtless of the Society; and even
some of the officers were not exempt from serious dereliction in
this matter. For a time it appeared that a crisis was approaching.

Many changes took place among the officers, and on October
4th Elder Solomon King announced that he would return East
for a season and that he had appointed Elder David Meacham his
successor, and on the 13th of the same month, in company with
Eldress Rachel Johnson, Eliza Sharp and Luther Copley, set out
for New Lebanon.

REIGN OF DAVID MEACHAM, 1835—1836.

The reins of government were assumed by David Meacham on the day that Elder King took his departure. The Ministry living in the Meeting House now consisted of David Meacham and Betsy Hastings, with Joshua Worley and Nancy McNemar assistants. The advent of Elder Meacham and Eldress Betsy gave great relief to the Society. While Elder King was a thoroughly good man, upright and pious, he did not possess the characteristics so necessary for one in his position. The rebellious.

EXTERIOR VIEW OF OFFICE.

and seditious met with a different reception with the new ministry, and were soon weeded out.

The heavy burden, which had grown to unbearable proportions under Elder King—that of entertaining and receiving visitors at the office—was done away with on October 7, 1835. It also had an undesirable effect upon the younger and more thoughtless members of the Society.

On November 30, Elder Meachem, accompanied by Elder Matthew Houston set out for New Lebanon. On the 27th Stephen Wells and David J. Hawkins arrived from the East, having been sent to assist in regulating the temporal affairs of the Church. After surveying the field, about the 1st of January, 1836, it was.

,decided to make certain radical changes. This matter was put to the vote of the Church and carried. It was decided to constitute two interests of temporalities in the Church; and to this end it was proposed that the first family should occupy the Brick House, South House and North House, the South House to be denominated the Second Order of the First Family. The second Family was to occupy the North Lot buildings. The young Believers were to move to the West Section, and the West Brick and West Frame families were to be the Gathering Order of the Society. The West Lot Family was to break up and move into the West Brick and West Frame buildings. The East House Family was to be scattered among other families and their former home vacated. Two whole families were broken up and their homes abandoned. The change began January 12th and required many days before the work was completed.

The officers now stood as follows: *Ministry*—David Meacham, Joshua Worley, Betsy Hastings and Nancy McNemar. *Elders, First Order*—Stephen Spinning, Andrew C. Houston, Lois Spinning and Mary Hopkins. *Elders, Second Order*—Joseph Johnson, John Babbit, Elizabeth Sharp and Nancy Milligan. *Elders, Second Family*—Eli Houston, James Darrow, Caty Boyd and Sally Sharp. *Trustees, First Family*—Daniel Boyd and Ithamar Johnson. *Trustees, Second Family*—William Runyon and David Parkhurst.

On the 14th of February, 1836, a letter was read from Elder Solomon King, who was still at New Lebanon, resigning his position in the Ministry. The same letter stated that the New Lebanon Ministry had appointed Freegift Wells, of Watervliet (near Albany, N. Y.), to be first in the Ministry at Union Village. The number of members at this time was 330, in the Church Order 256, and 74 in the Gathering Order.

REIGN OF FREEGIFT WELLS, 1836—1843.

Elder Freegift Wells arrived at Union Village April 27, 1836, and on the same day was installed as First Minister of the Society. On the Sunday following he received a hearty welcome. On August 7, Elder Freegift "bore a powerful and scathing testimony against hidden iniquity and all manner of sin, con-fessed or brought to light. Also the reading of newspapers on the Sabbath." In 1842 the circulation of newspapers was inter-dicted. On April 3, same year, "a very heavy restriction was laid upon the Church, with regard to meats, drinks, medical and dom-estic beverages, etc., under various degrees of limitation, accord-ing to age and infirmity; the cause to commence on the 10th in-stant. Under these restrictions (with the above modifications), the use was forbidden of pork, store tea, coffee, tobacco and strong drink." For fourteen years this was religiously kept, when tea and coffee were re-introduced.

During this reign, for the first time it is noted by our chron-icler that the men wore drab clothing, which, doubtless, had al-ways been the custom. Every man made his own hat (until 1873), which was made of braided straw, and some of them were so finely executed that they readily sold for $5 a piece. Fur hats were purchased in the markets in 1837. It is also revealed that there was a custom known as the "yearly sacrifice," which con-sisted of a "general opening of the mind and confession of all known sin, required of all in the Society."

The year 1837 "was one of the most remarkable periods in our whole history, at least up to this time. A remarkable revival of religious zeal was prevalent throughout nearly the whole year. The peculiar inspiration of the revival was that of pure love to-ward each other, and a sorrow for our shortcomings in regard to hard speeches and feelings toward one another. On Sabbath, February 5, the Ministry attended meeting with us, at the Center House, it being too inclement to use the Meeting House. Elder Freegift read a discourse delivered by Mother Lucy Wright in the East some years since. It was very solemn and impressive and well adapted to our situation. He also strongly urged the necessity of our gaining the gift of repentance of all wrong, and in humiliation of spirit to labor for a deeper inward work. Many of the brethren and sisters were deeply affected and wrought in their minds and strove to lay hold of the gift. And this meeting may be reckoned as the beginning of a very remarkable revival and a time of peculiar refreshing in this place, together with the

:preparatory work that preceded it. On the 12th the Church meeting was, according to a journal kept at that time, 'one of the most extraordinary of the kind we ever witnessed at this place. It was attended with many mortifying and humiliating gifts, calculated to unsettle and·to free souls and enable them to serve God in spirit and in truth. Surely the spirit of the Lord is striving wonderfully with this people! This remarkable revival, thus inaugurated, continued for many weeks without cessation, seeming to grow more intense with every meeting. I have seen many meetings wherein there was scarcely a dry eye, so overwhelmed were we, not with sorrow, but with the love of God and tender feelings toward each other. It seemed as though we never wanted to break up, but remain to bless one another with our tender feelings and forgiving spirit. I have seen, over and over, many parties kneeling and asking each other's forgiveness for unguarded words that had passed between them. I have noticed many times the floor of the meeting house wet all over with tears after the members had retired."

It was during the reign of Elder Wells that Spiritualism broke out among the Shakers and reached its highest tide. The first notice of it occurred on March 25th, 1838, when two letters from the East were read detailing the wonderful visions of Ann Mariah Goff, a girl of Watervliet, N. Y. On August 26th, in church meeting, Elder Wells remarked upon the wonderful works going on in other places, and added that it would eventually break out among them. Immediately "many were taken under the mighty shaking power of the Spirit."   -

Oliver C. Hampton was a pronounced Spiritualist and has much to say about the manifestations, and leaves us to infer that astounding circumstances took place during the first seven years of this phenomenon; but for the facts, and the instances and special work, he refers the reader to "the several books," the "Records" and the "Annals." It is claimed that the revelations were caused to be made by Mother Ann Lee, who continued among them until her final departure for Heaven; that even Jesus Christ silently and unseen made a special visit among them, and bestowed upon them "faith, charity and wisdom."

About the middle of May, 1839, "the Spirits of the Indians began to make their appearance to the Mediums, and this continued for many months."

Elder Hampton claimed that great good resulted from these manifestations; and yet he tacitly admits there were many extravagant features during the early period, for he remarks: "In looking back over the whole ground covered by it, we are able to see many things which happened during its advent that were the consequences of a want of wisdom in the leaders of the Society; yet when these untoward features are allowed their full weight and measure, there still remains a precious residuum, partly outweighing all the more eccentric, in some cases, unfortunate feature of this great work amongst us." Again he adds: " About the latter part of March, or beginning of April, of this year (1839), the work thus far having been kept within the limits of prudence and a Godly discretion, by the untiring efforts of the good Ministry and Elders, now for a time took on a phase, and was as it were pushed to an extreme, in several directions, which could not have been in unison with the Spirit of our Blessed Mother; but which the Leaders from some cause, seemed unable or unwilling to interfere with, and embarrassing the mediums; who also seemed conscientious to convey nothing that did not come from good and progressed spirits. But as I am no pessimist, and have not one atom of faith in sending the chronicles of ignorance, susperstition, or failure, down to future generations; and as recently, these indiscretions, were all finally corrected, condoned and reconciled among all parties, I shall draw the veil of oblivion over them, and let them rest in eternal sleep."

The Hampton MS. is so vague on the subject of these phenomena, and the subject, owing to its peculiar features among the Shakers, so important, that I design preparing a special paper on the subject. Hence I dismiss the subject here without further reference.

On the 19th of February, 1843, the Church was notified that Elder Freegift Wells, with consent of the Eastern Ministry, had resigned his office of First Minister of Union Village, in favor of John Martin, and would return to his former home at Watervliet, New York. On June 25, Elder Wells nominated Jesse Legier to the second place in the Ministry, and on July 9th took his final leave of the Society at Union Village, and set out on his journey the 13th.

REIÓN OF JOHN MARTIN 1843-1859.

According to the edict for the removal of John Martin, that worthy stood in the Ministry since June 25, 1839. It was not a

LARGEST RESIDENCE. CENTER FAMILY

quiet reign, nor was there anything but might have occurred in a period of sixteen years in any similar community. During the incumbency of Elder Wells the large Center House was projected. It was finished January 13, 1846. This is the most imposing building ever erected in Union Village. The walls contain 1.000,-000 brick. The next day after its completion the First Family consisting of 170 persons, 112 of whom occupied the building, took supper in it. Although the brick was burned on the Shaker property and the timbers from their woods, and the greater part of the labor performed by the Community, yet the expense was so great that retrenchment was made and economy strictly enforced on the estate. During its erection a sad accident occurred, which resulted in the death of Elder Andrew C. Houston, who, on October 7, 1844, fell from the third story and died the same day. His death was not only a shock but also a great loss to the Society, and by his attainments was equal to any office created by the Institution.

Malcolm Worley, the first Shaker convert in the West, and the recognized leader of the "Great Kentucky Revival" died, August 3, 1844, aged 82 years. His children, who had renounced Shakerism, consisting of Joseph, Joshua and Rebecca, commenced legal proceedings to recover the lands he had deeded to the Church in 1812. The claim was put forth that Malcolm was not sane. This suit dragged along until 1848, when the Supreme Court decided in favor of the Shakers. The suit cost the latter $1,200, and had they lost the case it would have taken the land on which the principal buildings stand.

In 1843 the use of meat on Sunday was interdicted. The question was seriously agitated of abandoning the use of flesh altogether, but was decided that every person must be their own judge. In 1848 all the hogs were sold, but afterwards a few were kept to eat up the offal. In 1843 the raising of turkeys was abandoned as a matter of economy.

As inventions increased and the population of the Society decreased, the various employments also changed. The stock was now imported from abroad, and the Durham stock of cattle, secured in England, gave the Shakers a great reputation for improved brands. A spirit of speculation seized some of the community, but was frowned down by the older members. Garden seeds and brooms became a great source of revenue. Development and growth intellectually, were more or less active; for the subject of literature and the acquisition of books received more and more attention, but resisted by the conservative leaders who held that science was destructive to religion and dangerous to Christian character.

Out of the Miller excitement of 1846, when it was declared that the time was at hand that all earthly things should end, there was added 200 souls, whose minds had been swept by the delusion.

7

These people found relief in Shakerism, and constituted the greatest accession ever had at one time.   They were mostly sent to
Whitewater, were faithful and active' adherents, and possessed
of the missionary zeal.

It has ever been a cardinal principle of the Shaker faith to be
charitable and benevolent.   They have been exceedingly generous to the various communities when in distress, and also to
individuals appealing for assistance.   During the great famine in
Ireland in 1847, the Society contributed 1000 bushels of corn.

That Quakers should become persecutors was not dreamed of
in our philosophy.   On April 11, 1847, a Quaker girl, whose
father had died a Shaker, " went to Lebanon to choose a guardian,
and persisted in choosing Elder Hervey L. Eads in spite of all outside persuasions to the contrary and could not be turned from her
purpose.   The Court had previously agreed that if the girl should-
choose the said Elder Hervey, they would sanction the choice, and
turn the said girl over to him. 'This however they did not do,
and so her outside relations forced her away.   She was taken to a
place about 14 miles distant, but ran away in the night, and was
back to the West Brick the next morning, having traveled the
whole distance afoot and alone.   But a few days after, the Quakers
came and took her away by physical force and violence.   And to
make assurance doubly sure, they sent her to the state of Michigan, there to remain till she was of age.   The persecuting spirit of
enmity shown by these Quakers on this occasion was astonishing."

During September, 1850, a sensation was caused about two
girls who had been bound to the Society, and on a writ of Habeas
Corpus were taken to Lebanon.   After a full hearing before the
Court they were remanded to the custody of the Shakers.   In the
early part of the year mob violence had been threatened (on what
pretext the Hampton MS. does not state), and even some des-
peradoes gathered at the cross-roads in a threatening manner.

An incendiary burned the cow barn at the West Brick, on
December 12, 1854, with all its contents, consisting of 22 cows and
4 calves.

April 1, 1857, a tract of land, containing 1,500 acres, was purchased in Clinton County, Ohio.   The object was to start a

colony, but as the enterprise proved a failure, some years later the tract was sold for $30,000, — the purchase price having been $18,000.

"Jehovah's Chosen Square" is first mentioned in the Hampton MS. for September 7, 1845, where the whole Society was want to meet in the summer season, and there preached, announced their faith, good resolutions, sang, marched, danced, etc., from two to three hours, — then marched home singing most of the way. This spot was an enclosed piece of ground of half an acre,

NEW COW BARN.

in the woods, about two-thirds of a mile from the Center Family, to the North East.

During the reign of Elder Martin the population is given as follows: In 1845 there were living at the Center House 107 persons, 74 at the South and 76 at the North, or 257 in all; in 1849 there were belonging to the First Order 153 persons, and 74 to the Second Order, or 227 in all; in December 1850 there were 164 belonging to the Center and 72 to the South Family; in May 1853, there were 241 members, and in April 1857 the membership numbered 264. "Up to this time, we had little foreboding of the fearful decimation we were destined to experience in later times."

Owing to pronounced eccentricities exhibited by Elder Martin, in 1859, the Eastern Ministry having been consulted, de-

·puted Daniel Boller, second in the Ministry at New Lebanon, to visit Union Village. On January 30, 1859, Elder Boller announced that Elder Martin was released from the first gift and Elder Aaron Babbitt should succeed him, with Peter Boyd as second in the Ministry and Elder William Reynolds was placed in the First Order of Eldership. These appointments were ratified and confirmed by unanimous vote of the Church, and Elder Martin was directed to place his mantle upon Elder Babbitt.

REIGN OF AARON BABBITT, 1859-1868.

Elder Aaron Babbitt, as First in the Ministry moved into the Meeting House February 3rd, 1859. For the first time, in several years, the Church Covenant was read, both to the First and Second Orders, on the 27th.

Elder Babbitt was called to pilot the ship through the stormy scenes of the Civil War. The war spirit, despite all efforts to the contrary, seized possession of some of the younger members, who enlisted. Others were drafted, and a fine imposed for not attending general muster. Through the machinations of Samuel J. Tilden, the entire local conscription at New Lebanon, fell on the Shakers. Secretary Stanton decided that the Shakers, as fast as drafted should be furloughed, which was afterwards confirmed by President Lincoln. Although the Shakers opposed war, refused pensions and grants of lands for military services, observed national proclamations for Thanksgiving or fasting and prayers, yet they were not unmindful of the distress caused by such conflicts. To the Sanitary Fair, held in Cincinnati, in 1863, the Shakers contributed the following: 1¼ barrels tomato catsup, 1 barrel sauer krout, 5 barrels dried apples, 1 barrel green apples, 4½ bushels dried sweet corn, 8 dozen brooms, 5 boxes garden seeds, 10 gallons gooseberry sauce, and 5 gallons apple preserves, — the whole valued at $158.50. Their energies were somewhat paralyzed by being called upon to relieve the distress of their brethren at South Union, Kentucky, who suffered from the horrors of war.

Occasionally the Shakers have received members who had gained considerable notoriety. In 1859 Richard Realf became a member. He had been John Brown's secretary during the Kansas troubles. He had undergone much suffering in establishing freedom in Kansas, and was often in the greatest of dangers. He announced he was weary of the world and wanted rest. Being a man of uncommon abilities, he was placed where he could rapidly learn the thoughts of Shakerism. He soon became the greatest preacher ever connected with Union Village, and was heard with delight by both believers and unbelievers. His stay, however, was brief. He soon longed for the ways of the world, became a Major during the Civil War; afterwards was entangled by the wiles of a woman and committed suicide.

In July 1859, an organized band of robbers, from Indiana, made preparations to rob the community, but the design was exposed by a member of the gang, and all necessary precautions taken to thwart the purpose. About the first of March 1860 quite a large amount of wheat and clothing were stolen, and shortly after a great number of shirts were taken. The thieves proved to be apostates.

On March 4th, 1865 the Society lost by fire the Old North House with its contents, which contained a tin shop, broom shop, carpenter shop, shoemaker shop and sarsaparilla laboratory. The loss was about $10,000. This loss was aggravated by the fact that the Society was now $12,000 in debt. Although the constitution forbid indebtedness, and many members were opposed to incurring such a burden, yet the leaders decided that such, at times, was wisdom.

Knitting machines were introduced in 1861. Previously the sisters and girls wrought goods by hand, and their work was sought for in the markets, knitted mittens and gloves sold readily at $6 per pair.

The industries consisted of raising garden seeds, preserving and packing herbs, manufacturing woolen goods, brooms, flour, oils, extracts of roots for medicine, sorghum and of cattle. In 1862 there was manufactured 2 barrels of grape wine, 30 gallons of currant wine and 60 gallons of strawberry for medicinal purposes.

There were many things that agitated the colony during Elder
Babbitt's reign. The Shakers had taken great care of children,
but nearly all of them had left the community on arriving at lawful
age; so that the care-takers were now few in number, and somewhat enfeebled by age. It became a serious matter whether any
more should be received. The questions of insurance against fire
and a change in the mode of dress were seriously discussed. In
1867, owing to the depleted condition of numbers, there were grave
fears expressed that the Colony might become extinct. In 1867
the Eastern Ministry reprimanded the Community for regarding
a proposition to have the Society incorporated. " Can it be possible," say the Ministry, " that either the leaders of people of
Union Village, have lost sight of the only true Order of the
Church of Christ, and now wish to recede from their loyalty to
Gospel Principles, and instead thereof, introduce a wordly form
of Government? We do not perceive that any temporal advantage
of importance would be derived from the introduction of laws governing corporate bodies, but we do see wherein it would sap the
foundation on which Christ's Church must stand. Should we
become a body politic, appointing our officers by ballot or vote,
we then should be left to drift with the worldly tide and the Powers of Earth and Hell would most surely prevail against us. But
while we stand firmly on the Rock of Revelation, and maintain a
Covenant — consecrated whole, our sacred inheritance will remain secure from the ravages of worldly influences. Never, while
reason remains with us, can we extend the least toleration as
union toward permitting any Society of Believers to become an
incorporated body."

The population of the Church on March 17, 1859 was 255;
on January 1st, 1865 it was 167, and 152 at the close of 1867.

On the 20th of July, 1868, the Eastern Ministry, then on a
visit at Union Village, divided the temporal interests heretofore
existing between the First and Second Orders of the Church,
and set off each Family to itself, as far as finances, lands and
houses were concerned. On the 26th, the same Ministry announced that Elders Aaron Babbitt and Cephas Halloway were
released from their gift in the Ministry, and should take the

Eldership at the First Family; Elders Amos Parkhurst and William Reynolds should be the Ministry, and Elder Philip F. Antes to be First in the Eldership of the Second Family.

REIGN OF AMOS PARKHURST 1868-1875.

The reign of Elder Amos Parkhurst commenced on July 27th, 1868. It was not marked by any special occurrence, although questions of vital interest to the Society transpired. The question of great importance was that of indebtedness, but the manner in which it was contracted does not appear. The blame is laid largely on the shoulders of Aaron Babbitt. There had been a large purchase of land, which the Hampton MS. condemned, owing to the paucity of their membership. Besides small tracts there was purchased 257 acres, in 1864, at $70 per acre, and in 1869 another tract costing $9,000. In 1875 the indebtedness of the Society amounted to $20,000, on which there was paid 8 and 9 per cent. interest. When the truth was revealed to the Society, all were appalled. Changes were at once made in the trusteeship. Money, at a reduced rate, was borrowed from other Communities of Believers, and the entire products of a portion of the estate was devoted to the payment of the debt. This was placed in the charge of Elder William Reynolds, and the first year liquidated $2,000 of the indebtedness. In 1869, the woolen factory was dismantled, as it could not compete with similar mills. August 6, 1870 an incendiary burned the large grain and stock barn, the loss about $25,000.

During the months of May and June, 1870, Durham cattle, to the amount of $11,535 was sold.

Singing school and instrumental music were introduced in 1870.

In 1871, a committee attended the Spiritualistic Convention, held in Cleveland, and participated in the proceedings. The Shakers and Spiritualists, on different occasions held conferences; but this was finally abandoned, for there was but little in common between them.

The MS. first specially notices recreations in the memoranda for 1871. During the whole period of their history the Elders of the various Communities were given to visits. The general members had their recreations in rides to neighboring towns, picnics in the woods, and the Harvest ride was always celebrated. The years 1873, 4 and 5 were marked by great agitation and speculation about the revision of the Constitution. It was urged that the leaders had too much and the lay members too little freedom, etc. It was left to Elder Hervey L. Eades of South Union, to draw up a new Constitution. This production was so faulty as to be rejected. During the depression in the money market, in 1874, the Believers at Union Village gave away 4,300 meals of victuals to the hungry poor.

On the 7th of July, 1875, Elder Giles B. Avery, second in the Ministry at New Lebanon arrived at Union Village, and seven days later the following changes took place: Eldress Sally Sharp, who for many years had stood first in the Ministry was released, and Eldress Naomi Ligier, was promoted from the Second to the First place, and Eldress Adaline Wells, of Watervliet, Ohio, was appointed Second in the Ministry. Elder Amos Parkhurst was made Second and Elder William Reynolds First in the Ministry.

REIGN OF WILLIAM REYNOLDS 1875-1881.

Elder William Reynolds became First in the Ministry on July, 14th, 1875. This change appears to have been made owing to the financial stress under which the Society was laboring. This distress was heightened by the failure of a bank in Lebanon, in 1877, in which the Shakers had deposited the sum of $7,568, which was a total loss.

This epoch notes three matters to the Shakers of much importance, that came under discussion. From time to time much commotion attended with acrimony, occurred between the progressive and conservative portion of the Society on the subject of the wearing of beard. From the beginning it was the rule that the beard should be shaved once a week, and oftener if the individual was so disposed. The Brethren of the progressives thought to allow the beard to grow immunity would be secured against throat and eye trouble. It was, after much labor and discussion, permitted to those who plead health; then allowed to all within a certain prescribed mode; and, finally, the whole subject was left optional. On January 1st, 1881, at a business meeting it was decided that some of the property should be insured. This policy has ever since been carried into effect. Lively dancing and the square step exercise had been a part of the religious exercises from the beginning. May 27, 1880, it was announced that these exercises would cease, owing to the decrease in numbers and the members being too aged.

The intellectual improvement had received quite an impetus. In 1871 a Lyceum was established, which interested the younger portion, and even some of the middle-aged. In it were taught, grammar, composition, declamation, and correct language in address. There were also rehearsals of comic and absurd pieces, as well as recitations of serious, dictactic, poetic, and sententious character. These proceedings were frowned upon by the Ministry, but in 1875, the Eastern Ministry being cn a visit, after witnessing an exhibition, gave it their approval.

The Shakers took advantage of the Ohio School laws, and came under its provision, so that in 1879, there was a liberal curriculum; a Shaker teacher employed, which returned to the Society $450 per year, which was not a large sum owing to the taxes they paid.

An incendiary, on January 2, 1876, burned the North cow barn with 39 head of cattle. This was supposed to have grown out of a law suit about a rented peach orchard, which the Second Society gained in Court, from an outsider. It was discovered that the employment of hired help was not conducive to the best interests of the Society. However, in later years, they were forced to it.

Our Chronicler for 1878, remarks: "We began to feel seriously, during this year, the want of more members and greater efficiency and talent among those who from time to time come in among us. They seemed to belong to a class that were not in possession of either talent, or strength of purpose, such as was necessary to the well-being and perpetuity of the Institution, but we had to do the best we could with them, thinking they might answer the purpose of tiding over our depressed condition, until better times might reach and favor us with better material." The middle of the year 1880, the entire Society numbered only 162 souls.

For the year 1877, the Hampton MS. speaks on the subject of funerals. "Our funerals have not thus far been described. They were, and are, devoid of all ostentation, and even the ground in which we are interred, would never be suspected of being a cemetery. It is leveled off and planted in forest trees, and the spot where the remains of our dear friends lay, is not marked by even a head or foot-stone. When one has deceased, the cadaver is washed and wrapped in a shroud. At the proper time it is placed in the coffin and allowed to be viewed by all who desire, and especially at the close of the funeral. All who reasonably can, are required to attend funerals, and if the weather is favorable, also the burial. When the members are assembled, a solemn hymn is sung, and then all are seated. The meeting is then addressed by the Elder, or some one appointed to this gift. This is generally followed by short and sententious discourse from any who feel so disposed. In these expressions of sentiment, as well as that of the chief speaker, an affectionate reference is had to the merits and good qualities that were characteristic of the deceased; and also to the necessity of living a life here, that shall recommend us to the Heavenly Home and the happy scenes to be enjoyed by those who faithfully live in obedience to their highest consciousness of right, while passing through the shades and shadows of this rudimental sphere. The funeral lasts sufficiently long to give every one an opportunity to speak who desires it, and a second hymn, and a last view of the corpse closes the ceremonies."

Eldress Sally Sharp died April 7, 1879, at the age of 80. Nearly her entire life had been spent in the Society. For 39 years she was one of the Ministry, during 35 of which she was First in the Order. She was just, upright and sincere, extremely sympathetic, and took upon herself the sorrows and tribulations of others.

Elder William Reynolds departed this life May 13, 1881, deeply regretted by all. His whole life, after joining the Shakers, was given to the upbuilding of the cause he had espoused. He joined the Society in 1837, and died in his 67th year.

REIGN OF MATTHEW B. CARTER, 1881-1890.

The Eastern Ministry arrived at Union Village on June 9th, 1881, and on the 15th appointed Matthew B. Carter and Oliver C. Hampton to succeed William Reynolds and Amos Parkhurst. The whole church, assembled for the purpose, sanctioned the appointment by the raising of hands.

The greatest event during the reign of Elder Carter, and which distinctly marked the decline of Shakerism in the West was the dissolution of the Colony at North Union, near Cleveland, after a career of 67 years. On May 23, 1889, the Union Village and Eastern Ministry met the entire Society of North Union, and then decided to break up the Colony and move the members to Watervliet, near Dayton, O., and Union Village. The dissolution took place on the 15th of the following October, the greater part of the members going to Watervliet. The following December the North Union property was sold for $316,-000. Then followed a long law suit. A part of the North Union property was consecrated by various members of the surname of Russell. Certain heirs, not Shakers, brought suit to recover the property. The court awarded the property to the Shakers, after costing them $12,000.

Other disasters were encountered. On January 22, 1884, the Elder at the West Frame Family, absconded with $500 belonging to that family, and probably appropriated still more. On July 24, 1890, John Wilson, acting in the capacity of Farm Deacon, took off and clandestinely sold $700 worth of stock and left for parts unknown. In 1885, the Society commenced loaning the Dayton Furnace Co. money, and all told $16,000. By 1890 they realized it was a case of misplaced confidence, and the work of a shrewd lawyer. This loss was total. Added to all this there must be mentioned a destructive cyclone that visited them on the night of May 12, 1886. Several buildings were demolished, and many chimneys of other buildings were blown down; hundreds of acres of forest, ornamental and fruit trees were uprooted;

miles of fences blown away, and some stock injured. So great
was the calamity that it required quite a period to recover from it.
Foes within did incalculable damage. April 12, 1890, the
woodshed at the South House with a two story building were
burned. On the 29th the dwelling, wash-house, with all the
laundry machinery, and several outhouses were consumed.
This calamity broke up the old South House Family, whose
members now became scattered among other families. This
was considered the most disastrous occurrence which ever
happened in the Community. Believing that the fire was
the work of an incendiary, a detective was employed, who,
in a few days, caught the wretch in the very act of
trying to burn the West Frame Family dwelling. The vil-
lain was living among the Shakers. He confessed all and was
sent to the penitentiary for four years.

During February, 1884, a liberal donation was sent to the
sufferers made by the sudden rise of the Ohio River.

Elder Carter died suddenly July 24, 1890. Almost from
the beginning of his career among the Shakers he filled many
important places of care and responsibility. He was strictly honest, modest and unassuming.

REIGN OF JOSEPH R. SLINGERLAND, 1890 —.

Dr. Jos. R. Slingerland.

The Ministry from New Lebanon
and Union Village, on August 21, 1890,
announced the following changes : Elder
Joseph R. Slingerland to be First and
Oliver C. Hampton Second in the Ministry. The first mention of Elder Slingerland, in the Hampton MS. is for the
year 1888, when he is on a visit from
New Lebanon to all the Western Societies. The second reference is for
April 19, 1889, when he arrives at
Union Village to make that his home;
and on the 12th of the following May
was appointed Second in the Ministry.

An effort was made in 1897 to start a colony near Brunswick,. Georgia, where previously, 7,000 acres had been secured. This proved a failure. In 1898 the Society purchased over 40,000 acres in Camden County, Georgia, and placed on it a small colony,. mostly from Union Village.

The membership having not only greatly decreased (60 in 1897), but also in all the other Communities, and the majority becoming old, the buildings began to show the effects of time in so much so as to need repairs. Elder Slingerland supported by the Eastern Ministry, although greatly opposed at home, in 1891, set out repairs and improvements, on a gigantic scale. Modern ideas and improvements now ruled the day. So extensive was the plan that it required several years to consummate it. Not only were the buildings looked after, but the same year ten miles of hedge fence was contracted for, besides miles of wire fence placed in order. The fields were now thrown into 100 acre lots. In 1893, pear, apple, cherry, peach and plum trees were set out to the number of 1,900. In 1895, practically all the lands had been rented, — the Society reserving the gardens and orchards.

A schism broke out in 1893, the nature of which is not mentioned. It was finally amicably settled. The custom of kneeling just before sitting down to dine, was abandoned in 1894. In 1895 the men were permitted to wear the hair in such style as suited the individual. The wearing of caps by the sisters, which had been rigidly enforced from the beginning, was abandoned in the same year.

The Hampton MS. ends with the year 1897. "At the commencement of this year (1897), we had become so reduced, that many serious thoughts were rife in the community as to the continuance and perpetuity thereof; if no better success attended our efforts in gathering in persons from the world, to fill the places of the fast declining members." It now became impossible to fill all the necessary offices with suitable persons.

The MS. evidently is left in an unfinished condition. But in a journal kept by Mr. Hampton, the record is brought down to May 8, 1900. In this record we are informed that on January 9, 1898, Oliver C. Hampton was released from his place as Sec-

Eliz. Downing.

ond in the Ministry, but continued preaching until his death.

The Ministry at Union Village, at this date (September 28, 1901,) is as follows: First in the Ministry, Joseph R. Slingerland, with second place vacant. First in the Ministry, on the Sisters side, Elizabeth Downing, and Second, Mary Green Gass.

Elizabeth Downing, a direct descendant of Oliver Cromwell, was born in Louisville, Ky., in 1828, and has been a Shaker since 1840, living with the Community at Pleasant Hill, Ky., until she was removed to Union Village in 1889, to succeed Louisa Farnham, as First in the Ministry, which occurred on May 12th.

Mary Green Gass was born in England in 1848, and from infancy has been a Shaker. She was removed from Whitewater in 1897, to become Second in the Ministry, having been appointed February 21st.

Mary G. Gass.

To the present generation of Shakers the name of Emily Robinson is sacred on account of her many virtues. She became a Shaker at the age of 8, and on May 12, 1889, was appointed Second in the Ministry and so continued until her death, January 17, 1897.

Emily Robinson.

Those who read my article on the Shakers of North Union (Quarterly, July, 1900) may be interested in the welfare of Clymena Miner, who has been an Eldress since 1860. She saw the North Union Society in all its power, and numbering 200 souls. She now sees the remnant with but seven in number. ·Eldress Clymena Miner was born in Painesville, Ohio, December 1, 1832; was taken to the Shakers of North Union, by her mother, in 1839; removed to Watervliet, October 15, 1889, and on the dissolution of that Society, removed to Union Village, October 11, 1900, and is now in full charge of the North or Second Family. Eldress Clymena is a bright, vivacious lady, and is as pleasant a person as one would desire to meet. She is well informed and an excellent conversationalist. She is devoting the remainder of her life to the care of the people under her charge.

One of the most interesting characters at Union Village is James H. Fennessy, who was born in Cincinnati in 1854, and became a Shaker in April, 1882; Farm-Deacon in 1887, and Trustee in 1898. In his honesty and business capacity the Society has unlimited confidence. They believe that he will extricate them from the most serious financial distress into which the Society has ever fallen. It is to be sincerely hoped that their expectations will be fully realized.

CONCLUSION.

As may be inferred the discipline of the Believers has been greatly relaxed. Even assent to the Shaker faith is no longer required. It is however demanded that the applicant for admission shall have a good moral character, and also to have a healthy body and be under 50 years of age. Owing to the paucity of their numbers, public meetings are no longer held and their Meeting House is practically abandoned. Religious services are now conducted in the chapel of the Center House. There appears to be a general feeling among the Shakers of Union Village that the days of their existence as a Community are drawing to a close. The Shakers of the United States, from a membership of 4,000 in 1823, have dwindled to less than 600 in 1901.

In closing I desire to state that I have received the utmost courtesy, in the preparation of this article, from the Shakers of Union Village. During its preparation I received a presentation of a complete set of Shaker books, from the hands of Elder Joseph R. Slingerland and Eldress Clymena Miner. By my solicitation, the former sent a selection of books to the Ohio State Archæological and Historical Society. May these kind Shakers, and all others of their faith, continue long in the land.

FRANKLIN, OHIO, Sept. 28, 1901.

RISE, PROGRESS AND EXTINCTION OF THE SOCIETY AT CLEVELAND. OHIO.

I. PRELIMINARY OBSERVATIONS.

The communistic societies of the United States continue to elicit more or less attention, and receive profound consideration from those engaged in sociological philosophy. Whatever religious or sociological problem these communities seek to solve, their progress or failure is carefully noted even by those who have not come in immediate contact with the advocates, or their special environments. The careful observer ever remains candid, looking for results, although not necessarily swayed by the opinions put forth and the practices adopted. With an intelligent conception of history he fully realizes that one failure, nor even a dozen abortive attempts, does not prove or disprove the solution of a problem. Circumstances embracing leadership have more or less influence in the ultimate success or failure.

When communistic societies that have endured for a period of a hundred or more years, and still retain their position, practically unchanged, their success, manners, principles and prospects become worthy of special notice. In the investigation the promulgators should have the fullest latitude to answer for themselves. The tendency of this age is to accord that right.

If a branch of one of these communities should exist for a period of years, gain wealth, practice their precepts, and then dissolve or become extinct, the position they maintained should not be forgotten, and their records should be preserved.

For a period of two-thirds of a century there existed eight miles east by south of the Public Square, in Cleveland, Ohio, a community known as Shakers, but calling themselves The Millenium Church of United Believers. Their location they called North Union, and by that name it was so designated by their co-religionists. Although the name Shaker was originally applied as an epithet, yet it has been taken up by the members of the United Believers, who now deem it an honor to be so characterized. It is no longer used as a term of reproach.

The North Union community has passed into history. Its former existence is entirely unknown to the vast majority of the inhabitants of Cleveland, and the greater part of those aware of such a community know it only as a tradition. However, the land owned by them is now called Shaker Heights, and as such is likely to be perpetuated. No one in Cleveland, so far as I was able to determine, could tell when the society was dissolved, and in what year the land was sold. They could tell about the time, but not the date. It was after much perseverance I was enabled to fix the time. These people, who secluded themselves from society, should be remembered for many reasons, and especially because they may justly be denominated as pioneers of the Western Reserve. It is also but just, in what pertained to themselves, they should be permitted to explain their position and submit their narration of events. Advantage of this will be taken through the labors of one of the elders, who has left a MS., now in the Western Reserve Historical Society.

It must be admitted that for a community or sect so small as that of the Shakers, the literature has been more extensive than the results. The believers deserve great credit in the enterprise exhibited in the publishing and spreading of their views. In point of numbers of believers, in this respect, in all probability, they are unexcelled.

It is not the purpose, in this account, to give a history of this sect, nor to discuss their doctrines. These questions are not hidden from the world. Their doctrines have been changed to a greater or less extent, and one important feature added, before the close of the first half century of their existence. However, in its proper place, the dogmas entertained by the

Shakers of North Union, will be given. A brief outline of the sect's history, in that particular, must here suffice. The Shakers owe their origin to Ann Lee, who was born in Manchester, England, February 29, 1736, emigrated to America in 1774, and died September 8, 1784. The first church building was erected in the autumn of 1785, and the first formal organization of the society was in September, 1787, at Mount Lebanon, New York, which still ranks as the leading one. The Shakers thus become the oldest of all existing communistic societies of the United States, besides being the most thoroughly organized, and in many respects the most successful. However, it cannot be said, at this time, they are in a flourishing condition, unless their possessions be accounted.

While the promulgation of the Shaker doctrines was taking root in certain localities in the states eastward, one of the greatest religious excitements that ever was enacted broke out in Kentucky in the year 1799. It began in Logan and Christian counties, on the waters of Gasper and Red rivers, and in the spring of the following year extended into Marion county. Richard McNemar, who was an eye-witness, published a descriptive account of the wild carnival. There is no reason for questioning his narrative. It was even claimed that a babe of six months was spiritually affected. It is outside our province to rehearse what has been written concerning this revival. Suffice it to say that engaged in it were Barton W. Stone, who soon after founded the sect called Christians, but generally termed New Lights. There were other strong men who changed their views, among whom may be mentioned Richard McNemar, John Dunlavy and Matthew Houston, who became leaders of Shakerism in Kentucky and Ohio. When the "Three Witnesses," from Mount Lebanon, were sent into the west, they found the soil partly prepared. Union Village, in Warren county, Ohio, the first in the west, largely owes its location to Malcom Worley. He was early converted and used his influence over his neighbors. His house still stands near the center of the society's estate. Union village may date its origin to the year 1805. The elders of this community have the general oversight of all the societies in the west.

II. ORIGIN AND HISTORY OF NORTH UNION.

The history of the North Union Society is the history of the elders. If the chief leader possessed judgment and was full of enterprise the society flourished. This is particularly true during the first twenty years of its existence. Then came the stationary period, followed by a rapid decline that ended in extinction. The origin, rise, decline and extinction must be extracted from the biographies of the elders.

The origin and location of the North Union Society must be accorded to Ralph Russell, who owned a farm on section 22, Warrensville township, Cuyahoga county, Ohio. During the month of October, 1821, he visited the Society of Shakers at Union Village, Ohio, and united with them with a view of removing his family there in the following spring. Although it is not stated, yet he probably knew of this community before visiting them, and the object of his sojourn was to become better acquainted with their manners and doctrines. He was advised to return home and wait until spring, which counsel, received from the elders of Union Village, was acted upon. He was filled with the same zeal that actuated those by whom he had just been instructed. On his return he immediately began to teach the doctrines he had just espoused, and employed the remainder of the winter in proselyting. When spring opened, the same elders advised him to remain where he was, and prepare to start a community in his own family and on his own farm. This was an undertaking he does not appear to have contemplated. The elders had not acted inconsiderately, for they not only had the means to favor the enterprise, but were willing to render such assistance as was necessary. To this end they sent two of their ablest advocates, in the persons of Richard W. Pelham and James Hodge, who arrived about March 25, 1822. Soon after their arrival a meeting was called, when Elder Pelham "first opened the testimony of the Gospel" at North Union. Under the eloquence of the preacher, supplemented by the influence and private labors of Ralph Russell among his kindred and neighbors, there was a visible result manifested. Ralph and his wife received the elders with kindness and he felt very strong and was positive that a society would be established on his and neighboring farms. As a reason for the faith that was in him he gave an account of a vision he had received since his return home from Union Village, which consisted in a strong, clear ray of light, that proceeded from Union Village, in a perfectly straight, horizontal line until it reached a spot near his dwelling, about where the center house now stands, and there it arose in a strong, erect column, and became a beautiful tree.

The first meeting for public services was held in the log cabin of Elijah Russell, on the Sunday following the arrival of the·elders. Instead of delivering a discourse the time was occupied in stating the principal doctrines, articles of faith, practical life, ending with an invitation to any one to talk over the questions in a friendly manner. Advantage was taken of this opportunity, and ˙for nearly two hours the discussion continued. The arguments continued in a lively manner, both pro and con, for the time specified. At the first lull, a small, keen-looking man, who had remained silent, though deeply interested, spoke out and said: "Christians, you may ground your arms, you are beat if you knew it." Elder Pelham's voice in the meantime had become hoarse, recognizing which the little man again spoke: "Neighbors, you ought to consider that a man's lungs are not made of brass. This man has spoke long enough and said sufficient to satisfy any reasonable people; but, if you are not satisfied, you ought to quit now and take another opportunity." Instead of this sound advice being quietly received it only served to irritate and caused some to become factious. A man now arose who authoritatively said: "Come, neighbors, you have gone far enough, and it will become my duty to use my authority and command the peace, unless you desist." Peace having thus been restored the meeting was dismissed.

The discomfited people, stung by having been overcome by one whom, from his appearance thought to be a boy, in order to excuse themselves circulated the report that "the lad" had been brought up by the Shakers, who had always kept him in

school, and he had done nothing else, in order that he might
out argue everybody.

For full six weeks the elders remained, and held several
other meetings. Ralph Russell's three brothers, Elijah, Elisha
and Rodney, united with him. The two former owned farms
adjoining that of Ralph, while the farm of Rodney was some
distance, but in the same township. Rodney, being single,
lived with his mother on Ralph's premises. To these believers
there were added Riley Honey and Chester Risley, the former
single and the latter married, each of whom owned land adjoining that of the Russells. All of these men, with their
wives and older children, adopted the forms, costumes, customs
and doctrines of the Shakers. Of the six men all remained
faithful with the exception of Ralph.

Immediately the believers commenced to organize, enlarged
their accommodations, erected log cabins, cleared lands and in
a short time there was an interesting group of houses, and the
smoke of their chimneys, in the winter season, assumed the
appearance, to a distant observer, of a rich cluster of wigwams.
The general oversight of the infant community was vested in
the ministry at Union Village. The local leader was Ralph
Russell, who proved himself very efficient.

A religion at variance with that to which people are generally accustomed, and especially one advocating radical measures, must, in the necessity of things, meet with opposition.
This was true in the case of the United Believers at North
Union, but not so violent as that encountered by the society
at Union Village. The first organization at North Union occa-
sioned much excitement, and their doctrines and method of
worship were subjected to ridicule, as well as opposition. In
due time this feeling entirely subsided by giving way to respect
for the people, who soon became regarded as honest in their
peculiar religious views and upright in their transactions with
the community at large.

The United Believers at Union Village were not remiss
in their obligations to those at North Union. Soon after the
departure of Richard W. Pelham and James Hodge to their
home at Union Village, the ministry there delegated Richard

McNemar, Richard W. Pelham, James Hodge, Anna Boyd and
Betsey Dunlavy to proceed to the new settlement and organize
the believers into a common family, to be known in reference
to the parent as "The North Union." It was soon after this
organization that public worship, after the manner of that sect,
was held in a log cabin near the residence of Ralph Russell,
and these meetings were so continued with satisfactory results
until near the close of the year. When the elders returned to
Union Village they were accompanied by some of the brethren
from North Union, who desired to study the doctrines and
observances more fully as exemplified in the usages of the older
community. Their report gave every assurance that The True
Millenium Church had been fully established, of which they
had now become an integral part. In the spring of 1823, section 23 of Warrensville township was purchased by the trustees of Union Village and formally consecrated. Other lands
were purchased and some received by donations.

After the society had been in successful operation for a
period of four years, and was increasing in strength and good
works, through the frequent visitations of the elders and
eldresses from the parent community, without a permanent organization, early in the spring of 1826, Ashbel Kitchell was
appointed presiding elder, and came, accompanied by James
McNemar, Lois Spinning and Thankful Stewart. The society
now began to assume the appearance of an organized body
well officered. The established order of the eldership was now
introduced for the first time. The equality of the sexes was
brought into exercise in the government of the community,
which consisted of two of each sex, each governing its own
side of the house. The one-man power, or one-woman power,
was thoroughly eliminated, and the practice was introduced of
all working together and in harmony, as the head of the body.
It was then and is still claimed that this mode of government
is founded upon the Gospel of Christ's second appearing.

In the year 1828 the time appeared ripe for the signing of
the Covenant. To this instrument no one was allowed to subscribe his or her name save those of lawful age and such as
had been "duly prepared by spiritual travel and Gospel experi-

ence," that no undue advantage should be taken of those who had not counted the cost sufficiently before making an entire consecration. This practical test of Shakerism was signed September 8 by the following persons: Elijah Russell, James S. Prescott, Samuel Russell, Chester Risley, Return Russell, Elisha Russell, John P. Root, Wm. Andrews, Edward Russell, Wm. Johnson, Daniel N. Baird, Ambrose Bragg, Benjamin Hughey, Barney Cosset, Riley Honey, Ebenezer Russell, Mary E. Russell, Prudence Sawyer, Emma H. Russell, Lydia Russell 1st, Lydia Russell 2d, Jerusha Russell 1st. Jerusha Russell 2d, Clarissa Risley, Clarinda Baird, Melinda Russell, Hannah Addison, Caroline Bears, Candace P. Russell, Mercy Sawyer, Esther Russell, Abigail Russel, Phebe Russell, Phebe Andrews, Almèda Cosset, Adaline Russell and Diana Carpenter. Later in the fall of 1828 sixteen more brethren and twenty-seven sisters signed the same document, making in all eighty members. The church was fully organized by the election of James S. Prescott, Chester Risley, Prudence Sawyer and Eunice Russell as elders and eldresses; Return Russell, Elisha Russell, John P. Root, Lydia Russell 1st and Huldah Russell as deacons and deaconesses. The duties of the above officers are mainly spiritual, the temporalities being controlled by a board of trustees, operating under the ministry.

The signing of the Covenant was not only consecrating their own energies to the cause they had espoused, but also the absolute surrender of all their possessions to the church. The act of September 8, 1828, placed under the absolute control of the society a large tract of land, which, together with some acquired afterwards, made the sum total of 1,366 acres, which continued in its possession until the final dissolution, all of which, save 126 acres, is located in the northwest corner of the township of Warrensville, in sections 11, 12, 13, 21, 22, 23, 24, 32, 33, 34. Of the remaining part 15 acres is located in section 414 and 102 acres of section 422 of East Cleveland township, and a fraction over 9 acres in section 422 of Newburgh township. A plat of this land is given in the accompanying illustration.

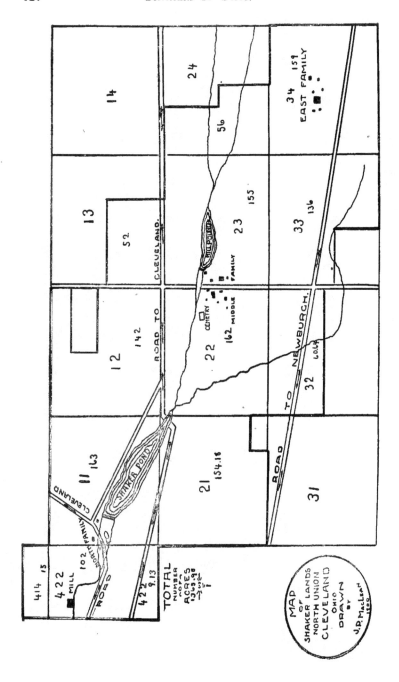

The land on which the society first started was owned by Ralph, Elijah and Elisha Russell, Chester Risley and Riley Honey, all of whom owned adjoining farms. Return Russell and the trustees of Union Village purchased farms adjoining these, already cleared. Other farms, at a distance, were exchanged for lands contiguous to the community, by John P. Root, Oliver Wheeler and Rodney Russell, all of which were under some degree of improvement.

This land is slightly rolling, through the center of which runs Doan's Brook, having a narrow valley, but of sufficient depth to afford admirable drainage. It is located upon the high tablebland overlooking the City of Cleveland. When first bought it was very heavily timbered with beech, maple, whitewood, oak, elm, birch, walnut, basswood and hemlock. On the border of the creek, between the site of the Mill Family and the ruins of the old grist-mill—notice of which will again be made—is a grove of native hemlock, which, in point of beauty, is not surpassed by any in the county. The Shakers left it just as nature made it,—unadorned and unimproved. The first settlers on this soil judged that land capable of producing such a growth and variety of trees, some of which were from four to seven feet in diameter, especially of the whitewood and chestnut, must be of the first quality for agricultural purposes. In this they greatly erred and were sadly disappointed. The deception may be accounted for from the fact that, owing to the great lapse of time since vegetation began to grow on it, the annual decay of the grass and the foliage of the trees gradually deposited the top soil, which varies in depth from five to ten inches. Below this is hard clay, resting upon sandstone. This top soil made the timber, the roots of much of which did not penetrate into the clay, notably the sugar-maple, which is easily blown over as soon as the forest is cleared and the winds have a full sweep, in consequence of which the roots run close to the surface of the ground. On account of the great abundance of the last-named tree it was not unusual during the early days of the society to make 3,000 weight of maple sugar annually.

The lesson was soon learned that the soil was better adapted for dairy and grazing purposes than for raising grain, although good crops were produced for several years after the first clearing of the land; after that it was figured that there was a loss of ten per cent. for every year it was ploughed, unless highly fertilized. Long experience taught the Shakers that the best way to manage this soil was to stock it down, put on fertilizers, top-dress it, sow on the grass seed, under-drain it, keep the water from standing on it and keep the cattle off. Then it will produce two tons per acre on the average. Nothing is more ruinous to this land than to let the cattle and horses tread it up when the ground is soft or full of water; for every footprint leaves a hole where the water settles, and not only kills the grass, but also the life of the soil. Hence the people learned that the ground should be seldom ploughed, and never when it was wet.

The leadership of Elder Ashbel Kitchell proved to be of great service to the community. He had an iron will and his word was law, and fortunately for the people they acquiesced in his plans. He was presiding elder for a period of five years, during which time the society made a great access in buildings and improvements, among which was the first frame house, called the Center House, 30 by 40 feet, two stories high, built by James McNemar, standing on the very spot of land where Ralph Russell saw the vision heretofore mentioned. There was also constructed the first grist-mill, built of wood, 30 by 50 feet, with two run of stone and all the apparatus for bolting wheat. There was erected a frame house, 30 by 45 feet, which was subsequently occupied for a church, or, as the Shakers call it, the Meeting House; also an ox barn, 24 by 50 feet; a cow barn, 80 by 40 feet; a grain barn, 40 by 70; a tan house, 30 by 35 feet, and an office, 24 by 36 feet, besides clearing off about ten acres of heavy timbered land at the grist-mill, and making various other important improvements. Nearly all these buildings were at the Middle Family, which was always the principal one.

Ashbel Kitchell was succeeded by Matthew Houston, and after two years he in turn was succeeded by David Spinning, who became presiding elder October 24, 1832, and held the office for a period of eight years, during which time the community continued to increase in numbers and grow and prosper in all things, both temporal and spiritual.

In June, 1834, a new ministry was formed, consisting of Elder David Spinning, Richard W. Pelham, Eldresses Lucy Faith and Vincy McNemar,—all save the first named recently sent from Union Village. A better selection could not have been

VIEW OF MILL-DAM FROM BOULEVARD.

made, for all were consecrated to the work, able in their exposition of the Gospel, of upright example, and could not be swerved from their duties. With such a coterie the impetus received under Elder Kitchell would necessarily continue.

But Elder David did not wait for this valuable accession to the ranks. In September, 1832, he caused to be erected a building called the red shop, 30 by 120 feet, two stories high, designed mostly for workshops, which was completed in 1833. It was subsequently divided into three parts, one removed and formed for a boys' house, one shoved south of the family house and used for a work-house, and the remaining one for a broom-shop. In 1836 a building was erected for a sheep barn, 24 by 50 feet, placed on the north hill. In the spring of 1837 a new saw-mill was built at the Mill Family, 21 by 43 feet, two stories high, the upper part of which was occupied for a coopershop, and there was made tubs, pails, churns, etc., of pine lumber, shipped from Michigan, from land owned by the society. Just above this mill an expensive mill-dam was constructed across the creek, forming a pond of water covering about twenty-five acres. The same year a barn was built for the Mill Family, 36 by 50 feet, located by the roadside south of the creek. In 1838 a dwelling house was erected for the same family, 34 by 50 feet, two stories high, with an underground room for a kitchen, making it three stories on the south side. It was during the eldership of David that spirit manifestations were recognized, a detailed account of which will be given under the consideration of religious dogmas.

On September 15, 1840, the leadership of the society was conferred on Elder Samuel Russell, who presided over its destinies for a period of eighteen years, during which time it progressed in things temporal and spiritual, in buildings and improvements. Under this administration the community reached its culminating point, both as to numbers and material development and growth. The advance had been steady, with but comparatively few drawbacks. The membership increased to nearly two hundred, living at one time in the three families. A marked decline set in at the close of this period which steadily increased until the final abandonment of the community. Thirty-six years saw the community growing in wealth, developing spiritually, increasing in numbers;—thirty-one years marked the period of decay, slow at first, but rapid towards the final consummation.

Among the first improvements was an addition to the residence at the Middle Family of a kitchen 20 by 60 feet, two stories high, with a bell weighing three hundred and twenty-six pounds, purchased in Cincinnati for $130. It cost an addition of $15 for transportation. The kitchen was very convenient, and later all necessary improvements were added, such as stoves, ranges, bakers, etc. It consisted of a dining-room, with two long tables; twenty-five persons could be seated at each, the sisters on the south and the brethren on the north side. Over the dining-room was a chapel, used three evenings in the week for family worship; also on Sunday. West of the

SOUTH-EAST VIEW OF RESIDENCE OF MIDDLE FAMILY.

cook-room was the bake-room, and over these were two dwelling rooms and two shops for the sisters.

These additions were made necessary, for the society had increased until in 1840 there were one hundred members at the Middle Family, about equal in numbers of each sex, including children, and in each of the other two families there were fifty members, making in all two hundred in this community.

In 1843 a new stone grist-mill was built on the north side

VIEW OF THE RUINS OF THE GRIST-MILL.

RUINS OF DAM AND RACE OF GRIST-MILL.

of the creek, near the extreme western part of this land and not far from the hemlock grove. On the south end it was four stories high. Its massive walls of the basement story was built of sandstone, four feet thick, quarried on the spot, or near by. The gearing was mostly of cast-iron. The penstock was hewn out of solid sandstone, to a depth of 50 feet. The front was laid with heavy blocks of stone, mitered in, laid with

SOUTH-WEST VIEW OF CHURCH.

hydraulic cement. There were three run of stone, cast-iron shafts, 50 feet long, running from the stones above down to the cast-iron arm-wheels below. Besides all this there were two new bolts and screen, smut-mill, and a place for grinding coarse feed. When it was built good judges pronounced it to be one of the best flouring-mills in Ohio. It was a monument of solid masonry and workmanship.

In 1848 a new church was erected, 100 feet long and 50

feet wide, large, commodious and built of wood. It was dedicated November 29, 1849. It is divided into three parts. At the south end are rising seats for the public, fenced off by a railing, occupying 20 feet of the floor room, used by the general public. At the north end 24 feet of the space is cut off for the use of the ministry. On first floor are two apartments. These parts are separated by a hallway 10 feet in width. This hallway is entered through a double doorway. The men's apartments have a doorway to the hall, the audience-room and an exit. The same is also true of the apartment of the women. Over these apartments are others for the elders and eldresses,

DEPARTMENT OF ELDRESSES (ABOVE)		GALLERY
PASSAGE STAIRS	SHAKER	PASSAGE
DEPARTMENT OF ELDERS (ABOVE)	CONGREGATION	GALLERY

FLOOR PLAN OF SHAKER CHURCH

or ministry, leading to which is a stairway through the hall. Each of the upstairs apartments is divided into two rooms and a closet. At both ends are double doorways, and the same on the west side, the latter seldom ever used. The arrangement gave the worshippers a space of about 50 feet square, surrounded by benches fastened to the wall. Wooden pins abound in the building, used for the purpose of suspending hats and coats. There is also a stairway leading to the attic and one to the cellar. The attic exhibits the massive timber used in its construction. The building was painted white.

The building of the church was followed by the erection of a shool house a few rods south of the former, constructed of brick, 21 by 36 feet, well furnished with stationary seats and desks, and teacher's platform on the north side near the middle. It was well ventilated and furnished with the best approved books, globes, maps, blackboards and all other apparatus in use in district schools.

The times also demanded a kitchen for the office, and one was built 15 by 36 feet, two stories high. About the same time a small two-story building was put up near the northeast

SOUTH-WEST VIEW OF OFFICE.

corner of the church, used by the ministry for a workshop, the lower story by the men and the upper for the women.

In 1854 the woolen factory was erected, 24 by 50 feet, three stories high on the south and four stories on the north side, including the basement, built of brick. The upper story was occupied by a spinning jack of 160 spindles, two power looms for weaving cloth and a twister. The next story below was used for the carding machines,—the most of their wool being manufactured into stocking yarn. In the story immediately under this last named was an iron lathe for turning broom handles, and in the basement was a large grindstone and a buzz-saw for sawing wood for fuel, which kept between forty and fifty fires supplied through the winter. The entire machinery was carried by water power supplied by an overshot wheel, with water drawn from the upper pond through an artificial race.

This is a narration of some of the improvements made under the immediate supervision of Elder Samuel Russell, who went further in this direction than any one ruling that community. His attention was also called to the better stock of cattle and horses. Of the former he secured the Durham and Devonshire breeds, of the most thoroughbred that could be obtained in either England or the United States. The horses adopted were those evenly matched in color, size and speed— it proving nothing whether they were Morgan, French, Canadian or Arabian.

The withdrawal of Elder Samuel Russell from the society in 1858 left his office vacant, which was immediately filled by the appointment of John P. Root in the ministry. In 1862 the ministry was dissolved.

About the year 1858, on account of some financial troubles, vaguely hinted at and their origin, Elder Richard W. Pelham was sent from Union Village to straighten it out. He remained two years engaged in this work. This mission did not interfere with the work of Elder Root.

There is no record of any special improvement after 1858. In 1870 the condition had become such that a rumor was current that an abandonment was contemplated. This met with an indignant denial. At this time the three families were kept up, having a membership of one hundred and twenty-five.

In 1874 the Novitiate Elder and Eldress were James S. Prescott and Prudence Sawyer.

In 1875 there were still three families, numbering one hundred and two persons, of whom seventeen were children and youths under twenty-one years of age. Of these last six were boys and eleven girls. Of the adult members, forty-four were women and forty-one men. Their number had recently increased, although during the previous fifteen years there had been a gradual diminution. Of the members then remaining about one-third were brought up in the society. Of the remainder most of them had been by religious connections Baptists, Methodists and Adventists. The majority had been farmers, but there were also sailors, whalemen and weavers. Some were Englishmen, others Germans, still others Swiss, but the greater portion were Americans. The buildings now began to exhibit neglect, showing a want of thorough painting and the neatness of shops. They had no steam laundry, nor provision for baths. They possessed a small library and took the daily *New York World* and *Sun*. They had no debts, but possessed a fund at interest. Their chief source of income was supplying milk and vegetables to Cleveland, as well as fire wood and lumber. Their dairy brought them the previous year $2,300.*

The Shaker for November, 1876, contains the following notice of North Union:

"Anticipated development of stone quarry at this place looks like a steady source of income to society. Grist-mill, built in 1843, has failed for years to be more than a convenience, and sometimes only an expense, is now running by steam and likely to be appreciated as one of the best in the country. Nearly 1,000 bushels of oats threshed. Early potatoes were a good crop; late ones not so good—bugs, etc. Roots and garden products coming in well. A dairy herd at the center family— forty cows—are unequalled in the state."

In 1879 the East Family had twenty-five members, of which John P. Root and Charles Taylor were the elders, and Rachel Russell and Harriet Snyder the eldresses. The Middle Family had thirty members, of which Samuel Miner and George W. Ingalls were elders and Lusetta Walker and Clymena Miner the eldresses. The Mill Family had twelve members, of which Curtis Cramer and Watson Andrews were elders and Lydia Cramer and Temperance Devan eldresses. The board of trustees consisted of James S. Prescott, George W. Ingalls and Samuel S. Miner, and the deaconesses of Candace Russell, Abigal Russell and Margaret Sawyer.

---

*Nordhoff's Communistic Societies of the United States. p. 204.

As the society had ever been dependent on Union Village for its ministry, and as there was no ministry resident, those who filled that position were, at this time, William Reynolds, Amos Parkhurst, Louisa Farnham and Adaline Wells.

The members of the community, for the greater part, had reached an age when they could not toil as of yore. Hence it

SOUTH-EAST VIEW OF RESIDENCE OF EAST FAMILY.

became necessary to employ laborers and the fruits were not of the increase. John P. Root ceased to be presiding elder in 1876 and was succeeded by James S. Prescott, who in turn was succeeded by Samuel Miner in 1878.

In 1889, owing to the age of the members and the numbers decreased to twenty-seven, and the East Family buildings having been abandoned, further struggle was deemed unwise. Matthew Carter, of Union Village, was made property trustee, who afterward turned the office over to Joseph R. Slingerland and Oliver C. Hampton, also of Union Village. On October

24, 1889, the society was dissolved, eight of the members going to Union Village and the remainder to Watervelt, near Dayton, Ohio. At the time of the dissolution of the society the elders were Samuel S. Miner and Clymena Miner at the Middle Family and Watson A. Andrews and Temperance Devan at the Mill Family. Then came the auction for the disposal of such chattels as the members did not desire to take with them. Two of the brethren remained to look after the buildings and collect the rent. Some three years later the land, by the trustees, Joseph Slingerland and Oliver C. Hampton, was sold to T. A. and Lawrence Lamb for the sum of $316,000. A few years still later the same land sold for $1,365,000. The park system of Cleveland, with its boulevards now (1900) takes in all of Doan Creek that once belonged to the Shakers of North Union.

III. THE SHAKER FAMILIES.

I have never seen any description of the three families that constituted North Union. The description that here follows depends almost entirely on my own trips to the locality, made March 8, 27 and April 1, 1900. My first walk was for the sole purpose of locating the village and obtaining a general view. The second trip was for the purpose of obtaining definite information concerning such things as I was unable to determine during my first visit. Fortunately I learned of Mr. John Ubersax, who was in the employ of the society from 1861 to 1869, and he accompanied me and readily gave me such information as I required. He was the peddler for both the brethren and sisters, carved thirty-four of the head-stones in the cemetery, and laid the stone walks at the Middle Family.

Approaching the lands from the west the first object that attracts the eye is the ruins of the old grist-mill. It is one corner of solid masonry, rising to the height of 45 feet. When the mill ceased to be of value it was sold. The new proprietor blew it up with dynamite, in order to extend his stone quarry underneath it. The dam is at a very narrow part of the stream hard by, composed of heavy beams. The mill race was covered from the dam to its junction with the mill. A part still remains. A few feet north of the mill may be seen the foundation of the miller's home. The first miller was Jeremiah Ingalls, a member of the Mill Family.

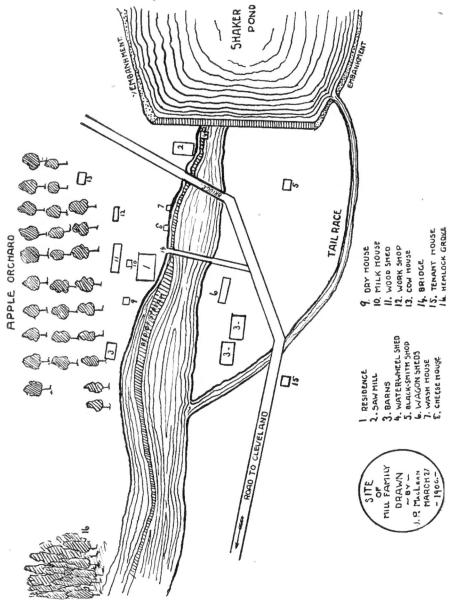

Proceeding eastward, leaving the Hemlock Grove, we next came to the site of the Mill Family, not a single building of

which remains; nor are the foundations in a good state of preservation, save that of the saw-mill, close by the great dam of
earth and stone. All this destruction has taken place since its
desertion by its last inhabitants. These buildings were all of
wood, with sandstone foundations. The mill building proper
was removed, while the remaining buildings were destroyed by
fire. While Doan Creek is narrow at this point, yet there is
a marked declivity of the land towards the banks of the stream.
The residence was on the bank, so built, in all probability, for
the purpose of having a basement kitchen. The wall for the
cheese house commenced at the bed of the stream. The never-
failing spring ran through the wash house. The barns (marked
3, 3, in the accompanying diagram) were on the south side on
high land overlooking that on which the other buildings were
placed. These barns were connected with the residence by a
roadway, now abandoned. The bridge remains in a ruined
condition. This was the bridge crossed by the patrons of the
saw-mill from the south. The buildings were arranged for the
two-fold purpose of health and convenience. The dam, although well built, at times was a source of some danger during
freshets. But such breaks as occurred were repaired without
delay, unless unavoidable. As an additional protection willows
were planted, which also extended along the embankments. At
the present time there is a broad space enlarging the dam,
built as an extension of Cleveland's boulevard system. Another
arm of the same system extends a bridge and roadway between
the site of the mill and that of the residence.

The family sometimes called the North, also the Second,
but generally known as the Mill Family, for its existence depended largely on the grist-mill to the west and the saw-mill
at the dam. When in the highest degree of their prosperity
they were great sources of income. The saw-mill turned out
lumber, and vessels of various kinds that met with a ready and
profitable sale. The water from the spring was carried to the
residence through pipes, and being soft, was used for such purposes as cooking, washing and bathing. In everything the sisters were favored as well as the brethren, not only in the matter
of convenience, but in the power to produce and sell.

Of the Center or Middle Family the greater number of buildings still stand, a faithful witness of good workmanship and heavy and solid timbers. These have stood for a period of

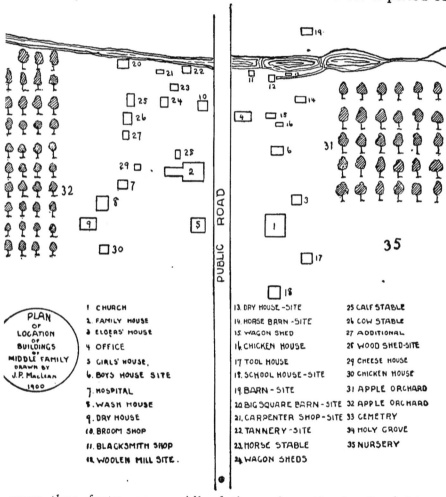

PLAN of LOCATION of BUILDINGS of MIDDLE FAMILY DRAWN BY J.P. MacLean 1900		
1 CHURCH	13. DRY HOUSE -SITE	25 CALF STABLE
2. FAMILY HOUSE	14. HORSE BARN -SITE	26 COW STABLE
3 ELDERS' HOUSE	15. WAGON SHED	27 ADDITIONAL
4 OFFICE	16. CHICKEN HOUSE	28 WOOD SHED-SITE
5 GIRLS' HOUSE,	17 TOOL HOUSE	29 CHEESE HOUSE
6. BOYS HOUSE SITE	18. SCHOOL HOUSE - SITE	30 CHICKEN HOUSE
7. HOSPITAL	19. BARN - SITE	31 APPLE ORCHARD
8. WASH HOUSE	20 BIG SQUARE BARN - SITE	32 APPLE ORCHARD
9. DRY HOUSE	21. CARPENTER SHOP - SITE	33 CEMETRY
10. BROOM SHOP	22 TANNERY - SITE	34 HOLY GROVE
11. BLACKSMITH SHOP	23. HORSE STABLE	35 NURSERY
12 WOOLEN MILL SITE.	24 WAGON SHEDS	

more than forty years. All of them show the hand markings of neglect. Decay of the buildings commenced with the decay of the community. With the exception of the broom shop, painted red, there is scarcely a trace of paint on any of the buildings. Even the white church has the appearance of unpainted boards long exposed to rains. The buildings have every appearance of a long deserted village. Most of the buildings are not used and those in use are neglected. Amidst the ruins, even the unpracticed eye can read the testimony of former prosperity.

My first approach to the village was from the northwest. The family residence and office appeared familiar when I caught the first distant view. I had seen them before. There can be no mistake. The impression was too vivid. That was my first appearance in that vicinity. Perhaps years ago I saw them in a dream, which dream was laid up in a substratum of my brain. I do not know. I only know I had seen them before.

In this village were two brick buildings, the woolen mill and the school house. The former was blown up to make room for the boulevard, and not a trace remains, although the mill race is practically intact. When the children were too few in number to have a teacher the school building was sold and the brick removed. The buildings are connected with sandstone slabs regularly laid, so that in the muddiest season there was no effort in passing to the school house, church, office, nursery or hospital, girls' house, wash house, etc. With a few exceptions these stones are still in place. The buildings that have been removed, besides those already mentioned, were dry house (13), horse barn (14), big square barn (20), carpenter shop (21), tannery (22), and woodshed (28). Some of the buildings could be put in repair at comparatively small expense, notably the church, the office and the residence; but as there is no necessity for this, they will vanish in a few more years, even as those who erected them have passed away. A German family now lives in the office and a Hungarian family in the residence.

Besides agriculture the Middle Family depended on the sale of brooms, stocking yarn, leather and broom handles. The principal resource was broom making, which was carried on quite extensively, the brush having been bought in Illinois. The sisters manufactured bonnets, stockings, mittens, socks, gloves, etc., besides canning and drying fruit, making apple butter, etc.

The buildings of the East Family practically remain intact, although decay is written over all of them. The family residence is of about the same size and construction as that at the

Center.   When the buildings were erected and when the family
retired to the Center I have no record.   It was abandoned since
1879, and probably not long anterior to the dissolution of the
society.

This family was originally the Gathering Order, which consisted of four elders, two of each sex, where all were directed
to go who desired to join the community, and where strangers

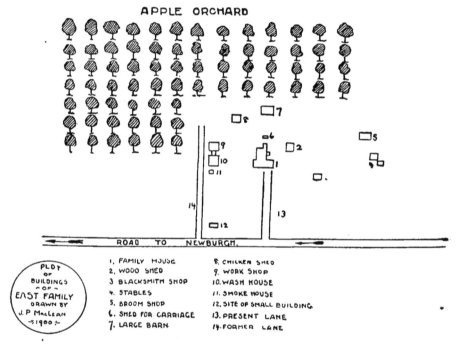

called to secure information respecting future membership.
Many called in the fall of the year and when spring opened
would withdraw.   These were called "Winter Shakers."   The
principal resources of this family were the manufacture and
sale of brooms and the selling of milk at the door.

The third and last trip was made with Mr. Ralph Hogan,
who accompanied me for the purpose of taking such photo-
graphs as I desired, which accompany this work.   In the three
trips I found the ground muddy and in places almost impassable.   It is probable that the Shakers improved their own
roads, although the evidence is wanting.

IV. MANNERS AND CUSTOMS.

The arts and sciences have already been indirectly treated. and need not be specially pointed out. Their dress was not unlike that of the Quakers. The men wore their hair long behind, and the women had their heads enclosed in caps. Their dress was plain, severely so. In this that of the women was more striking and least attractive.

They did not associate with the world, save in the matter of gain. They sought no acquaintances, but lived strictly within themselves; but having frequent visits and communications with the parent Union Village.

The Western Reserve Historical Society possesses three MS. letters, which are here inserted, being of sufficient interest for preservation. These letters were not enclosed in envelopes, but endorsed on the back, one having a broken seal. The first is endorsed, Rhoda Watson.

"UNION VILLAGE Dec. 2d 1828.

Kind Sister Rhoda I received your handsome little present by the hand of the Brethren together with your kind love &c, for which I truly feel thankful for I wish to remember & be remembered every faithful cross-bearer, — I likewise was very much pleased to read your good determinations as expressed in the conclusion of your little letter; and I can assure you if you abide faithful in the calling whereunto you are called the end of your faith will be the salavation of your soul,—I am glad to hear of any one setting out to save themselves from this untowered generation.—

As to any Kindness or charitable feeling manifested by me while I was there I can make you heartily welcome I remember very well of paying a visit to your house when James was on his deathbed.—I felt willing to show kindness but I had but little opportunity that I remember of If I remember right you was unwell yourself when I was there and besides that and attending on James you had a young child, & was obliged to neglect it a little sometimes—perhaps on one of these occasions I might have tried to help a little, but I cannot re-

member of much, — however it seems that ·you accepted a willing
mind—

It is a time of general health which blessing for one I
enjoy and have since you saw me (in general)—So as a token of
my well wishes I send you this little present,—I thought I must
send you something that would be of use to you as probably
you are in the habit of wearing a cap before now.—The chest-
nuts are quite a rarity with us, of course taste very good. — I
have sent you a hymn noted down. — This may suffice to express
my faith and determination—

Be so kind as to accept of my best gospel love and give
it to as many as you feel — but in particular to Elder Ashbel — &
Bro Rufus—Eldresses Lois & Sister Thankful & Sister Polly,
&c,—for I do love them—

ANDREW C. HOUSTON."

The next is without date, but addressed to Thankful, Union
Village. It is on paper that bears greater age than the above.
How it was returned to North Union is unknown. "Thankful"
is probably Thankful Stewart.

"Kind Sisters Thankful and Polly I cannot express the
sensations of love and gratitude I owe you with the rest of my
kind Elders for the blessings the kindness & good ministrations which I have received from you ever since my first acquaintance with you for which may I never cease to be thankful though tongue cannot express As we are now to be left
destitute for a little season of the kind care and protection of
our Elders O remember us in your prayers. that we may be
enablled to walk agreeable to your desires and not leaving a
wound upon so glorious a cause as we are called to obey I
feel like one among my Brethren and Sisters that means to be
faithful while you are absent from us and through life for I
do feel thankful for the privilege which I now enjoy through
the blessings of the gospel O may we again have the privilege
of seeing all our Elders that we may be the better enabled to
make our thankfulness more clearly manifest be so kind as to
accept of my best love and give it to all with whome I have
had any acquaintance and all that belong to the family of Christ

and Mother for may I ever esteem love and union as the greatest treasure on the earth—In haste.

So kindly Farewell,

RHODA WATSON."

The third letter is of a different nature and calls up traveling of other days. It had been sealed and on the back was "To
Sister Rhoda North Union Center Family."

"SECOND FAMILY UNION VILLAGE, Oct. 6, 1848.

Respected Sister Rhoda.—I now undertake to write a few
lines to let you know how we got along on our journey. The
Brethren both turned sick soon after we left the shore and
could not sit up part of the way. Elderess Sister did not own
that she was sick.

The swells were so high and rough that I became sickened
though not so much as to vomit. By dinner time we were some
better & eat some. after this we were well enough, with the
exception of a dizziness in the head. We left Cleveland at 9
o'clock and reached Sandusky half past 2. here we put up
at a carr office, took supper and learned that the morning train
did not leave until 10 oclock Friday, and at Springfield stay
over night, then reach Dearfield by 8 oclock Saturday morning.
Rather than tarry so long by the way, we chose to go along
with the train that ran in connection with the boat that we
had left. This train had but two passenger carrs attached to it,
and think there were about 50 people in the one we were in
and not so many in the other. We left Sandusky a little before 6 evening and got to Springfield half past 3 morning.

Our tickets told us that we were 134 miles from the Lake.

This train runs no farther than to this place & back again.
therefore we all moved ourselves & baggage out, and into
another that runs from this place to Cincinnati. We started I
think, about 4, passed through Xenia soon after day break and
reached Dearfield* just at 8 oclock Fri morning. No one
but ourselves stoped here, and at that moment the Lebanon
Hack drove up and took us in. We had no rain on our way,

*Now South Lebanon.

and here we found the roads as dusty as they were when we left home, and a great change as far as the eye could behold the leaves on the trees were mostly red or yellow, the earth and grass seemed parched and dry. The Hack landed us safe at our door by 10 Oclock Friday morning. The Brethren and Sisters were not looking for us untill next day. Nothing very especial took place while we were absent, and we found the family in tolerable good health, and glad to see our safe return. The next day after we got home it began to rain and was showery for three days. Since that we have fair weather and a pleasant time for our good friends from Pleasant Hill,* a carriage load of them have come to Union Village, and are visiting the Second Family to-day. we have learned some pretty little songs from them. Their names are as follows Elder Brother Joel Shields and Henry Daily Elder Sister Sophia Vooris & Elenor Hatfield.

Brother Timothy wishes to send a pleasant spinner by the Brethren, and he has not sufficient time to make one before they start, therefore he sends one that has been in use long enough to be proved very good.

With much pleasure we will long remember our visit at North Union, and not at this time return our warmest thanks and best love love love.

I would like to have my particular love given to all the Sisters, and especially to the young Sisters. Were it not for being so tedious I would love to name them all, one by one, but I think I have already been tedious enough so

Farewell in love,

JULIA DARROW.

SISTER RHODA."

These letters are written in a clear, legible hand, and probably indicate the general nature of the correspondence between the communities of North Union and Union Village.

It is not to be inferred that their interests were wholly within themselves. The general reputation of the Shakers is that they are kind to the unfortunate and needy and never

---

*A Shaker Community in Kentucky.

turn away one empty handed from their door. Unfortunately, however, when one leaves them, even though he or she may have been a faithful follower for years and rendered most excellent service, that one is abandoned and "given over to the world, the flesh and the devil." While this is equally true of all the religious sects it does not redound to their credit. It is not the Spirit of the Great Exemplar.

On the other hand, it must be noted that while the Shaker was capable of driving a sharp bargain, yet in his dealings he was honest. His wares were exactly as represented. Shaker goods have always been synonomous with honest productions. Their fabrics were made of the best material, and always found a ready market.

As may be inferred, the sexes lived apart, although in the same building. In reference to the Middle Family, the brethren lived on the north and the sisters on the south side of the main building. In the days of greatest prosperity those who made brooms lived over the shop and some at the office. At first the children were at the East Family; when removed to the Middle Family the boys had a house not far from the office, and the girls a residence across the street from the church. The children were under the immediate charge of a keeper. No child under ten was taken into the family unless accompanied by its father or mother, or both.

The separate families had their own dining-rooms attached to the main residence. In 1870 there were two long tables, the brethren served at the one and the sisters at the other. The ministry always was served at a separate table, and the children had their repast after all the others had finished their meal.

It was the practice for all to kneel before and after eating; no loud talking was permitted during meals, and only such conversation as became necessary for the serving of the food. They had breakfast at six o'clock, dinner at twelve and supper at six. The signal for rising in the morning and for their meals and meetings was given by a bell. All were supplied with wholesome food in sufficient quantity. Pork was eschewed, on the grounds that it was not wholesome. Some of the members refused to eat meat in any form. Alcoholic stimulants or ardent spirits was not allowed to be used, save when prescribed by a physician as a medicine, and even that toleration became almost obsolete.

The children were cared for with great kindness, and the government was strict, and the force usually applied was moral suasion. At the proper age the child was sent to school, under the instruction of one of the community, where the common branches were taught. The last teacher was Miss Elmina Phillips, daughter of Elder Freeman Phillips, of the Mill Family, who joined the society in 1841. Miss Phillips passed so good an examination before the county board that it was always received without further trial. She left the community in 1875, and now resides in Cleveland. As the Shakers had enough children to form a district under the law they drew money from the public funds, but when the children became few in numbers the district was divided and assigned to others. The salary for the teacher's services, like that of all others, went into the common funds.

Labor was honorable amongst them. Whatever position one might hold, still he must labor with his hands. But the general spirit was to move slowly. There was not that incentive to energy, push and daring characteristic to the man of success. In the allotment of labor due consideration was allowed to adaptability, and when any one displayed an ingenuity in a certain line restrictions were not placed on him. Whatever growth and development that occurred were due to the energy manifested by a leader in that line, as already noted.

As the people lived up to their best ideas of health, there was, in consequence, but little sickness. Among them contagious diseases were unknown. In the early stages of the community their mode of practice was Thompsonian more than any other, but in later years they paid more attention to ventilating their sleeping apartments and dwellings, and by the reforms instituted sickness became almost unknown, and hence there was but little use for drugs and doctors. Still there were two doctors among them, one of whom was a graduate of Yale College and took lectures under Professor Silliman. In extreme cases they were known to take the Water Cure. A hospital, called the Nursery, was provided for the sick, and there all attention demanded was administered with the utmost kindness. As already intimated, the hospital was seldom used, but under the laws regulating their manners and customs such a place, when needed, was of the utmost convenience.

Under the regulations adopted it must go unquestioned that the whole tendency was towards longevity. During the first

SOUTH-EAST VIEW OF HOSPITAL.

forty-eight years of the society's existence, there were ninety-two deaths, fifty males and forty-two females. The average age was over forty-nine. Nine were over eighty, thirteen over seventy, twelve over sixty and ten over fifty years of age. Besides these there were three children under two years, and one boy under eight who was killed by an accidental fall from a steep bank below the grist-mill.

The funerals were attended with but little ceremony. When a person died among them the body was kept from twenty-four to forty-eight hours, and even longer if circumstnces so required. The friends and relatives of the deceased outside the community living at a reasonable distance were notified of the hour of the funeral. The body was laid out and placed in a plain coffin, having a lid at the head, and was then placed in the lower hall of the dwelling, just before the commencement of the ceremony. The members of the society then assembled in their chapel, usually with those from the other families. The meeting opened with a solemn song, or an appropriate hymn composed for the occasion, after which the elder stepped out and addressed those present, in which he endeavored to impress the thought that they too were born to die, and whatever things were lovely and of good report in the life or character of the deceased, they should be imitated by the living. Short addresses were sometimes made by others, in which the brethren and sisters participated. At the close of this ceremony all proceeded to the burial. As they passed out of the hall they took the last farewell look at the remains of the departed by passing on either side of the coffin with noiseless tread, until they formed two abreast, brethren with brethren and sisters with sisters, and in this way they moved slowly and silently to the grave. Arriving at the place of interment, the coffin was carefully removed from a vehicle and then lowered into the grave. The brethren then filled the grave, in which all usually bore a part. While this was proceeding there was either singing or speaking. They claimed, in their later history, that the spirit of the departed often attended the obsequies and communicated, through some inspired instrument, words of cheer and comfort to the living.

The grave having been closed, the one in charge, then doffing his hat, dismissed the attendants in the following words: "Having performed the last kind act to our departed friend, we may all return to our homes." No badge of mourning was worn, but the dress or suit worn on Sunday was donned.

The burial ground is located in the extreme northwestern corner of the apple orchard connected with the Middle Family.

The space so attached is eighty feet square, surrounded by pine trees. On the east and south exterior is an avenue of thirty-five feet hemmed in by a row of mulberry trees, the leaves of which they used for silk-worms. The burial plat proper is divided into four sections by two avenues, ten feet in width, running north and south and east and west. The females were buried on the north and the males on the south side. The

SOUTH-WEST VIEW OF BURIAL GROUNDS.

burial was in ridge rows. The place, while kept plain, yet was attended with care.

I visited this spot every trip I made. I found the burial ground fully in keeping with the deserted village. The word ruin, or dilapidation, was written everywhere. The tombstones were in all positions, from the erect to the one flat on the surface. One grave had been opened, and others bore indications of the same.

148   Shakers of Ohio.

They commenced the interments at the extreme west side.. All the graves had the headstones in the first row. There were 21 headstones in the first row, 19 in the second, 17 in the third,. 16 in the fourth. Then came the avenue. There were 12 in the fifth, 3 in the sixth and 2 in the seventh. I counted 13 graves without stones in the sixth and 9 in the seventh. There were probably other graves, but I failed to identify them.
 .   With but few exceptions the only inscriptions are simply initials of the name. All are made out of sandstone save one. In the extreme northwestern corner, lying flat on the grave is a marble stone, with the following inscription: "Our Mother Lydia Russell consort of Elisha Russell died June 29, 1839, aged 63 yrs. 10 ms. 28 ds. This stone was erected by her daughters in memory of a dear mother."

In the fourth row, eighth stone from the south: "Elisha Russell died October 15, 1862, aged 83." In the same row, third grave from the north: "O. M. T.* died May 23, 1858, aged 39 years." In the seventh row, fifth grave from the south: "In memory of Sewel G. Thayer who departed this life. Feb. 27, 1881 aged 78 yrs. 7 mo." Same row: "In memory of Rodney E. Russell who departed this life Sept. 3, 1880, aged 84 yrs. 3 mo. 3 ds."

V.   GOVERNMENT.

The government is a theocracy, all the various communities in the United States being subservient to that at Mt. Lebanon, New York. The ministry is the highest order in the selection of which the general membership has no choice. The community is under their immediate jurisdiction. Then come the elders. The legal trustee is the one in whom the land is vested that the laws of the state might be complied with. The ministry was a higher, spiritual state than that of the other elders. To a certain degree it was removed from the others, and such associations as occurred was formal. While the first ministry in the incipient stage preached openly to the world, it was not true when the organization had become completed. They delivered discources to the membership, but during the religious

---

*Olive Melvina Torrey.

services known as Public Meetings, when non-members were admitted to the worship as spectators, the ministry remained in the second story of their apartments. About six feet above the floor there was in each apartment—men and women—an aperture in the wall through which the ministry could see the worshippers below.

Their mode of government, as already intimated, was to combine everything within themselves. They were a law unto themselves. They did not go to law if the same could be avoided, but sometimes were drawn into it by seceding members. In such cases they defended themselves by employing the ablest counsel that could be obtained. Their standing counsel, on all legal questions, for nearly forty years, was Samuel Starkweather, of Cleveland. They never lost a case, for the reason that he never undertook one for them unless he was positive that they were in the right.

An extraordinary case occurred in the courts of Cuyahoga county, which was a test one in regard to the validity of their Church Covenant. It originated by a sister, who, after having been a member of and residing in the society for the space of fifteen years, withdrew from it and married a reckless man, and they connived together to sue for the services which she had rendered during her membership. It was admitted that the services had been rendered, but inasmuch as she had signed the covenant, in which she had voluntarily pledged those services to a consecrated purpose, the society was thereby released from all pecuniary obligations.

The interest excited by the trial of this case was very great, as manifested by the crowds attending the hearing. as it presented for the first time for decision, in northern Ohio, a question which involved a cardinal principle of Shakerism. Eminent counsel was employed on both sides, the defendants having retained Governor Reuben Wood and Judge Starkweather. The plaintiffs attempted to avail themselves of the popular prejudice which then existed, but their arguments were based on the assumption that the existence of such a society was against public policy, by its alleged opposition to the union of the sexes in matrimony, and by their advocacy of celibacy.

Governor Wood, in an able argument, overthrew the proposition of the opposing counsel by expounding the law, and referring to the decisions of the Supreme Court in the states of Maine and New Hampshire. He was followed by Judge Starkweather, who, in the ablest speech of his life, showed that the tree is known by its fruits, that these people called Shakers, by the simplicity and purity of their lives, by their exemption from the strife of worldly ambition, and by the consecration of themselves and all they possessed to their religious faith, but imitated the example of the Christians in Apostolic days, more than any other sect in Christendom, and that their views on the subject of matrimony were in no way variant from the teachings of the Apostle Paul.

The result of this trial was a victory for the Shakers, and settled a question over which they could never again be disturbed. It is but a matter of justice to Judge Starkweather to state that for the valuable services he had long rendered them as legal adviser, he never made any charge or received any compensation, save what the society deemed best to bestow upon him.

They never took any part in politics, nor voted at elections, but paid their taxes according to law. They took no oaths in the courts of law, but affirmed to tell the truth of what they knew concerning the case at issue. They bore no arms, nor studied the art of war. During the Civil War two were drafted into their country's service. Although a release could have been procured by the payment of a certain sum, yet this they refused, because, as they claimed, it was contrary to their principles. One of them maimed himself and thus escaped. The other went into the hospital service and took care of the sick, owing to his scruples about bearing arms.

It would be unreasonable to claim that under a system as practiced by the Shakers all would live up to their ideals. Every community has its weak membership; but those not in harmony with the ideas promulgated sooner or later retired from the organization.

They were very fortunate in the selection of their legal trustees, for they never suffered materially by defalcations.

VI. RELIGION.

Public meetings, in the days of their strength, were held every Sunday at the church, opening usually about the first of May and continued until the first of September. The services commenced at half-past 10 o'clock A. M. Their exercises consisted in singing, marching and sometimes in dancing, according to the movement of the Spirit. They believed in the Bible as a revelation from God, but not in plenary inspiration. They believed it was a record of God in past dispensations, but not the word itself, for they claimed that could not be limited nor circumscribed to the boundaries of any book. They believed in books as records of the word of God, of present revelations, from which they read and expounded occasionally on Sunday, in their public meetings, in the attempt to prove from the Bible that they had the word of God given to them in this day, adapted to the age in which we live, of which they kept a record.

On such occasions the elders did most of the reading and speaking, although others, of both sexes, were not prohibited when impressed by the Spirit. They believed that "where the Spirit of the Lord is there is liberty."

Other meetings were held in the family during the week, on Wednesday and Friday evenings, at half-past 7, called Union Meetings, where the brethren and sisters met together in different rooms, for the purpose of having an hour's social conversation on temporal or spiritual subjects, and whatever tended to promote union, peace and harmony.

On Wednesday and Thursday evenings, at 8 o'clock, they had family meetings, where they went forth in their usual manner of worship, in singing and marching, two abreast, motioning with their hands, and sometimes toward the close of the meeting they had a lively dance, quickened by the Spirit.

Their solemn meetings were not wholly confined to the church and the family chapels. When Shakerism was at its highest pitch they assembled in the church and there formed a procession and marched to the Holy Grove equidistant between the Middle and East Families, and in the woods worshipped God in His first temple. It must not be inferred that all their services were simple, for in the early history of that *ism* there were extravagant performances, but time gradually eliminated them.

VII.   SHAKER THEOLOGY.

Men are more sensitive in regard to their religious views than any other opinions held. Every man should be accorded the right to express himself on this point, if for no other reason than that, owing to the bias of the human mind, it is so easily misjudged or misinterpreted. On this subject I shall follow the exact language of James S. Prescott, their historian. In the Prescott MS. it is stated:

"*First*—They hold that God is dual, male and female, Father and Mother; that these two attributes exist in the Deity; that these two principles are exhibited throughout the universe of God; wherever we turn our eyes, we behold these two principles, male and female, throughout the animal kingdom; if we turn our eyes to the vegetable kingdom we find the same; if we turn our eyes to the universal kingdom, we find there the same two great principles, 'positive and negative'; if we look into the Bible we find the same principles recognized from Genesis to St. Paul's epistle to the Romans, where he says, 'For the invisible things of him from the creation of the world are clearly seen, being understood by the things that are made, even his eternal power and God-head, so that they are without excuse,' Romans I, 20. According to Moses, among the things which are made was man: 'So God created man in his own image; in the image of God created he him; male and female created he them,' Genesis I, 27. Thus the duality of God is established by holy writ.

"*Second*—They hold that 'Christ was the Lord from heaven a quickening Spirit; created male and female in the image of God; that his first appearance was in the male, in the man Jesus; his second appearance was in the female: Ann Lee, born in Manchester, England, in 1736, on the 29th of February; received the revelation of Christ in 1770; came over to America in 1774. First church was organized in 1792.

"*Third*—They recognize two orders of people on the earth. 1st, The rudimental or Adamic order, where all who wish to marry and populate the earth are required to keep the law of nature, *i. e.,* have no sexual intercourse except for offspring; whatsoever is more than this, cometh of evil. They do not condemn marriage where there are fit subjects to improve the race, if they keep it where it belongs, in the Adamic order. They say it is not a Christian institution, but a 'civil right,' therefore they abstain from it, as Christ and the Apostles did. 2d, The spiritual order is where all who enter it are required to keep the 'higher law,' 'the law of grace and truth'; have no intercourse between the sexes, except social, and that which can be enjoyed and perpetuated in the 'spirit world.' They hold to living lives of virgin celibacy, as being the highest, holiest and happiest life a person can attain to while in the form. They hold to a separation between these two orders, and between church and state.

"*Fourth*—They hold to a community of interest in all things, where 'no man has aught of the things he possesses he calls his own, but they have all things common.'

"*Fifth*—They hold to the doctrine of an oral confession of sins to God, before living witnesses, as a door of hope into the church, and as indispensable to finding the power of salvation. This is the first and initiating step into their order. Not because the Catholics have derived and retained the form of confession from the primitive church; not because it is written in the Bible 'confess your faults (*i. e.,* sins) one to another, and pray one for another, that ye may be healed.' When souls are laboring under deep convictions of sin, they want some confidential friend before whom they can open their whole lives, without fear or reservation, and make a clean breast of it before God. And this friend they can always find in both sexes in the Shaker order. As Joshua said to Achan: 'Make confession unto Him (*i. e.,* God), and tell me now what thou hast done: hide it not from me.' This was typical of a true Gospel confession. Here was a confession made to God before a living witness. Joshua VII, 19.

"*Sixth*—They hold to dancing as an act of divine worship. The first founders of the institution were led into it by spirit influence, and many times by an irresistible power, which attended them by night and by day. Hence they were greatly persecuted by their orthodox neighbors, it being so new and strange, and so contrary to the fixed creeds, lifeless forms and ceremonies of the churches,—Christian in name, but pagan in practice.

"They say that dancing was the original mode of worship of God's ancient people, and that it was only fulfilling ancient prophecies that it should be restored in the latter day (See Jeremiah XXXI, Psalms and various other Scriptures). Hence dancing and marching have become their established form of worship.

"*Seventh*—They believe the resurrection is synonymous with regeneration; that it is a gradual growth and rising out of the death of the first Adam, into the life and Spirit of Christ,—a resurrection of the soul and not of the body. They believe with St. Paul 'that flesh and blood cannot inherit the kingdom of God'; 'that there is a natural body, and there is a spiritual body'; that when they put off the former, the natural, they put on the latter, the spiritual; that when the natural body once dies and returns to dust, it can never be resurrected, changed or transformed into spirit, without counteracting the immutable laws of nature.

"*Eighth*—They believe in a probationary state after this life, that God is just; that the millions of earth's inhabitants who have died and gone into the 'spirit world,' who never had a chance to hear and obey the Gospel of salvation in this life, will have an offer of it there; as it is written, 'For Jesus Christ also hath once suffered, being put to death in the flesh, but quickened by the spirit, by which He went and preached to the spirits in prison,' etc. 1 Peter III, 18, 19; and in IV, 6; 'For this cause was the Gospel preached also to the dead, that' they might be judged according to men in the flesh, and live according to God in the Spirit,' etc.

"*Ninth*—They believe that Christ is to judge the world through His people, as it is written, 'Do ye not know that the saints shall judge the world?' 1 Corinthians VI, 2, 3. Know ye not that we shall judge angels? They believe that this work of judgment has begun on the earth, that the hour of his judgment is come, Rev. XIV, 7; 'And Jesus said, For judgment I am come into this world,' John IX, 39; 'And judgment was given to the saints of the Most High,' Daniel VII, 22; some men's sins are open beforehand, going before to judgment; and some men they follow after. This work is also progressive and is inseparably connected with the resurrection of the soul.

"*Tenth*—They believe that every man will have to atone for his own sins, and work out his own salvation; that Christ came to set us an 'example that we should follow his steps,' and thereby save us from our sins, and not in them. They believe in being saved by the blood of Christ, *i. e.,* by living his life: 'the blood is the life thereof'; 'this is eating his flesh and drinking his blood,' John VI, 53, 54: thus becoming incorporated into his spirit, and being *at-one-ment* will ever avail him anything, and every one will have to become personally righteous by doing right. 'He that doeth righteousness is righteous, even as he is righteous,' 1 John III, 7."

VIII. SPIRIT MANIFESTATIONS.

The Shakers claim that communications from departed spirits occurred among them several years anterior to the Rochester rappings. Elder James S. Prescott was requested by the editor of the *Cleveland Weekly Herald* to write out an account of these early manifestations at North Union. His article was copied into the *Shaker and Shakeress* for April, 1874, and was made use of by Nordhoff in his "Communistic Societies of the United States," published in London in 1875. As the Prescott MS. contains some important features not given in the *Herald* article, I will more closely follow it than the one already published.

During the latter part of July, 1838, some young sisters were walking together on the north bank of Doan Creek, between the Mill Family and the grist-mill, near the hemlock grove, when they heard some beautiful singing, which seemed to be in the air just above their heads. They were taken by surprise, listened with admiration and then hastened home to report the phenomenon. Some of these girls afterwards became mediums. Prior to this manifestation word had come to the elders by letter that there was a marvelous work going on in some of the eastern societies, notably at Mount Lebanon and Watervleit in New York, and when it reached those in the west all should know it; and every individual felt that there was a heart-searching God in Israel. These manifestations were the greatest they ever expected to witness on the earth, being more than an ordinary revival of religion.

The invisibles commenced their work one Sunday among

EAST VIEW OF HEMLOCK GROVE.

the little girls in the childrens' order, while in meeting of their own with their care-takers, the doors were closed, when suddenly involuntary exercises commenced, such as going with great speed across the room, back and forth, with great velocity, nor could they stop, nor be stopped, by any human agency. A messenger was dispatched in haste to the elders, with the message that something uncommon was going on in the girls' department. The elders, then engaged in the regular religious services, brought the same to a close just as soon as circumstances would permit, hastened to the scene to witness the phenomenon. They saw the little girls were under an influence not their own. They were hurrying around the room, back and forth, as swiftly as if driven by the wind. When attempts were made to arrest them, it was found impossible, because that which possessed them was irresistible. Suddenly they were prostrated upon the floor, apparently unconscious of

SCENE ON SHAKER DAM TAKEN FROM MILL-DAM.

what was going on around them. With their eyes closed, muscles strained, joints stiff, they were taken up and laid on beds, mattresses, etc. Then they began to hold conversations with their guardian spirits, and others, some of whom they once knew in the form, making graceful motions with their hands and speaking audibly, so that all in the room heard and understood, and formed some idea of their whereabouts in spiritual realms they were explaining. Alternately and at intervals they would sing some heavenly and melodious songs, motioning gracefully with their hands, which surpassed anything they ever heard before. Sometimes they would appear to be flying, and their arms and hands would go, apparently as swift as the wings of a humming bird; at other times they would appear to be swimming across a river, beyond which was a plain, *i. e.*, the rudimental sphere; beyond this was a beautiful country, far surpassing anything language could describe. They were taken to the cities of the redeemed and to the mansions of the blessed.

About the same time the boys began to see visions, and their gifts were similar to that of the girls. These children were, for the greater part, between ten and twelve years of age, and entirely incapable of feigning these manifestations, nor could they have been guilty of collusion, trickery, fraud or anything of that description. All they had to do was to be passive in the power that enveloped them. Adults of both sexes, whose physical organization would possibly admit of mediumship, were soon under the same influence.

The following is the first song given direct from the "spirit world," sung by a young sister while in a vision, which occurred in August, 1838. Her guardian angel called the poem

THE SONG OF A HERALD.

Prepare, O ye faithful
  To fight the good fight.
Sing, O ye redeemed,
  Who walk in the light,
Come low, O ye haughty,
  Come down and repent.
Disperse, O ye naughty,
  Who will not relent.

For Mother is coming,
  O hear the glad sound,
To comfort her children
  Wherever they're found,
With jewels and robes
  Of fine linen
To clothe the afflicted withal.

In the year 1843, when the Millerites were looking for Christ to come literally, through the literal clouds, he was among the Shakers spiritually, in spiritual clouds of his witnesses, accompanied by legions of the invisible hosts. He took up his abode at North Union for the space of three months, during which time none were allowed to go off the premises, except the trustees on public business, or needful occasion. During this extraordinary visit he made himself known through mediums of both sexes, and by inspired communications, among which were brief sketches of his own life, written by his own hand, corresponding with what is written concerning him in the New Testament. Likewise a short communication from each one of his beloved disciples, bearing testimony to the truth of what the Holy Savior had written, all of which they had in MS. copied from the original.

The most important event to the Shakers in "spirit manifestations," took place at Mount Lebanon, New York, in 1843, "which will sooner or later interest all mankind." It was in the giving of the SACRED ROLL AND BOOK, as a word of warning to the inhabitants of the earth, that the judgments of God were nigh, even at the door. Of what has taken place since that time let the world be judge. They are called calamities by the world, and these have not yet ceased, but grow more and more serious every year. What will be the end of these things no one can tell. As true as God spake by Noah to the antediluvians, even so has he spoken to the world in these days through the Shakers by the SACRED ROLL AND BOOK.

The Shakers believe that this ROLL might be called the Bible of the Nineteenth Century, adapted to the day and age in which we live, and, as such, no doubt will be handed down to generations yet unborn,—that in the ages to come God's own book, written by His own Hand, may be left as His handprints on the sands of time!

The Shakers claim they have as much evidence to believe that the SACRED ROLL AND BOOK were given through a holy man of God, raised from his childhood in the church at Mount Lebanon, who wrote and spake as he was moved by the Holy Spirit, as they have that any part of the New Testament was so written, and more too; because the former has never been perverted by commentators and translators from their original meaning.

In this new Revelation the doctrine of the trinity is exploded, and two great principles established, viz., a FATHER and a MOTHER in the DEITY. On these two hang all the law and the prophets, and are the foundation principles of Shaker theology. All others are tributary to them.

The Shakers did not withhold this new Revelation from the world; but performed as they were commanded at the time it was communicated. Five hundred copies were distributed gratuitously to the nations of the earth as follows: One copy each was sent to the president and vice president of the United States, the various heads of the different departments at Washington, to the governors of the various states and territories of the American Union, to all the crowned heads of Europe and the heads of all foreign countries, so far as civilization extended and access could be had through their ministers and consuls at Washington. Of all these sent out, the King of Sweden alone responded.

The spirit manifestations continued for a period of seven years in succession, in different forms and phases, in which nearly all nations were represented by the spirits of their dead, taking possession of living mediums, speaking in their own language, and acting out all the peculiar characteristics of the nations to which they beolnged.

IX. CHRISTMAS FESTIVAL.

Miss Elmina Phillips, at my request, placed at my disposal her unpublished MS. entitled, "Christmas Among the Shakers in the Olden Time."

Probably the English founders of Shakerism in America brought with them the English custom of celebrating Christmas, and introduced it among their American converts. Certainly fifty years ago, when the congregational descendants of the Puritans in New England were going about their usual employments on Christmas as on any other day, their Shaker descendants in northern Ohio were keeping it as the one great holiday of the year.

There was a stir of Christmas preparation in the air two or three weeks beforehand. Individual members had no money to spend for Christmas gifts, since all the purchasing for the community was done by the trustee deacons and deaconesses; but it was understood that it was to be a day of good cheer and that there would be gifts for all.

The eldresses and trustee sisters might be found occasionally in private consultation, likely to result in a trip of the latter to the little town, now grown to be a great city, where such things as they could not raise or manufacture for themselves were obtained. And sometimes a rap at the eldress's door would bring the family deaconess to the door with an air of Christmas mystery, and through the crack she opened to receive your message might be heard the click of shears, indicating that new goods were being cut.

The kitchen deaconess was busy superintending the picking over of the apples, setting the barrels of choicest ones convenient for Christmas day, inspecting the pickles and preserves, and honey, etc., consulting with the trustees and the cook and baker, which consultations were likely to result in cakes and puddings and chicken and other pies, etc., in due season.

You are thinking, perhaps, as is probably true, that the New England housewives must have brought recollections of Thanksgiving to Ohio, where Thanksgiving day had not yet been introduced. But this was only one phase of the preparation—chiefly the day was kept as holy day. Much of the worship of the Shakers consisted of singing, and they made their own hymns and tunes; and Christmas would hardly have been Christmas if a company of the young people had not gone around in the early morning singing a Christmas song to awaken the family. So the favorite hymnist was quietly reminded, now by one young singer, then another, that a new song for Christmas morning would be wanted. And the company of singers must be chosen, and copies of the new song privately written and distributed to each one, with the music for those that could read it; for opportunities must be caught to practice it on the quiet, since it would not be Christmas like if there were no mystery about it.

11

There were many musical young people among them at that time, and I have known one hymnist to be applied to for a new song for two separate companies of singers, neither company knowing of the other till they met on their rounds in the morning.

And, as the day drew near, the elders did not fail to counsel the people in meeting that if there were any differences among them they should be reconciled, that there might be nothing to mar the Christmas good-will.

On Christmas eve, at half-past seven, at the sound of the bell, all retired to their rooms, and one read aloud and the others listened to the story from John XIII of the washing of the disciples' feet. Then each two washed each other's feet, "and when they had sung a hymn they went out," if they chose, to make any final preparations for the morrow.

This was the time usually chosen by the Christmas singing band for the final, and probably the only full rehearsal of their morning song; and, as if casually, by twos and threes, they took their way to some shop sufficiently remote from the dwelling house that their voices would not be heard there, and in which the brother in charge of the building had agreed to have a good fire, and to let the members of the company in by signal. When they were satisfied that all knew the song, some young brother volunteered to waken all the company in due time in the morning and they separated for the night. At nine o'clock all was dark and silent in the village.

Next morning as early as half-past four the singers met, perhaps in the kitchen, and partook of some light refreshment, set ready the night before just to put them in voice, and then started out to sing, first in the halls of the principal dwelling, then at every house in the little village, in which several people lived.

By the time they had gone all around the family, if there was sleighing, a span of horses and sleigh was likely to stand convenient, and the company merrily started off to sing their song at one of the other families a mile away. If they met a sleighload from the other family coming to sing to them, as they sometimes did, they hailed each other and kept on their way, sure of a warm welcome, though not of surprising and waking the friends where they were going.

And after breakfast, as all rose from the table and kneeled for a moment in silent thanksgiving together, the new song was probably sung again in the dining-room, the kitchen sisters coming in to listen to or join in the singing.

At 9 A. M. the singers met to select and rehearse the hymns to be sung at the church meeting at the meeting house.

At 10 A. M. came union meeting, which was a number of social meetings held at the same hour, the brethren usually going to the sisters' rooms.

The brethren and sisters were seated in two rows facing each other at opposite sides of the room; doubtless it sounds more stiff to alien ears than to one brought up from childhood in the customs of the community. There was cheerful chat of this and other Christmas days, and singing of new and old songs, and passing around of pans of cracked nuts and pop-corn, etc.

At 11 o'clock lunch was carried around to the rooms in big pans by some of the young brethren and sisters—great quarter sections of the most delicious cake, if memories may be trusted, and slices of creamy, home-made cheese and whitest bread and pie.

At 1 P. M. all the families assembled at the meeting house. The services were the same as at the usual Sunday meetings, except that there were special hymns and special readings from scriptures, old and new.

After meeting baskets of choice apples were carried around and the gifts which had been prepared for each one—usually some article of clothing somewhat nicer than common.

At 4 P. M. came the principal meal of the day, and after-wards a big basket was carried around to the rooms to receive offerings of clothing for the poor. All were expected to give something from their own store. And the day closed with quiet talk, probably interspersed with singing.

A SHAKER CHRISTMAS SONG.

Hail, hail, the beautiful morn hath dawned
    The joy of angels and men;   '
The star of the east, with beauty beyond
    All others has risen again.
Awake, disciples of Christ, and sing,
    Your robes of gladness put on,
And precious gifts and offerings bring
    Our loved Redeemer to crown.

Not gold, nor myrrh, nor frankincense sweet
    Our Savior asks from our hands,
But hearts that with love and tenderness beat
    To bless and comfort his lambs.
Go seek and feed my wandering sheep,
    Forgive the erring and lost,
Thus prove your love for me, and thus reap
    The precious fruits of the cross

X.   BIOGRAPHICAL SKETCHES.

The actions of men make history. In order to understand
history the lives of the principal actors in making it must be
given. The history of North Union is practically summed up
in the lives of a few. Of the following characters depicted I
confess I have no other knowledge save that given in the Prescott MS. In fact, I never heard of these men until revealed to
me in the above record. It is but just to follow closely what
is therein written of the lives of the founders of North Union.
Their characters must be presented in the view held by those
the best acquainted, however fulsome the praise may be. The
order as given is also preserved.

The Russell Family.—As the origin of the North Union
Family was largely due to the Russells, both in point of zeal
and number, they naturally stand first in the record. There
were three brothers, who emigrated from England between the
years 1730 and 1745 and settled in or near Hebron and East
Windsor, Connecticut. Their names were John, Jacob and William Russell. William once lived in West Windsor, Connecticut. His son Samuel, born about 1714, died in Windsor at the
age of 65 years, and was buried in the cemetery of West Windsor

Square, Connecticut. He had four brothers, Ebenezer, Ellis, Jonathan and Hezekiah. Samuel had six children, Jacob, Stephen, Cornelius, John, Elizabeth and Rachel. Elizabeth married a man by the name of Ebenezer Young, one of the fourth generation from Miles Standish, of Plymouth Rock memory. Rachel married a man by the name of Cook, who once lived in Cherry Valley, New York. John, the fourth son of Samuel, married Polly Thrall, brought up a family and died in Rodman, Jefferson county, New York, June 22, 1844.

Jacob, the eldest son of Samuel, was born in West Windsor, Hartford county, Connecticut, April 26, 1746. He married Esther Dunham, of Hebron, Connecticut, where he lived about 66 years, and brought up a large family, consisting of six sons and six daughters, one of whom died when about two years old, named Jerusha. The names of those who survived were as follows:

Elijah, born July 18, 1773.
Esther, born October 23, 1774.
Jerusha 1st, born July 7, 1776.
Return, born March 1, 1778.
Elisha, born November 14, 1779.
Samuel, born January 15, 1783.
Jerusha 2d, born February 24, 1785.
Content, born May 7, 1787.
Ralph, born August 3, 1789.
Roxana, born March 10, 1792.
Obedience, born May 23, 1794.
Rodney, born May 15, 1796.

In the year 1812 Jacob Russell, with a number of his sons, emigrated to Ohio and settled in the township of Warrensville, Cuyahoga county, where he died on August 29, 1821, aged 75 years. His grave is not far from the site of the woolen-mill at the Center Family. It is marked, enclosed with pailings and has a pine tree growing over it. His wife Esther died in Solon, September 16, 1835, and was buried at Chagrin Falls, aged 85 years.

On his way to Ohio he was accompanied by the families of Elisha Russell and Nathaniel H. Risley, his son-in-law, in all about twenty persons. They started on June 13 with three ox teams and heavily loaded wagons, and had not proceeded far before news came that war was declared between the United States and Great Britain, and, if they did not want to be massacred by the Indians, they must turn back; but not in the least intimidated, they continued their journey under the rays of the scorching sun, determined to see the end of their journey, each one contributing a full share in making the way comfortable, cheerful and happy. In many places the roads were new and almost impassible, especially after leaving Buffalo. At Cattaraugus Creek, in driving into the boat one team jumped overboard, and after much difficulty it was rescued. The next morning the party started again with the same fortitude and courage that actuated the pioneer, neither turning to the right nor left, but determined to accomplish the object sought. The roads were in a deplorable condition from Buffalo to Cleveland. On their arrival in the latter place they were informed that "there was but one frame house and that was a log cabin." They first stopped at Newburgh, and thence to Warrensville, and settled on sections 23 and 34. After a tedious journey of 600 miles all arrived safely at the destination during the latter part of August, 1812. They set at once to work and constructed shelter, making houses out of logs, cut and rolled together, notched at the corners. They had puncheon floors. The houses were roofed with elm bark. The chimneys were made of mud and sticks. Their neighbors consisted of the families of James Prentiss, who lived about half a mile south, and Asa Stiles and Daniel Warren, about a mile south. For a whole year they felt they were in jeopardy every hour, not knowing what might befall them, especially when the army, upon which they depended for protection, had been surrendered to the enemy at Detroit. They then believed that the Indians would be let loose upon them, and a general massacre would overtake them. Under this state of excitement the people were expecting the British and Indians to fall upon the country about Cleveland. They packed up their goods and prepared to move, but did not know in what direction. During the excitement the settlers in and around Cleveland threw away in the woods over $1,000 worth of provisions. As provisions were scarce this greatly added to their discomfort. Wheat was worth $3.50 per bushel; salt, $24 per barrel, and mouldy at that. The only method they possessed of grinding their corn was to excavate a hollow in the end of a log, and placing the corn therein, pounded it with a heavy pestle hung to a spring pole. Such was the fear and consternation brought on by the war that people were afraid to work without keeping up a constant and vigilant watch, day and night, in order that the alarm be sounded.

Under such a consternation they worked as best they could, cutting down trees, cleaning off land and fencing their farms.

In 1810, Samuel Russell, son of Jacob Russell, emigrated from Chester, Massachusetts, to Aurora, Portage county, Ohio, where he lived to a good old age. In 1813, Elijah Russell, the oldest son of Jacob, emigrated from Rodman, New York, to Warrensville, where he lived and died at the age of 83 years. Return Russell, son of Jacob, emigrated from Rodman, New York, to Warrensville, in 1822, and died October 5, 1834, aged 55 years. Ralph came to Ohio in 1812. After being separated a distance of six hundred miles, most of them were gathered together and settled in Warrensville. Some of them asscribed this "to the overruling providence of God, that they should be the first founders of a branch of a community of people commonly called Shakers."

Ralph Russell.—The subject of this sketch was born in Windsor, Hartford county, Connecticut, August 3, 1789. In 1812 he emigrated to Warrensville. As previously noted, he visited Union Village in 1821, and became a convert to that form of faith usually called Shakerism, and at once set about its practice and promulgation. He was the originator and for a season the active and efficient leader of the North Union Society. It was said of him that "he was a burning and shining light, and many were willing for a reason to rejoice in his light;" but when a superior light and gift came from the church at Union Village in the person of Ashbel Kitchell, in the spring of 1826, Ralph could not vie with Ashbel, and hence Ashbel's light and gift increased, while that, of Ralph gradually decreased, until he lost his influence and leadership among the people.

Ralph subsequently withdrew from the society, went to Solon, a few miles distant, bought a farm, moved his family, and there lived until his death, which occurred December 28, 1866, in the 78th year of his age.

Ralph Russell was tall and straight, about six feet in height, well proportioned, dark complexion, black hair and eyes and of a winning manner, mild and persuasive in argument, naturally of a sociable and genial disposition, and was kind and hospitable to strangers.

Richard W. Pelham.—Although Richard W. Pelham was a member of the society at Union Village, yet he figures so largely in the formation and history of North Union that he may be said to have been a member of the latter also. He was born May 8, 1797, in what is now Indiana, two miles above the Falls of Ohio. He was the youngest of eight children, and his mother dying soon after his birth, his father gave him to his uncle, E. L. Pelham, a physician and Methodist preacher. Not having any children of his own, the uncle adopted Richard into his family and reared him with great care and tenderness. He then lived on the east side of the Chesapeake Bay, called the "Eastern shore of Maryland," in Talbot county. When Richard was eleven years of age, the uncle removed from Maryland to Lyons, New York. At the age of thirteen, during a religious revival, he joined the Methodists, but before reaching his twentieth year, he was dissatisfied with his church relations. Being disappointed in not finding that holiness of life, that purity of heart, that power over sin and a sinful nature, which he had expected to find, he proposed to his uncle to leave, and seek his fortune in the wide world; but his uncle being wealthy, and unwilling to part with his only adopted son, a young man so useful and full of promise, and one on whom he had placed his chief dependence and reliance for support in his old age, offered to make him sole heir to his entire estate, and showed to him the document that would secure to him this great prize. All this was no more to the young man than a blank page in a book. His religious nature had taken the turn of an intense yearning of his soul, and he craved salvation, and nothing short of this would satisfy him. Go he must, and go he did. After traveling hundreds of miles, he brought up as a weary traveler to the hospitable roof of Elder Matthew Houston, who at that time stood at the door of entrance into the church at Union Village. Here, for the first time, he found that for which he had desired, a true apostolic church, where "no man had aught of the things he possessed he called his own, but they had all things common," after the example of the primitive church. Here he found a church, consisting of both sexes, living lives of "virgin" celibacy." To him this was more satisfactory than silver and gold. After being thoroughly initiated into this order he felt anxious to go out and proclaim it to the world, which impulse is natural to all converts to a new form of religion. On representing his feelings to Elder Matthew Houston, and others of the family, he was advised to wait for a propitious moment, with which counsel he readily consented, believing that his advisers were competent to decide. When the tidings came he was sent to North Union. With James Hodge he was directed to go to Warrensville, and in March, 1822, set out for that place, two hundred and fifty miles distant, as the roads then ran. They had one horse and a heavy Dearborn wagon, and the roads, at that season of the year, were almost impassable, so that they were compelled to walk on foot the greater part of the distance, but through their zeal and perseverance they overcame all obstacles and arrived in safety at their point of destination.

After a six weeks' successful mission the two evangelists, in May, returned to Union Village. "I could tell," says Mr. Pelham in his autobiography, "of many thrilling incidents, accidents and hair-breadth escapes, through which myself and colaborers passed in this and after visits to North Union and other places; but the account might seem tedious, and must mostly be omitted. Suffice it to say, that I traveled the road over twenty times between Union Village and North Union, making an aggregate of over 5,000 miles, besides going to the State of New York and other places as a missionary. This distance seems trifling in this day of railroads; but in those days of mud roads and corduroy bridges, when the 'rail' laid the other way, that is, across the road, it took eight days of hard labor for man and beast to travel the road between these two points. Taverns were then few and far between, many of which were mere log huts infested with fleas, mosquitoes and bedbugs, so that sometimes we had to lodge in our wagons, at other times on the hay in the barn. We carried our provisions with us and cooked and ate our meals by the roadside."

Elder Richard W. Pelham was considered by the Shakers to have been an extraordinary man, and intellectually had no superior among them. Under the tuition of Elder Matthew Houston he mastered the Greek and Hebrew languages and translated the Bible into English, which enabled him to cope with any of the theologians of his day. As a critic and author he had but few equals among his own order, and as a public speaker he was among the best, both at North Union and Union Village. His discourses were eminently practical, argumentative and instructive. But his voice was feeble and his manner of delivery unpleasant. As a writer among his brethren he ranked high. They point with pride to his tract on "What Would Become of the World, If All Should Become Shakers," and allege that "it is generally conceded to be one of the ablest productions among believers, on that subject, and is irrefutable and unanswerable." •

Richard W. Pelham was not only one of the first founders of North Union, but also of the communities of Groveland, Livingston county, New York (formerly located at Sodus Bay, near Lake Ontario, New York,), and White Water, Hamilton county, Ohio. In person he was of the average height, large hazel eyes, black hair, also beard, and weighed about one hundred and thirty-five pounds. He died at the Second Family, Union Village, Ohio, January 10, 1873.

Ashbel Kitchell.—The success of North Union, during its first period, was largely due to Ashbel Kitchell, who was born August 21, 1786, in Morris county, New Jersey. His panegyrist declares that "he was a noble specimen of humanity and an honor to his profession. One of earth's rarest productions; a gifted man in nature; a man of great muscular strength, and·

of great executive ability; a Napoleon of his day, and a giant in intellect. It was said of him, if he had received an early education he would have made an excellent judge in the Court of Common Pleas. But his talents were of great use in the church militant in fighting the battles whose weapons are not carnal but mighty through God to the pulling down of strongholds."

In person he was above medium height, large head, self-esteem quite prominent, veneration large, large ears and eyes, deep and broad across the chest and shoulders, corpulent, weighing about two hundred and fifty pounds, and of a dignified and commanding appearance.

Early in the spring of 1826 he was appointed presiding elder at North Union, and under his administration the community was organized and greatly prospered, and his authority extended over a period of five years. This growth was largely due to his practical business methods and indomitable will. Decision being a prominent feature of his mind, he never faltered. His word was law, and when he willed to do a thing it was done without question. His wonderful will-power may be illustrated in the following special instance:

Elder John P. Root was sick in a log cabin and given over to die. The brethren and sisters generally had been to see him and taken their final leave, not expecting him to live from one hour to another. Elder Kitchell had just returned from a visit to Union Village, and learning of his illness, immediately repaired to his bedside, and when he arrived the sick man's mouth and extremities were cold and his jaws set. Looking intently on the outstretched form he said, in a firm voice, 'Pomeroy, live.' 'I will,' replied he. 'There is no gift for you to die,' said Kitchell. Thus uniting his will-power and positiveness with Pomeroy's faith and passive obedience, a barrier against death was formed, which had to yield its victim to a further extension of life. From that hour Pomeroy began to mend and soon recovered.

In his discourse his favorite theme was a Mother in Deity, which he handled with power, and at times was carried beyond himself. Although he reproved sin and disorder with severity, yet he was tender-hearted, sympathetic and easily touched by the sorrows and griefs of those around him. In all his dealings with mankind he was no flatterer, but open, frank, generous and candid. He died at Union Village, March 27, 1860, in his 74th year.

Matthew Houston.—In the early days of the Shakers, there were but few, if any more prominent, or as well educated as Matthew Houston. He was born in Virginia, December 25, 1764; educated for a Presbyterian clergyman and was one of the leaders in the Kentucky Revival, which commenced in the beginning of the Nineteenth Century and continued for several years in succession. He was a man of high standing in society, of great influence, possessed a classical education, which aided his naturally superior intellectual endowments. He had been a slave-holder, but subsequently manumitted them. Under the spirit of the Revival, together with others, he embraced the principles of Shakerism and became one of its leading founders in the west, both in Ohio and Kentucky. He had the rare gift of entering the hearts of the people and gathering them around him. He was a great and good man. His greatness consisted in his humility, self-denial and shild-like simplicity and obedience to that order with which he had covenanted.

He succeeded Ashbel Kitchell as presiding elder at North Union and continued in that office for two years. In person he was of medium height, light complexion, large head, but well balanced, small, round eyes, wide apart, which sparkled with intelligence and good humor, broad across the chest, long body, short legs, fat and corpulent, which gave him the appearance of an English nobleman, but by no means aristocratic. In manner he was affable and courteous, easy and graceful, naturally of a mirthful turn, but not vain, social and generous, warm hearted and always carried with him the sunshine of pleasantness and made all happy around him. Everybody loved Elder Matthew Houston. He died at Union Village, March 18, 1848, in the 84th year of his age.

David Spinning.—Although not one of the fathers of North Union, yet Elder David Spinning's work is a part of its history. He was born September 17, 1779, and succeeded Elder

Houston as presiding elder at North Union, October 24, 1832, and held the office for eight years, during which time there was a steady growth of the community. He had been a Presbyterian layman and took an active part in the Kentucky Revival.

In June, 1834, a new ministry was formed consisting of Elder David Spinning, R. W. Pelham, Lucy Faith and Vincy McNemar, all thoroughly prepared for the duties involved in their office. When this valuable contingent arrived from Union Village, Elder Spinning was greatly gratified and took courage, because all were examples that could be followed. Such an acquisition would strengthen him in his purposes.

Elder Spinning was a conscientious and devoted man. He was slow in his judgments, preferring to arrive at conclusions after thorough investigation. From principle he practiced self-denial, curtailed all unnecessary expenses, lived on a plain, simple diet, dressed plain and cheap, refused tea, coffee, tobacco and all other superfluities. He condemned excess of every description, and became a strict vegetarian. His view of man was also extreme, holding that all were universally lost in selfishness, and there was no possible way whereby the selfish desires could be so effectually destroyed or overcome as to place it upon the altar of self-denial. The principal reason he assigned for this course, which he rigidly imposed on himself and fearlessly taught to others, was that a portion might be saved for the poor, and, further, that by such a practice he could lay up treasure in heaven. He held to the idea that when he entered the future state the question would not be asked him what he believed, but what he had done to benefit suffering humanity.

In person Elder Spinning was of medium height, dark complexion, black hair, dark hazel eyes, veneration and benevolence large. In manners he was simple, modest, unassuming, courteous and agreeable. As a public speaker he had no equal at North Union. He was natural in his delivery, abounded in figures of speech, in natural similitudes, and in symbolic language. However, his discourses, though logical, yet were so simple that a child could understand him. Such a speaker was calculated to please and instruct his audience. It was during his administration that spirit manifestations first occurred at

North Union. He departed this life at Union Village, December 22, 1841, in the 63d year of his age.

Samuel Russell.—The successor of Elder Spinning was Samuel Russell, who was born in Rodman, Jefferson county, New York, May 14, 1807, being the son of Return Russell. He was admitted in the North Union Society in the fall of 1823, being about 16 years of age. On September 15, 1840, he was appointed presiding elder, and for eighteen years continued in that office. Under his guidance improvements were introduced and the character and growth of the community maintained.

He was a man of rare talents and great executive ability. But his genius was better adapted to that of a trustee than a Gospel minister, because the spiritual part of his nature was subordinated to that of business.

In person Elder Russell was about five feet, eleven inches in height, well proportioned, evenly balanced head, hazel eyes, black hair, of a quick and active mind, easy address, a high sense of order. He withdrew from the society August 19, 1858, when in his 51st year, took with him the Church Covenant and only yielded it after securing a compromise.

John P. Root.—Another of the prominent men was John P. Root, born in Pittsfield, Berkshire county, Massachusetts, June 28, 1799, and admitted into the North Union community March 15, 1825, and thus may be ranked as one of its early founders. He had been a classleader among the Methodists, and of the most zealous kind. When he first emigrated to Ohio he settled on some wild land in Grafton, Lorain county, for which his father had exchanged his farm. He passed through all the hardships of pioneer life almost alone and single-handed.

In July, 1825, he was appointed farm deacon, which place he occupied three years and gave good satisfaction. On the organization of the church in 1828 he was appointed the third legal trustee, which place he filled for five years. In 1833 he received the appointment of first elder in the Middle Family, which place he filled for many years. In 1858 he was appointed successor to Samuel Russell in the ministry, which appointment was ratified by the members. As the ministry was dissolved in 1862, he continued to be presiding elder. Among his brethren he was known as Elder Pomeroy. He was deeply imbued with a religious baptism while among the Methodists, and this undiminished he carried into his new faith and always held the temporal to be subordinate to the spiritual. The principle that actuated him was the golden rule. He believed in the doctrine of "live and let live," which he daily practiced. He would ask no one to do a thing he would not do himself. In him the poor always found a generous friend, and he never sent away any one empty handed, but relieved all whenever it was in his power. Although a farmer by education he had a turn for mechanics. In the Middle Family, where he was first elder for many years, he showed his aptitude for mechanics by making bureaus, tables, stands, drawers, chests, joiner-work, etc., etc., which could have been seen in every room.

In his preaching his favorite theme was the same that delighted the ear and heart of every preacher, viz., "A Mother as Well as a Father in the Deity." , From that he became an uncompromising defender in woman's rights, which he did not fail to impress on his auditors.

In stature Elder Root was about six feet in height, fair complexion, large blue eyes, high forehead, language easy and flowing, veneration large, bald head, tender hearted and an open and frank countenance. He ceased to be presiding elder in July, 1876, and was succeeded by James S. Prescott. Elder Root died in August, 1881, in his 83d year.

James Sullivan Prescott.—It is with more than an ordinary degree of pleasure I turn to the biography of Elder James S. Prescott, for without his zeal in trying to preserve the history of his little colony, it would have sunk into oblivion. The lovers of history owe him a debt of gratitude. He first wrote out his sketches, placed them in the hands of Judge John Barr, of Cleveland, who, over his own signature, caused them to be published in the *Cleveland Daily Herald* for June 13, 21, 28; July 5, 11, 18, and 25, 1870. Afterwards Elder Prescott wrote another MS., in which he corrected the typographic errors and discrepancies which occurred in the published account. He wrote that MS. "expressly for the Western Reserve Pioneers' and Early Settlers' Association, in Northern Ohio," The MS.

is written in a clear, bold hand, in blue and black ink, and covers 121 pages. Great care has been exercised to have it go to the printer and published as written. Unfortunately he failed to separate the history of the community from that of the ruling elder. As he has recorded it, the history is simply a series of biographical successions. Many important features are left out entirely. Although living in sight of the East Family scarcely a record is made. Why this family was overlooked must forever be unaccounted for. But, as has been previously intimated, the writer of this owes nearly all his information concerning North Union to the writings of Elder Prescott. His MS. closes with the year 1870. What I have learned of the community since that period was secured after much diligence. That the recent period is greatly lacking in this record, is admitted, but not the fault of the writer.

Elder James S. Prescott was born in Lancaster, Worcester county, Massachusetts, January 26, 1803. In the usual acceptation of the term his father was not orthodox, but his mother was a pious, devoted woman and belonged to the Congregational Church in Lancaster. She brought up her children under the pastoral care of Rev. Dr. Nathaniel Thayer, Unitarian. She taught them their Bible and catechism, and that after the strictest manner of the Puritans. On Sunday her children were not allowed to play until after sundown, on which question her word was law. At the age of ten James went to live with his uncle, Brigham Prescott, in West Boylston, about ten miles distant. At the age of sixteen he went to live with Charles Stearns, of Springfield, Massachusets, on the border of the Connecticut River, to learn the mason's trade. After spending one season there, he then went to Hartford, Connecticut, and engaged himself to Danforth Rogers, a practical mason, with whom he continued four years, during which time he assisted in the construction of some of the largest buildings in that city.

The winter of 1820 saw him the subject of a religious revival, and then connected himself with the close communion Baptists, under the pastoral care of Elisha Cushman. The following year he became a teacher in the African Sunday school and so continued for three years. While still a minor, and serving his apprenticeship, in the winter season he attended the "Literary School and Female Academy," taught by George J. Patten. At the age of twenty-one he entered Westfield Academy, Massachusetts, and there completed his education.

In 1825 he was employed by the executive committee of the Baptist Missionary Convention of New York to teach the missionary school at Oneida, consisting of about forty Indian scholars of both sexes, instructed on the Lancastrian plan.

In July, 1826, he emigrated to Cleveland, Ohio, and there went to work at his trade. While engaged as a journeyman, Elisha Russel came from North Union to hire a mason to lay the foundation of a dwelling house. James Prescott responded, and leaving his trunks in Cleveland, took his tools under his arms and went out afoot and alone. On arriving at the Shaker settlement he found them living in log cabins, similar to Indian wigwams, but kept neatly and cleanly. Immediately he set about the work he was to perform and laid out the foundation and started the corners of the building. The Shakers helped lay the cellar walls, and in about two weeks they were ready for the framework, and in due course the house for the Center Family was ready for occupation. That house still stands and is given in the illustration.

While engaged with the Shakers, and looking with great favor upon them, he received a letter from Frederick Collins, an old classmate, requesting him to come to Unionville, about ten miles from St. Louis, Missouri, as a missionary. On that mission he started to go, but being out of health he stopped in Cleveland to work at his trade and recuperate. While thus engaged he investigated the doctrines of the Shakers and compared the same with the Bible, and found he had no cause to seek further. When he saw the purity of the lives the Shakers led, and the power of God attending their meetings, the heavenly inspiration of their singing, and a flaming testimony against the licentiousness of the world, he was satisfied that he had "found Him of whom Moses and the prophets did write," and to this he would hold until he could find something better. As he viewed the various sects of Christendom he could find no people.

12

on the earth that came so near the Pentecostal Church, in their principles and practices, as the Shakers. Under this conviction he did not wait long before he made up his mind to prove the work for himself. On making his determination known he was admitted into the society in the fall of 1826. In 1827 he was appointed second elder in the Cabin Family. The brethren, to show their approval and to ratify the appointment, took him on their shoulders and carried him around the meeting-room, exclaiming, "the lot has fallen upon Jonah."

After continuing in the elder's lot for four years he was released in order to take charge of the district school. For a period of about fifty years, when not engaged in teaching school, he was in the elder's lot in the different families, sometimes first and sometimes second, and for about forty years was one of the legal trustees. He was thus not only one of the early advocates, but continued long as one of the pillars of the community.

The only notice, "The Manifesto," June, 1888, gave of this faithful laborer was as follows: "James S. Prescott died at North Union, Ohio, April 3, 1888, age 85 years, 2 months and 8 days. Brother James has been in the community sixty-two years. He was a faithful laborer in the Gospel field. S. S. M."

In the little graveyard at North Union the body of James S. Prescott rests in an unmarked and an unknown grave. There are none to weep over him or plant a flower to lessen the monotony of his surroundings. His friends either lie buried around him or else have taken their departure. He saw the colony in its infancy; he was with it in its strength and decline. Had he lived another year he would have seen its dissolution. He was spared that sorrow, yet he must have realized that the inevitable hour was near at hand. Rest, sweet saint, thy labors are over. The society which thou didst give thy life for its welfare and promotion, like thee, has passed away. But thy life was not a failure, and the course thou didst pursue will be an admonition to generations that must follow.

Return Russell.—One of the important members of the society was Return Russell, born in Windsor, Hartford county, Connecticut, March 1, 1778. He emigrated to Ohio in 1822.

.

He had a wife and eleven children, six sons and five daughters, viz., Luther, Edward, Samuel, Sanford, Robert, Henry, Huldah, Abigail, Mary Ann, Roxana and Lydia, all of whom, save Luther, were gathered into the Shaker fold, and out of that numerous family only one remained in the society in 1870, and that was Abigail, otherwise called Rachel, was, in above named year, the elder sister in the Middle Family.

IEAST VIEW OF GIRLS' RESIDENCE.

Return had been a Baptist and a highly esteemed member of that church. He did not relinquish his sentiments without a thorough investigation, and when convinced he yielded to the testimony and joined the Shakers in 1823. He purchased a lot in Warrensville, which included the land about the saw-mill, for which he paid one thousand dollars. This land, and that purchased by the trustees of Union Village, on which the center house still stands, were adjoining the lands of Ralph and Elijah Russell.

When the church was organized in 1828 Return was appointed first legal trustee, which place he held until 1834. He was a laborious man, and in constructing the dam across the stream at the grist-mill, his zeal to do good work carried him beyond his physical powers of endurance, although of a strong constitution. He was above medium height, broad across the chest, square shouldered, large, open countenance, high forehead, dark complexion, and black hair. He was of a social and genial disposition, intelligent and agreeable in conversation, possessing faculties by nature superior to the ordinary class of men, and eminently calculated for the position he filled. He departed this life at the Middle Family on October 5, 1834, in the 56th year of his age.

Elisha Russell.—On November 14, 1779, Elisha Russell was born in Windsor, Connecticut. He emigrated to Ohio in 1812, and was one of the first pioneers to settle in Warrensville. He had a wife and five daughters,—Mary, Candace, Abigail, Hannah and Adeline. He was a man of great activity and usefulness. In point of muscular strength he had but few equals. Unfortunately, when a young man, he cut his kneejoint, which made a stiff leg for the rest of his life. For many years he was one of the legal trustees. Although a farmer by occupation, he was useful in repairing wagons, carts, buggies, sleighs, etc. He was industrious, quick and active. He died October 15, 1862, in his 83d year.

Riley Honey.—One of the first, if not the first, child born in the Western Reserve, and one of the first pioneers of Warrensville, was Riley Honey. He was born in Burton, Geauga county, Ohio, December 31, 1798. He could wield an axe among heavy forest timber in cleaning off land, erecting log cabins; he could boil down sugar water, catch raccoons, find wild honey, and further, was the equal of any of his neighbors. His early training gave him an advantage over those who had not endured the hardships of pioneer life. He was prepared in an eminent degree to become one of the first founders of a community whose principles are based upon sacrifices and daily cross-bearing.

He entered the society in 1822, while it was still in embryo. He came alone and single-handed, without any family, in the prime of his activity, and devoted a long and useful life in building up the cause of truth and righteousness. He was appointed first legal trustee September 15, 1840, which place he still occupied in 1874, during which time he gave general satisfaction, and at two different periods was, at short intervals, appointed second in the ministry. He was universally known as an honest man.

In 1835 he was taken sick and given up to die. He was emaciated and reduced to a skeleton. The lingering look, the parting word, the silent tear, the last farewell, were reluctantly given. His grave clothes were prepared and the funeral hymn composed. He requested to see the elders of the church. David Spinning, then presiding elder, immediately responded, and arriving at the bedside was moved with compassion and tender sympathy. Elder David prayed in spirit, in low humility, in deep supplication and silent yearning. That prayer was heard and answered, not by any outward manifestation, but by a deep, silent, invisible power, and Riley Honey began to recover from that very hour, and soon after was able to take his place in the ranks of the faithful, and resume his labors in all his daily avocations. In his old age he began to take a deep interest in bee culture. He died August 7, 1884, aged 85 years, 5 months and 6 days.

Elijah Russell.—Windsor, Connecticut, was also the natal place of Elijah Russell, and was there born July 13, 1773. In 1813 he emigrated from Rodman, Jefferson county, New York, and settled in Warrensville, Ohio, and thus became one of the western pioneers. He purchased a farm heavily timbered, and at once set apart to clear it for cultivation. In 1822 he embraced the testimony of the Shakers, and the first meeting of that order took place in his cabin. His family consisted of a wife, six daughters and one son, the children named Melinda, Eunice, Esther, Adeline, Caroline, Emeline and Marcus, all of whom were gathered into the Shaker fold. His wife was a member of the Baptist Church, an excellent woman and an ornament to society.

Elijah was old-fashioned and eccentric, but made himself useful in the cultivation of fruit trees, in which he was success-- ful. After the church was organized he devoted his time ex- clusively for many years in planting nurseries, setting out or- chards, pruning and grafting in the proper season, sparing no pains to procure the best varieties of apples, peaches, pears, plums, cherries, etc. When a tree did not bear fruit to suit him, or was of an inferior quality, he would cut off the limbs near the body with a fine saw, smooth the top with a sharp knife, put in one or two scions of some choice variety, and within a few years that tree was seen bearing different kinds of fruit of a superior quality, size, color and flavor. All of the old or- chards, of which there were two quite extensive ones, at all the three families, owed their origin and subsequent cultivation chiefly to the labors of Elijah Russell. In times of drouth he was often seen carrying water from a distance to moisten the roots of the young trees. His time for pruning was in the spring, after the sap began to flow, and from that time on until the fruit became too large to admit of any further en- croachments. Although he pruned sparingly and cautiously, yet he believed in pruning to some extent. By close observa- tion he learned that the best way to set out an orchard was to place the trees on top the soil, and then bank up around them, instead of setting them down on the clay, as he had formerly done. In winter he was frequently seen stamping the snow down around the trees to prevent the mice from gnawing the roots, and in summer he would remove the turf from around the trees.

Elijah Russell was a practical man, and contributed more towards furnishing the community with good, wholesome fruit, both for the table and the market, than any other man who be- longed to the society. He departed this life February 26, 1857, in the 84th year of his age.

Chester Risley.—The next after Ralph Russell who started in the work of the faith at North Union was Chester Risley, who was born in East Hartford, Connecticut, December 6, 1794. He embraced the faith March 30, 1822, and set out to obey it. He had a wife and a daughter Lucina, both of whom subse--

quently became adherents of the same faith. When the Shakers found Chester he owned a small farm adjoining that of Elisha Russell on the east, and lived in a log cabin.

Chester Risley was a practical man,—a man of deeds and not of words. He had no faith in being saved by grace through faith, without having corresponding good works. Hence he was often heard to say, "We must work out our salvation. We cannot talk it out, nor sing it out. An apostle hath said, 'Faith without works is dead: it being alone.'" He believed in being saved by the blood of Christ, *i. e.*, by living his life—"the blood is the life thereof."

After the church was organized Chester Risley was called to be an elder, which place he occupied for many years in the different families, and was highly esteemed for his works, for his devotedness to the cause, and for his pious and godly example. By occupation he was a farmer and shoemaker. He departed this life May 6, 1855, in the 61st year of his age.

William Andrews.—In the formation of the society the founders filled some important station. Such was the case also with William Andrews, who was born January 16, 1776, in Little Hoosett, or Stephentown, Renssellaer county, New York.

In July, 1825, he was admitted into the community. He had a wife and four children,—Phoebe, Harriet, Louisa and Watson—who were subsequently gathered into the society. He had been brought up at Mount Lebanon, New York, and consequently was indoctrinated into the principles of the community. As he had that faith implanted in him when young he never got rid of it, and thereby found no true peace and comfort until he was brought under its obedience. So he put away a wife, and she a husband that they might live according to the principles they accepted.

By occupation William Andrews was a tanner and currier, and for many years was useful in this line. He departed this life March 22, 1850, in his 75th year. In 1870 the entire family was dead, with the exception of Watson, who was still living at the time the society was dissolved.

Oliver Wheeler.—Although not a member at the beginning, yet Oliver Wheeler might be classed as one of the founders of

North Union Society. He was born in Preston, Connecticut, August 14, 1790. He had been an exhorter in the Methodist Episcopal Church. Deeply imbued with the religious element, and not finding Methodism that which he sought, he became a member of the United Society of Believers, January 22, 1825. His three children, William, Sally and Hester Ann, then living in Aurora, a few miles distant, chose to come with him, but his wife decided to remain where she was. A mutual separation took place.

Oliver was a pious, devoted man. He made himself useful, first as a caretaker of children, then as an elder, and finally as second in the ministry. He died from the effects of a surgical operation for hernia, September 12, 1848, in his 59th year.

Rodney Russell.—The youngest son of Jacob Russell was Rodney, who was born in Windsor, Connecticut, May 15, 1796. In 1870 he was the only surviving male member of the Russell family at North Union. He was a single man, and owned a farm a little distance south from the settlement, which he exchanged for land lying north and adjoining land owned by the community.

He entered the society with his four brothers and consecrated his property, his time and his talents and all he possessed to build up and support his religious faith. To that cause he devoted a long and useful life and blessed many an orphan and poor widow, who had been brought into the community and permitted to partake of the fruits of his labor. By occupation he was a farmer and shoemaker. He died at North Union, September 3, 1880, aged 84 years, 3 months and 7 days.

Daniel N. Baird.—No Shaker was better known in Cleveland than Uncle Daniel, as Daniel W. Baird was usually called. He was born in Grandville, Jefferson county, New York, November, 7, 1801, and was admitted into the society in October, 1823. By occupation he was a wheelmaker, was of an inventive turn of mind, and took out several patents, among which were a brace and bit; but none yielded him much profit. As soon as the society began to use machinery he found some soft metal, supposed to be composed of tin, pewter or lead. He found that

NORTH UNION SOCIETY.   185

this composition was excellent for gudgeons of the wheel to his turning lathe to run in without heating by friction, and subsequently became quite extensively used at North Union.

Some years afterwards a man by the name of Babbitt invented a box for this same kind of metal to run in, and then commenced a suit against Ward & Co., of Detroit, for infringement of his patent. The defense summoned Daniel as a witness, who appeared in court with his box and soft metal, and testified that he had invented that box and composition and used it for years prior to Mr. Babbitt's patent. He turned the scale for the defendants, who, feeling under great obligations to him, offered to reward him handsomely, but he would take only his expenses in attending court. However, he did accept a free pass which they gave him over all the railroads and steamboats in their jurisdiction and as far as their influence over other companies and conveyances extended. This privilege he was not slow to improve; he visited some of the principal cities both east and west and was in Washington a short time before his death.

Daniel never enjoyed good health, and was dyspeptic from the day he entered the society to the time of his death. He was a very useful man, and for several years was acting trustee for the society. In buying and in selling and peddling their home manufactures, in most things he exercised good judgment and gave general satisfaction. A short time before his death he started to go to Cleveland on foot, and got as far as the Mill Family, when taking sick, in a day or two he expired. He died June 2, 1867, being in his 66th year.

Sisters.—Among the first founders of North Union were some pious, devoted, active and intelligent sisters, whose services were eminently successful in the cause espoused. These sisters, should have found a biographer and sketches of their lives, would have been just as useful and entertaining as those of the brethren. The Prescott MS. states that the data was not at hand for such a purpose. Such data as exists is here given. Those who were most prominent in the inception and who lived at Union Village were:

Anna Boyd, Betsey Dunlavy, Charlotte Morrell, Susannah Stout, Melinda Watts, Lucy Faith, .Lois Spinning, Thankful Stewart.

Anna Boyd, Thankful Stewart and Lucy Faith were remarkably gifted in song. They seemed to "sing with the spirit and the understanding." There was an inspiration about their singing that would inspire a whole assembly. The rich melody of their voices, at a little distance, could hardly be distinguished from a well-tuned instrument. Those who heard them were extravagant in their praise.

There were other noble souls who subsequently were called into the work, who may be justly ranked among the founders of the community, but have long since passed away. They were:

Lydia Russell, Betsey Russell, Jerusha Russell, Eunice Russell, Esther Russell, Caroline Russell, Roxana Russell, Harriet Andrews, Melinda Torrey, Polly Torrey, Cynthia Bevin, Clarissa Risley, Susannah Sawyer, Permelia Torrey, Polly Sawyer, Huldah Russell.

Among those living in the society in 1870, may be named:

Lucy Cooper, aged 97; Arabella Shepard, Phila Copley, Mariah Pilot, Hannah Addison, Laura Russell, Ruth Butson, Melinda Russell, Rhoda Watson, Jane Bearse, Harriet Shepard, Margaret Swayer, Harriet Snooks, Elizabeth Deree, Laura Houghton, Sylva Tyler, Elmina Phillips, Henrietta Wallace, Harriet Snyder.

Those occupying places of care and trust were:

Rachel Russell, Abigail Russell, Candace Russell, Prudence Sawyer, Lezette Walker, Clymena Miner, Temperance Devan, Lydia Ann Cramer, Mary Pilot, Charlotte Pilot.

Hannah Addison was the mother of H. M. Addison, one of Cleveland's most devoted and influential philanthropists, and universally called Father Addison.

Brethren.—Among the brethren whose biographies are not given and who have long since passed away, are the following:

Jeremiah Ingalls, Hugh McQuead, Christian Stade, William Johnson, Ambrose Bragg, Benjamin Sawyer, Hiram Young, William Devan.

Those living in 1870 and holding positions of care and trust were:

Freeman Phillips, Samuel S. Miner, Charles Sweet, Joseph Montgomery, Charles Taylor, George Hunt, Henry Summerfield, Sewell G. Thayer, Jacob Walker, Jacob Kimbal, Curtis Cramer, Cornelius Bush, Christian Lyntz, Thomas Giles.

At the time of the dissolution of the society the elders at

SOUTH-EAST VIEW OF WASHHOUSE OF MIDDLE FAMILY.

the Middle Family were Samuel S. Miner and Clymena Miner, and those at the Mill Family were Watson W. Andrews and Temperance Devan.

The members of the community had their choice whether they should be transferred to Watervleit, near Dayton, Ohio, or to Union Village, near Lebanon, Ohio. Those transferred to Watervleit were:

John Pilot, Christian Lyntz, Charles Taylor, Cornelius Bush, Daniel Dunning, Maria Pilot, Mary Shepard, Clymena

Miner, Harriet Snyder, Margaret Swayer, John Morton, Sam-
uel Miner, George Hunt, William Dunn, Ferdinand Budinger,
Robert Budinger, Lizzie Budinger, Lulu Budinger, Harriet
Snooks.

Those who cast their lot with the society at Union Village
were:

William Sheppe, James McQuigan, Watson Andrews, Lis-
zette Ryder, Thomas Mylrea, William Lincoln, Temperance Devan, Harriet Shepard.

A short time prior to the dissolution of the society Melinda
and Rachel Russell were removed to Watervleit.

XI. CONCLUSION.

In parting with the history of the United Believers of
North Union, I desire to repeat what has been intimated in this
record, that of the people herein portrayed I had no personal
acquaintance, and hence was bound in justice to allow their
spokesman, James S. Prescott, to state the facts as he saw them.
I have restrained myself from offering comment, leaving the
reader to do that for himself. In these concluding remarks I
will closely follow the opinions of them as given by Judge John
Barr, as published in the *Cleveland Herald* of July 25, 1870.

By the people of Cleveland the Shakers, who came in contact with them, were regarded to be a strictly moral class, very
industrious, male and female, in the various duties assigned to
each that was able to labor, while the children were sent to school
in order to acquire a reasonable education. They were noted
for promptness and integrity in their dealings and faithful per-
formance of contracts. They studied the laws of health in the
construction of their dwellings, in the selection and preparation
of food, and noted for neatness and cleanliness. They eschewed the use of all intoxicating drinks as a beverage, and
used only when prescribed by a physician; and any violation of
this rule by any member was a matter of strict discipline. The
use of profane, obscene, vulgar or harsh language to each other
or to the world was not tolerated. Sunday was regarded as a
holy day and observed as a day of rest from all secular pursuits,
save those of necessity and mercy, just as strictly as did the

Puritans, and devoted the day to religious worship in praise and thanksgiving exclusively. They were kind and liberal to the sick and unfortunate, and the stranger who was overtaken by disease or casualty in their midst, in them found the good Samaritan. To the members of their respective families no pains were spared or expense avoided, in sickness, or infirmity of any kind; and the aged and infirm were cared for to the full extent of parental affection. They were averse to strife or litigation, and avoided going to law if possible. During their existence they appeared in court but once as plaintiffs, and were successful. They carefully obeyed the laws of the land, punctually paid their taxes, and fulfilled all other requirements of them, patiently and cheerfully. None of their members were ever accused of an offence. They were opposed to anything like pomp or ostentation, or useless parade or ceremony. They regarded the practice of wearing mourning of any kind as a relic of paganism, and religiously discarded it. They laid out their burial grounds in a proper manner, ornamenting the same with beautiful trees and planted shrubs and flowers around and over the graves of their departed friends.

On what has been written a liberal interpretation must be given. Recently speaking to a lady who was a member of the North Union Society for a period of thirty-four years, and still had a very warm place in her heart for them, I asked her if there were not jealousy among them, and if the various offices were not desired by those who had not attained to them. She replied: "The Shakers must be judged just the same as others, for human nature is the same everywhere."

Being further pressed she said that those refusing to sign the Church Covenant were subjected to a very strong and irritating pressure. This class was brought up in the society and on the very day any one became of legal age the Covenant was brought and the party urged to sign it.

Cleveland, Ohio, April 14, 1900.

WATERVLEIT, OHIO, SHAKER COMMUNITY.

The extinct Shaker community, called Watervleit, was lo-cated about six miles east by south of Dayton, on sections 13 and 14, VanBuren Township, Montgomery County, Ohio. The lands are on both sides of Beaver Creek, which divided the es-tate. The stream afforded most excellent drainage for the lands on either side. The estate was located partly on the second river terrace that encroached upon the adjacent hills. To these lands was a strip of one hundred acres adjoining in the county of Greene.

In the early Shaker documents the Society is variously called Beaver Creek, Beulah and Mad River. In the same papers these terms are used indiscriminately, and in such a way as to leave con-fusion in the mind of the misinformed reader. It was among the first stations instituted by the Shakers in the West; for just two months and six days after the arrival of the propaganda (Issa-char Bates, Benjamin S. Youngs and John Meacham) the place was visited by two missionaries. So far as my information ex-tends, none of the Shaker documents state why Beulah received their attention.

The first settlers on Beaver Creek were Scotch Presbyterians, having mostly come from Bethel congregation, on the North Elkhorn, between Georgetown and Lexington, in Kentucky. The first to arrive was John Patterson (a brother of Colonel Robert Patterson), who settled on the southeast quarter of section 14, in the fall of 1799, where he built a cabin made of logs notched at the corners. In 1805 he built a two-story hewed log house 20 by 30 feet, with brick chimneys and shingle roof, which was the best that the county, at that time, could afford. The next arrival was John Huston, a brother of Judge David Huston, of Greene county, Ohio, a single man, entered a quarter section and began to im-prove it. In the spring of 1801, John Buchanan and his family arrived. In 1802, James Milligan, his wife Peggy, William

Stewart, his wife Sally, with their connections, arrived. The cabin built by William Stewart stood near where the Shaker gristmill afterwards was built. The records of the Washington Presbytery show that the Beulah church was taken under its care as early as 1800. The first preacher appears to have been William Robinson, but in 1802 Richard McNemar was assigned for two Sabbaths to this church. This was during the midst of the excitement caused by the Kentucky revival, and the bitter feelings then engendered began to exhibit themselves.

Richard McNemar began his public ministrations about the last of May, 1802, at the house of James Patterson, a large congregation having assembled. About the middle of June, 1803, a camp-meeting was held, with Richard McNemar, Robert Marshall, John Thompson and James Kemper as preachers. Although all belonged to the Washington Presbytery, yet so wide a difference was exhibited in the doctrinal preaching that the people were divided, a part holding with Kemper, who was a sober, rigid Calvinist, but the principal part of the multitude held with the other three. On Saturday Mr. Kemper preached from Isaiah xxii, 23, "making predestination the nail in a sure place." On Sabbath morning Mr. Marshall followed, and literally fulfilled the context, verse 25, for in that day was the nail fastened in the sure place removed, cut down and fell, and the burden that was upon it was cut off. The contest grew so warm and the exercises so powerful that in the afternoon Kemper and his company withdrew from the meeting and retreated homeward.

"The effect of this meeting served to excite a spirit of free inquiry on the doctrinal points of difference, which ultimately prepared the congregation as a body for the approaching event, which was a separation from the government of the Presbyterian church, which took place in the month of September following. After this separation the place of meeting was changed to the stand about half a mile west of John Patterson's, on the Dayton road, where a general camp-meeting was appointed about the last of July, 1804. At this meeting the work was powerful, the gifts and exercises singular, and the light transcendent. The jerking and barking exercises were astounding, and the effects of a sermon preached by McNemar, from Zech. xi, 7-14, are well remembered. The breaking of the two staves (the creed and form of government) excited the most un- bounded enthusiasm. The breaking to pieces a beautiful system and a beautiful order of government on which millions were resting for support was so emphatically announced and so rhe- torically pictured that it seemed as if the old heavens were al- ready passing away with a great noise and the elements melting with fervent heat." *

SOURCES OF INFORMATION.

A wise edict went forth from the Mt. Lebanon Ministry that full records of the different communities should be kept. Doubt- less such records were made by all the Societies. But nowhere, either directly or indirectly, do I find an injunction that such rec- ords shall be preserved. Nor do I find a scratch of a pen inti- mating that the Ministry ever inquired into these documents, or saw that they were in a proper condition.

The records of the Watervleit community do not appear to have been properly arranged until Richard McNemar assumed the task in February, 1832. When the Society was dissolved the records were brought to Union Village. The first volume ends with June 30, 1880. The second volume is in existence, but mis- placed. The first volume was commenced by Richard McNemar, but in no sense is it a journal until January 1st, 1833, when the writing is in another hand.

From the very inception of Shakerism in the West, Union Village has been the chief and ruling community. Its Ministry, first established there on Monday, July 29, 1805, has not only been continuous, but ever since regarded as the first. It would be supposed that the principal center would guard all the archives with care. It is positively known that some of the records have been purposely burned. Even no church journal can now be found dating since April 30, 1861. Whether destroyed or loaned no one can tell. There were pamphlets published, but afterwards forgotten, and no attempt made to preserve a copy of each pro- duction. All this dereliction of duty must be laid at the door of

---

* MS. Records Watervleit Society.

the former Ministry. When it is considered that some of those chosen to the leadership were not particularly gifted in lines that required peculiar qualifications, we are not at a loss to discover where the culpability should rest.

For the early history of Watervleit I have depended almost entirely on the South Union Records from 1805 to 1811, with such light as those of Union Village may throw on the subject, and certain references from books. The Union Village records have many references to visits of brethren and sisters, to and from, between the two Societies, but rarely any practical information; and even then, none until Jan. 23, 1808. I find the Union Village Ministry, especially during the reign of John Martin, were frequent visitors; but the object of the visit is never explained, nor the names of the parties given. In nearly all other cases, the names of the visitors are preserved, and occasionally the title of "Elder" occurs. But little satisfaction can be obtained from those now living, for the reason that transfers were rapidly made; persons removed from office, afterwards restored, then sent to another community, which could only breed confusion and uncertainty in their recollections.

There is a book that contains the journals of five of the Elders, beginning with that of Ebenezer Rice from Sept. 23, 1856, to Nov. 17, 1859. This contains more information, given daily, than any Shaker document I have yet examined. Matthew B. Carter's journal begins Nov. 27, 1859, and ends Sept. 21, 1860. Stephen W. Ball's can hardly be considered a journal. It contains but very little, — beginning Aug. 14, 1871, and ending Dec. 25, 1879. This is followed by that of John Sauerborn, beginning Jan. 6, 1880, and closing Oct. 25, 1884. Then Elder Ball resumes the task from Jan. 1, 1889, to Oct. 21, 1891. The last is that of Henry W. Frederick, which begins Dec. 16, 1891, and closes Aug. 31, 1894. This is the most replete of all, covering 158 MS. pp., but really says the least. It may be of some interest to those who lived at Watervleit during the period covered, but can be of but little effect to others.

All the above documents are still at Union Village. A very large chest of documents was left at Watervleit at the time of

13

the removal of the people from there. These documnts were all turned over to me October 19, 1903, by James H. Fennessey, general manager at Union Village. From these papers I have gathered some things relating to the community. Most of the archives, however, related to North Union.

EARLY MISSIONS.

It is not a difficult problem to solve why the Shakers should seek converts in the settlement along Beaver Creek. The great excitement during the camp-meeting of June, 1803, swept the greater part of the congregation into the Christian (New Light) church. It was then nurtured and sustained by Richard McNemar, and through him, it would naturally follow, that efforts would be put forth i that direction. An incident greatly hastened the event. The turbulent camp-meeting held at Turtle Creek (present site of Union Village), commencing April 7, 1805, attracted a great multitude of people, among the rest a principal part of the Beulah congregation, "of whom none were more distinguished for good sense and spiritual discernment than Phoebe Patterson and Peggy Buchanan, who happily came divested of prejudice, and willing to hear and judge for themselves regardless of popular opinion; and the result was a united and settled conviction that the testimony then and there opened to them was the everlasting truth of God, and pointed out the only way of salvation. This impression they never lost, altho' it was nearly a year after before the way was opened for them to obey their faith. William Stewart and others, at the same time received a measure of faith, insomuch that William invited Issachar and Benjamin to make a visit to Beulah as soon as convenient."

In compliance with the above request at 5 :30 A. M., May 28, 1805, Issachar Bates and Benjamin S. Youngs set out from Union Village to Beaver Creek, and on Friday, the 31st, preached at the residence of John Buchanan, which, in a measure, served to confirm the faith in those who already were disposed to believe. This effort served to stir up to redoubled zeal the Revival (New Light) preachers, that their congregation might be held back, "and the people were so linked in their family and social connection that it required time and patience for the leaven to work."

The missionaries were encouraged to make another attempt, and on Saturday, June 22nd, Youngs, Richard McNemar and Malcolm Worley set out from Union Village for Beaver Creek and returned the 24th.

The first avowed convert was John Huston, an amiable young man, a wheelwright by trade, but a farmer by occupation. Sometime in October, 1805, he visited Union Village (then called Turtle Creek), declared his faith in Shakerism and then returned home, and for nearly five months was the only resident there openly to confess his faith.

On December 9th, 1805, Daniel Mosely, Youngs and Worley set out for Beaver Creek and returned the 11th. During the month of February, 1806, John Stewart openly espoused the new faith. On Wednesday, March 22, 1806, "Elders Issachar, Benj. & Richard went 22 miles to Beulah or Beaver Creek. — Had meeting at Wm. Stewart's, as usual spoke some two hours. After meeting Richard went home with John Patterson, who had been an opposer — his wife Phoebe, having faith but held back on his account. Thurs. 27. Wm. Stewart confessed to Benjamin — evening went to John Stewart's — Next day to Dayton at mouth of Mad river—forded the Miami—went thence to Wm. King whose wife refused to tell us the way to Nathan Worley's,* because she had heard we were deceivers — Her husband told us the way — We remained two hours at Nathan's — their opposition was great and returned to John Stwart's, thence to Jas. Milligan's & John Patterson's. Saturday, 29. Peggy Stewart confessed to Issachar and Jas. Milligan and Elizabeth and Caty Stewart (John's mother) confessed to Benjamin — On our way to John Pattersons, Phoebe Stewart confessed to Richard — soon after he returned to Turtle Creek — thence we went to Wm. Stewart's and Sally his wife confessed to Benjamin. Sab. 30. Abm. Patterson confessed to Benjn. — We went to John Patterson's. — A large collection of people assembled, to whom John Thompson preached from Acts iii, 22, 23. He observed 'that once the Jews were God's peculiar people, but since Christ's

---

* Then a prominent New Light preacher.

time, the whole world was God's people — God with us — the whole world! — no one ought to work on their sins so as to feel guilt — but lay hold of faith in the promise of God,' etc., etc.— a great deal of hypocrisy and foolery. In his prayer however, he desired God would preserve the innocent lambs from the ravening wolves (alluding to Shakers) that were going about the country in sheep's clothing, etc. John Patterson opened his mind, confessed to Benjn. — Mon. 31. Peggy Buchanan confessed to Benj. — did not wish, but was advised to return to her family and do her duty to them and keep her faith — which she did — though her husband had said to her she should never enter his house if she joined the Shakers — but said not a word when she informed him of the fact — We went to John Patterson's — thence to Wm. Stewart's — thence to John Houston's where we kept out horses — thence to Abrams — thence to James Milligan's in Co. with J. Houston — 12 have opened their minds in this place of the most respectable people — stable and upright in their faith — Numbers of them having had in the revival great views of the present work of God." * The two companions arrived at Turtle Creek on the evening of April 1st.

In reference to John Thompson, in the Watervleit Church Records, Richard McNemar says: "John Thompson came on for his last effort, if possible to check their progress; being there to retract the steps they had taken, or at least deter the remnant from taking the same course. For his purpose he chose for his text, Acts iii, 22, 23, 'A prophet shall the Lord your God raise up unto you," etc. After exhibiting Christ as the great prophet and the awful penalty of disobeying him, to be destroyed or cut off from every fellowship with God's people, he observed that under the law, the Jews were the only people of God, but under the gospel there is no distinction between Jew and Gentile, but God claims all the world as his people; of course that to fall under the awful sentence now, must incur a fatal and final cutting off, or separation from the whole world. This logical paraphrase was rather diverting than alarming to the Believers, as they felt prepared, with much composure to meet the terrible

---

* MS. journal of Benjamin S. Youngs, copied into the South Union, Ky. Church Records.

sentence of excommunication. After meeting Thompson asked his old friend Patterson what he thought of the sermon. To which the Captain replied: 'You did somehow blunder into the truth; perhaps you did not intend it.' At which Thompson was so offended, that he immediately got on his horse, gathered his company and moved on to George Patterson's, to hold their evening meeting.

"Issachar and Benjamin being present on this memorable occasion, the Believers were much strengthend and confirmed in their faith, and John Patterson, for his disobedience to Thompson, being excommunicated, or cut off from the whole world, sought his relation to the little company, and from that period to his death, filled a respectable lot among Believers."

It will thus be seen that the way to the Watervleit Society was paved by Richard McNemar, and the superstructure was largely due to Issachar Bates† and Benjamin S. Youngs.

While the efforts were being put forth to found a Society on Beaver Creek, an interest was awakened there in the progress of the community at Turtle Creek. From April 13, 1806, James and Betsey Milligan and Ezekiel and Eunice Patterson paid a visit to Turtle Creek. The interest increased so much so that on the 26th, both Issachar and Benjamin went to Beaver Creek, where all the Believers met together and "for the first time all went forth to worship in the dance." On the following day Rachel Southard confessed to Benjamin, and that night the two companies reached Turtle Creek.

For some reason, unexplained, the infant society was left alone until July 8, when it was visited by Daniel Mosely, Bates and McNemar, who staid until the 14th, but with what results, we are left uninformed, though owing to the presence of McNemar, and the length of the stay, it is probable that plans for the stability of the Society were discussed. This view is plausible from the fact that on Aug. 29th, David Darrow,* Ruth Farring-

---

† Issachar Bates claimed to have been the father of the Watervleit Society, and greatly desired that it should be the parent of all the Western communities, in which he was overruled.

* David Darrow was a Revolutionary patriot, being second lieutenant, 4th company, 17th regiment, New York, commissioned March 6, 1779, in

ton, Prudence Farrington, Ruth Darrow, Daniel Mosely and Solomon King went to Beulah in a wagon and there remained until Sept. 10th.

I find no farther record until Dec. 2nd, when "Daniel Mosely, Samuel Turner, and Benj. S. Youngs set out to visit Believers at Beaver Creek or Beulah near Dayton, returned the 27th." Other Shaker documents affirm that Watervleit took its rise in 1806, and it must be inferred that steps towards a permanent organization, before the close of the year, had been seriously taken. Although the Shakers had the example of John Wesley before them, who placed a leader for every flock that numbered three or more, yet they appear never to have taken advantage of it. Yet the work was kept moving at Beulah, for on Jan. 17, 1807, Solomon King, Issachar Bates and David Hill arrived here and staid until the 30th. I find no further record for 1807, but that is no indication that the movement was in a dormant condition.

Jan. 23, 1808, there arrived at Union Village 16 Believers from Beulah and Eagle Creek, — proportion of each not stated. It is more than probable that the Beulah Believers were still living in their own cabins.

Mar. 7, 1808, Solomon King and Malcolm Worley were at Beaver Creek. May 31st, Solomon King, Archibald Meacham, Molly Goodrich and Ruth Farrington went to Beaver Creek on horse-back and returned June 3rd, bringing with them David and Polly Greene. Eight visitors from Beaver Creek arrived at Union Village June 25th, but names not given.

The next and last reference for 1808 is dated Dec. 28: "Mathew Houston, Malcolm W. and John Rankin go to Mad River and Staunton.* returned Sat. the 7th of Jany. 1'09."

I find but one reference for 1809 and that dated April 12: "Issachar and Richard McNemar set out for Beaver creek,

---

place of John Smith. His estate he gave to the Shakers of Mt. Lebanon, N. Y., and is now owned by the North Family, and the residence is on the same spot on which his was located.

* This may refer to the small village of that name that once stood about two miles east of Troy, in Miami county.

and Mad River and Pickaway — some at Pickaway now obey their faith — returned the 22nd."

Apr. 30, 1810, "Eld. David Darrow, Eldress Ruth Farrington, Solomon King & Molly Goodrich in a wagon to Beaver creek & returned the 3d of May."

Sept. 12, 1810. "Twenty-seven of the brethren set out for Beulah (now Watervleit), to help that small society to raise a log meeting house." This indicates that the organization had been completed for some time. As their church building was of logs, it is probable that their sole industry, at this time, was agriculture. The starting of a saw mill would mean the commencement of frame buildings.

Sept. 7, 1811, John and Phoebe Patterson moved to Union Village, and on Sept. 12, John Houston, John Hutchison, Rosanna Shields and Miriam Worley went to Beaver Creek to live. This is the last reference in the South Union Records. Previous to this date there are but two references in the rcords of Union Village. What follows must be largely culled from the latter down to 1861.

The first reference in the Union Village Record is for Jan. 23, 1808; the next, Sept. 12, 1810, and the next, Feb. 2, 1813, which states: "About this time, the Journal (Peter Pearse's), in speaking of the Society on Beaver creek (sometimes called Beaulah) calls it Water Vleit. It is likely the name was changed about this time. Hereafter it will be so called." The name was taken from the Shaker Society of Watervleit, New York.

ORGANIZED AS A SOCIETY.

The above visitations would indicate a well organized Society, though not standing alone. The Believers were strong enough to have a permanent order in March, 1806, and at that time John Stewart was appointed first Elder, and with much acceptance, filled that office for two years and four months. In the beginning they did not own the property in common, some of whom still remained in Dayton, though frequently warned to leave through the papers. Opposition to some extent continued which culminated in a mob, of the baser sort, in May, 1811. The Shakers boldly met the mob as it intruded on their premises, and drove them away, without causing violence. After this open opposition ceased.

The deeds to their lands were carefully entered upon the Church Records by Richard McNemar, which in 1882, amounted to 800 acres of land.

The Society was under the direct supervision of the Ministry of Union Village and so continued up to the time when Issachar Bates assumed the reins of power. The Society never was numerically large, nor could it so have been under the rapid and useless changes in the officers made by the Union Village Ministry. Whenever temporary assistance was needed Union Village was always very prompt in sending the necessary number of brethren. Visits were very frequent between the two Societies, which were kept up until the general decline became quite marked, when they gradually grew less.

A sawmill must have been early in operation and the log cabins abandoned for frame dwellings. The grist-mill was running in 1812, and in July, 1813, the tannery was in operation, and in 1814 the cooper shop, wooden ware industry and woollen factory were doing business. In 1815 brooms were made for the market, and in 1819 blacksmithing was done for the public, while the wagon shop had become quite a source of revenue. In all probability the above industries were in operation before the respective dates mentioned.

On March 8, 1813, Richard McNemar arrived in the village, and taking sick on the 15th Nathan Sharp arrived to bring him home.

Elder John Houston died September 21, 1817, aged 46.

In 1820 there was a Mill and a School Family, but in 1823 one Family is called the West and the other the North, while the following year there appears to have been a West, a North and a Center Family, besides a residence for the Young Believers. In 1823, Alexander Hughey was elder and Jean Patterson eldress at the West Family. The same year William Martin was elder and Prudence Grunin eldress at the North Family. Oct. 30, 1823, Electa Morrell succeeded Molly Kitchell as eldress, but I know not at which Family. The trustees in 1822 were Jethro Boyd and Thomas Johnson. In 1825 William Burnham and Nathaniel Taylor were deacons, and on June 1, 1826, the latter was transferred to the Center Family. In 1827 Joseph Eastwood was an elder and Jean Patterson an eldress, probably at the North Family.

THE BLESSING AT DAYTON.

The most amiable relations had been existing between the people of Dayton and Believers, insomuch so that the incident of the mob of 1811 had been fully forgiven. The great difference accorded to the Shakers by the denizens of Lebanon and those of Dayton was a matter of remark among Believers. About the year 1820 a Shaker brother of Union Village had a vision, in which it was revealed that the Shakers should place a curse upon Lebanon and a blessing upon Dayton. In their early history Shakers were ever obedient to heavenly commands. David Darrow felt that the command must be obeyed. The first messenger selected was Francis Bedle, who demurred and even refused to perform the mission. Finally he gave his consent provided Richard McNemar should be his attendant. McNemar disapproved of the whole scheme and thought it should be passed over; but, being obedient to higher powers, he reluctingly consented. Together the two brethren rode on horseback through the principal street of Lebanon, waved their hats and pronounced woe upon all persecutors. The same day they appeared on one of the streets of Dayton, riding rapidly, waving their hats, and pronounced the blessings of God upon the town and all its inhabitants. News of the action of the Shaker missionaries, in Dayton, spread upon the wings of the wind, over the banks and hills of the Miami and Mad rivers. The farmers regarded the Shakers as possessed of deep religious foresight. Dayton had made but slow progress. There were farmers who now believed the town having been blessed by holy men of God would become prosperous. Some rented and others sold their farms and moved to the town, giving it an impetus which has ever so continued. Of Lebanon and its enterprises, on the other hand, its local historian, in his "Centennial Sketch," has been forced to proclaim that its population has remained stationary for four decades.

BRICK DWELLING.

On January 15, 1820, a number of joiners arrived at Watervleit from Union Village to give a week's work towards finishing the new brick dwelling, which was 44 x 50 feet. This house was occupied on the 31st October following. Assistance must have been further needed, for July 9 there were 14 sent to assist in the harvest.

July 12, 1821 a company arrived from Union Village to help raise a large barn, and returned the 14th.

October 9, 1822, Robert Baxter and a number of recent converts were transferred to Watervleit.

SICKNESS.

The summer of 1823 was a very sickly one, but the nature of the disease is not stated, but probably some form of malaria. As early as August 9th there was much sickness and several deaths. By September 19th it became very sickly. The disease must have again broken out the next summer, for on September 19, 1824, there were many sick.

THE GOLDEN AGE.

The Western Societies enjoyed their golden age, or greatest degree of prosperity when the future appeared to be bright and full of promise. The golden age of Watervleit commenced during the eldership of Issachar Bates and continued through that of Richard McNemar, his successor.

The Society at Watervleit had become discordant. There was confusion, and strong opposition made to the Elders, the Deacons and to one another. In order to bring peace and submission, David Darrow sent Issachar Bates to take general charge, as first Elder, with Joshua Worley for second. Both arrived at Watervleit Oct. 24, 1824. Soon after John Martin and James Ball were appointed trustees by the Union Village Ministry. At once Elder Issachar commenced regulating matters, insisting upon the Shaker rule of confession, and settling all matters of difference between them. It proved a difficult task to per-

CENTER FAMILY RESIDENCE.

form; but Issachar so adroitly managed the affairs as to retain the confidence and respect of all. While thus engaged the trustees paid off the indebtedness of the Society, and the last of the year the North brick house was completed and a family constituted in it. By January 1, 1825, affairs had been so righted that it was agreed to build a new meeting house, — a frame 40 by 50 feet. The frame was raised May 25th and 26th, assistance being rendered by a large number of brethren from Union Village. It was occupied in June. This is a large frame, two-story building facing the large Center Family brick building. The upper story was never finished, — it being designed for the use of the Ministry, in case that order should ever be assigned to them separately.

Elder David Darrow was buried on June 27, Elder Issachar was present with a large number of Watervleit Believers. He returned on July 4th, accompanied by the Ministry, who now put forth efforts to quiet all contentions that existed. In a good degree this was effected. On being asked if they were satisfied with Elder Issachar as their successor, all responded in the affirmative.

The possessions were now extended by the purchase of 100 acres of land for $2,000, and the erection of a two-story dwelling house on it, 40 by 30 feet, for the use of recent converts, called Young Believers. A saw and grist mill were built, with other improvements.

Joshua Worley proved himself to be a good assistant; but in February, 1826, he was transferred to Union Village, and his place was taken by Robert Baxter.

In 1827 an unfortunate schism broke out among the young and ambitious. They contended for a division of the property, which meant the end of the community. Being defeated in their designs, quite a number withdrew from the Society; which however did not take place until 1832. These were mostly young people of both sexes. This division was largely due to the mismanagement and breaking up of the West Union Society.

March 19, 1832, David Price was sent from Union Village to act as gardener and peddlar.

LITERATURE.

The reign of Issachar Bates imperceptibly passed into the hands of Richard McNemar. Early in the year 1832 he removed to Watervleit and at once engaged in correcting and straightening out the records of the Society. On April 1st he assumed the principal burden and care of the Society, which was not favorably entertained by Issachar.

September 29th, Malinda Watts, Samuel Tuttill and his son Bostwick removed from Union Village and took up their residence at the West house with a view to keeping up a Gathering Order.

Wherever the hand of Richard McNemar was felt literature and the dissemination of truth were brought to the front. Publishing interests commenced with him within two years after the founding of Shakerism in the West. When he died it was the practical death of Western publishing interests among the Shakers of Ohio. Within three months after he became lead at Watervleit he republished "Brief Exposition of Shakerism" that first appeared from the press at Albany in 1830. To this he added 22 pages of additional matter, partly his own, but mostly from the pen of David Spinning, devoted to answering sundry inquiries and objections that had been offered by non-believers.

In 1832 McNemar published quite a number of Covenants, among which were those adopted at Watervleit December 7, 1818, and January, 1833; the one at Union Village in 1810, January 15, 1812, and December 31, 1828. The first Covenant in Ohio, drafted by Benjamin Seth Youngs, in 1810, I have given in full in my "Bibliography of Shaker Literature." As that book fully discusses Shaker literature in Ohio, it is not necessary further to enter upon that subject in this connection.

COVENANT MEMBERS.

To the Watervleit Covenant of 1833 the following names were signed:

SISTERS' NAMES.	BRETHREN'S NAMES.
Salome Dennis	Issachar Bates
Eunice Bedle	Richard McNemar
Malinda Kitchell	Robert Baxter
Betsey Milligan	Ashbel Kitchell
Eliza Davis	Henry Miller
Peggy Naylor	James Ball
Mary Ann Duffey	William Phillips
Jane Patterson	James Milligan
Rachel Zane	Alex Hughey
Caty Eastwood	David Grummon
Eleanor Jackson	Thomas Williams
Kezia Hughey	John Rue
Elizabeth Simonton	James Martin
Esther Ball	John L. Eastwood
Elizabeth Maxson	James Grummon
Esther Eastwood	John Maxson
Peggy Patterson	John Davis
Matilda Rue	David Price
Polly Dewitt	Samuel Tuthill
Betsy Eastwood	John M. Eastwood
Matilda Williams	Noah Spafford
Edith Gee	William Slater
Polly Ball	Daniel McLane
Sally Kimal	Isaac Houston
Jane Gallagher	James M. Patterson
Hannah Mayze	Alvah West
Frances Silence	David Eastwood, etc.
Polly Rice	
Abbey Rice	
Nancy Rice, etc.	

This list does not include those in the Gathering Order.

The Covenant of 1818 shows that James Patterson and Nathaniel Taylor had immediate charge at that time, of the Society. The probability is that there were, even then, three families, viz., Center, North, and West, or Gathering Order. In 1833 the Chief Eldress was Salome (Edith) Dennis, who had previously been at West Union. At this period the public speakers in the Society, besides Issachar Bates and Richard McNemar, were Henry Miller and William Phillips. These four took regular turns, two speaking each Sunday.

CONCLUSION OF M'NEMAR'S REIGN.

Not only did McNemar look after the spiritual welfare of the Society and literary productions, but the temporal outlook received his attention. On May 7, assisted by a number of brethren from Union Village, a large barn was moved.

June 30, 1835, the Union Village Ministry made the following changes: Eldress Salome Dennis is removed to Union Village and Eunice Bedle takes her place, and Eliza Davis to live with her; James Ball becomes an Elder, second to McNemar; and Alexander Hughey removes to the Office as trustee in place of James Ball. On December 28, McNemar was released from the Eldership, but did not return to Union Village until January 13, 1836, and with him came Ashbel Kitchell and Malinda Watts-Kitchell.

The only other reference for 1836 I find is that on May 26, the Ministry at Union Village set out for Watervleit in their new carriage but the "springs did not do well," but their object or what they accomplished must be of no moment, for the result is not mentioned. Perhaps a mere junket. However, on January 24, 1837, the Ministry, accompanied by Matthew Houston and James Ball, proceeded to Watervleit, where Matthew was installed to be "a counselor resident."

CHRONICLES.

On March 25, 1837, "Matthew Houston and the Lot of Elders from Watervleit arrived (at Union Village) on a visit. (27.) The Watervleit Elders attended meeting this evening at the Centre family; this evening was overwhelming in point of spiritual gifts and sensation, — The heartfelt humility and contrition, together with the melting expressions of thankfulness and love to the way of God, caused the tears to flow from our Watervleit Elders." They returned home the 29th.

The meat having spoiled, the Union Village brethren sent them 250 pounds of salt pork on Oct. 3rd.

The Union Village Record for Aug. 30, 1838, shows that James Ball was the Elder Brother at that date, and it is probable that he was the immediate successor of McNemar. Elder Sister

Eunice Bedle went to Union Village April 25, 1838, to receive medical treatment, and returned Aug. 30th.

SPIRITUALISM.

Spiritualism probably did not break out until 1839, judged by a paragraph in the Union Village church journal for April 10, 1839: "This morning the Ministry, accompanied by some others, set out for Watervleit. This visit was signified by inspiration, & intended to help the people in that place. The same marvelous work has commenced at W. Vleit, & moves rapidly." The Ministry staid until the 16th. This is the only reference concerning this phenomenon. In all probability its history here was the same as at Union Village, only in a lesser degree. Freegift Wells was now on the throne, Watervleit was easily accessible to Union Village, and doubtless he worked this matter for all that could be obtained from it.*

OFFICERS.

January 2, 1841, James Darrow was appointed Elder Brother and that day removed from Union Village to Watervleit. The Ministry arrived on December 30, previous, and staid until January 17th. As it is stated, under April 10, that "Br. Matthew Houston removes home from Watervleit, where he has resided in care for a considerable time," and James Darrow "supplies his place as Elder Brother," it is proof that Matthew immediately succeeded McNemar. The record for July 2, 1841, shows that James Darrow was then the Elder Brother and Eunice Bedle was still the Elder Sister. James Ball and Matilda Williams are mentioned in same connection and in such a relation as to indicate they stood second. By other documents it is affirmed that Bates was the first of the Ministry at Watervleit; then succeeded by McNemar, who, in turn, by Houston.

Sometime during the year 1840 Ithamar Johnson became

---

* The spiritual communications were taken down on separate sheets and afterwards recorded in book form. What became of these books I have been unable to discover. I recovered 68 revelations and turned the same over to the Historical Society. Peggy Patterson appears to have been the principal medium.

manager of the real estate, for under February 3, 1842, it is stated that he "removes back home (Union Village) from Watervleit, — having been there a little more than 2 years, assisting them in the management of their temporalities." We also find that on August 2, 1841, that John Martin, James McNemar, P. F. Antes, Timothy Bonnell, Levi McNemar, Wm. N. Redmon, Aaron and Amos Babbitt went to Watervleit to help shingle several buildings, and returned (to Union Village) on the 7th.

On December 12, 1842, Elder Sister Eunice Bedle deceased. I find no mention of her successor, but on Aug. 11, 1853, Eliza Davis was Elder Sister. How long she had so acted is unknown.

CHRONICLES RESUMED.

On Monday, February 13, 1843, Andrew C. Houston and Lewis Valentine arrived from Union Village "to serve as witnesses at the execution of their revised Covenant," and departed the 15th. On June 2nd, assisted by twenty-nine Union Village brethren, a frame building, 36 x 76 feet, was raised north of the main dwelling. On October 18, James Ball and William Phillips set out for Union Village, in order to secrete there Frances Ann Cushwaugh, that she might be saved from being taken forcibly away.

No record for 1844, and the only one for 1845 is the note (March 29) that four horses and harness had been stolen.

November 20, 1846, the mill was burned by an incendiary. The loss included 600 bushels corn, 60 of oats and some buckwheat.

January 20, 1847, Richard W. Pelham moved from Union Village to become assistant in the Elders' order. April 15th, Oliver C. Hampton arrived in order to assist in schooling the children. He staid until June 11th.

No references for 1848 and 1849.

February 20, 1850, "Moses Eastwood returns to Watervleit, there to continue." March 25th, James Darrow returns to Union Village, after serving as "first care about nine years." Presumably he was succeeded by R. W. Pelham, although I do not find his name until April 14, 1853.

January 1 ,1851, Oliver C. Hampton arrives to assist in the

school, and remains until March 4th. April 7th, Abner Bedle arrives to assist in the trusteeship." During the early season the Society was assisted in cording and spinning by Sanford Russell, of Union Village. October 15th, the Office was robbed of $20.

No reference for the year 1852.

March 14, 1853, O. C. Hampton arrived "to assist in the management of the children, and staid until May 16th. March 7th Oliver Hampton visited the Spiritualists at Mechanicsburg, and on April 14th "Elder Brother R. W. Pelham at Watervleit writes about the arrival there of four families from Mechanicsburg, numbering of men, women and children twenty-two." September 26th Elder Sister Eliza Davis is taken to Union Village for medical treatment and remains until November 3rd. During the summer Elder Pelham was taken with chills and fever. Was attended by C. D. Hampton.

January 19, 1854, Rachel Hall, of Whitewater, became Elder Sister. June 10th, Daniel Miller arrives in order to officiate as deacon, but returned to Union Village December 10th. On December 31st, Persis Hoag arrived to teach school.

Nothing recorded for 1855.

ACCESSIONS FROM WHITEWATER.

A necessity arose for the strengthening of the Society; and to do this the members must be drawn from the Whitewater Community. "For some time back, there has been an anxious feeling by the beloved Ministry & Church at Union Village that the little flock at Water Vleit, might receive help & strength, that they might be able to gather & save souls. Accordingly in the fore part of last month (September, 1856), the beloved Ministry communicated their feelings to the believers at White Water, who universally expressed their good union in this matter & felt willing to do all they could to help carry out the feelings of the Ministry & Church at U. V., by giving up as many Believers from W. W. to go to W. V. to live, as the beloved Ministry should think best."

The Union Village Ministry together with the Elders at Whitewater made choice of the following: Ebenezer Rice and Matthew B. Carter, for Elders; Adaline Wells and Matilda A.

14

Butler for Eldresses; and Ezra Sherman, Lewis Packer, Mary Adams and Mary Ellen Stroud for Trustee, Deacon and Deaconesses, with the addition of Ramuth G. Bunting, Thomas Streets, Francis Vann, William Adams, Matthew Traber, Charles King, Mary Jane Lewis, Hester Ann Revox, Rebecca Adams, Sally McBride, Emily Adams and Bethynia Williams. On the morning of September 23, 1856, the entire party, with Ministry, left Whitewater, in five carriages, for Union Village. Near Hamilton the party was met by 40 Believers from Union Village, and all arrived the same evening at the latter place, where they were welcomed with the greatest friendship. The next day at 10 A. M. there was a general meeting of the Believers, when many spoke of their faith. Elder Rice represented the faith and spirit of the migratory band. The Ministry and Church extended "their great portion of love and strength in this meeting to help them to do the work that they were called to do, and a firm assurance was manifest that the time had fully come for the Believers at W. V. to be helped, and that the little company of 20 from W. W. were called of God for the express purpose, and no doubts were entertained but that they would be blessed in the undertaking, and be able to perform what they were called to do."

On the morning of the 25th the little band set out for Watervleit, and first reached the North Family, where the party was welcomed with cheering songs and suitable words. Accompanied by the members of the North Family, all proceeded to the South House, where they were welcomed by 13 Believers, most of whom were young in the faith. Here the pilgrims took up their abode, constituting a family of 33 persons. The house was well furnished, and everything had been placed in readiness for their reception.

The journal shows that all settled down to work as though they had been accustomed to the place. There was the cutting of corn, mason work at the North Family, sowing of wheat, digging potatoes, carpentering, work in the factory, etc., etc., all in rapid succession. Then there were "expeditions" to Dayton, and more distant parts, for the gathering in of new believers and children, in all of which the participants were very successful. The journal shows many accessions through their efforts, — the

North Family Residence.

names being specified. Six months before the arrival of the party 100 acres of land had been bargained for at $53 per acre, and on October 3rd the first payment was made. At the Dayton Fair, which commenced October 6th, the Shakers' cattle took 5 prizes. The week commencing the 11th was spent in cutting clover seed, repairing cellars, picking and drying apples, putting in pump, etc. The new addition of members put vim and vigor into the Society, and had the same momentum continued, the Society would still have been a tower of strength.

CHRONICLES RESUMED.

November 1, 1856, Richard W. Pelham was released as first Elder and Moses Eastwood was appointed in his place, with Ramuth G. Bunting to live with him.

The record shows there were peddling trips, especially in the line of yarns, which had probably been instituted years before. In December there was a large increase in members, probably most of whom may be classed as "Winter Shakers," —desiring a good home only during the cold weather. During the fall and early winter of 1856, John Sherman was in care of the boys. Provisions must have been scarce during the winter of 1856-7, for a load was sent from Whitewater and arrived January 3rd, consisting of sauce and butter, and a load of potatoes from Union Village on February 7th.

It was found necessary to put an engine in the mill, to use when water was scarce. In January, 1857, an addition to the North House, 30 x 60 feet, was commenced. February 20th, Matthew Carter went to Whitewater in a wagon for willows. apple trees, grape cuttings, currants and raspberries. Returned the 28th.

ADMISSIONS AND SECESSIONS.

As a sample of admissions and withdrawals I give the following for the year 1857:

"January 9th. An Irishman by the name of John McDaniel, 36 years old, a farmer.
    11th. A Dutchman by the name of (came here), 51 years old. Weaver. Went off.

24th. Virginia Harris is brought here by her ————, she is four years old.

27th. George Grub was placed under our care by his mother.

29th. David Eastwood, E. Sister Adaline and Peggy Patterson brought home from Dayton two girls, one by the name of

30th. Two boys came here from Dayton.

26th. Eliza Welchhammer went to the world taking her five children, and Peters' child.

26th. Martha Parker turned off to the world.

February 1st. John McDaniel turned off to the world.

4th. Joseph Barret came here a boy 10 years of age without father or mother.

12th. John Short, Henry and George Grub and Joseph Barret ran off to the world.

12th. Two boys and two girls was brought home from Dayton by David Eastwood, Elder Sister Adaline and E. S. Matilda Williams, by the names of Wm. James Edmond, aged 16 years; Thos. Wardlow, aged 10 years, they both set out on the 14th of February, 1857. Names of girls, Hester Ann Petitt, 10 years, Caroline Wardlow, 10 years, they both set out.

14th A girl came from Dayton with David Eastwood, by the name of

18th. Geo. Grub came back and obtained another privilege.

25th. Geo. Grayham turned off to the world.

27th. Wm. Boswell went to the world.

March 4th. Godlib Myers and his family moved away, to the great joy of us all.

5th. John Carrol and John Hayden went away to the world.

7th. Martha Harris turned off to the world. But received back in three months.

February 27th. Richard Murphy an Irishman came here and set out.

March 16th. John Sherman turned away to the world, has had three privileges.

19th. Wm. Adams went to the world.

20th. Richard Murphy went to the world having two privileges, he coveted and took.

23d. John Carrol came with a wagon and took his wife and three children away.

April 14th. Charles McCormick (aged 12 years last December 12th) came here to live, from N. Port, Ky. His mother is a widow.

29th. Wm. Nichols went to the world, having had three privileges.

30th. America Hughes went to the world.

May 8th. Joseph and Lydia Ann Stoker was taken away by their parents.

9th. Mary Carrol came and took her two girls, the first of May.

14th. Wm. Harris, or Barret, came and obtained a privilege, and on the

18th. he went off. We considered him not a fit subject, about 12 years old.

18th. Sarah Ann Turbavill went to the world. Marvin Banister turned off to the world April 15th. Joseph Edmonds came here and obtained a privilege.

25th. James McLaughlin, an Irishman, obtained a conditional priviledge.

June 1st. John Thompson, an Englishman, came here.

6th. Hiram Hughes was taken away by his Father.

12th. Henry Grubs went away.

July 1st. John Thompson, an Englishman, united.

4th Ann Flemon moved here for the purpose of uniting.

4th. Wm. and Joseph Edmonds went to the world. George Grubs and Charles Shorts going along. Emma Jane and Frances Virginia McNichols (four and six years old) were bound to us by their mother the last of June, 1857.

8th. Wm. Williams, an Englishman, shoemaker, set out.

13th. Elder Brother E. Rice visited Springfield, and found Reuben Miller struggling for freedom, but his age and surrounding circumstances will operate to keep him in bondage.

16th. Thomas Wardlow was taken away by his parents.

20th. Elder Sister Adaline, and David Eastwood, bro't home from the Dayton poorhouse two boys, viz., Washington Montgomery and Stephen Martin, the first 12 and the other 4 years old.

24th. Thomas Williams and Elder Sister Adaline, bro't home from Xeny Poorhouse 2 boys, and a girl, the oldest 13 years, Name Howard Ransbottom, youngest boy 4 years old, Name Stephen Martin, and a girl 7 years old, Name Clarry Dore Stephenson.

26th. Elder Br. E. R. brot home a widow, (by the name of Catherine ———) and her 2 children, viz., (and Aug. 19th she was taken away), and a boy by the name of Jacob Banjest, who was bound by his mother until 16 years old.

26th. John Thompson and Wm. Williams went to the world.

20th. McClothling, James, came here; James got sore eyes and went to get them cured.

August 12th. Wm. Hirsch, a boy about 12 years old, German.

10th. Dianna Morehouse came here, and set out (Irish), 58 years old.

25. Wm. Hinch ran away to his mother in Dayton.

September 18th. Washington Montgomery was taken back to the poor house (thief).

18th. Elizabeth Hill (from Cincinnati) and her 4 children, viz., Robert G. Hill, born May 24th, 1847, May Hill, March 15th, 1850, Frances

Elizabeth, January 14th, 1854, Henery S., November 22nd, 1856. and on the 22nd Elizabeth set out to be a believer.

20th. The Grub girl was taken on trial. October 14th George Grubs went off.

21st. James McGothling came back and obtained another privilege, the last of September.

29th. A boy about 11 years old by the name of Edward Hill, came here to live, from London.

November 4th. Sent a boy home to Cincinnati by the name of Joseph Pursell.

5th. Walter Vann, and Ann his wife, with their two girls by the name of Anna M. and Eliazbeth M., came here from Phila. to be Believers.

4th. James H. Oliver came here desiring to see Elder John (Martin) for to get a gift to live either at Union Vill. or here, he lived at N. U. (North Union). Joseph and his sister — Edmonds came here and obtained a priv. on trial, until they were secured to us by Indenture.

10th. Richard Wilson (coulered) and coulered girls by the name of Martha and Sophrona Melone, aged and 13 years, these girls were adopted into his family, he gave them to us to bring up.

16th. Michael Brant set out, he came from Cincinnati (40 years).

16th. Evans Williams, Welshman, set out, from Portsmou', 24 years.

17th. Patrick Doul set out (Irish) from Hamilton.

December 4th. Barney Rourka set out, he is Irish, 31 years old, shoemaker, gone to world.

5th. George Smith set out, he is typesetter, 21 years old, from Dayton.

Hester Ann Pettitt came back, was bound until 18, November the last.

13th. Michael Shandly (Irish), 48 years old, set out with us.

George Smith (typesetter) backed out December 9th.

19th. Lucy Lemmons was kindly invited to go to the world. She went.

Lydia Ann Edmonds was taken to her mother (sister to Wm).

20th. Boy by the name of Wm. Green, 2 years old, without father or mother; he united.

20th. Englishman by the name of Robert Wilson united, turned off soon.

22nd. Henery Bankman, German, 66 years old, he united.

21st. Mary Elizabeth Ryley was taken to the world.

30th. Ambagini Harris went to the world.

VALUE OF JUDICIAL DECISIONS IN OHIO.

Under date of July 13, 1857, I find it recorded that Elder Ebenezer Rice was in Columbus. What he records is significant and needs no comment: "Visited ex-Judge Swan, who pronounced the decree against Elder Brother Ebenezer* some 32 years since for joining the Shakers, which was that he should cease to have from that time forward any parental authority in his family, and the little of this world's goods in his possession should all be given to the wife. The judge said that we had outlived those prejudices, and took quite an interest in helping me to get orphan children."

CHRONICLE RESUMED.

September 16, 1857.   Finished burning 120,000 brick at a cost of $2 per thousand.

The year 1858, similar to the two previous years was noted for admissions and withdrawals.   The journal naively records that they were "thronged with visitors both from the world and Believers."   The mill race and forebay received repairs.   On April 28th it was learned that the $1,000 loaned to "a paper maker" was lost, as he had failed.

From March 18th to 26th, 1859, the Union Village Ministry was present, during which time it made the following changes: "Moses Eastwood was released from being Elder Brother and Matilda Williams released from Elder Sister title, but still remains as lead of the aged family who live at the North house.   Thomas Streets released from being Deacon, and Charles Flagg appointed to fill his place.   David Eastwood removes to Office at South Family."

November 27th.   Ebenezer Rice was released from the first Eldership and Matthew B. Carter appointed in his place, and William Britten to live with him.   Ephraim Frost was chosen Elder at the Gathering Order, Moses Eastwood to live with him. Matilda Williams and Mary Ann Duffy to be Eldresses in the same order.   Ezra Sherman, on December 4th, was appointed Deacon and Warren McCain assistant.   During the year a kitchen was put up at the North residence.   On December 26th commenced making brooms, although the extensive trade in yarn was still pursued.

---

* Sally Rice, June 3, 1823, petetioned the court of common pleas for separation, custody of children and property.

The journal for 1860 is a record of what usually takes place during the year. There is an item which shows they were somewhat given to superstition. Under date of July 5th it is recorded that "Moses Eastwood, Eldress Matilda Williams and Betsey Kripe went to Miss Fulk's, the charm doctress, to get her to charm a wen off of Moses and the big neck off of Betsey." September 4th the record further states that "Moses Eastwood, accompanied by several sisters from the North, went to Doctress Fulk to be charmed for the last time." The final outcome is not stated. From the Union village record we learn there was a new building put up at the North House. The same record, for August 4th, informs us that "Rachel Hall moves home to Whitewater, after an absence of six or seven years, part of the time as Elder Sister at Watervleit, and the remainder at the first family U. V."

The journal of Matthew B. Carter abruptly ends at September 21, 1860. The Union Village record for February 9, 1867, speaks of "Elder Ephraim Frost, Eldress Adaline Wells, and a girl here from Watervleit."

In 1865 Matthew B. Carter was elder at the South and Moses Eastwood elder at the North family. Under the supervision of the latter the North family became financially prosperous. January 3, 1872, he loaned Union Village, for the benefit of North Union, $3000 in government bonds, and on March 19, 1873, had $2050 in bonds in a Dayton bank. On January 1, 1875, the family consisted of Elder Moses Eastwood, Francis Vann, Peter Post, Eldress Mary Ann Duffy, second Eldress Peggy Patterson, Jane Tucker, Eliza Read, Mary Haselden and Betsey Kripe.

In a letter written by William N. Redmon to Erastus Finney and dated Watervleit, Ohio, January 1, 1865, the following occurs:

"We have a joint inheritance (no man having aught or anything to call his own) in real and personal estate. Our land is a dedication to the service of God, — an inheritance to those who will live godly in Christ Jesus; each person possessing and enjoying the benefit of said estate, acording to his needs. The clothing of the brethren is generally alike; the sisterhood dress very modestly and in uniformity, having their heads covered. The sexes partake of the same food, at different tables, and at the same time. We breakfast at 6 o'clock, dine at 12, sup at 6 P. M., and retire at 9 P. M. We have worship on the Sabbath at 1 o'clock, union meeting of the sexes at 7, of the same evening, and singing meeting at 9 in the morning. Also we have worship and meetings every evening in the week, if conditions of health, etc., permit.

"The family consists of 4 elders, two of each sex; 4 deacons, two of each sex, — the female called deaconess. Elders have charge in the spiritual administration and a supervision of the schools; the deacons and deaconesses manage the temporal concerns of the family. We have trustees who stand as a sort of door to the world, — doing the trading of the family and keeping the money of the same. To them the landed estate is deeded IN TRUST for the Society. There is a Children's Order, of the sexes, and a school for the same, — the boys generally attending in winter and the girls in summer. These children, principally are orphans. They are kindly and tenderly brought up; living, eating and wearing the same as the family, only some difference in clothing of the youngest girls of calico, etc., in their little dresses."

On August 1, 1868, the Mount Lebanon ministry, in company with that at Union Village, arrived at Watervleit. The former was astounded that the meeting-house had not been used for services since 1865, and that no public meetings had been held since 1834. The church building was ordered to be cleaned immediately, and on the following day a service lasting two and one-half hours was held. The Union Village ministry, for this dereliction of duty, was deposed and a new one appointed. On the 9th a public meeting was held which, during the proper season, was continued until 1873.

The journal was renewed by Stephen W. Ball, beginning August 14, 1871. For that year it covers but nineteen lines. The journal of Matthew B. Carter abruptly ends with September 21, 1860, and nothing further occurs until the journal is renewed by Stephen W. Ball, August 14, 1871. The Union Village Record for February 9, 1861, speaks of "Elder Ephraim Frost, Eldress Adaline Wells and a girl here from Watervleit." This is the last reference from that record.

The journal for 1871 covers but 19 lines of manuscript and alludes simply to usual duties, by which we notice the yarn and broom trade interest was still uppermmost. Elder Stephen Ball probably became first elder at the time his journal begins.

For 1872 there are 32 lines. It is related that on June 12th

"Ephraim Frost and Fannie Ball went to the world." The whole year is embraced in 16 lines.

The year 1874 is comprised in less than a page. From it we learn that Eldress Matilda Williams passed away January 27th; April 18th fenced in the 30 acres bought of Fulkerton; June 15th bought 1,169 pounds of wool at 30 cents per pound at Union Village, and same day commenced building a new dry-house, 18 x 30 feet, two stories high." Nordhoff, in his "Communistic Societies," written in 1874, in speaking of Watervleit says it "has two families, containing 55 members, of whom 19 are males and 36 females, and seven are under 21. They own 1300 acres of land (mistake), much of which they let to tenants. They have a wool factory, which is their only manufactory. This society was founded a year after that at Union Village. It had in 1825 100 members and is now prosperous pecuniarily, having no debts and money at interest. One of its families once suffered a slight loss from a defalcation." (p. 206.)

On July 16, 1875, Elder Giles Avery, of Mount Lebanon, N. Y., accompanied by Elder William Reynolds and Eldress Sallie Sharp, of Union Village, arrived at Watervleit and made important changes. Eldress Adaline Wells, July 23, 1875, was promoted in the second place in the sisters' lot, in the ministry of Union Village; Hester Frost became elder sister, with Emily Adams standing second.

Eldress Mary Ann Duffy died November 9, 1875, and was succeeded by Eldress Peggy Patterson and Ann Anderson, of the Center family, became second eldress at the North family, but left the society April 29, 1876. January 9, 1877, Lavina Rollins, from Union Village, became second eldress at the North family. December 25, 1876, the North family consisted of Elder Moses Eastwood, Francis Vann, Peter Post, Stephen Jones, Joseph S. Bands, Eldress Peggy Patterson, Eliza and Betsey Read and Betsey Kripe.

The year 1875 was noted for its great floods, and much damage was done to the estate.

The journal for 1876, though more lengthy than for any previous year, makes no special record other than the usual routine.

June 24, 1877, "opened public meeting. Elder Oliver Hampton spoke to the people. We had a good meeting." July 8th, "Public meeting to-day. A large audience of attentive people. Elder Oliver opened the testimony to much acceptance." August 9th. "About this time the sleeping room of Elder Moses was entered by two burglars, at midnight, and demanded his money, threatening to kill him if he made any noise. They rifled the desk, containing mostly old papers of no value, and some small change, amounting to about $2.00. They made their entrance by the west window, second story, by means of a ladder belonging to the place. After threatening Elder Moses, they clubbed him severely about the head, and then left, taking the drawers of the desk with them, which were found the next morning scattered along the pike. No clue to the robbers could be found."

February 12th, 1878. John Sessman was released from farm Deacon and the care given to Stephen Ball. November 24th, Sessman was released from the trusteeship and Elder Ball accepted the gift. June 4, the foundation for the new horse barn was laid. October 30th, the cattle barn at the North Family was burned. Insured for $945. April 3d. "Calvin Marsh left for Manchester, N. H., to settle his affairs. It has since been discovered that this man is a fraud, passing under an assumed name; he having lived at Groveland, N. Y., under the name of Charles Merriam, with his wife, passing her for his sister. Description: He is above medium height, dark hair and eyes, of good address, and claims to be a machinist by trade. His aim in coming here was to get money."

July 10, 1879. John Sauerborn was appointed farm Deacon in place of Elder Stephen Ball. December 25th: This day was held as a day of yearly sacrifice. Holding prayer meeting in the evening, the Ministry announced important changes in the leading gift of the family, as follows: Elder Stephen to be released from the first Eldership, and be transferred to the Center Family at White Water, in the same gift. Bro. John Sauerborn to fill the order vacated by Elder Stephen, and Alfred E. Doyle to stand with him as second."

Thus ends the journal of Stephen W. Ball.

MEMBERSHIP IN 1880.

BRETHREN.	BORN.	BRETHREN.	BORN.
John Sauerborn	Nov. 25, 1824	Edward Richards	July 22, 1826
Alfred E. Doyle	Oct. 25, 1856	T. Jefferson McKinney	Dec. 15, 1858
William Hislop	Aug. 5, 1813	ohn H. Sessman	Oct. 27, 1844
J. Wallace Lloyd	Nov. 26, 1816	Geo. R. Romaine	Sept. 21, 1860
Thos. M. McKinney	Oct. 22, 1822	Edmund E. Sauerborn	Aug. 14. 1862
George Hutton	July 18, 1825		

SISTERS.	BORN.	SISTERS.	BORN.
Hester Frost	Mar. 1827	Eliza M. Jameson	May 25, 1825
Mary A. McBride	April 1832	Catherine Sauerborn	Apr. 8, 1826
Rachel Butler	Jan. 6, 1807	Sarah Romaine	Jan. 22, 1831
Mary J. Lewis	June 1808	Sarah A. Cripe	Apr. 10, 1836
Mary Hazleton	Dec. 10, 1810	Martha Evans	1842
Mary Adams	Oct. 14, 1814	Katie Sauerborn	Sept. 8, 1855

CHILDREN.

Annie L. Windle	Sept. 1, 1867	Annie M. Reed	May 1, 1868
Nettie Kennen	June 2, 1868	Mary Fetter	1870
Emma Dunbar	Nov. 7, 1870	Elnora Reed	Feb. 26, 1870
Lillie D. Newcom	Nov. 12, 1868	Lottie Dunbar	Nov. 1, 1874
Nannie B. Kennen	Jan. 2, 1873		

ADMITTED IN 1880.

Thomas Mann,	Kaspial G. Bieler,
Otto Kunks,	Frederic Mills,
Maud A. Michener,	Louisa Swartz,
Stella M. Billings,	Annie E. Mills.
Etta Mills,	

CHRONICLE RESUMED.

On April 3, 1880, the Sisters commenced marketing in Dayton, receiving 35 cents per pound for butter, 13 cents for dried apples and 12½ cents per dozen for eggs. From the sheep was clipped 180 pounds of wool, and purchased at Union Village and Whitewater 2790, paying 30 cents per pound. On November 19–22 the mercury ranged from 10 to 20 degrees below zero. The cold was steady until February 1st, following. The ice house was filled with blocks from 10 to 13 inches thick. During August and September there was much sickness, the complaint being chills and fever.

April 3, 1881, there was a heavy snow-storm, the snow ranging from 6 to 8 inches in depth. In February Elder Moses Eastwood purchased 60 acres from the Boroff estate, but as he did not have "the proper gift" it was sold March 10th. April 3rd, the year's supply of sugar (650 pounds) was purchased at 8 1-3 cents per pound. The supply of wood (135 cords) at 75 cents per cord for chopping, was paid for The December taxes amounted to $525.

Owing to "some tribulation," the nature of which is not stated, the Union Village Ministry arrived February 3rd, 1882, and moved Elder John Sauerborn to the North House to take charge there, and J. Wallace Lloyd is appointed first Elder at the Center, or South Family. Complaint is made of the paucity of numbers, and more land is let to renters.

GROUP OF NORTH UNION SHAKERS, REMOVED TO WATERVLIET.

Wheat was sold at $1.40 per bushel, corn at 80 cents and potatoes at 30 cents.

Eldress Peggy Patterson died January 13, 1883. November 7th. John Sessman was appointed Trustee and Manager of Center or South Family. As the wool crop was sold for 16 and 20 cents per pound, the inference is that the manufacture of yarn and cloth had ceased.

October 25th, 1884. Alfred E. Doyle becomes Elder at North Family. April 25th, 500 panes of glass were destroyed by a hail storm. The records show various attempts, by different parties, to impose on the Shakers. As an instance: On February 4th, Marion and Henry Scarborough came to unite. They had been members at Pleasant Hill, Ky., and married two women from that Society. They tried to pass off their wives as their sisters, but were foiled.

The journal abruptly ends with October 29, 1884, and we have no further record until January 1, 1889, when Stephen W. Ball again takes it up. It is probable that on that date he became first elder, with residence at South or Center family.

ACCESSION OF NORTH UNION.

The ministry, both at Mount Lebanon, New York, and Union Village assembled at North Union to take into consideration the status of that community. It was the united opinion of this body that the society should be dissolved, although 37 in number and amply able to look after the estate. Eldress Clymena Miner was given to understand that if she would accept the North house, at Watervleit, she should also have the lands pertaining thereto. On this promise she decided to move there, but was disappointed in not realizing the promise.

September 10th, 1889, Eldress Clymena Miner arrived at Watervliet, bringing two aged sisters with her,—Rachel and Malinda Russell. This was "the first installment of a Ministerial Gift," as the record puts it. On the 12th Eldress Clymena returned to North Union. On the 16th "John Hufman and Lotta Pilot came from North Union to help prepare for the move;" both returned. October 10th, six brethren and four sisters arrived from North Union. The last to arrive was Samuel S. Miner, who came the 18th, making a total of twelve brethren and nine sisters. "In the organization of the family at the North, all the North Union family was placed in it, with the exceptions

·of Samuel Miner, and two aged sisters, Malinda and Rachel Rus-
·sell; Stephen Ball, who was the Elder Brother in the South
family, was released and placed as Elder Brother in the North
family, with general temporal care both families. Samuel Miner
was installed as Elder in the South Family. Hester Frost as
Elder Sister in the South and Clymena Miner as Elder Sister
at the North Family." But the North Union people were destined
to seek still another home.

CHRONICLE RESUMED.

During the month of November, 1890, a two-story frame house,
with kitchen and porch, 30 x 16, was built on one of the rented farms,
at a cost of $500.

The Mt. Lebanon and Union Village Ministry had a gift, and by
·consent of the Trustees, 60 acres was sold to L. Moler at $100 per
·acre. As the people depended largely on their rentals for their sus-
tenance, it would appear that the Ministerial "gift" was not in accord-
ance with ordinary prudence. The money thus obtained was to build
a house and out-buildings for a tenant, and what remained "to be placed
safely in the hands of the Trustees."

February 12, 1891, the north end of the shop was fitted up for a
dwelling to be used by a tenant. In May a barn 54 x 34 and 18 feet
high was commenced at the South Family. Same month a wind-mill was
put up to force water into the North dwelling.

October 20th, the Union Village Ministry visited Watervliet and
moved Stephen W. Ball to the Central or South Family as Elder
Brother, and Samuel Miner was released.

October 21st, 1891, the journal of Elder Ball apruptly stops, and
that of Henry W. Fredrick begins December 16th, 1891.

On December 16th, 1891, Henry W. Fredrick took charge as second
Elder, Deacon and Trustee, having been brought from Whitewater.
Elder Stephen Ball was moved to the North Family and Elder Lloyd
became first Elder at the Center Family. The year closed with much
sickness, mostly la grippe.

October 21, 1892, Elder Stephen W. Ball left for Whitewater,
where he still resides. He was very happy to be at his old home again.
April 23, the sum of $1,600 was deposited in Fourth National Bank of
Dayton. May 15th, Eldress Clymena Miner was released from the
North Family and Harriet Snyder put in her place, with Elizabeth
Buddings to live with her. This was the time when Elder Slinger-
land removed Eldress Clymena to Union Village to act as Office
Deaconess. At the same time he brought Eldress Jane Cowan from
·South Union. Eldress Clymena left for Union Village on the 20th.

ELDRESS CLYMENA MINER

That the strict rules were departed from is evidenced from the fact that on May 26th, Henry Fredrick, Moore S. Mason, John Minogue, Ferdinand and Robert Buddinger, Eldress Hester Frost, Florence Bostwick and Louisa Buddinger went to Dayton to see Barnum's show. November 15th, Henry Fredrick, Eldress Hester Frost and Mollie McBride went to Dayton to see a medium, but were disappointed."

The year 1893 shows many visits from Union Village and Whitewater.

August 27th, "we had a very good meeting. The Whitewater friends brought a great deal of inspiration with them. We had quite a spiritual manifestation, — Elder Matthew Carter came and spoke through Elder Lafayette Parker. Such meetings as this one creates union and love among the brethren and sisters." December 25th, "we had a very enjoyable time, it being Christmas day. We had a meeting this afternoon and had a great deal of inspiration flowing among the brethren and sisters. Some of the brethren and sisters sang a few songs while the family were eating breakfast. We also had a Christmas tree for the children."

January 1, 1894, was ushered in at midnight by five of the brethren singing songs in the Hall of the South House, and from there they went to the North Family. The day was spent in singing and playing, while two of the brethren were sent to Dayton for oysters and other edibles. Cyrus Teed had visited the Society in the interests of his sect, so this year members of the Koreshans were again present. The Christian Science people, this year, took a deep interest in the community, and some of the Shakers attended their meetings in Dayton. March 17th, finished setting out 1,000 raspberries, 500 blackberries, 6 plum trees, 50 currant and 2 cheries. August 12th, Oliver C. Hampton announced Henry W. Frederick as Elder at the South and Moore S. Mason as Elder at the North Family.

The journal abruptly ends October 31, 1894.

CLOSING PERIOD.

There was nothing special that occurred from 1894 to the dissolution of the society, except the return of Eldress Clymena Miner to take charge once more of the North family, which took place September 12, 1895. During the fall of 1900 Elder Joseph Slingerland announced to the community that it should disband and the members must go to Union Village. He stated there was no hurry about going, so the society began to dispose of its surplus effects at private sale. Then came the sudden order that the removal must take place at once. There was hurrying, and a public sale immediately advertised.

There was no reason why this community should have been disbanded. The members were fully able to manage their domain. There is a strong suspicion as to the reason, but as it is not absolutely known, it will not be stated here. The removal to Union Village took place October 11, 1900. Those who left the North family were Elderess Clymena Miner, Margaret Swayer, Harriet. Snooks, Moore S. Mason, Cornelius Bush and George Hunt, all of whom except Cornelius are at the North family, Union Village. Those from the South family who moved into the Center family, Union Village, were Eldress Hester Frost, Mary - McBride, Eliza Jemison, Sarah Ann Cripe and Hattie Snyder. Eldress Clymena Miner is in full charge of the North family,* which consists of 12 members. Eldress Clymena is the youngest in the family save three. All have the greatest respect for her and defer to her in all things. She is a broad and liberal minded woman, prudent in all things, a splendid manager, and economical. While she has great decision of character, she establishes no rules, but governs by the power of love. When promoted to. the office of second in the ministry, she accepted on the condition that she should not leave her North Union people. One of the sisters said. to me: "We are a happy family. I have a good home and I am thankful for it."

At the present time the Watervliet lands embrace 667 acres. The number of acres varied at different periods. Without warning Elder Slingerland sold 60 acres, and the same amount at another time. What was done with the money thus secured the office books do not reveal. The land is under control of the trustees of Union Village. Mr. James H. Fennessey, general manager, was forced to place a mortgage for $40,000 on the property to meet Slingerland's debts. But this has been liquidated and the last of the Slingerland obligations has been met. To Mr. Fennessey the Shakers owe a debt of gratitude for saving Union Village from financial ruin. He withstood difficulties which would have crushed a fainter heart. To narrate what he passed

---

* This family was disbanded October 10, 1906.

MOORE S. MASON.

through would read more like fiction than an actual experience. I have met him when he was enduring blows which would have brought down a less courageous man. I have found him, under all circumstances, a gentleman. He commands the respect of all who know him.

NORTH UNION PEOPLE.

I have taken special interest in the North Union people, not only because I first essayed to chronicle their history, but also because of my associations with them since I published their story. Ten of the members are still living, and all are at the North family of Union Village, save three who make their home at the Center or Church family. Having been interested in the longevity of the Shakers, I took the life line of seven of the North Union family. Of the other three two were absent and one refused. Such as it is I give it, recognizing that the full value depends also on other considerations.

LIFE LINE OF NORTH UNION SHAKERS.

Name.	Age.	Length of Membership.	Life Line.	
Eldress Clymena Miner	70 years	64 years	1	inch
Harriet Snooks*	79 "	66 "	1½	"
Margaret Swayer*	86 "	72 "	1½	"
Lizette Ryder	30 "	20 "	⅞	"
George Hunt	68 "	50 "	1 1/16	"
Thomas Mylrea	64 "	24 "	1	"
Harriet Snyder	66 "	59 "	1¼	"
Sarah Corcoran	80 "	78 "	1⅜	"

The last named has always lived at Union Village, and, in point of service, is the oldest member in Ohio. It will be noticed that the life line indicates that old age is not due to a Shaker life, for under ordinary circumstances all would have reached their present venerable years. This is not a test. To prove that Shaker life conduces to longevity, the life line should be drawn at the time of admission, when young, and the subject should live continuously until death among the believers. Doubtless children

---

* Died in 1905.

15

die of old age among the Shakers, as well as under other principles of living.

FRANKLIN, OHIO, August 28, 1903.

NOTE — The account of Watervliet was written at a time when the Church Record had been misplaced, but afterwards found. I was in hopes to have said record before me in revising the MS., but unfortunately it is in the possesion of the Common Pleas Court of Montgomery County, Ohio. The lands were sold for $50,000, the deal to be consummated July 1, 1906. Then came the scare that the title must be quieted, though the Shakers had undisputed possession of the lands for more than eighty years. The lawyers caused delays, which continue at this writing. As a large sum is at stake, there is no knowing when the case will be decided. Questions of Shaker property have been frequently adjudicated, and their covenant has been held to be binding. Franklin, June 14, 1906.

Since the above was ready for the printers it has been revealed that the matter referred to in above note was a hold up to extort money from the Shakers.

ORIGIN, RISE, PROGRESS AND DECLINE OF THE WHITEWATER COMMUNITY OF SHAKERS LOCATED IN HAMILTON COUNTY, OHIO.

While engaged in collecting the material for the article on West Union, I engaged in a correspondence with Elder Charles H. Sturr, general manager of the Whitewater community. He invited me to make him a visit, and I should have the freedom of all the archives of the society. I determined at once to accept the invitation, and although the distance is about forty miles I decided to drive through. The route took me diagonally across Butler county from northeast to southwest, which was quite hilly, and the greater part of the distance the roads were muddy. The worst mudhole I struck was Hamilton, the streets being full of chuckholes. The lower road from Hamilton to Millville was so out of repair I had difficulty passing over. Early on the morning of May 30, 1903, I started on my journey.

Fifteen years before, I was familiar with every nook and corner of the county. I had geologized all its fossil beds, and searched out all its archæological remains. Either I or the general aspect had changed, for the views did not have the same appearance. There was a wornout air almost everywhere. The roads were in the worst condition I ever saw them, and the poorest I had seen in years.

Although I had never seen the Shaker lands, the moment I struck them I knew I was on their possessions. The fences were in good condition, the lands cared for, and there was the general aspect of thriftiness. When I caught sight of the first house, my opinion was confirmed that I was on the lands of the Shakers, for the same style of architecture, solid appearance, and want of decorative art were before me. I knocked at the door, which was opened by a small lady. I asked her name, and she replied "Adaline Wells." I was astonished. I had supposed she was no more. She is eighty years old but could pass for sixty. She is spry, animated, and possessed of a clear mind. I passed on to the Center family, and was there greeted by Elder Sturr, who made me feel at home without any ceremony. I was assigned quarters in what is called the Office. My lodgings consisted of two rooms, of three beds, with good furnishings. I was here under the care of Eldress Julia Ann Bear, who has been a member since 1846. My meals were furnished me separately, and as I partook of the viands, two ladies engaged me in conversation.

The Shaker lands are situated on the Dry Forks of the Whitewater, in the northwest part of Hamilton county, with 400 acres in Butler county. The farms, for the most part, are level, composed of black soil, with a circular ridge of hills surrounding them. The view is pleasing to the eye and furnishes ample material for a beautiful landscape painting. The possessions comprised, in one body, are 1457 acres. In 1825, there was purchased on Dry Fork Creek, 215 acres at $6.50 per acre; in 1827, 40 acres at $1.26 per acre; 305 acres of Congress land at $1.20 per acre; in 1829, 135 acres for $2,000; 1835, 137 acres for $3,000; 1838, 197 acres for $7,000; 1847, 30 acres for $1,000; 1850, 200 acres for $10,000. In 1827 Joseph Boggett, a member, deeded his farm of 160 acres.

During the daytime, Elder Sturr was with me the greater part of the time, conducting me over the premises and through the buildings. He showed me all their collections of books, with the invitation "If you see anything here you want, take it." I obeyed the mandate. I was not invited to the services on Sunday, and knowing that public meetings were no longer held, I did not seek admittance, although I should have been present otherwise. I staid in Elder Sturr's room during the service, examining old documents. I could hear the singing and noted there were excellent voices among the young sisters. After services Eldress Amanda Rubush and Matilda A. Butler, called on me, and engaged in conversation. Eldress Amanda's private room is handsomely decorated and her collection of china shows off to advantage. In the afternoon I called on the venerable

Henry Bear, now in his 91st year. He joined the society during the Miller excitement in 1846, and from that time till 1901 was an officer in continuous service. He is still hale and hearty, and ever ready with a reason for the hope that is within him. He undertook to make a Shaker out of me, but his efforts fell on unfruitful soil. However I enjoyed my little visit with him.

The Society has forty-three members, including minors. The Society takes children out of orphan asylums and rears them; but few become permanent members. Elder Sturr has been a member of this Society since he was three weeks old, and for twenty years was a trustee, and during the last two years has filled the office of Elder, succeeding Elder Bear. He is sociable, well-informed, and utterly devoid of all ostentation. If it were not for his "yea," and "nay" you would not suspect his creed. This, however, is true of nearly all of the Ohio Shakers.

My visit to Whitewater will be remembered as one of the most pleasant incidents in my life.

MANUSCRIPTS.

There are comparatively few MSS. at Whitewater. Elder Sturr found the church record in parts, thrown into the coal bin, ready for the furnace. The scattered pages he carefully arranged in their proper places, and then copied the same into a separate book. Into the same book he has copied from other MSS., especially the diaries of Ebenezer Rice, Stephen Ball and Henry Rice. The early church records are made up from the MS. of Calvin Morrell. 1884, Elder Sturr commenced a journal which he has continued down to the present. After consolidating the various MSS., Elder Sturr has taken the pains to classify some of the important transactions. But owing to the loss of a great part of the church records, his consolidated MS. is neccessarily incomplete. What follows, in this article is almost wholly taken from the Sturr MS.

DARBY PLAINS.

In 1801 a movement commenced in Lyndon, Vt., which gave rise to the Christian (New Light) Church in New England. Believers of this order from Connecticut and Rhode Island settled on Darby Plains, Union township, Union county, Ohio, seventy miles northeast of Union village. Their leader was Douglass Farnum, but known among his adherents as Elder Farnum. There was also a young preacher, by name of Nathan Burlingame. In the year 1818 the work of confession of sins broke out among them, which was blown into an excitement, and within ten days, several hundred were drawn into the movement, all of whom set about to right their wrongs. Unfortunately some of these confessions were made in the presence of those who were destitute of that charity that covereth a multitude of sins. This resulted in many forsaking their good resolutions and turning against their former friends.

The work among the people at Darby Plains became known at Union Village. Continued reports finally caused David Darrow to send forth messengers of inquiry. During the month of June 1820, Richard McNemar and Calvin Morrell were dispatched, with instructions to find out their state without committing themselves. Elder Farnum received them with an affectionate embrace and saluted them with a kiss. There was an interchange of good feeling, during which Elder Farnum gave an account of the revival work they were engaged in. On the following day, in presence of some of the neighbors, the nature of confession was under discussion. In the afternoon, in an adjacent grove, a public meeting was held, addressed by both McNemar and Morrell. The third day the messengers returned to Union Village.

On August 5, Douglass Farnum, Samuel Rice, Sr., and Elijah Bacon, arrived at Union Village from Darby Plains, and next day (Sunday), Farnum spoke in public meeting. On the 9th, Ebenezer Rice and others from the Plains arrived. Darrow was greatly pleased with Farnum and declared him to be "the weightiest man that ever came to the Village." He "appeared to be a man of great government over himself, and notwithstanding great plainness of speech was frequently used towards him, he remained a mild, quiet spirit, and in all things behaved himself discreetly. He acknowledged the weight of our testimony and did not venture to contradict in a single instance." Two years later he died on the Plains of Sandusky.

Samuel Rice made a most excellent impression on all who saw him, "His unfeigned simplicity and honesty created in all who conversed with him universal esteem and good will. He drank deep of the living waters, and appeared to be perfectly satisfied with our testimony."

Late, in the same summer, another visit was made to the Plains, and in return, (probably August 9), a wagon load came to Union Village, consisting of Ebenezer Rice (son of Samuel), Archibald Bates and their wives, and Almira Burnham. Early in the spring of 1821 another visit was made to Darby Plains, but as all the preachers were absent, except Bates, "who was a quibbler, we found it would be of very little use to continue our visits."

Calvin Morrell "never felt released in relation to the people" on Darby Plains, and as "some circumstances took place which brought the Darby people once more into remembrance," it was decided by Darrow that he and Samuel Sering should make another effort. On October 3, 1822, they proceeded on their journey. Upon their arrival at the Plains they learned that Nathan Burlingame had started that day on a preaching tour and would not return for two weeks. "Nathan, being warned of God in a dream, returned next day, and was greatly pleased with the Shakers' visit and conversation." After laboring a few weeks, with fair prospects of success, the two brethren returned home, bringing a good report. While discussing the feasibility of another mission, a letter was received from Samuel Rice, Sr., stating that many of the people were sick of fever. The next morning the same two brethren started posthaste for the Plains. "When we arrived there all was gloomy indeed. Many who a few weeks before were rugged and cheerful, were now reduced to skeletons, and felt weak in soul and body.' We made the best of the situation. The sickness had begun to abate and the people looked and felt much better every way, when we had discharged our duty." After an absence of three weeks they returned home.

On November 23, 1822, Nathan Burlingame made his first visit to Union Village, and with him came Samuel Rice, William and Zilpha Burnham and others. They were kindly received, and anxious for the decision of Nathan, knowing that his people were waiting to see what course he would pursue. He keenly felt the responsibility of his position, but after due deliberation, he cast his lot with the Shakers, and was followed by all who came with him.

On January 8, 1823, Issachar Bates and Richard McNemar started to Darby Plains, and returned the 24th. No farther record of this trip.

In March, William Burnham and Nathan Burlingame and his wife were at Union Village. "This was a profitable visit to Nathan, for he received much counsel from us, especially in relation to the order of gathering young believers together." Nathan returned and gave his whole time, with great devotion, to the work. Within a few weeks he had converted several families. It was now decided to form a community on Darby Plains, and the plantation of Samuel Rice was selected as the most eligible for a beginning. Nathan was instructed to give up his land, with all that might accrue from it, to Martin Simmons and Gideon Brownell, who were very poor, and move to the new gathering order.

On April 23, 1823, Calvin Morrell, James McNemar, Nancy Rollins, Phoebe Seely and Samuel Sering set out for Darby, —four in a carriage and one on horseback. Owing to the condition of the roads the journey was very tedious. Some places the mud was knee deep to the horses, and this continued for a mile at a stretch. On the fourth day the party reached its destiny, and found the people in high spirits, and determined to work in union and obedience. The visitors held public meetings, and bore "a heavy testimony to the world; so that persecution was stirred up and the wicked did some mischief to our wagon and stoned us with stones." The missionaries extended their labors to the Scioto, where they visited John Sell. The party returned to Union Village, May 29th. The Darby people were left making every arrangement for laying the foundation of a society and village, with bright prospects of success.

On August 5th, Calvin Morrell, Samuel Sering, Charity (Peggy) Houston and Thankful Stewart set out for the Plains. The people were found to be doing well, and the brethren assisted them in building a meeting house. Also a second missionary trip was extended to the Scioto. The believers on Darby now numbered forty. Having completed the work allotted, the party returned to Union Village on the 29th.

INTEREST IN WHITEWATER.

Whilst the energies were being devoted to Darby Plains, a woman by name of Miriam, wife of Joseph Agnew, in the spring of 1823, visited Union Village. She came from the dry fork of the Whitewater, and reported that some time previously a great revival of religion broke out among the Methodists, and that the work was now on the decline and likely to leave the subjects of it short of the object desired. Her story was affecting, and produced intense interest in all who heard it. She united with the Shakers, and then returned to her family, after extending a very pressing invitation for a visit to her neighborhood. Soon after Richard Pelham and George Blackleach were dispatched to the new field, who opened the testimony, and among those who believed were Joseph and Brant Agnew. Several other visits were afterwards made. Samuel Sering and George Blackleach set out July 10th and returned the 16th. By autumn the number of believers, including their children, amounted to about thirty.

ORGANIZING AT WHITEWATER.

The Darby settlement was an enterprise that required profound attention. By the fall of 1823 it was realized that the location was a sickly one, and that the district was held by military claims, and that the rights in many cases proved a source of litigation. The Shakers were fearful that if they made extensive improvements their labors might be lost. On the other hand the country about Whitewater was not only a good locality, but the rights were indisputable. By combining the two settlements into one, a good foundation would be laid for a strong Society. These considerations decided the authorities at Union Village to remove the Darby people to the Whitewater.

According to previous arrangements, on December 2nd,. Calvin Morrell and Stephen Williams set out for the Plains in order to give notice and administer the gift felt for them. On the way they met Nathan Burlingame and James Thompson. The gift was cordially received at Darby, and the party returned on the 9th, bringing Martin Simmons and Jefferson Rice along with them. On the 10th, the whole party started for the Whitewater with the addition of Matthew Houston. All put up with Brant Agnew, who received them cordially.

Almost immediately persecution showed itself. One of their horses had one ear cut off and the other partly so; the curtains of the wagon were nearly all cut away and the inside defiled; the gears were injured, and the doubletrees thrown into the creek, and were not recovered until months afterward.

Nothing daunted, the brethren were called together and the object of the visit presented. The news was received with every manifestation of good feeling and satisfaction. Having surveyed the field and visited the several families the party returned to Union Village.

On January 1st, 1824, Calvin Morrell set out alone for Darby Plains. He found the people in high spirits. He dispatched Martin Simmons to Whitewater in order to procure a small place for a temporary residence for the people. The money was principally furnished by Samuel Rice, Sr., yet such was the zeal manifested by all, that every one cast in their money that they might have an interest in the joint investment.

Having completed the necessary arrangements for the removal, Calvin and Nathan started for the Plains of Sandusky in search of widow Susan Farnum and Polly Clark. On their arrival they learned that both had removed to Kingston, forty miles distant. Thither the brethren went and after much serious labor with them, gained their consent to move to Whitewater.

The first move appears to have been made in February,. by Nathan's family. He hired a team, and with a two-horse wagon moved the most valuable part of his property, and settled on the forty-acre lot that had been purchased by Martin Simmons on the Whitewater. This property cost $200 and the deed made to the trustees for the good of the whole. The party proceeded by way of Watervliet, near Dayton, where it received much kindness and help. Another part of the Darby people began to move on February 9th. They proceeded by way of Union Village, where a four-horse wagon load of provisions joined them. In the meantime (January 22) Richard Pelham and George Blackleach had been dispatched to Whitewater as advance assistants.

At Union Village the Darby people were joined by Thomas Hunt, who went with them to Whitewater, where all arrived in safety. They first stopped with Anthony McKee, but after ten days got possession of their new land, and moved into a cabin eighteen feet square, with a lean-to in the rear. Necessity compelled them to use this until larger quarters could be obtained.

Calvin was now dispatched to the Plains again to superintend the removal of other families, mostly poor people who had to be helped. For this purpose several teams from Union Village were sent. "Nothing worth mentioning took place until they were all landed at the place of destination, where homes were provided for them as speedily as possible. Some crowding and scolding naturally took place, but no one was materially injured in soul or body. Most of the people seemed pleased with their new situation, and seemed in high spirits. The moving continued throughout the summer, and near a year had elapsed before all got down." The following are the names of those who moved from Darby Plains, and who remained faithful to their cause: Nathan and Emma Burlingame, Samuel, Sr., Samuel, Jr., Jefferson, Ebenezer, Caleb, Lucy and Mariah Rice; John and Lucy Easterbrooks, James and Dorcas Wells; Zilpha and Polly Burnham, Polly and Susan Champlain, Susannah Farnham, Sarepta Henman, and Martin and Charlotte Simmons, with their children. Those who believed at Whitewater were Joseph Brant, Caty and Miriam Agnew, Joseph and Peggy Boggett, Sarah McKee and Samuel B. Crane, with their children. There were others who finally seceded, but their names are not preserved.

DISCOURAGEMENTS.

In the early history of this community there were a number of circumstances that produced discouragements and other uncomfortable feelings, all of which, by due perseverance, were overcome. Those who came from Darby Plains were subjected to the same fever that afflicted them formerly, which made them feel that their constitutions were broken down. For the most part, these people were poor and the land procured for them was thin and not calculated for raising grain, and only of that three acres cleared. The land rented did not produce well, principally owing to sickness, the brethren were not able properly to cultivate it. Added to this, they were destitute of proper nourishment for the sick. None, however died. What little they had was husbanded for the winter. They had no hogs and no money to purchase meat. The help they received from Union Village, and what could be spared by those previously on the ground, in a measure tended materially to relieve their wants. Calvin Morrell has preserved the following: "Meat with them was scarce. Sugar they had little or none, and milk but seldom. Bread was greatly lacking, while tea and coffee were out of the question. It was *Lent* with them nearly all the year round. Their common manner was to buy a side of bacon and make sop for their johnny cake. The sop was made by mixing a sufficient quantity of milk and water with enough meat cut in small pieces to make the composition somewhat greasy, and the whole was fried together until the meat had nearly vanished. This was used morning and noon. For breakfast they had herb tea. For dinner potatoes and sauce. For supper milk porridge, but more commonly water porridge. When wheat could be procured it was mixed with Indian meal, with rye mixed with the Indian corn for a change.

In the summer of 1825 a spirit of infidelity crept in among the believers, which caused confusion and distress. Under the labors of Calvin Morrell, Phœbe Seely and Mary Bedle—sent from Union Village—this reign was ended by a portion withdrawing and others restored to the faith.

LANDS PURCHASED.

It was a matter of great anxiety to have a sufficient number of acres lying contiguous in order that the colony might have proper support. Calvin Morrell, Nathan Burlingame and Ebenezer Rice traversed the surrounding country in search of suitable lands. There were offers of land, but none seemed desirable.

It was finally decided to purchase the lands of Mull and McCance lying on the dry fork of Whitewater, which presented a good mill site. Union Village purchased the 100 acres lying on the west side of the creek of William McCance at $6.50 per acre. The Whitewater believers bought the land on the east side of George Mull for $1,200. It contained 115 acres.

These purchases put new zest into the hearts of the believers. The winter of 1825-6 found the people making preparations to take possession of their new farms. Many thousand rails were made and hauled. The fences, on the little place they were about to leave, were put in good repair. Improvements were first made on the west side of the creek, for there the settlement was to be made. The crops were put in, and two of the sisters came to cook. Then the cabins were moved and some new ones put up. In June some of the Union Village brethren arrived, in order to assist in building the houses. Just as fast as the cabins were constructed they were occupied, and this was continued until all had been moved.

They found the soil favorable to agriculture, and their crops were abundant, and their gardens produced beyond expectations. Apples were plenty and peaches abundant. The corn averaged sixty bushels to the acre. Of broom corn they planted eight acres. Hogs were also raised.

During the month of July the children were gathered in the school order, and over them were placed James Wells and Susannah Farnum.

The records are silent as to the first officers. It may be inferred that Calvin Morrell had general oversight, with William Davis as farm deacon and Phoebe Seely and Mary Bedle in charge of the sisters. Nathan Burlingame was the preacher.

It was he, with Polly Burnham and Susannah Farnum, that furnished the money to pay for the Mull farm.

In 1827 a lot of 40 acres, adjoining the first purchased lot, was bought at $1.26 per acre, after first buying off the parties who made claim to it. In September, 305 acres of Congress land, lying near New Haven (Preston P. O.) was entered at $1.25 per acre.

During the month of March, the principal part of the young believers of West Union arrived for the purpose of making Whitewater their home. This was done because, owing to the fever-stricken locality, West Union was broken up, and the members scattered among all the western societies, save that at North Union.

This year the brick meeting-house was constructed, 45 x 35 feet and two stories high. The time occupied from its commencement to its being finished was four months. The first service held in it was December 2, 1827.

OFFICERS APPOINTED.

The first specific reference to officers occurs both in the Union Village and Whitewater records for May 24th, 1828. The latter states that "E. Archibald and Sister Eunice moved to Whitewater, and with them came Joanna Wallace. From this time the Society was considered under the care of the two first-named persons. Calvin still continued here."

On account of ill health Phoebe Seely went back to Union Village, and Mary Hopkins—late of West Union, on April 19th, 1827, was sent to take her place.

The eternal fitness of things was not always—perhaps rarely — observed in the appointment of officers. Elder Archibald Meacham was now appointed at the head of affairs, although he was a conspicuous failure at West Union. His appointment and that of John Meacham, as first at Pleasant Hill, Ky., and David Meacham as first in the Ministry at Union Village, in 1835, must be ascribed to a gross abuse of favoritism. All the documents that have come under my inspection have led me to infer that these three men were mediocre. Certainly they per-

MEETING HOUSE WITH NORTH RESIDENCE BEYOND.
(Elder Charles Sturr in Foreground.)

formed no service of value to Shakerism in the West. Back of all this, we find that Joseph Meacham was among the early converts of Ann Lee, and was the senior Elder after the death of Ann Lee and the first Elder, and it was he who began the organization of the several Societies. He brought his wife and entire family into the Shaker fold. John, Archibald and David were the sons of Joseph, and thereby hangs the tale.

The same day Eldress Eunice Sering started for Whitewater to take first charge of the sisters, having removed out of the Ministry's order at Union Village.

On September 18, 1828, "Mary Bedle moved back to Union Village, having lived here three years as one of the Elder Sisters."

On October 30, 1828, Archibald Meacham, Calvin Morrell, Eunice Sering, Mary Hopkins, Susannah Stout and Joanna Wallace moved into the upper part of the meeting house which indicates that they were in the Ministry order.

During this year a large frame building was erected for the family. Assistance, in the way of artisans, was rendered from Union Village. The village at Whitewater, at this time was what now constitutes the North Family. The Center Family then had no existence.

IMPROVEMENTS AND EXTENSIONS.

During the month of September, 1828, a dam was commenced across the creek and timbers prepared for a saw mill, in which work the brethren generally participated. As the race was long several interruptions occurred before its completion. By April 29, 1829, the work had sufficiently advanced as to enable them to commence sawing. On November 5th a grist mill, 30 x 36 feet was framed.

Brant and Joseph Agnew sold their farm of 160 acres for $1,000. Samuel Rice, Sr., also sold his farm, on Darby Plains, for $800. Eli, a brother of Ezra Sherman, who was a West Union believer, sent word he had sold his farm, fifty miles up the Muskingum river, and desired to move to Whitewater. Calvin Morrell and Ezra Sherman were sent to assist Eli. They tarried in the neighborhood some days and held a public meeting. When they started on their return many of the friends and relatives collected and set up a general wailing and uttered threats against the Shakers for ruining Eli's family, and for two miles followed the wagons. Thirty miles down the river they stopped at Josiah Sherman's, who also wanted to join the Shakers. They built a boat and in it the two families descended the river. All were kindly received at Whitewater.

The farm of Joseph Sater, comprising 135 acres, was next purchased for $2,000. In April, Brant Agnew moved on this land. It proved productive and there was a good yield of corn, oats and potatoes.

During the year (1829) the Shakers continued selling brooms and garden seeds; and during the winter made mats in sufficient quantity to pay for all the meat purchased by the Society. These mats sold for from $2.25 to $2.35 per dozen, the same price received for their brooms.

LEGAL AND MILITARY TROUBLES.

At Union Village, October 22, 1829, just as he was ready to start to Whitewater, Elder Archibald was arrested by a constable for a claim of $99.99, made by an apostate, James Wallace, for work done at Whitewater, while he (Wallace) was a member at Union Village. The justice allowed the claim.

As the Shakers were always averse to war, the militia officers caused a lot of oats to be seized and sold for failure in military duty. In turn the Shakers prosecuted the constable and captain in action for trespass and damages. On the day of trial the justice called to his assistance another squire, who was major of the regiment. The testimony of the Shakers was set aside and the decision was, "No cause for action." An appeal was taken but never brought to trial.

On April 19th, 1830, another military order was received demanding fines. This being refused, all their hogs were driven off. The next day Ebenezer Rice, one of the trustees, went to Cincinnati to consult a lawyer. The upshot was the Shakers

16

paid $20 to have the suit withdrawn. This would indicate that the Shakers — Quakers also — had no redress in law.*

THE COVENANT.

For some reason unexplained the Covenant had never been signed by the Believers at Whitewater, although all the deeds had been made to the trustees; though the names of the first trustees are not given. On February 9th, 1830, Richard Mc-

---

*The militia officers did not always have their own way. The Quakers often outwitted them. Springboro, Ohio, has long been known as a Quaker community. The colonel of militia was one Sweeny, who lived at Ridgeville, and he was particularly severe on the Quakers for not mustering. Among the Quakers were three rollicking brothers, young and full of mischief, viz., Alfred, Hanse and — Thomas. Sweeny had the regiment drawn up in a large field, armed with cornstalks, broom handles and other makeshifts. He straddled a small horse possessed of a spike tail. At the proper time the three brothers, well mounted, leaped the fence, two of whom galloped up on either side the doughty colonel, and the third in the rear. At the same instant all plied their whips to the spike-tailed steed, which gave a bound, with the lashes descending thick and fast. Around the entire field three times the racers ran, and then the boys spurred their horses over the fence and were soon out of reach. Military dignity must be upheld. As the reins of justice in Clearcreek township was in the hands of the Quakers, redress must be sought elsewhere. · Sweeny went before a justice in Lebanon and swore out a warrant charging the boys with riot. The father retained Tom Corwin, who had even then gained a national reputation. The trial was held in the court house which was packed with interested spectators. Evidence all in, at the proper time Corwin arose, all eager to hear what he might have to say, for the case was plain against the boys. The speaker paid a glowing compliment to the militia, and in the very midst of his panegyric, he stopped, waited a moment, and then in his inimitable way, described the race around the field, which brought roars of laughter from the audience. Then he resumed his laudatory praise of the militia, pictured it in glowing terms as the arm of defense of our homes and native land. Again he stopped short and gave another description of he race around the field. Once more he launched into an eulogium of the valiant militia, described their uniforms, their gallant bearing and redoubtable courage. Suddenly, with the gravest of faces he again pictured the race around the field which brought forth another storm of applause. Corwin saw that the crowd and migistrate were with him, and he rested his case. The boys were immediately discharged.

Nemar arrived, who had been instructed by the Mount Lebanon Ministry to visit all the western communities in the interests of the new covenant that had been recently adopted. In this mission Richard devoted all his time while sojourning at Whitewater. This was not fully accomplished until March 1st, when he returned to Watervliet, Ohio. No record is preserved of those who signed the Covenant.

CONFLAGRATION.

The brethren, when time could be spared, devoted their energies towards buildings and other improvements. On May 17th (1830) they began to frame a barn which was raised June 14th, its dimensions being 70 x 35 feet.

At 11 o'clock on the night of June 19th, a fire broke out in the kitchen, in the building occupied by the children, and in less than twenty minutes three of the buildings were completely wrapt in flames. Nearly all the household goods and clothing were consumed. Happily no lives were lost. Evidence pointed out that it was the work of an incendiary.

On July 13th, Abner Bedle and three sisters arrived from Union Village in order to inquire into the extent of the loss. Having obtained an inventory of the same, after two days they returned. On the 21st Joshua Worley arrived from Union Village with a wagon-load of property, consisting mostly of clothing and provisions, to the amount of $157.00.

The school family being left without a home, the brethren, on August 30th, laid the foundation of a Tapia house, 40 x 20 feet, on the land purchased of Sater. By September 21st about half the second story was completed. On a dark night, the wicked tore down the four corners level with the ground. The season becoming late for such kinds of buildings, the work was covered and left for the ensuing summer. This necessitated the removing of cabins and fitting them up for winter usage.

CHRONICLES.

In 1831 it was concluded to put in two run of stone in the grist mill. Ezra Sherman and Edward Burnham were sent

on October 1st to West Union, with a yoke of oxen for a pair
of stones that had been abandoned here in 1827. They were
gone a month. During the fall the first land purchaseu (40
acres) by the Darby people, was sold for $225. May 27th, on
his personal request, Calvin Morrell returned to Union Village,
having been with the Whitewater people from the fall of 1825,
zealously devoting his time and talents in building up the little
colony. On November 11th, previous, Daniel Sering had been
sent as aid to Elder Archibald, and he remained till January
16, 1838. After the departure of Calvin, Richard McNemar
remained for several days, arranging matters for the permanent
security of the estate. On the 30th the trustees named were
Samuel Rice, Ebenezer Rice and Brant Agnew. Deeds of trust
were made and subscribed to by Ebenezer Rice and Ezra Sherman.

In February a frame house for the South family was commenced, 18 x 40 feet, with a stone cellar. The first account of it
was in the year 1824 when it was a log cabin 18 x 18 with a
lean to; in 1826, there were other log cabins, but number and
dimensions not stated; the meeting house, 45 x 35, erected in
1827; in 1829 the first saw and grist mill; in 1830, a barn
70 x 35; in 1830 a frame house 40 x 20, afterwards used for
the boys' residence.

In 1832, August 8th, commenced constructing a brewery.
September 1st, commenced a dwelling 30 x 52 feet. The brick
house was finshed in April 1833.

In January 1834, a frame barn, 30 x 60 feet was commenced
at the South family, — carpenter work contracted for $65, and
oak shingles made and put on $40, all material furnished on the
ground. The barn was finished in July; August 25th commenced
building a brick work house 24 x 40. September 28th, Rachel
Hall was appointed to succeed Mary Hopkins, the latter being
recalled to Union Village.

March 1st, 1835, the farm of Aaron Atherton, consisting of
175 acres was purchased for $3,000, payable in three installments.
It was decided to raise the money by fattening hogs; so all hands
assisted in raising corn. At Center family, June 18th, a horse
stable 28 x 45 was raised; August 27th, a brick kitchen 20 x 38,

was built at South family. On December 20th, 75 hogs sold for $1,425. The amount owed on Atherton farm was deposited in bank, so successful had the society been during the year. This left no outstanding debts.

For this year (1835), we first have a list of members, and also the information that a new covenant had been signed. The list of inhabitants, with ages, is thus given:

CENTER FAMILY.

BRETHREN.		SISTERS.	
Archibald Meacham	58	Eunice Sering	42
Daniel Sering	45	Rachel Hall	32
Ebenzer Rice	43	Sarepta Hinman	31
Ezra Sherman, Jr.	32	Emeline Jackson	21
Samuel Rice	74	Peggy Boggett	70
Joseph Boggett	77	Sarah McKee	72
Joseph L. Carson	65	Lyda Woodward	53
Ezra Sherman, Sr.	72	Lucy Easterbrooks	42
John Easterbrooks	50	Anna Sherman	41
Thomas Ganes	55	Polly Burnham	43
Nathaniel Massie	32	Zilpha Burnham	68
William Easterbrooks	20	Minerva McGuire	46
James Callahan	24	Susanna Champlain	45
Edwin Burnham	22	Sally Tucker	39
William Agnew	20	Elizabeth Callahan	25
Fisis Jackson	16	Nancy McKee	25
Samuel Easterbrooks	16	Louisa Farnham	21
Samuel Agnew	15	Eliza McGuire	19
George Gray	15	Phœbe Agnew	18
Jacob Brown	15	Hortincy Brown	18
Theodore Agnew	9	Lyda Gray	17
William Herington	11	Hannah Boggett	29
Benjamin Hill	18	Emma Burlingame	17
Moses Allen	42		
Micajah Banze	34		

SOUTH FAMILY.

BRETHREN.		SISTERS.	
Joseph B. Agnew	49	Amanda Agnew	12
Manly Sherman	37	Saloma Brown	12
James A. Agnew	32	Rachel Tucker	7
Aaron Stroud	16	Phœbe Howard	7
Josiah Burnham	15	Ann Hall	31

SOUTH FAMILY — Concluded.

BRETHREN.		SISTERS.	
William Agnew	15	Susannah Farnum	51
John Whitney	15	Polly Champlain	40
Calvin Easterbrooks	14	Louisa Jackson	24
George Woodward	12	Susan Easterbrooks	19
Isaac Sherman	10	Louisiana Stroud	19
		Marietta Agnew	18
		Rebecca McGuire	17
		Lucy Woodward	16
		Rhoda Hinman	15
		Adaline Wells	14
		Eunice McGuire	12
		Jane Sherman	11
		Martha Tucker	6

Total males 35, females 42; or in all 77.

The records of Union Village for May 25, 1837, speak of Ebenezer Rice, Ezra Sherman, Sarepta Hinman and Emaline Jackson "of the deaconship of Whitewater" being on a visit. If they were "office deacons," then their office possibly was that of trustees.

January 24, 1838, Edwin Burnham moved into the Elder's lot, having succeeded Daniel Sering. A little later Louisa Farnum moved into the lot with Eldress Eunice Sering.

December 20, 1838, the farm of Daniel Long, comprising 197 acres was purchastd for $7,000.

In the fall of 1839, a horse stable, 45 x 28 was built at the South Family. Same year 17 acres of broom corn was raised and made into brooms. This had already become one of the regular sources of revenue.

ARRESTS EXTRAORDINARY.

As late as 1840, the great mass of mankind, even those supposed to know the general policy of the Shakers, were ready to believe incredible stories concerning them, and even mob violence feared. In the fall of 1839, a widow, named Mary Black, with her two boys, aged respectively 14 and 9, and a girl still younger, left the Whitewater Believers and went to Kentucky. In March 1840, the officers of Bracken county notified the authorities in Cincinnati that the county was in a great uproar on account of two boys who had been emasculated by the Shakers. The boys were ordered sent to Cincinnati and there examined by Drs. Hiram and Jackson, who pronounced the report to be a fact. On the 25th of March the marshal of Cincinnati came with a state's warrant, and the deputy sheriff with a capias for Elder Archibald Meacham, Joseph Agnew, Manley Sherman, William A. Agnew and John S. Whitney, who were arrested and that night at five o'clock were incarcerated in the jail at Cincinnati. So great was the excitement that the prisoners were hurried through the streets as privately as possible on account of the multitude. No food was given them and they were locked in filthy cells, where emanated such odors as almost suffocated them. For bedding one small dirty blanket was furnished. On Thursday morning the 26th, they were let out of the cells after spending a wakeful night, and about 8 o'clock breakfast was served them in small black dirty tin pans, on each of which were very hard pieces of coarse cold cornbread, about four inches square and a piece of cold boiled beef's heart. All declined eating. At 2 o'clock, came bread with soup. Some eat a little of it, but others refused. A little later, Mr. Brook, the inn-keeper, on Main street, who had always been a friend of the prisoners, sent in a good dinner, for which all felt very grateful. That night all were again locked up in cells. Friday morning Mr. Brook sent them a good breakfast, and soon after Ebenezer Rice came and conversed with them through the grates, and handed a letter to Elder Archibald from Eldress Mary Hopkins, who wrote words of comfort to the distressed and persecuted brethren. But the brethren were not cast down, for they believed that God would open a way for their deliverance. At noon they were visited by a number of the brethren and sisters, and some of the neighbors called, shook hands through the grates while tears coursed down their cheeks. At four o'clock, the afternoon of the 27th, the brethren were conducted to the court house where their trial was already in progress, and witnesses testifying. The room was crowded. At sunset the brethren were hurried to the jail followed by the rabble venting out their curses and reproaches, and yelling that hanging was too good for them. Supperless they were again thrust into their reeking cells. On the morning of the 28th, Ebenezer Rice and James Agnew furnished them with an ample breakfast. At 9 o'clock, by a different route they were again conducted to the court house, but in going up stairs, the rush of the multitude was so great that the party was kept together with difficulty. They were surrounded by officers for protection.

Ezra Sherman had not been idle all this time. He had retained Bellamy Storer for the defense. He labored hard with the mayor and marshall to have the boys examined by other physicians. After a great amount of pleading and intercession the marshall finally agreed that the boys might be examined by Drs. Groce and Lakey. These physicians soon saw that the boys labored under a natural deformity, and no privileges had ever been taken with them. While the trial was going on they entered the court room and stated to the mayor the true status of the case. All the officials and lawyers arose and shook hands with the brethren individually, and with tears in their eyes dismissed them with congratulations of joy. The brethren embraced each other on their happy deliverance. Storer declared publicly that it was a manifestation of the power of God.

But the trial was not yet over. The two boys and their cousin, who appeared to be their guardian and the principal in the prosecution, were examined, and then sent to jail. The brethren, with the other believers, fourteen in all, immediately set out for Whitewater, where they arrived at 5 P. M., greatly to the delight of the entire community.

I have been informed by members who had lived at Whitewater, that there was great distress of mind in all the community during the incarceration of the brethren; that even the hoary head of Elder Archibald was not respected by his tormentors.

Anxious to know what the Cincinnati papers of that period had to say on this outrageous persecution, I wrote to Mr. Eugene H. MacLean to look up the matter. He replied. "I looked up the back files of the Chronicle and Gazette for March 1840, and can find no mention of any such occurrence as you mention, although I went over the papers column by column. Indeed there was no local news at all, save brief mention of ward meetings."

I have seen accounts of this in some books relating to Cincinnati, but I am unable to give the titles. I think "Bench and Bar" is one of them.

The Union Village records, in commenting upon the affair adds, "As if to add injury to insult, the greedy cats charged $300 for fees; besides incidental expenses that would of course accrue in the prosecution."

The Whitewater records contain no farther information for 1840, and nothing for 1841, save a few changes in members. The Union Village Records give accounts of visits between the two communities, and also of certain members going to Whitewater to instruct and assist in making brick.

IMPORTANT CHANGES IN OFFICERS.

The Union Village Ministry, on a visit to Whitewater, August 11th, 1842, announced the following changes: Elder Archibald Meacham should be released from his office and return to Mount Lebanon, and Eunice Sering is also released and to return to Union Village. The eldership and trustees to be reorganized and composed entirely of their own members. Edwin Burnham was appointed first elder and Ebenezer Rice second. Joseph Agnew was released from the care of the South Family and moved to the Center to act as a trustee. Ezra Sherman was released as a trustee, and moved to the South Family as first Elder, and Allen Agnew as second. Hannah Boggett succeeded as first elder, and Louisa Farnum as second. Polly Champlain as Eldress with Susan Easterbrooks at the South.

The weeding out of all the officers does not in itself imply that circumstances demanded it, nevertheless such was sometimes a necessity. Sometimes it was simply expedient, sometimes the abuse of arbitrary power. In the present instance it was probably felt that a general change would be in the best interests of the society. Elder Archibald "did not wish to be removed, but it was thought best, although it was regretted by many."

250   Shakers of Ohio.

CHRONICLES, RESUMED.

In 1842 a shop 40 x 18 feet was built; also a two-story house 24 x 17, with a porch on one side, now called the Nurse House.

In 1843-4 the large dwelling house was built 54 x 44, with an extension 60 x 30 feet, — the first three stories high and the second two stories. On April 1, 1844, twenty-eight of the Union Village brethren arrived to assist in raising the house.

August 22, 1844, Joseph Agnew released as a trustee and moved to South Family as First Elder with Ezra Sherman second; Edwin Burnham was transferred to Union Village and went November 27th. On December 3d Moses Eastwood arrived from Union Village to become Second Elder at South Family,— Ezra Sherman removing to the Center Family. The Union Village records state that on October 29th Philip F. Antes was established as Elder Brother. This would make him Burnham's successor. He continued in office until September 11, 1847. March 15, 1845, Ezra Sherman became trustee in place of Philander Banister. A general move in the families took place October 1st. Harvesting lasted forty days,— the acreage for the year was, rye 3, oats 30, grass 80, broom corn 25, potatoes 5, pumpkins 4, corn not stated. Commenced doctoring by the water cure method which proved a great success. Previous to this the botanic or Thompsonian system was used to great satisfaction. This last was introduced by Calvin Morrell who gave much time to its study.

March 4, 1846 the use of tea, coffee, tobacco and intoxicating liquors were renounced. Built a new saw mill.

SECOND ADVENTISM.

While the doctrine of the second visible, personal coming of Christ is no new doctrine in the Christian Church, yet it remained for William Miller to create a wonderful excitement on that subject during the nineteenth century. The earliest date fixed upon for the advent was February 10, 1843, and the next was the 15th, and then April 14th. The disappointment

CENTER RESIDENCE, WITH GIRL'S RESIDENCE ON LEFT AND BOY'S ON RIGHT

in not realizing the promised event did not relax the zeal of the
preachers engaged in this promulgation. In all parts of the
country the cry of warning was raised. Farmers left their
crops unharvested, and mechanics forsook their tools.*

A commotion such as that of Miller and his followers
would elicit the Shakers' attention. Four Second Adventists visited Whitewater in March, 1846, and on the 6th
Joseph Agnew went to Cincinnati with them. Their meetings
in Cincinnati were attended by Joseph Agnew, Ebenezer Rice
and Ezra Sherman, and several were brought to Whitewater
by the brethren. Joseph went to Rising Sun, Ind., to see some
of the Adventists there. On the 18th, Joseph brought home
with him, their principal preacher, Enoch Jacobs. The interest manifested by the Shakers brought numbers of the Adventists to Whitewater. Meetings were held in union and both sides
took an active part. At one time twenty persons came. These
sojourners became quite a tax on the Shakers, and it became a
question of what to do with the visitors. Among them was Henry
B. Bear and his wife, Julia Ann, both having expressed a determination to give up all for God. In 1846, there were 200 of the
Adventists gained to the Shakers of Union Village and Whitewater, most of whom were assigned to the latter place. Eldress
Julia Ann Bear informed me that she never had seen any of
the reputed "white robes" in which to be clothed to receive
Christ, nor did she ever hear of such a thing until some time

* During the month of February, 1869, I heard two Second Advent
preachers holding forth at East Jaffrey, N. H. They were uncouth looking
men, but gave every evidence of sincerity. Their whole burden was to
prove that we were living in the last day. One took his argument from
Nahum II. The "flaming torches" (v. 3) were the head-lights on loco-
motives; the "chariots" (v. 4) were passenger coaches; "they shall jostle
the one against another," refers to cars coming together while trying to
stop them; "they shall run like the lightnings," means their great speed;
also a train on the N. Y. Central called "the Lightning Express;" "He
shall recount his worthies" (v. 5), means the conductor collecting the
tickets; "they shall stumble in their walk," refers to the inability to walk
straight in cars when in motion; "they shall make haste to the wall thereof," refers to passengers entering their seats and leaning against the
side of the car; "the gates of the rivers shall be opened," means draw-
bridges.

after she had become a Shaker. The new members proved to
be zealous workers. A list of the names of those Adventists
who became Shakers was made out and placed in the archives,
but cannot now be found.

SPIRITUALISM.*

Strict orders had been given out by the Mount Lebanon
Ministry that the revelations made during the reign of spiritualism should be kept. Nothing is mentioned of these manifes-

*On October 19, 1903, I came into possession of the archives of
North Union and Watervliet. Among the loose papers I found a brief
record of Whitewater Spiritualism, of which the following is an exact
copy, taken from first leaves detached from a book:

"Where as, We have lately received in structions from the Ministry
of Union Village that it was the will and in structions of our heavenly
Parrents, that all of those Sacred Communications which had been
given Through our Heavenly parrents and there Ministering angels,
for a few years past, should be carefully recorded and as far as it is
is in our power we will labor to it as we had heard By letters from New
labanon that there was a powerful Work of God going on among the believers in the Eastern Societys and that the work was very hart touching
and a wakening and Many Promises given through Visions and inspired
Instruments, that our Heavenly Mother wold thougraly purch and purify
her children on Earth and fit and prepare them for the in crease of the
gospel. Also that Mother wold Visset every Sosiety of believers both
East and West.

"The above information from tne East, Caused us to Look and wait
with great anxiety for the fulfilment of those pretious Promises which
we firmly believed wold certainly com to pas as Mother had promised,
and our earnest prayers was that our Blessed Mother wold pour out her
Spirit upon us at White water for we fealt poor and needy and so our
prayers cotinnued without much mannifestation, of the fulfilment of the
promises which we had received, Until the 16 of August in the
year one thousand Eight hundred and thirty Eight At which time the
power of God was showered down upon the boddy of believers at this
place like a mighty rushing wind, it being Sabbath Day while attending
publick Meeting and Many Spekaters present, That remarcable Manne-
fest of the power of God Seamed to Seaze the greates part of the assembly of believers, Such Mighty Shaking we never will before it wold
Seam Sometimes that some individuals wold be Shaken all to peascis, This
Mighty Shaking continued till the Close of the Meeting and with a num-
her much longer, and for this Notice of the power of God we felt exceeding thankful and that our blessed Mothers hand now began herewith.

tations until 1847, or after the marked decline had commenced. All of the Western Societies had been favored by the angelic

in every deed, and from this time the good work gradually increased, and there soon began to be chosen Insrements who ware inspired to deliver the Council and instructions of our Hevenly Parrents, through whom we received Many Pretious gifts from the Spiritual world, which to us has fealt to one of the greatest Blessings that was ever given since Man dwelt on Earth. Thease blessings finally became so frequent and in such a bundance, that for Sumtime we kept no correct record of those wonderful communications, But we labored to treasure them up in our harts as Much as we was able, and We can truly say that we have from the first commencement of our Blessed Mothers good Work, fealt thankful with all our Souls for the kind notice of the Many blessings which we have received from our Heavenly parrents, All of which has been calkulated to purge and purify our souls by an honest confesson and bring us dow in to a Spirit of humiliaty and simplicyly and true obedience so that we could larn to fear god and walk humbly and gain true love and union with one a nother and Larn to set a good examble before all people, and thus this blessed work continued to progress in till the latter part of the year 1839 at which time we began to receive books and litters through Mothers chosen and in Spired instruments, but it was some time before there was any gift for thease books letters to be read and written by Mortal power. But in January in the year 1840 we received a gift from the Ministry at union Village to have those Spiritual Boks and leters written by mortal power. And after we received the gift to have them read, we received a great many written communications from our Heavenly parrent and others. Ministering Spirits, which we hace Mostly committed to record. Nearly every individual through the Sosiety has been blesst with some written communication to Strengthen and in courrage them to be faithful and truly obedient to their Vissible lead.

"The Lot of Elders at this place have received Many pretious communications, in the form of book and litters and a number of theas comunications seamed to be of a publick nature, and a number of others seamed to be to us as individuals, so that we feal at los to now how to make the right Selection, not fealing our Selves to be competent judges in this matter. Therefore we have concluded to coppy all those that appear to be the Most of a publick Naure and such as we have received nearly as we received them, and leave the matter to the judgment and desisson of that gift and authority that is apointed in the East for that purpose, as we do not wish to hide our one tillant.

"We feal that we have been Noticed and blest by our heavenly parrents for more than we felt that we was worthy of, yet we can testify with thankful harts that the believers at White water have been greatly Blest with Many heavenly Blessings fead our Souls."

hosts, before visitations were made at Union Village. There the heavenly messengers were anxiously looked for and when they came it was like a "whirlwind." According to the Church Record there, the break-out commenced on William Moore August 8, 1838. So the influence must have been felt at Whitewater ere that date. All that I find is under date of September 26, 1847, as follows:

"Sabbath was announced by Mother (The Holy Spirit), through two witnesses, Rhoda Hinman and Aletha Percel that four mighty Angels of judgment would make us a visit shortly to help every honest soul to awake and prepare for an increase in the work of God, by putting away all sin, and laboring for an increase in the true fear and love of God and for each other. Every soul in this part of Zion that would not hear and obey would be cut off. 30th. was announced through four witnesses that the Angels of judgment had come according to promise. The instruments were commanded to not sleep until the Angels had made their visit in the different room and done their work. At 12 midnight the Angels and Mother Ann visited every children and all. Ezra Sherman was chosen to speak for the Angel of Light the other three to be witnesses. Stephen Ball, Aletha Percel and Rhoda Hinman witnesses. The same Angels and witnesses went to the North Family and the same testimony was to them to prepare for a great increase in the work of God, by confessing all sin and laboring for love and union, to be prepared to gather in souls who would shortly come. Had a meeting admitting outsiders. As many as 200 came and was present to hear the instruments proclaim from the

Then follow six pages of narratives of Spirit doings, giving a daily record for January, March, April and May 1839. I give some extracts.:

"Sabbath evening while Eldress Eunice was sitting in the Room there was a light seen to encircle her around for a number of minutes And in that time, she could not move, a number more lights seen in the Room that evening, and musick heard."

"There was singing heard in the kitchen, it moved from place to place Around the room, it was very heavenly."

January 17. "A good many different operations, and lively exercise. A voice was heard, saying, good spirits dwell with you all the Time. Some lights seen, resting on the people, all manifesting That mother's spirit was with us."

mighty Angels the same testimony, the meeting lasted over three hours causing many to fear and tremble.

So far as I have pursued any inquiries, I find that Spiritualism has a stronger hold at Whitewater than in Union Village. Still, there may be more of it in the latter place than I conjecture.

JUDICIAL PERSECUTION.

The free exercise of religion is guaranteed by the Constitution of the United States. What the Constitution of Ohio was from 1811 to 1847 I have not taken occasion to examine. But whatever that constitution was, or whatever laws might have been enacted, all must conform to the Constitution of the United States, and the judiciary is sworn to obey the principles of the General Government.

Stephen W. Ball, — still a member at Whitewater — desired the possession of his two daughters, — his wife being dead, and children with their maternal grandparents. On October 6, 1847, Judge Moore decided that Stephen could not have his minor children because "the law of Ohio was if a man joined the Shakers, he forfeited all right and title to his children." The case was carried to the full bench, and set for the 9th, then the 23d, and finally November 5th, when the bench was equally divided, two for and two against. Case was again assigned for February 4, 1848, and again for the 26th, when Judge Johnson decided that Stephen could not have his children unless he would leave the Shakers. An appeal was taken to the State Supreme Court, where on April 19th, five judges decided "that any person joining the Shakers, deprived them of their natural right to their children." Two judges dissented. Comment is unnecessary. The record does not state why the case was not carried into the Federal Courts. In after years one of Stephen W. Ball's daughters joined the Shakers. Fannie became a very successful teacher at Watervliet. While teaching there she consented to marry Ephraim Frost, and on June 12, 1872, both withdrew from the Society. Later, with their son, they re-united at Whitewater. Ephraim desired again to leave, though Fannie was satisfied to stay, but under threat of having her son taken from her if she did not comply, she left the Society once more to accompany her husband. She is now a widow.

GARDEN SEED ENTERPRISE.

It was in 1847 that the Whitewater brethren started on a successful career of raising garden seeds for the markets. Trips for selling the seeds were made in different parts of the country. One trip was called the Northern, another the Missouri River, another the Western Land, another the Kentucky, etc. The greatest amount received for one year — if I correctly notice,— was in 1857, when $5,704 was realized, with a total traveling expense of $416. This enterprise came to an end in 1873, because many firms began to put out garden and flower seeds in fancy colored papers and boxes, also in different size packages. "That our seeds did not take, as they were put up in a brown colored paper and a plain stained box. It was conclusive we must keep up with the times or step down and out, which we did."

CHRONICLES RESUMED.

In 1847 the floods in the Miami and Whitewater were the highest ever known and attended with great damage to property. In consequence, on February 1st, the Shakers commenced grinding breadstuffs for the public, because other mills were either destroyed or damaged. During the year a two-story brick wash house 30 x 60 feet was built. Bought of Michael Shuck 30 acres for $1,000. August 20th, Phillip Antes was released from the First Eldership and Ebenezer Rice was appointed to succeed him. December 25th, it was decided to give up the eating of pork, which has been maintained to the present. However pork is set before visitors. I was favored with it at every meal while at Whitewater.

In 1848 a horse-power shed, a wagon shed and a dye house were built.

In 1849 a two-story wood house, 20 x 60 (for Center Family), milk house with cellar (North Family), and sheep barn 30 x 120 feet were built. Spinning machines started. Julia Ann Bear, on June 23d, became Eldress in place of Susan Ann Easterbrooks. December 26th, small-pox broke out.

17

A farm of 200 acres, containing a brick house and barn was purchased of William Walker for $10,000 on February 1st, 1850. During the high water of March 6th, the stone dam was washed out and fences gone. August 24th, thirty brethren from Union Village came to help rebuild the mill dam. November 19th, George Rubush was appointed first Elder and Lewis Gordon second at the North Family.

In 1851, burned 140,000 brick, and December 11th, for first time used a circular saw.

DEATH OF AN EASTERN MINISTER.

The only notice I have seen of the death of one of the Mount Lebanon Ministry is that of Rufus Bishop, at Whitewater, August 2, 1852. The Mount Lebanon Ministry, then consisting of Rufus Bishop, Amos Stewart, Eliza A. Taylor and Asenath Clark, arrived at Whitewater, July 30th, from Pleasant Hill and South Union, Ky. "August 3d, at half-past two in the afternoon, the funeral began, attended by this Society generally, and some 20, mostly Elders from Union Village. The meeting continued some two hours, — first by singing some verses composed by Elder Harvey (H. L. Eads), and Elder Oliver Hampton. Elder John Martin (first in the ministry at Union Village), spoke some very appropriate remarks for the occasion, followed by the Eastern Ministry. Two verses given by inspiration was sung of Elder Rufus' welcome into the company of the Redeemed, followed by testimonies from the Elders of the different families,— first Union Village, then Whitewater. Several messages were given out by inspiration. More verses were read, — other speaking. Elder John Martin made the closing remarks. All moved to the grave: Western brethren going before the carriage, four at the sides. Western Ministry followed the carriage containing the corpse: Eastern Ministry followed next; the Elders of Whitewater, then Union Village Elders next, then the elders from the different families; then all the folks, old and young, followed, marching four abreast. After the corpse was buried, the singers sang a hymn; a message given by inspiration through

Elder Oliver Hampton. All returned home in the same order as they went. Several hymns were sung on the return to the house.

"The order in the East at this time was to appoint some twelve or more brethren to go before the corpse. These were the persons that performed the duties at the grave. Since that time, owing to lack of members, that plan has been abandoned." On the following day the Eastern and Western Ministry started for Union Village.

CHRONICLES RESUMED.

During the year 1862, a house for drying fruit, 20 x 28, and a cowbarn 40 x 168, were built. On January 1st, commenced making broom handles, and in February commenced running the saw mill day and night. December 23, Louisa Farnum became Elder Sister at Center Family and Julia Ann Bear, Eldress at the North, with Elizabeth Gass as second. December 24th mill dam and fences carried away.

In 1853, a brick school house 20 x 30, and a two-story brick house 18 x 36 were built. On January 3d, it was decided to abandon water power at the mill, and introduce steam. The cost of the change was $2,000. Had $87 worth of sheep killed by dogs, for which damages were received. A McCormick reaper was purchased. August 4th, a company of sixteen went to Lawrenceburg, Ind., to see the telegraph and railroad trains.

In 1854, a brick henhouse 17 x 44 and 14 feet high was built. Bought the Mering mill lot of 70 acres for $1,300. Purchased twenty China chickens ranging from $1 to $20 each; also a bull and heifer for $1,000; two cider mills for $80; barn burned by lightning and another unroofed at South Family.

In 1855 a brick office, front three stories, 45 x 30, kitchen part two-story, 43 x 22, a milk and loom house at South Family 12 x 16, and a frame at the South Family house 18 x 36 were built. The Society now numbered seventy persons. The Gathering Order was removed on May 17th, from the North to the South, and the children to the North. Elders and Eldresses at the South, George Rubush, John Hobart, Elizabeth Gass and Polly McClain, and at the North, Matthew Carter, E. Frost, Julia A. Bear and Hester Frost.

THE OFFICE.

(Elder Charles Sturr on Extreme Left.)

In 1856 a wood house at the Office, 24 x 18, a house for dyeing cloth, and a one-story frame at North were built. Purchased near Cleveland 2,500 evergreen trees at two cents each. The Union Village Ministry arrived on September 17th, and decided that a part of Whitewater people should remove to Watervliet. Those selected were Ebenezer Rice, Matthew B. Carter, Ezra Sherman, Lewis Packer, William Adams, Thomas Streets, Francis Vaun, Charles King, Matthew Traver, Mary, Rebecca and Emily Adams, Adaline Wells, Matilda A. Butler, Mary Ellen Stroud, Sally McBride, Hester Ann ReVoux, Mary J. Lewis and Berthany Williams. All left on the 23d September. The Union Village records add the name of Ramuth G. Bunting. This removal necessitated certain changes. Stephen Ball was made first Elder, and with him John S. Hobart second. Josiah Burnham and Frederick Faulhaber, Trustees. On October 12th Frederick Faulhaber, Joseph Agnew, Louisiana Stroud, Lucy Woodward, Susan Rubush and Polly Burnham moved into the Office. On December 1st commenced to weave bonnets.

In 1857, built a two-story addition of brick to the nurse house. Bought 944 acres of land for $15,000, in Clinton County, Ohio, adjoining that purchased by Union Village. In April, Josiah Burnham and Marion Moss took cattle there to pasture.

April 3, 1858, grain barn was burned by an incendiary, losing threshing machine and 120 bushels barley. On 17th, a robber entered the office, threatened one of the sisters and Joseph Agnew, broke open the desk, scattered the contents on the floor, and escaped, securing but little booty. October 1st, Henry Bear transferred to the Center as Elder and Stephen Ball to the South as Elder.

March 3, 1859, Louisa Farnum was released as first Eldress at Center and Lucy Woodward took her place. Lewis Gordon moved from the North to the South and Stephen Ball from the South to the North, changing places as Elders.

April 14, 1860, John S. Hobart became crazy and on 28th was taken by sheriff. June 4th, he entered suit against the Society, for $10,000 damages, alleging that he was injured by being dragged through the streets of Cincinnati, and also for false imprisonment. June 25th, had Henry Bear and Stephen Ball arrested by the U. S. Marshall and taken before the U. S. Commissioner at Cincinnati on the accusation of opening and detaining his letters, but being unable to prove his charges, the case was dismissed. The suit for damages was heard November 16th, and decided in favor of the Shakers. During March, set out 165 apple and 200 pear trees.

December 21, 1861, "Stephen Ball released from Elder at the North, George Rubush first. Josiah Burnham at the North, Ebenezer Rice as second at Center with Elder, H. B. Bear."

NAMES OF MEMBERS IN 1862.

The Ministry from Union Village arrived October 16, 1862, and changed the three families into two; the South, Gathering Order, changed to the North, and the South to be a part of the Center. George Rubush, Ezra Sherman, Elizabeth Gass and Amanda Rubush, Elders at the North; Stephen Ball and Manley Sherman, Polly Burnham, Mary Midldleton, Lucy Devolve, Margaret Nickles, Molly Dupler and Eliza Cook to live with the boys at the South.

At Center with the South — Elders Henry Bear, Ebenezer Rice: John Easterbrooks, Joseph Agnew, Lewis Gordon, John Clark, George King, John Atcheson, John Wisenborn, Charles Wortman, Charles Faraday, Josiah Burnham, Frederick Faulhaber, Elmer Butler, Washington Rubush, Oliver Atchison, Isaiah King, William Burnet, Edward McBride.

Brethren and boys at South: Elder Stephen Ball and Manley Sherman, with following boys, Elijah, Ora and Daniel Starkey, Thomas Andrews, Charles Brock, Charles Almon and George Merrick. 'Boys under Ann Vann at Center near Office: Charles Sturr, Robert Morrison, Edward Donaldson, Lafayette Packer and Alfred Doyle. Sisters: Eldress Lucy Woodward, Nancy McKee, Susanna Farnum, Minerva McGuire, Susan and Polly Champlain, Lucy and Susan A. Eastabrooks, Susan and Martha Rubush, Elizabeth Sharp, Ann Vann, Louisianna Stroud, Eliza McGuire, May A. Wheeler, Rachel Hall, Julia A. Bear, Julia Middleton, Harriet Thompson, Lucinda Packer, Jane Starkey, Matilda Butler, Susanna and Marietta Faraday, Emily Flagg,

Sarah E. and Hannah J. Bryant, Fanny Ball, Amelia Dobson, Josephine Deming, Polly McClain, Lottie Wheeler, Sisters at South, seven, previously given. Girls at Center: Caty Walker, Ovanda Brock, Arecia Columbia, Olive Flagg, Lamora Brooks, Betsey Allman, Luella Carpenter, Aurilla Lacy, Antonette King. These two families were under one interest of the Center.

Of the North Family, — Elder George Rubush and Elder Ezra Sherman, John S. Hobart, Dennis and William McBride, Alexander Butler, Wilson Davis, John Freeman, James Starkey, William Merrick, Nelson Atchison. Eldress Elizabeth Gass and Eldress Amanda Rubush. Eliza Carter, Mary Faraday, Priscilla Rubush, Isabella and Mary E. Merrick, Mary Donaldson, Rebecca Clark, Melissa and Catherine Carpenter, Lydia Brock, Albina Kilgore, Jane Allman, Mary Gass, Rosetta Worts, Rhoda Gray, Catherine Sturr, Emaline Brooks, Eliza Hobart, Marinda and Lotta Sirk, and Adelia Doyle. The total population at this time embraced 118, persons.

THE MORGAN RAID.

On July 13, 1863, "one of the boys was at the mill at Harrison and saw Morgan's raiders coming down the hill west of town. He came home and reported the news. Frederick Faulhaber, on a fleet horse, rode out until he came in sight of them, and then hurried back as fast as he could, — receiving the fire of the enemy, but was soon out of sight. He spread the alarm, warning the neighbors to hide their horses. Several heeded the warning and took their horses above the North Family and there hid them. They took from the South Family two horses, but this was the extent of their damage to us, save a few meals and hindering us in the harvest. The main army encamped on the main road between Harrison and New Haven (Preston, P. O.), but extending their pickets and horse thieves for several miles each way, searching the cornfields and thickets for horses, robbing private residences of such things as they wanted, and if any refused they were roughly treated. At Harrison they entered all kinds of shops and stores, taking whatever they chose. At Leonard's store they took $4,200 in money besides $6,000 worth of goods. At Davison's about $6,000 all told. The loss in Harrison was about $50,000. At New Haven they cleaned out both the stores. At Frost's $300 and Thompson's some $500, and in the vicinity 100 horses. They treated our folks very respectfully, and did not enter our buildings. They departed towards New Baltimore, and burned the big covered bridge across the Miami.

"After the aiders had departed we supposed our troubles had come to an end. But the next day the Union Army, some 500 or 600 on horses,—Home Guards of Indianapolis—headed by John S. Hobart, claiming to be authorized by the Government, to take all the horses he could find. John threatened to burn and kill if we did not bring in our horses from where we had hid them. Elder George Rubush ordered his horses brought to the house, where John and his companions selected the two best, as he agreed only to take two, if they were brought in.

"This time of excitement continued for days, owing to false reports being received that more of Morgan's men were coming, — then it was the Union men."

CHRONICLES RESUMED.

February 29, 1864, Henry B. Bear, Ezra Sherman and Frederick Faulhaber were appointed trustees.

In 1865 sold brooms at $6 and $7 per dozen, and 200 bushels of strawberries ranging between $6 and $7.50 per bushel.

December 31, 1868, Ezra Sherman became Elder at Gathering Order and Stephen Ball succeeded him as trustee.

February 7, 1870, Stephen Ball was removed to Watervliet, and Matthew B. Carter removed from Watervliet to Whitewater to take first charge as trustee. In 1871 steam laundry was put in at both the Center and North Families.

In April, 1872, Ebenezer Rice was released from second Eldership, and George B. Amery appointed in his place to live with Henry Bear. Alexander Butler from the South moved into Office to act with Matthew B. Carter.

December 23, 1873, Eliza McGuire was appointed Eldress at South Family in place of Polly Burnham.

March 23, 1874, George King appointed Elder at South in place of George Rubush. October 29, Matthew Carter transferred to Union Village to act as trustee there. November 4th, George Amery removed to Office to act as trustee; Alexander Butler becomes first Elder at North; Ezra Sherman removes to Center, and Charles H. Sturr becomes deacon.

In 1875, bank grain barns were built, both at the Center and North. March 6th, donated $1,000 to Mount Lebanon to assist them in the great loss the Society there had sustained by fire. June 1st, Amanda Rubush becomes second Eldress at South and Amelia Dobson becomes second at Center. November 16th, suit instituted against George B. Amery for selling onion seed not as guaranteed. On the 22d, suit against Society by Harrison Turnpike Company. Action on account of George King using a road along and by the side of the turnpike and toll gate, and striking the toll-road beyond the gate. The claim was for $40, for passing the gate eight times. As nothing further appears, it is probable these suits were settled.

In 1876 a shop for making brooms and carpenter work was set up. September 6th, Frederick Faulhaber becomes Elder at the North and Charles Faraday the same at the South.

March 25, 1878, George Amery released as trustee and appointed second Elder; Wilson Saffin becomes first Elder at the North in place of Alexander Butler, and the latter removes to the Office as trustee, and Charles H. Sturr to live with him. August 22, George Amery removes to the South, and succeeded by Charles Faraday at the Center. October 8, on account of the secession of Eldress Lucy Woodward, Amanda Rubush and Susanna Faraday become first and second Eldress, respectively at the Center; Julia Ann Bear becomes first Eldress at North, and Eliza McGuire moves into the Office; George Amery having left the Society, Joseph Usher moves from the North to the South.

March 25, 1879, Louisa Farnham moved to Union Village to become first in the Ministry in the Sister's Lot. Ezra Sherman becomes first and Wilson Saffin second Elder at the North. December 29th, Stephen Ball returns from Watervliet to become first Elder at the Center, with Henry Bear second. The latter also becomes a trustee. As the Shakers had been schooling their own children besides paying taxes they attempted to get a special school district, but failed. It was not until April 20, 1891, that the school board established a school at the Shaker school house.

January 27th, 1880, Wilson Saffin removed from the second Elder at the North and goes to the Center. July 2, Nancy McKee second Eldress at Center in place of Susanna Faraday, and Kate Dennis becomes second at the North. November 2d, Henry Bear is released as trustee and moves to the North as first Elder; Ezra Sherman removes to the Office as trustee; Charles Faraday becomes second Elder at Center, and Charles Sturr, bookkeeper at Office.

In December, 1881, the sorghum house was removed to the Boggett farm to be used as a dwelling.

January 1st, 1882, the Union Village Ministry arrived and made the following changes: Henry Bear becomes first Elder at Center and trustee; Stephen Ball becomes second, and Charles Faraday first Elder at the North. May 13th, Julia A. Bear is released from first Eldress at the North and moves to Office in place of Eliza McGuire. Susan Faraday as first with Carrie Burk as second at the North.

February 4, 1884, Charles Sturr succeeded Henry Bear as deacon and trustee. May 21st, commenced roofing cow barn. It took three men twenty-nine days to put on the 65,000 shingles. Put up wagon scales. Made two fish ponds. Dried 54 Barrels of sweet corn. Began to ship first by express for stock purposes.

October 24, 1885, raised a new sheep barn on same spot where previous one stood. August 19th, Matthew B. Carter and Julia Ann Bear appointed trustees for the Society. A strange freak of lightning occurred June 13th, during a heavy storm. It struck the wash house, going in at the door on the west side; thence up through the floors to the attic, tearing a hole through the roof by both chimneys; then down the south end to the cistern, and on its course it took off most of the ceiling in the ironing room, doing damage all the way. In the upper room were 20,000 silk worms about ready to spin. The children had just left the ironing room.

November, 1886, Eliza McGuire became second Eldress at Center. In August hot air furnaces were put in at both the Office and Center dwelling.

During April, 1887, an orchard containing 400 apple trees and 200 peach trees was set out north of the Office. In September a stone walk was placed around the Office and another connecting it with the residence of the Center family.

June 25, 1889, Louisa Farnham returns from Union Village, where she had lived in the Ministry, and became second Eldress at Center. The South Family was broken up and moved to the North. This is the first acknowledgement (though indirect) of the visible decay of the community found in the Sturr MS.

July 1, 1890, Lafayette Parker becomes first Elder at the North, in the room of Charles Faraday. August 19th, the Mount Lebanon Ministry arrives and appoints Mary Gass, Eldress at the North in place of Elizabeth Sharp, — the latter moving to the Center.

In 1891, a new engine house of corrugated iron was built. A new boiler and engine for the wash house at North Family. March 14th, purchased threshing machine and traction engine.

In 1893, a new threshing machine and a traction engine of 15 horse power were purchased. Threshing was done in the vicinity. This was carried on for some years.

June 25th, 1894, another thresher was purchased, and later a clover huller, and during the season threshed 33,461 bushels of wheat, 9,731 of oats and barley and 355 of clover. The house on the Williamson farm having been destroyed by fire, within forty days a new two-story with kitchen, was constructed, for the renter. This is the first indication of lands rented out. Doubtless, owing to age and the paucity of numbers, the Shakers had commenced renting out their lands ere this year.

The Sturr MS. is utterly silent on the subject of manners, customs and dress, save two items in the year 1895; one of which (January 6th), states "began to kneel once after meals, after eating," and the other (July 14th), "change made of worship, first stand singing a hymn, then sit down, speak, sing or read." As all the manners, customs, etc., are prescribed by the Mount Lebanon Ministry, the edict goes out to all the Societies at the same time, and hence Shaker Zion is supposed to be blessed with a general uniformity in all things. During the year, at the Center a 40-foot steel tank tower, holding 75 barrels, was put up to supply house and stock.

February 15, 1896, Lafayette Parker was released from the Eldership at the North, and soon after withdrew, taking his children with 'him. The temporal affairs of the entire estate were now assumed by Charles H. Sturr. The year was one of tribulation, presenting great trouble with the Ludwig family; all the boys leaving; all the work and affairs to be looked after by Charles Sturr; could not run threshing machines because none at home to call on for assistance; sold one of the machines.

In 1897, steam heating at Center Family and hot water at Office were introduced.

September 25, 1898, Charles H. Sturr was appointed sceond Elder at Center, Henry B. Bear being first.

March 21, 1899, the Shakers' suit against the Birdsell Huller Company was decided in favor of the former. Particulars not given. Under one roof was constructed a wagon shed and corn crib. This is the last item of building.

July 5, 1900, John Tyler removes from Watervliet to live at the North to take charge of affairs there. July 8th, Charles H. Sturr succeeded Henry Bear as first Elder, and moved into the building of the Center Family, having lived in the Office since March 25, 1878. This closes the Sturr MS.

The Sturr papers inform us that the telephone was in use at the Center Family in 1901, and the windows of the dwelling were enlarged in 1902.

OFFICERS AND MEMBERS.

The Elders of the Center Family take rank over the North Family — the South Family extinct. Charles H. Sturr is first Elder at Center, likewise Amanda Rubush first Eldress, with none standing second. John O. Tyler is first Elder at North; Adaline Wells, first Eldress and Sarah Smith second. The trustees are Henry B. Bear, Charles H. Sturr, Amanda Rubush and Matilda A. Butler. Besides the above, the Covenant members are Frederick Faulhaber, Lewis Robbins, Stephen Ball, Julia A. Bear,

Elizabeth Sharp, Mary Middleton, Lucinda Parker, Catherine Sturr, Emaline Brooks, Rebecca Clark, Eliza Cook, Carrie Burk, Susanna Rooney, Louisa Gass and Cora Stevens.

CONCLUSION.

In all the documents I have examined I have seen no evidence of any defalcations in the community. The affairs appear to have been well managed, and the Society has moved along in harmony. I asked Elder Sturr how the Society escaped the financial troubles in which Joseph Slingerland involved Union Village. In reply I was informed that he had a premonition and immediately saw every Covenant member, and all expressed themselves as being satisfied with the present board of trustees. When Elder Slingerland came to remove Elders Bear and Sturr, he was informed that the present board was satisfactory to all those concerned. The matter was not pressed. Nearly all the lands are rented. Harmony prevails in this community.

NOTE.—In 1907 the Mount Lebanon Ministry ordered the dissolution of this Society.

SHAKERS OF EAGLE AND STRAIGHT CREEKS.

PRELIMINARY OBSERVATIONS.

All reforms, whether in the cause of religion or efforts intended for the betterment of humanity, have been more or less opposed by those for whom the labors have been put forth. The cause of religion has ever called for its martyrs. Nearly every sect has been persecuted, and in the tempest, choice spirits are born, destined to become honored and revered by those who reaped the fruits of their toils. In the building up of the walls of Zion, self-sacrifice has been displayed to such an extent as to call forth the admiration of the just and all lovers of the progress of mankind.

The attempt will not here be made to pay tribute to a band of Shakers who once lived among the beautiful hills of Adams County, Ohio. They made sacrifices and suffered for what they believed to be the true expression of the teachings of Christ. Their own chronicler has portrayed their sufferings, disappointments and disasters. An impartial observer cannot help being aroused to feelings of sympathy by the recital of the unfortunate experiences of this devoted band of sincere followers of the teachings of Ann Lee. The fortitude, patience and hope under the most trying difficulties must appeal to the better parts of our nature, and call forth unstinted praise and approval. The record of the Shakers of Adams County is a part of the history of Ohio, although their sufferings were imposed upon them in other commonwealths.

SOURCES OF INFORMATION.

The official records, of what was known as the Shakers of West Union, have been lost or destroyed. In 1827 these records were in possession of the Shaker Community at South Union, Logan County, Ky., but after diligent inquiry among the Western communities I have failed to obtain even a trace of them. For-

(270)

tunately the journal has been practically preserved by Samuel S. McClelland, who made excerpts from the original document for a member of the Society at Union Village. This MS. was placed in my hands by Mr. Moore S. Mason, of Union Village, with permission to make such use of it as I might determine. As the MS. is very defective, I set about accumulating such information as would make the narrative more complete. In this I was seconded by all in authority in the Western communities. Eldress Jane Cowan, of South Union, placed the record of that Society in my possession. The early part of these records is made up from the private diary of Benjamin Seth Youngs, a member of the first Shaker propaganda to the West. It is rich in dates and the principles that form the basis of history. Elder Charles H. Sturr placed in my possession the records of the Whitewater Community, located in Hamilton County, Ohio. With the records of Union Village I was already familiar. I had the histories of Knox and Sullivan Counties, Indiana, searched in the same behalf. Having seemingly exhausted every corner, and presuming nothing had ever been published relating to the West Union Society, I was most agreeably surprised on June 6, 1903, by receiving a present of a complete set of "The Manifesto" (1871-1899) from Alonzo G. Hollister, Mt. Lebanon, N. Y., which contains two separate accounts of the people with whom we are now concerned. The first is in the form of five articles, purporting to be written by Samuel S. McClelland, placed in a readable form, prepared at the Shaker Society at Pleasant Hill, Ky., and appears in "The Manifesto" for May-September, 1885. The second is a short account in "The Manifesto" for January, 1890, written by Louis Basting, of West Pittsfield, Mass. The MS. autobiography of Issachar Bates I find to be very valuable. Before receiving the published accounts I had transcribed the McClelland MS. preparatory for editing and was engaged in selecting and arranging my notes. In the notes and the Introduction I have freely drawn on such sources of information as I have been able to obtain.

EAGLE CREEK AND STRAIGHT CREEK BELIEVERS.

Our history opens in Adams County, Ohio, in the year 1805. That region was sparsely inhabited, the people having mostly come from Virginia, Kentucky and the north of Ireland. On Eagle Creek, some ten miles from the Ohio River and three miles from West Union, Rev. John Dunlavy lived and settled over a parish there and another on Straight Creek, now Georgetown, Brown County. Dunlavy was a man of liberal education, had belonged to the Presbyterian Church, and was a pronounced participant in the Kentucky revival. Whether or not he had previously held views at variance to the Confession of Faith, I am unable to determine, but in all probability he was "not sound in the faith." He joined the reform movement with enthusiasm, and the opening of the year 1805 found him with the Christians (New Light) working to upbuild the new order of things. That he was skilled as a theologian may be seen in his "Manifesto," a book of 520 pp., first published in 1818, at Pleasant Hill, Ky., where he remained as preacher until his death. This book was reprinted in New York in 1847, and is one of the standards of Shaker theology.

ADVENT OF SHAKERISM.

The Shaker propaganda which set out for the West from Mount Lebanon, N. Y., on January 1st, 1805, took advantage of every camp-meeting that came under its notice. Where a camp-meeting was advertised, a Shaker missionary promptly made his appearance, and lost no opportunity to instill his doctrines. Some of the reformed preachers looked upon this attitude as in harmony with the spirit of freedom to worship; while others regarded it with great disfavor, and even descended to hostile proceedings. When the pulpit or the platform was closed against them, then private conversation was resorted to and homes visited. It was also deemed expedient to visit such neighborhoods as had accepted the faith of the revivalists, and these places appear to have been made stations or resting places during the longer journeys.

The first Shakers to visit Eagle Creek were Benjamin Seth Youngs and David Spinning, who left Union Village June 27, 1805, for Kentucky via Eagle Creek. In company with Issachar Bates and Richard McNemar, on their return, they were again at Eagle Creek July 26th. On the 29th, Rev. John Dunlavy became a convert. The vicinity was again visited by Bates, McNemar

and Malcolm Worley on their way to Kentucky, having left
Union Village August 8. By this time the principal people at
Eagle Creek had embraced the Shaker faith. From September
11th to 16th Youngs was with the Believers propagating the faith.
From October 10th to 13th, Youngs and John Meacham were
at Eagle Creek, and the 14th at Straight Creek, where they
must have remained several days, for they did not reach Cabin
Creek, Lewis Co., Ky., until the 24th; and on November 30th
were again at Eagle Creek. Youngs, Bates and McNemar
reached the same place December 31, and on January 1, 1806,
were stopping at the residence of John Knox, from whence they
visited the families of Dunlavy, Joseph Painter and William
Knox. On the 2nd, Bates and Youngs visited the homes of Nai-
lor and Judge Edie. On the 4th to Jonas Shrizes and Daniel
Redmon. On Sunday at John Knox's the three elders, together
with John Dunlavy, addressed an audience of 60, of whom 30
were Believers. At the evening worship, A. Dunlavy was taken
with shaking, jerking and dancing, while Redmon and Sally
Moore fell. Though the weather was very cold, visits were made
to McCawley's, Painter's, Shrizes', Straw's and Edie's. Services
night of 8th when Peggy Pangburn confessed. Meeting the 12th
at Knox's, whence confessions from S. Redmon, A. and S. Moore.
On the 13th converts were William and Nancy Clark and William Moore. The missionaries proceeded to Kentucky and returned March 5th. During their absence the following confessed
to John Dunlavy: William Gallagher and Adam, his son, Garner
McNemar, Elizabeth and Eliza Sharp, Jenny Boyles, William
Sharp, Hary Hall and F. E. Knox. At Cabin Creek, while
on a visit, Alexander and Sally McGehan confessed. Owing to
the conversion of his wife (Nancy) and daughter, James Duncan
left for Kentucky. On the 7th a large meeting was held at
Knox's, when Betsy McNemar, Rebecca Gallagher, Fielding Martin and Polly Sharp opened their minds. On the 10th Betsy Gallagher and Joseph Cospey confessed. July 30, Bates and McNemar set out for Eagle Creek and returned to Union Village August 9th. They found the people "under great weakness and
loss for the want of nothing but a privilege — numbers are going
back, and the wicked taking great power over them — they un-

18

wisely run wild at their meetings for want of a guide." August 2nd the Believers were threatened by a mob who desired to take away Peggy Knox and Anna Carr. On the 31st a meeting of about 100 was addressed by Bates and John Davis. John Edgington and wife, (recently reconverted) sang in the service. Preaching and visiting on the 2nd, 3rd and 4th of September, converts being Nancy and Jane Gallagher. December 9th, David Darrow, Solomon King, Bates and McNemar set out for Eagle Creek and returned to Union Village the 25th. January 15th, 1807, Worley, Spinning and John Wallace went to Eagle Creek. April 25, 1808, Worley, Matthew Houston, James Hodge and Francis Whyte set out for Eagle Creek and from there, with John Dunlavy, to South Union. May 23rd, McNemar, Spinning and Samuel Rollins to Eagle Creek. Youngs and Houston were at Straight Creek the 26th of April, 1809; on the 29th at Eagle Creek, where they held services in a log meeting house and addressed 90 Believers. As they staid May 1st with John Dunlavy, that person must have been still in charge of the congregation. Worley, Wallace, Peggy Houston and Jenny McNemar, September 3, went to Eagle Creek and returned the 20th. Youngs and Daniel Mosely visited Straight Creek January 26th, 1810, and hold meeting at John Sharp's; 27th, visit Thomas Vance, Nicholas Devoe and Edward Hall; 28th, preach to about 100, of whom 27 are Believers, and Nancy Scott confesses; 30th at Eagle Creek; visit William Gallagher and Elijah Hall; 31st at Richard Naylor's, J. Painter's and John Miller's; consult George Legier and William Gallagher respecting a final gathering, as the time had come for something to be done; February 1st, at Legier's, Joseph Johnson's, John Johnston's, David Eddie's, David, Alexander and Jerry Burn's; 2, at Daniel Rankin's; 3, at John Naylor's, Thomas Kallaghan's, Andrew Dragoo's, John Dunlavy's and John Edgington's; 4, about 220 people at meeting, 120 of whom were Believers; 5th, at Reuben Morris's, James Bromfield's, Knox's, — addressed 70 school children; 7th, permission given to George Legier and William Gallagher to purchase 1,000 acres of land half way between Eagle and Straight Creek; thence 12 miles to Baltashazzar Dragoo's and from that to John Sharp's on Straight Creek; 9th, confession of William and

Jenny White, and James Hodkin's children. "After two more visits, one in April and another in May — and taking Ruth Darrow and Hortency Goodrich in the April visit — Elder Benjamin thus-sums up the matter. He says: It is most evident that the people have run thro' and are at a full stop in this place — and also that their general and particular feelings are to be up and gone out of it. — After a trial of about 5 years every endeavor to find an opening for a foundation has failed — tho' the present opening proposed for consideration, meets the feelings of the greater part and finds a weighty objection in none." May 11th, at Union Village there was a consultation with John Dunlavy relative to removing the Eagle Creek Believers to Busro (West Union). On the 28th, Youngs and King start for Eagle and Straight Creeks "to ascertain more particularly the minds of the people respecting their continuance in those parts. Their removal to Busro proposed." June 21st, there arrived at Union Village from Eagle Creek, William Gallagher, George Legier, David and Peggie Eddie, Alexander Hughye, and Sally McGehan, and on the 23rd George Legier, William Gallagher and Robert Gill and John Stover set out for Busro. December 26th Youngs and Archibald Meacham arrived at Straight Creek and put up at John Sharp's; on 31st, at Amos Moore's, spoke to the Believers on "their condition; unless they turn about they are lost — Elijah Halls gone — but profess faith — Edward Halls they are also turned as a dog to his vomit — Reuben Watts still faithful — Devoes halting — A most pernicious & destructive has prevailed among some (Eld. & John H are the movers) which is setting up a political school among the youth, who have been sincere — a very flattering & certain way to ruin — & disgrace added."

At the time of the removal of the Believers from Eagle and Straight Creeks they numbered 150 souls, of which 70 moved to Union Village and 80 to Busro. The following minute of those to Union Village is made: April 1, 1811, Garner McNemar and family, Reuben Morris and family and Reuben Wate and family; 3, John Sharp and John Naylor and family from Straight Creek; 4, John Dunlavy and family, Betty Dragoo and Jenny Burns, and the remaining, whose names are not recorded.

No plausible excuse is recorded why the 150 Believers should have been removed from Adams County, and the majority taken to the Indian frontier. Shakers must exist by converts made from outside their communion; and if placed on the edge of civilization, the existence must necessarily be precarious. The numbers and wealth of the Adams County Shakers gave every encouragement for a prosperous community within their own vicinity. Issachar Bates did not approve of a permanent settlement at Busro, and plainly told David Darrow that it would "take the wisest man on earth to lead that Society." He farther records that "the Busero Society of themselves was a mixed multitude, white, black and yellow," and the mixing with these the Believers from Eagle Creek and Red Bank (Ky.) would be attended with difficulties; that while the country was beautiful to the eye, yet it was "naturally sickly," besides being on the extreme frontier, and upon the eve of a war with the Indians. But those in authority looked with favor upon the country, and the rich soil and extensive range for pasture bid fair for a community that might obtain great wealth. As early as 1809 the 30 Believers at Red Bank, Ky., had taken up their abode at Busro.

BUSRO, OR WEST UNION.

The name of the Indiana Society of Shakers I find variously spelled, in the earlier documents, Busro, Busroe, and Buserow, and in the later documents the name of West Union universally occurs. Union Village was the center or home church of the Western Shakers, and there was a tendency to name the societies with respect to the parent. Hence the Society near Cleveland was called North Union, being north from Union Village; that on the Gasper, in Logan County, Ky., received the name of South Union, and by the same logic the Busro Community was called West Union. The Community was first called West Union in 1816, as I learn from the Church Record of South Union. In that year, under July 21, is the following memorandum: "This morning Elder Benjamin starts on a journey to Busro or West Union as it is now called."

The West Union Community was located in the northwestern corner of Knox County, Indiana, in Busseron Township, on

ELDRESS NAOMI LEGIER.

Busseron Creek, and about sixteen miles north of Vincennes. In July, 1813, the main body of land was entered by William Davis, Adam Gallagher and Nathan Pegg, as trustees for the Shakers. The entire tract owned by the community embraced about 1,300 acres, all tillable and of deep rich soil. Here, for a while, the people were very prosperous. On Busseron Creek they built a saw mill and a grist mill, and manufactured many kinds of lumber, and out of walnut and cedar made various cooper ware; they had carding and fulling machines and a tannery; there was a cocoonery, and silk was manufactured; cattle and sheep were raised extensively. The village proper consisted of several buildings used for dwellings, various industries, and a house of worship. The meeting house was a frame structure 48 x 50 feet, two stories high, with a floored attic. The ground floor was all in one room, with seats, of walnut planks, extending around the walls. The second story, reached by two flights of stairs, was divided into nine rooms, and used as a place of residence by the Ministry. The ground floor had no heating accommodations, but the second floor was warmed by four fire places. This structure, as well as all the other residences, was finished with walnut, and displayed remarkable mechanical skill.

ORIGIN OF WEST UNION.

The Shaker missionaries not only made it a point to be present at camp-meetings, but also visited the Christian (New Light) ministers, hoping in them to find encouragement. Families were visited in expectations of making converts. Many of the converts had friends whom they desired to be of the same faith, and the missionaries would search these parties out. It was on such an errand that Issachar Bates, Mathew Houston, John Dunlavy, Malcolm Worley and James Hodge, arrived at the Busseron country, from Gasper, South Union, Ky., on June 3rd, 1808, where they remained until the 26th. They had been urged on this expedition by Jesse McComb, because his half brother, John McComb, had recently moved to the Wabash. Jesse McComb was the largest land holder that embraced the faith at South Union.

The following memorandum of the meetings on the Wa--
bash is preserved in the South Union Record:

"June 8. Robert Gills — Confession — Mary Shaw to John Dunlavy — James Shaw to Malcham.

"Tuesday, 9. Confession — Nancy Boyles to Malcham Worley.

"Wednesday, 10. Confession — Nancy Gill to Malcham.

"Thursday, 11. Confession — Wm. and Betsy Hill and Nancy
Jenkins to Malcham.

"Sab. 12. Robt. Houston's — Great meeting — 4 or 500 spectators.
Jno. Dunlavy and Matthew preach — Confession — Sally Jenkins to Malcham.

"Monday, 13. Over the Wabash River — Meeting at Enoch Davis'.

"Wednesday, 15. At Robert Gills.

"Friday, 17. Confession — Rachel Duncan to Malcham — at R. Houstons.

"Sab. 19. Wm. Price's — large meeting — Jno. Dunlavy preached."

"Sab. 26. Confession — John Hadden and Thos. Beard to Malcham."

On September 19th, Issachar Bates, Matthew Houston, Malcholm
Worley and James Hodge left Union Village for Busro; and on the 27th
William and Betsy Houston confessed; on January 16, 1809, Issachar
Bates, Benjamin S. Youngs and Richard McNamar set out for Busro.
Their journey was a perilous one, the particulars of which I have re-
lated in a sketch of Issachar Bates. The missionaries did not return to
Union Village until April 30th. On January 16th, the party arrived at
Robert Gill's.

Thus the journal is continued:

"Feb. 4. At Robt. Gills — a number of the Believers came to see us.

"Thursday. 2. At Nancy Jenkins — thence to Robt. Houston's held
meeting.

"Friday, 3. At Leonard McReynolds, late from Red Banks, Ky.
."At Matthew Neelys and Wm. Berrys.

"At Robt. Houston's held another meeting. About 30 souls.

"Tuesday, 7. At Robt. Gills — made ourselves a pair of Moccasins
each—

"Wednesday, 8. Wm. Brazzleton goes with us across the river
thence to Joseph and Sally Shaws — thence to James Shaws — Wm. Waldrups — thence to Jas. Evans where believers assembled 40 in number —
thence to Enoch Davis's.

"Sab. 12. At Robt. Gills — held meeting — 100 spectators. Believers
went forth and labored 2 songs —

"Monday, 13. Wm. Price's — A number of world came in, we addressed them — thence to Smith Hansburys.

"Wednesday, 15. At John Youngmans — thence to Robt. Gills.

"Thursday, 16. Meeting — About half the Believers assembled in or
under great death and stupidity —went to Matthew Neelys.

"Friday, 17. All at Robt Gills.

"Sab. 19. At Robt. Houstons — Held meeting, 'mockers and scoffers walking after their own lusts' attended —

"Tuesday, 21. At Harry Prices a sensible Black man—

"Wednesday, 22. At Robt. Houston's — old and young John Slover and Nelly his wife from Red Banks came here —

* Famous Indian fighters.

"Thursday, 23. Meeting at R. Houstons — in the afternoon at Wm. Brazzletons — having left Richd at Roberts in order that he might start Saturday morning for Red Banks, Ky., to visit Believers there and counsel them respecting their removal to Busro — John Slover and Abm Jones to accompany him.

"Friday, 24. At Joseph Shaws — evening at James and Polly Shaws.

"Saturday, 25. At Wm. Waldrups and James Evans.

"Sabbath, 26. At Enoch Davis' — Held meeting — Two visitors exercised Wm. Hoag and wife—

"Monday, 27. At Jas. Duncans — John Fowlies or Fowlgers thence back to Charles Boyles' — Gabriel Burches to Anthony Tamis, east bank of Wabash — thence Jas. Duncans.

"March. At Jas. Hopkins — John Slovers — Nancy Jenkins.

"Saturday, 4. Robt. Gills.

"Sabbath, 5. Meeting at Robt. Gills.

"Wednesday, 8. Indians (Creek) at Robt. Houstons, were on their way to visit the Shawnee Prophet to find out if he was of God —

"Thursday, 9. Confession — Leoden Naulin opened his mind.

"Friday, 10. At Matthew Neelys—

"Saturday, 11. Crossed the Bayou on a raft — Went to Roberts thence to Leonard McReynolds—

"Sabbath 12. Meeting at Robt. Houstons — The waters of the Wabash overflowed its banks — Believers on the west side came as they could — some 4 or 5 miles — in canoes — on horses and wagons — After meeting to Robt. Gills.

"Wednesday, 15. One hundred and ten believers — assembled at Robt. Houstons and we made our last labors in this visit — Benj. and Issachar staid at Roberts' Richd at Matthew Neelys —

'Thursday, 16. We met at Nancy Jenkins — Thence to Robt Gills.

"Friday, 17. Wrote to J. McComb and the Brethren coming from Red Banks, Ky. — Having finished our labors here all things prepared — A number of Believers met with us at Robt. Gills, where we took our leave of them for Ohio — Having traveled here in Indiana abt 186 miles."

The missionaries left Busro on Saturday, the 18th, and arrived at Union Village, Wednesday, the 31st.

The prospects at Busro were now so brilliant that on August

29, Elder David Darrow, Arichbald Meecham, Solomon Henson, Ruth Darrow and Rachel Johnson, set out on horseback, from Union Village, to Busro and returned Sept. 24th. On Aug. 31, William and Rebecca Brazzleton and David Price, and on October 7, Joseph Shaw, Smith Hansborough, Leaden Noulen, James Neeley, James Price, Jenny Houston, Sarah Jenkins and Rachel Duncan arrived at Union Village from Busro on a visit, and started on their return the 17th. On December 12th, Issachar Bates, Richard McNemar and John Hancock leave Union Village for Busro, the last named to make his home there; January 27th, 1810, Archibald Meecham and Richard McNemar set out for Busro, and on May 10, to Union Village, accompanied by John Slover; June 12, Robt. Gill, Sarah Jenkins and Anne Hill arrived at Union Village from Busro. On September 13, Benjamin S. Youngs, Archibald Meacham and Calvin Morrell left Union Village for Busro and arrived at Robt. Gill's on the 18th; on the 19th visited the families of John Hancock, James Duncan, James Evans, James Shaw, Nancy Jenkins, Robert Houston, Joseph Shaw, Joseph Worthington, Charles Boyles, William Harris and Anthony Tanns; 20th, visited the residence of Benjamin, David, William and James Price, Smith Hansbury, Thomas Anderson and Zecharia Bowles; 24th, received the confession of Davis Hadden, a black man; 30th, spoke to about 20 spectators at William Brazzleton's; and on October 1st all were startled by rumors that they were to be expelled by a mob before the end of the month.

The journal again is continued:

"October 12. Robert Gill and Wm. Harris arrived from Ohio with 7 men and boys from Eagle Creek — some sheep and cattle — They lost in the wilderness 40 sheep and 5 head of cattle. They left Wm. Gallagher and John Edginton to hunt them.

"14. Wm. Gallagher and John Edginton arrived, bringing 53 sheep and two head of cattle.

"Thursday, 18. Rumors of war with the Indians is very great, they have forbidden the surveyors from further operations — Unless a kind providence interferes, the time is nigh at hand when we will undoubtedly see trouble.

"November 7. Surveying — 800 acres on the great Prairee—
Sabbath, 11. Meeting — Wm. Brazzleton spoke to spectators. It

is difficult here to get anything accomplished here, everything is in confusion — no lead — no order — every thing behind hand — vast fields of corn lie untouched — winter close at hand — no preparations to meet it."

This data brings us near the time of the consolidation of the Eagle and Straight Creek Believers with those at Busro, and, hence, we now rely on the journal of Samuel Swan McClelland.

"MEMORANDUM OF REMARKABLE EVENTS.

INTRODUCTION.

"On the first Sabath in August 1805 There was a camp-meeting[1] held in John Dunlavy's Congregation, on Eagle Creek, Adams County Ohio To which Elder Benjamin and Elder Issachar, went from Turtle Creek Warren County Ohio — During the course of the meeting They found an opportunity of opening the Testamony to the people — WHICH THEY DID. — And it was believed and received by a considerable number — Among the first of whom John Dunlavy was one — And from that period the gathering of a society of Believers went on with a gradual increas for about five years — During which time the Ministry spent much labour on the subject of makeing a permanent settlement in that place and after mature consideration, It was thought to be almost Impracticable.—

In the month of May 1810 Elder Solomon, and Elder Benjamin[2] — visited the believers at Eagle Creek, and first proposed the Idea of a general move — To Turtle Creek Ohio — Shawney run[3] Ky — Bosserun, Indiana and so forth — In June George Legier,[4] and William Gallagher, was appointed to go to the Wabash country and view the situation — and accordingly they went to the Big Prairie, on Bosserun Creek — and to the houses of Robert Gill — Robert Houston — Joseph Worthington — and others, where the Testamony had been openeed in June 1808 by Elder Issachar — Malcham Worley — John Dunlavy — Matthew Houston and James Hodge, and a society of considerable magnitude gathered to the faith of the Gospel — And after thus forming a short acquaintance with the place and people, They returned with a favourable report — It was then concluded and agreed on by all partyes — to rise with one consent and move to

those several places with the prospect of finding a more permanent Settlement for life — And accordingly — a part was-
distined to move to Union Village — a part to Pleasant Hill Ky.
— But far the greater part was distined for Bosseron (or Busro)
Indiana —

A company of Brethren was then selected to drive the cattle·
and sheep to Busro, a distance of about 300 miles — which they
did and mowed Prairy grass for their winters forage — Two
of them stayed to feed and take care of the stock — and all the·
rest returned home — They next, proceeded to sell off their lands·
and other immoveable property, which was the principal business, of the latter part of the summer and fall of 1810. —

Early in the winter of 1811 they began to make calculations
and preparations for the journey — The commencement of which
was the beginning of the following short

"MEMORANDUM OF REMARKABLE EVENTS —

By

SAMUEL SWAN MCCLELLAND.[5]

"Beginning in January 1811, and Ending in March 1827.

'A MEMORANDUM OF REMARKABLE EVENTS — 1811.

During the month of January boats were prepared and brought
from Maysville down to the mouth of Red Oak, where they were har-
boured and held in readiness for the reception of the property.—

During the month of February the people were mostly employed
in making preparations for the journey — Such as packing up what they
intended to take with them, and disposing of other articles to the people
of the country — The hauling was chiefly done in about two weeks —
altho the distance was from 9 to 11 or 12 miles — All things now appeared to be as nearly ready as possible — and on the 4th ·of March
The Keel boat and one flat boat set sail for the mouth of Wabash —
They stopped at Jeffersonvile, unloaded and set up the waggons —
(the horses having gone by land) so that on the 9th three waggons with
seven families started from Jeffersonville for Busro, a distance of 120·
miles, where they arrived safe on the 16th — 26th Elder Archbald
Meacham[6] and James Hodge arrived on the Big Prairie at Busro.

The boats went on to the mouth of the Wabash — where the Keel-
boat received all that was in the flat boat, except one pair of Millstones

which was left on the bank, and afterwards was sold—The Keel boat went on up the Wabash to the mouth of Busro — which the French boatsmen said was 200 miles — where they arrived safe on the 29th —

As there was but few accounts kept of the journey of the first company that went to Busro — we will now look back to the 20th of March and start with the second company of boats.

March 20th. Eldress Ruth Darrow[7] and Saloma Dennis[8] with James Price and Samuel McClelland started from Union Village for Cincinnati in order to meet the second company of boats which was to come on from the mouth of redoak — We arrived in the city before night and put up at the Columbian Inn — where we remained till 8 o'clock on the morning of the 22nd when the boats landed, and all went on board — We bought another boat and made some arrangements in the loading — And pushed off late in the afternoon — We landed for the night on the Kentucky shore, just below the mouth of Big Miami —

23rd. We pushed off early — the day quite unpleasant — we landed just about dark at a house on the Indiana shore — The Elder sisters with a few others stayed in the house — This was the dreadfulest night of wind, thunder, lightning, and rain that we had remembered of seeing — the river raised eight feet plum water —

24th. We pushed off about 8 o'clock with a fair wind down the river, but a great bend soon caused the wind to blow quartering up — which drove us violently against the Kentucky shore about 10 o'clock, where we were compelled to stay all day and night — this was Sabbath.

25th. We pushed off about 6 o'clock in the morning — passed the mouth of Kentucky river at one — went on 34 miles below and harhoured all our boats in the mouth of a small creek on the Kentucky shore. The day was clear and pleasant and we had a comfortable night's rest —

26th. We pushed off at 6 and landed at Jeffersonville at 2 — Stayed about two hours and then passed over the falls and landed just below for the night — some rain fell, the boats were crowded and lodging uncomfortable.

27th. Eldress Ruth and Saloma, with James Hodge[9] and Wm. Price set off from Jeffersonville for Busro — We lowered our boats to the mouth of Silver Creek — and with our Battau and Pereauger commenced boating the property to a landing 3 miles up the creek where the waggons could receive it — the river very high and the low grounds all covered with water, so that our passage was much obstructed by the drift wood—

28th. Continued boating property up to the landing all day — and as we returned the last time night came on, and it was cloudy and dark. We got lost among the drift wood, and run aground in an old field where we were obliged to leave our boats and make the best of our way through water and mud, logs and brush to our camp at the mouth of the creek —

'29th. We found our battau Perogue in the old field and the water had fallen away from them and left them some distance on the land. However we put them off and brought them round to the camp — And in them and two flat boats we loaded up the rest of the plunder, and pushed off about 9 o'clock — The waggons also started from the landing on Silver creek for Busro — With two flat boats, battau and Perogue all lashed together we floated along pleasantly — passed the mouth of Salt river at 2 o'clock. Concluded to sail all night — about 3 o'clock in the morning we run on the head of an Island, and were quickly obliged to cut the lashing of our boats, when they immediately parted and one went on either side of the Island, and could not get together again till after sun rise.

30th. We floated along pleasantly all day and landed for the night seven miles above the yellow banks — This day Eldress Ruth — Saloma — James and William arrived at Busro —

31st, Sabbath. We floated well till about 11 o'clock when the wind raised violently against us, so that we were obliged to land, which was quite difficult on account of the water overflowing so much of the banks — here we lay the balance of the day and night.

April 1st. The wind still blowing some — however we pushed off early passed the mouth of green river about 9 — The wind ceased, the river became smooth and we had a fine day — Passed the Red-banks about one o'clock — and landed for the night just below the Dimond Islands — the bottoms nearly all covered with water —

2nd. Floated on without interruption till about 2 o'clock, when we landed about half a mile above the mouth of Wabash — that spot being the only dry ground within that distance — the bottoms being chiefly covered with water. Here we lay the balance of the day and night —

3d. We made some preparations for loading the Keel boat — which come to us in the evening with a rugged set of hands on board, having come from Busro in three days — a heavy rainfall this night —

4th. Loaded the Keel boat, Battau and perogue — made some oars and other preparations for ascending the Wabash — left the two flat boats at the landing and about 3 o'clock — all set sail for Busro — we encamped for the night on the Bonebank 9 miles from the mouth of Wabash —

5th and 6th. We moved along up the river about 12 by pulling the oars and brush — the river is very high, so that we can not use the poles, except to spike a tree once in a while — Heavy thunder and rain a good part of the night —

7th. All wet this morning — however we put off and got along 10 or 11 miles by spikeing the trees and halling brush —

8th. We pulled up 9 or 10 miles by the brush — The second company of waggons arrived at Busro this day.

9th. Went through the lower cut-off. This was a very hard day's

work tho' the distance is but 3 or 4 miles — but the water was so very
rapid, but it counted 15 miles by the way of the river —

10th and 11th.   We made out to get along about 15 miles.   The
water very swift and the wind blowing down the river.

12th and 13th.   Nothing material — we got along by hard work —

14th.   Sabbath — passed coffee Island and encamped on the west
bank of Wabash opposite the mouth of White river.

15th.   Passed over the grand rapids — went on 14 miles and encamped just below the mouth of River DeChee —

16th.   Pushed on 12 miles and encamped just above mouth of the
river L Emborres or (Annbrau) fine weather and the river has fallen
so much that we use the poles on the sand bars pritty well —

17th.   Pushed on and landed at Vincennes at 3 o'clock and after
resting about an hour we pushed on 4 miles and stopped for the night
on the west bank —

18th.   Pushed on and landed at the mouth of Busro about 4 o'clock
— and after resting a few minutes — pushed on up the creek about 3
miles and landed for the last time at that well known spot called the
Boat landing —

19th.   The boat and other crafts were all unloaded and the property halled to the settlement about six miles — Thus the journey ended
on the 19th of April, 1811 —

20th.   And so on — unpacking, regulating and distributing — people
and property till all were settled and ready for business, etc., etc. —

The Eagle creek and Busro were now united in one splendid community as far as local situations would admit of — The principal gathering was on Robert Gills[10] place, where the meeting house also stood and
was considered the center of the society — As the upper (or Prices)[11]
settlement lay about 4 miles off a little North of East — And the lower
settlement where Robert Houston — Joseph Worthington and a number of
other families lived, lay about 3 miles off a little west of South and
near the banks of Busro creek — The first family lived in two houses a
short distance apart, and was styled George Legier's family, where the
elders also lived, and were busy all the while makeing arangements for
the comfort and satisfaction of the people all round—

21st.   Wm. Price come to live in the family —

23rd.   Peggy Knox[12] come to live in the family — And so the
month of April passed away —

May.   The people all being settled the summer work was commenced which was mostly farming — The principle care of which was
consigned to George Leegier for that family.   They had 150 acres of
the big Prairy in cultivation and raised a great quantity of produce.

27th.   John Youngman removed from James Duncan's to John
Knoxes family —

June 10th.   Polly Edie came to live in the center family, which

then consisted of 72 members — the whole society was something over
300, — Dates of Arivels and departures, of brethren going to, or coming from other societyes, was taken but little notice of in those days, the
general Idea was, when any one or more would come, that everybody was
glad to see them — and a great-dale of love to be handed round — and
frequently some new songs to learn — And that was the end of the
matter —

However about this time Elder Issachar[13] came to Busro to Abide
with Elder Archabald — One hewed log house was finished with four
rooms, and all seemed to be going well for the present —

About the first week in June some few were taken sick with fevers
— And on the 17th Anthony Tann[14] (coloured man) Departed this life
leaving Peggy (his wife and a white woman) with six children among
the believers — This was the first death that occurred after the Eagle
creek people was settled in the Prairy — his age was not accurately known.
Elder Joseph Allen[15] and Tilar Baldwin Arived at Busro some time
near about the first of August for the purpose of building a saw mill and
on the 22nd the work was commenced under their direction —

August 25th. Tamer Handcock Departed this life — quite an aged
woman.

30th. Mariah Britton Departel this life — a little girl in the 5th
year of her age —

Elder Archebald had went to Union Village some timeinSeptem-
ber, and on the 30th he returned with William Davis[16] Peggy Stewart
and Patience Naylor[17] — if the account be correct.

October 11th. By the fall of a large piece of timber Samuel Mc-
Clelland had the three forefingers of his left hand stripped of the flesh
to the bones from the second joint to the ends —

October 18th. Joseph Allen, Filer Baldwin and Enoch Davis set
off for Jasper Spring (South Union, Ky).

During the summer the rumor of an Indian war was sometimes almost frightful — reports was frequently industerously sirculated that they
were collected at different places and were expected on in a few days,
with all the distruction common to their kind of war-fare — But none
of those false prophecyes come to pass.

In July Governor Harrison appointed a treaty at Vincennes[18] which
amounted to but little good — for the Indians went away about as Ill-
humored as they came — A company of rangers followed them to see
them safe out of the settlement.

Some time in September the Indians stole four of our best waggon
horses (the team that was halling timber at the mill) and as soon as
it found to a certainty how and which way they were gone — James
Brownfield (the waggoner) and Abraham Jones a coloured man and
a Linguist, with a hired man by the name of Robins — started with two
horses to follow them (but without firearms) and get the horses upon

peaceable terms if they could — And after traveling two days and half they overtook the Indians and found the horses — Abram told them that they had come for the horses, that they had no guns, and would not fight, &c., &c. — But the Indians gave no satisfaction. They would not talk much but appeared to be mad and was very busy fixing their guns, &c. However after a short time the brethren loosed the horses, made ready and started as quick as possible — each man having two horses to take care of.

After they had got about the distence of three miles they discovered the Indians coming after them with speed — They immediately started to make every possible exertion to keep out of their way — But after running some 7 or 8 miles through a long Prairy the horses began to get short of breath — and having a kind of flag swamp to cross before they could find any chance of hiding themselves — the time began to get too short for the distence — they being so far dun out they could hardly get their feet out of the mud — The Indians got close enough to fire on them, but as none of them got shot and the prospect of saveing the horses any longer was out of the question — and fearing that another flash of the gun might put an end to the contest (on their part) about horses and every thing else * * * They jumped off and made to the brush with all possible speed — leaving all the horses with their saddles, saddle bags, blankets, big coats and provision — The mud in the swamp robed them of their shoes — and in their extreem haste to save their lives they some how lost their hats — And after six days hard fatigue they got home pritty well famished and almost naked, by the action of the brush and briers on their few remaining clothes — And was then compelled to sustain the loss of six horses — besides all disappointments —

About this time the militia were called on to go a three month tower of duty up the Wabash, and I (Samuel) was drafted just at the time that my hand was useless from the hurt that my fingers had got on the 11th of October. The officer ordered me to attend according to malitia rules, which I refused telling him that my hand was entirely useless — but notwithstanding they took advantage of my absence more than a year afterwards, held a court martial — and fined me 30 dollars — and then abated 10 on account of my lame hand — And so went on, executed and sold — of my tools enough to pay the fine of 20 dollars —

Next an army of 1400[19] men was raised and marched on to Busro — they encamped on Snaps Prairy about one mile from our meeting house and our afflictions on this occation could not be easily described — However in a few days they marched on up the Wabash — and on the 7th of November the Battle of Tippecanoe was fought — after which they soon returned with many wounded — and all greatly fatigued — we give them all the comfortable usage we could — and they went on to Vincennes —

In November — some Brethren went to Smalls Mill on Ambran
with the Keel boat — cut timber, sawed plank, and brought home enough
to plank up the breast of the Dam — which was done and the business of
the mill pursued as fast as circumstances would admit of —

On the 16th of December the whole nation was suddenly awakened
at 2 o'clock in the morning — By the shakeing of the Earth — there was
two more shakes after daylight tho not so heavy as the first —
These occurrences about closed the year 1811.

1812.

* The beginning of this year may be singularised by the shakeing of
the Earth, which occurred so frequently that it would be boath tedious
and useless to have noted every one — On the 14th of February two
hours before day, was the heavyest shake that was felt on the Wabash
— A number of Brick Houses were cracked and the tops of some chimneys fell off, &c —

From correct information we learn that the shaking occurs almost
daily in New Madrid[20] — that the Earth motion appears to be about 12
Inches horizontaly, in a North and South direction — That large casms
can be seen in many directions — some of which are a mile or more in
length — from which muddy water and sulphurious vapors sometimes
ishue most frightfully and almost strong enough to suffocate the inhabitants —

Nothing material took place during the months of January and
February the shaking excepted — which was felt occasionally all winter —

The following few lines was taken from a newspaper and was an
extract of a letter from a man in South America — City of Carracces [21]—

March 1812 "The affects of the shaking in this part of the country
is truly distressing — On the 26th of March there was ten thousand ΔIn-
habitants perished in a few minutes. in the city of Carracces — besides
several other villages that was totaly distroyed. Two thousand five hundred perished in Laguira — four more shocks were felt on the night following. but not so hard as to do any material damage — On the 27th
the survivers were imployed in diging the dead bodies from under the
ruins and puting them in large lighters and carrying them outside of
the shipping and burying them in the Sea — On the 28th the sea was so
rough as to prevent them from taking off the dead — they even built large
fires near the wharf, and commenced burning them — about forty at a
time on one fire — On the 29th the stench had become so bad that they
quit diging the dead from under the ruins — All the survivers pitched
tents on the plains ot Magetere — The vessels trembled as if they had
been on a reef of rocks in a heavy sea — And from on board the Independence the mountains were seen to move and large peices to cleave off
them. The accounts were more lengthy than this — I only took down a
few of the most particular circumstances — See MS.

March 3d The sawmill finished and started to work — The school-house was now on hands and was finished about the first of May — and on the 3d Thadeous Jenkins Departed this life aged 12 or 13 years — having a few weeks previous got one of his knees badly hurt by being struck against a tree when riding on a horse — he took cold, his thigh healed — was opened — and after a long tour of sore sufferings it cost him his life —

May 7th. The children were gathered to the schoolhouse — 75 Boys and 56 girls — with a suitable number of Brethren and Sisters to take care of them — the house was double — of hewd logs and two stories high with four spacious rooms — and a stack of chimneys between —

In June — The Fever began to invade the Society in different quarters. and some began to get verry sick — On the 18th the President of the United States declared War against great Britain — The news of which, together with rumors of Indian war. and our settlement being almost the very frontier — added no little to our fears of impending danger — The fever went on with increasing violence till numbers were brought under sore and unusual sufferings — and some even unto death —

July 16th. Joseph Worthington Departed this life in the 49th year of his age — leaving Betsy and six children among believers

— 28th. Pheby Sparks Departed this life — a single woman — age not known exactly but must have been something near 30 —

August 1st. William Gallagher Departed this life in the 63d year of his age — leaving Rebecca and eight children among the believers.

12th. William Brazelton Departed this life in the 35 year of his age — leaving Rebecca and two children among believers.

From the 13th to the 18th A frame house was raised just below the sawmill — on the same side of the creek — two storyes high — intended for a grist mill — but was afterwards moved away and used for a shop —

Fevers still raging — the same that were taken first are getting a little better —

— 28th. David Edic. Departed this life some time in Augus Eldress Rachel[22] and Calvin Morrel[23] arrived at Busro — War — with the British and Indians — was the general talk in the country — To which our faith and practice was entirely opposed — And of course we need not build forts, unless we intende to defend them — And our settlement was almost the very frontier — All these circumstances (and a great many more) had their baring to our general center — which was that we had better abandon the ground in peace than to stay and fight for it. or even to run the risk of being insulted and abused by malitia troops — or of being massacreed by the Indians —

The spirit and feeling of those times can not be written at all — let it therefore suffice to say — That after much and difficult labour among the Elders and people — It was conclude best for us to quit the place altogather for the present —

19

Malitia troops were now almost dayly collecting — they made their encampment in the comons close by our houses — In, and out, of which they come and went without molestation — and without regart to even common good behaviour — Our gardens and fields were rich and afforded plenty for them and their horses — Our cattle and hogs they butchered and destroyed in a most savage wasteful manner —

While all this (and a great deal more) was going on we were very industriously imployed in preparing for our journey — and right in hurry the Press Gang come on and seized a number of our horses some saddles and some axes — as they were in haste to get up to Fort Harrison it being then besieged by the Indians — This circumstance caused us considerable trouble by breaking our teams &c.

However we got up some riding horses — some plow horses — and some oxen — with all of which we were only able to start fourteen wagons.

The Keel-boat and Perogue was prepared at the mouth of Busro — and property enough halled to load them — after which the waggons were all prepared for the roads and all were busy packing up and loading and making all possible speed to leave the ground —

On Monday 14th of September Elder Issachar and Joseph Lockwood,[24] started to Union Village in order to have the council of the Church conveyed to us some place on the road as soon as convenient that we might know how far to proceed —

All things now appeared to be as nearly ready as it was possible to get them — for the baggage was increasing every hour. and at last it seemed as tho we were leaving almost every thing torn to wreck and in a fair-way for being lost — However William Davis and some other Brethren stayed on the ground to take care of what ever they could among the tumultious multitude — The army was soon increased to about 1000 — our houses was converted to Barracks. our nurcerys into horse lots, and our fields into race grounds — In short the whole place looked as tho' a host of Pharos plages had passed over it —

And on Tuesday 15 of September 1812[25].. we hoisted our baggage and started for Kentucky — Red banks — Calvin Morrel — Eldress Rachel and Peggy Houston had come from Union Village some time in August — had stayed till the general move took place, and concluded to go the rounds with us.[26]

The whole camp consisted of about 300 human souls — 250 head of sheep — 100 head of cattle — 14 waggons — and one Keel boat — and Perianger — and one canoe —

The waggons were so crowded with plunder that it was difficult for the sick to be taken along with any tolerable degree of comfort — tho' a number of sick went on board of the boat —

As the company is now divided the journal must appear in two columns — the first will show a sketch of the movement of the waggons

— and the second of the boat — so that we can see where and what each company was about on the same day.

SEPTEMBER

1812.

OF THE WAGGONS.

— 15th. The waggons, foot company cattle and sheep, all started about 9 o'clock — Traveled about ten miles and encamped for the night — The sick were now quite uncomfortably situated having exchanged their houses and beds, for camps and bunks in the woods —

— 16th. Went on at a slow rate and encamped for the night four miles .below Vincennes —

Some of the sick appeared as tho' they could not live much longer —their sufferings were almost extreme —and probably, but for Eldress Rachel, they might have been buried in the wilderness.

— 17th. Traveled about 9 miles to white river which we got over safe bag and baggage. for 18 dollars — a little more than half price — the sick are still suffering — Tho' the appearance is not much different yesterday —

— 18th. Left White river and went on as fast as we could — the weather very warm and distressing to .the sick —

OF THE BOATS.

— 15th. The Keel boat, Perogue and canoe, started from the mouth of Busro about 3 o'clock in the afternoon — and floated down to Old Fort Knox and encamped for the night just below The soldiers fired a gun to bring us too —

— 16th. We floated along till in the evening. the river being very low we got fast on a shole and had to unload and encamped on the Lousiana shore.

— 17th. We loaded up and left camp about 8 o'clock — got fast of sholes a number of times in the cours of the day— and had to lift our boats over them with poles and handspikes

— 18th. We floated along till in the afternoon — when we got fast at the place called the Little Rock — and after working in the water about two hours, with poles and handspikes we found it impossible to get the boat over — And then began to unload, and had to take the plunder about a mile down the river before we could find water deep enough to carry the boat to shore — when dark came we were obliged to leave the boat fast in

OF THE WAGGONS.

— 19th. We moved along slowly the weather is very warm — and some of the sick are very low — the cattle and sheep much fatigued with the hot weather

— 20th. Nobody dead yet — tho' some of the sick are a good-deal worse — and some are geting a little better —

Fanny Price was so far gone that we did not expect she would live till morning —

21st. Fanny Price could not bear to ride any further in the

OF THE BOATS.

the rocks all night — encamped on the Indiana shore

— 19th. Continued unloading till the boat was light enough to pass over the shole — and down to the landing —

By examining the river below we found it would be impossible for the boat to pass the sholes with all her load on board — We then went down the river about 2 miles and hired a horse-boat and large Perianger, which we brought up. and loaded — then pushed off altogether and made the best of our way down to and over Ramseys Ripple — through which we had to wade and lead the boat — because the water was so low and the channel so crooked by that time it was night and we had got along only about 2 miles — for that day —

— 20th. We found we could not pass the grand-rapids without some assistance and for that purpose we kept possession of the horse boat and perogue — and hired four hands to go with us as far as the mouth of white river — the distance was 9 miles. 6 of which was quite rocky and bad and the last three is occupied by the Grand Rapids — We had a very fatigueing days work — great part of the time in the water — and just before sunset we landed a little below the mouth of white river — where we unloaded the two hired crafts for the use of which and the four hired men we paid nine dollars and they started home and we encamped for the night —

— 21st. Loaded up and pushed off in pretty good spirits — we had

OF THE WAGGONS.

waggon — we then made a horse litter and carried her to the Ohio river — where we arrived about the middle of the day

Mars, the ferry man was very cleaver. he give us his flat and canoe and told us to get over as cheap as we could — the brethren made him a present of four sheep and he appeared to be well pleased — We commenced crossing and kept the boat a going till near midnight —

— 22d. The boat was early in motion and kept a going all day

— 23d. We continued running the boat all day and just about dark we got all safe landed on the Kentucky shore. 3½ miles above the Red-banks — Town of Henderson —

— 24th. The malitia troops were crossing over to the Indiana at the same time that we were crossing to Kentucky, but as they had crossed at the Red banks, they had to come up the river to Marses and cross again before they could come to us — And accordingly t h e y marched up to the ferry and called a halt, and ordered the ferry man to set them over — which he did, and in a short time there was 40 of them landed close by our encampment[27]

And after makeing ready they marched into camp, and said they had orders to press 80 Blankets — but in this they were disappointed for the boat had not yet arriven, and the most of such plunder was on board of it —

OF THE BOATS.

to wade and help the boat over a number of shallow places in the cours of the day — but we got along without unloading —

— 22d. We made all the speed we could among the rocks and logs — and by close attention and hard work we got along safe —

— 23d. The water quite shallow but we got along safe by close watching

— 24th. We pushed on to the Grand-chain which was the last dangerous looking rapids we had to pass, which we did with care and good attention, and encamped for the night just below.

However they plundered about till they found 16 which they praised themselves — and left an order on the Paymaster for 71 dol-- lars — $4,4¾ cents a piece — which was afterwards paid

— 25th. We removed our encampment down the river to within 2½ miles of the town — where we found plenty of cane for the cattle — and to make tents of — The sick are some times better, and some of them are recovering —

— 26th. Nothing material — our chief employment was fixing our tents, and takeing care of the sick

— 27th. We are still fixing and most of whom are getting better — trying to take care of our selves as well as we can — John McComb arrived from Busro — and said the army was makeing sad distruction all over the place —

— 28th. A heavy rain fell this morning two hours before day which wet almost every thing in camp — The rain ceased a little after daylight and the day was mostly clear, and all hands were busy drying wet clothes and furniture

The boat landed about 10 o'clock at night —

— 25th. We went on passed the little chain and with some difficulty made our way to the mouth of wabash and got into the Ohio about the middle of the day — pushed up a short distance and encamped for the night

— 26th. Pushed on without much difficulty

— 27th. Pushed on passed the Dimond Island and camped for the night 15 miles below the Red-banks

— 28th. A while before day we were suddenly awakened by a heavy shower of rain and against daylight our camping ground was all afloat with water — about 9 o'clock the rain ceased, the clouds broke away and we had a fair afternoon — We pushed on within sight of the town before sun set. We had warning of the Press Gang and stoped till nearly dark, then pushed up on the opposite side of the river very silently and crossed over to the camp at about 10 o'clock —

— 29th. We are now all together and all most every thing wet with the rain for the boat had no cover on it only what was made by coverlets and such kins of cloths —

John Woods arrived from Union Village — with the good news of love and incouragement from the Church —

Samuel G. Whyte arrived from South Union with another message of love and good feeling to all the suffering Pilgrims — all of which felt quite refreshing and animating to us at the present[28]

— 30th. Six of the Brethren started back to Busro on some business

October 1st. Nothing material — our chief imployment was fixing our tents — taking care of the stock, and provideing something to live on for our plentifull fields and gardens were at Busro and the disorganized malitia rideing over them without remorse —

A heavy rain fell last night which rendered our situation more uncomfortable — so much stuff wet and all to handled over, and over till it was dryed — and the ground wet and muddy — the sick were in quite a disagreeable situation —

By this time we understood that the council of the Church at Union Village was, for us to move on by the way of South Union Logan county Ky, a distance of 112 miles from the red banks, thence on to Pleasant Hill Mercer County K. y. 40 miles from South Union and so on to Union Village Warren County Ohio — 150 miles from Pleasant Hill —[29]

It now became necessary to send back to Busro for some property that had been left — for so it happened that, in the hustle that there was more halled to the boat than could possibly be put on board of it — and so a great part of the beding of our pritty large family — and a great part of the wareing cloths of another was left — For which James Brownfield started back to Busro on the

— 2d of October and took some horses with him intending to get some more horses there that had been returned by the Press gang of the first company that had went up to the relief of Fort Harrison. And so pack as many horses as he could manage with such articles as were most needed at the present — At the same time some of them were makeing shingles and puting a roof on the boat and preparing it for ascending the Ohio river to Cincinnati — And on the

7th Joel Shields and James Neely arrived from Pleasant Hill with two big waggons and five horse teams — And besides 1500 pounds of flour they brought us many blessings of love and friendship. for all of which we felt very thankful — for we could not get flour in the settlement even for the sick and weakly —

8th. The waggons were partly put together and nearly ready to start — The boat is also loaded and ready to push off — All were now waiting for the return of James and the rest of the brethren from busro — We felt anxious to leave the Camping ground — in consequence of being afraid of the Press gang — Our cattle and horses were all scattered and concealed among the cane — and part of the waggon wheels taken off and rolled into the water — so that we were all the time in jeopardy —

Friday, 9th, the waggons and foot people, with the cattle and sheep, all started — leaving the Elders with a few others to wait the return of James and the rest of the Brethren from Busro —

— 10th. All the Brethren returned but James — He had hired a waggon and was fetching on a load of those articles which he intended to pack on horses when he started to Busro —

And so Elder Archabald, Eldress Ruth, and Eldress Rachel, with some that had just come from Busro, started on after the waggons — and left the boat ready to start the next day — and the load that James was comeing with had to be left in store at Squire Marses — The ferryman —

So the waggon and foot people started on friday and the boat started on sunday following — and the journal must now go on in two columns as it was begun —

OF THE WAGGONS.

October 9th after we left camp about a mile one of the waggons over-set, with one of the Sisters on board of it — but she was not hurt nor any thing broke — it was soon set up and in motion again — we went on about 7 miles and encamped for the night —

— 10th. The road was very muddy, and it was with difficulty that we got along about 13 miles

— 11th. Just after we left camp, a heavy rain came on, and in about an hour the foot people were all dripping wet. and the road extremely muddy and bad — an other waggon over set, but without any material damage — The ground and woods was so wet at night that it was difficult to get fires a going, and a great part of the night was spent in drying wet clothing — lodging uncomfortable —

— 12th. Some time after we left camp two of the oxen give out in the yoke, which caused some delay — however two horses were procured to supply their places, and so went on till night

OF THE BOATS.

October 11th. With a fair wind and a good sail well rigged, we pushed off from the old encampment — and with 36 passengers on board we stemed the current of Ohio 24 miles all in good glee — except the rain made some what against us — tho' not much

— 12th. We had to put our shoulders to the poles, and by hard pushing we got along 15 miles —

SUSANNAH COLE LIDDELL.

OF THE WAGGONS.

— 13th. After we had left camp about a mile the oxen that had been released from the yoke were missing — which caused a halt of about an hour, and considerable hunting — however they were found, and we moved along slowly — till near camping time, when the rain began to fall freely — we had a wet night and bad lodging —

— 14th. All wet this morning. boath Bed and wearing clothes — the rain still increasing — the road extremely muddy and slippry — The foot people have a very disagreeable tramp of it indeed — we traveled only 7 miles this day, and stoped for the night at Mager Willsons, who was very clever — he let us put the cattle in an vacant field, and give us all the shelter he could boath in his house and horsemill — so that we were tolerably accommodated —

— 15th. Soon after we started from Willsons we met Matthew Houston[30] and Samuel Whyte just from South Union with four led horses, on which some who were the most needy. Set of for South Union immediately —

About the middle of the day we met Francis Whyte and Robert Gray from South-Union with a waggon nearly loaded with provision — They brought a quantity of the largest sweet potatoes we had ever seen —

About two hours before night the rain began to fall bountifully, which prevented us from getting but little good of our fires till after midnight — We encamped at a meeting house in which all the chil-

OF THE BOATS.

— 13th. We pushed on 14 miles. had some rain through the day and a wet uncomfortable night — Our Perianger, we find is somewhat troublesome

— 14th. We had to lay too all day on account of the rain were kindly treated by a clever Old man and two of the brethren helped to make a coffin for a woman that had died in the settlement — Here we got some potatoes —

— 15th. A wet disagreeable day to walk the runing boards of a keel-boat — however we pushed off early and poled along about 10 miles and encamped for the night—

OF THE WAGGONS.

dren and most of the sick found
shelter from the rain — about one
O. clock the rain began to slack,
and we made up our fires and began to dry our clothes, so that by
daylight we had got tolerably well
dryed —

— 16th. Against 8 o. clock all
were on the road and in motion,
and in pretty good spirits — one
waggon wheel broke down, which
caused some difficulty, but soon
started again — About two o. clock
Samuel Whyte met us the second
time with nine led horses — which
was a great relief to the foot people — we traveled 14 miles — the
day was clear and pleasant

— 17th. Early this morning the
wheels were all in motion and went
on well too, for just about sunset
we arrived safe at Jasper Spring
where our kind friends received us
with every degree of friendship
they possibly could manifest — they
devided familyes—moved into close
quarters and cleared out some of
their mechanical shops to make
room for us — In short they done
every thing in reason to get us all
into their houses — ror all of which
we felt very thankful — for it was
the first spot that we had found
to rest on, in any kind of peace,
since the 15th of September — The
weather clear and fine —

— 18th. We are now, all at
South Union among strange people,
which many of us never saw before — but notwithstanding all that
— we were cordially entertained
among them for three days free of
all expenses on our part — A number of our horses were shod —

OF THE BOATS.

— 16th. Pretty hard poling but
we got along slowly — We sold
our Perogue for 9 dollars and was
glad to get clear of it — for it had
become troublesome —

— 17th. Pushed off early and
went on well till in the afternoon,
when we met with some difficulty
by running on logs that was partly
concealed in the water however we
got through without receiving any
injury — it was late before we
could get to shore, and then had to
camp among the rocks after pushing 15 miles —

— 18th. We had some fair wind
up the river — of which we were
very glad for it floated us along
pleasantly about 15 miles Some of
the company are yet afflicted with
chills and fevers —

OF THE WAGGONS.

some of our waggons repaired —
our shoes were mended, and more
such like deeds of charitable kindness, than could be writen on many
sheets of paper — for all of which
we surely felt very thankful —

On this occasion the four following short lines were written by one
who had more feeling than poetical
genius of expression —

What thanks to our friends do we
    owe
Their love we shall ever retain
We cannot forget all their kindness
    bestowed
Though we should nere see them
    again   William Douglass —

Here we received a very great
pledge of love from Union Village
— Elder Peter Peas,[31] with three
other brethren came to our assistance with four waggons — some
barrels of bread and biscuit—some
bags of shoes &c. besides many
other blessings of love and encouragement from the Church —
for all of which we surely felt very
thankful to our good friends —

Our company was somewhat reduced at South Union — some being sick and not very well able to
travel — After mature consideration
it was concluded for 30 to stop and
make South Union their home[32] —
The sheep were also left —

— 20th. Early this morning all
were in motion, we began to hoist
our baggage and make ready for
the road — And after taking a kind
and affectionate fare-well of our
strange friends. and those of our
own company that stayed at South

OF THE BOATS.

— 19th. We had some wind by
the help of which and the good use
of our poles and oars we got along
about 12 miles during the night we
caut some fish — which helped to
make us a good breakfast next
morning —

— 20th. After taking a good
breakfast, we pushed off, and poled
15 miles. our hunters killed five
turkeys And the boarding appart-
ment was surely well directed by
the Sisters on board — for which
they have our sincere thanks —

OF THE WAGGONS.

Union — we marched out to the road and started for Pleasant Hill — soon after we started the rain began to fall — which continued all day — the road was muddy and walking quite disagreeable — we traveled 15 miles to Big Barron river, and got about half the waggons over before dark — and so we encamped on boath sides of the river —

— 21st. The remaining part of the waggons were got over, and after breakfast we moved along 16 miles and encamped for the night in the barrons

— 22d. One material circumstance that affords us considerable comfort, ought to be noted here — which is this, that the weather and road is both very good — this occurence is almost entirely new — We traveled 17 miles —

— 23d. The road and weather is still good and we have got along tolerably well —

— 24th. Nothing material — we

OF THE BOATS.

— 21st. Passed Blue river Island, had very strong waters and by hard pushing we got along 12 miles — and stopt for the night —

— 22d. We had some fair wind which helped us along considerable. This day may be remembered by a little scrap that took place between us and another boats crew — We overtook them, but soon found that they would not admit us to go before, and we did not want to be laging behind, neither did we like their company — And in order to get clear of them on reasonable terms, we concluded to cross the river — which they soon discovered — and started across too — they found we were going ahead and strove to give us a broad side with the bow of their boat — W. P. threw a spike pole at her stem, but missed his aim and fell overboard — but soon got in again — And after exchanging a few boat-mens compliments — we pushed off and saw them no more — we made out 23 miles — a good days push —

— 23d. Fine weather and all in good spirits we pushed along 18 miles — and encamped —

— 24th. We had some pritty

OF THE WAGGONS.

moved along tolerable well till we passed over 21 miles of the hills and valleys of Kentucky — and encamped for the night —

— 25th. Was rather a wet day, tho not with heavy rain — the road somewhat muddy — but we got along pritty well — some 10 or 15 miles — we encamped half a mile from the road, in order to get forage for the horses and cattle more convenient — had a shower of rain in the night — which disturbed us some little —

— 26th. We traveled 15 miles, crossed Mulders Hill—the day was rather wet and disagreable — whe had an uncomfortable night — chills and fevers returned on some that had got nearly well —

— 27th. Nothing material, the road muddy and slippry — all in pretty good spirits, and got along tolerable well considering —

— 28th. One of t h e waggon wheels broke down — the load was distributed among the other waggons — and as the body was much woren we concluded to burn it with the broken wheel and save the Irons—This day we had to face a cold Northwest Storm of wind and rain — the road was very bad. and we made but little progress —we encamped early at a convenient

OF THE BOATS.

strong water — and very hard pushing to get along 10 miles — Some rain — This evening we landed just below the Falls — more than half our journey is over —

— 25th. We lay by all day just below the Falls, rested what we could, and made some preparations for geting up over the falls as soon as we could —

— 26th. Unloaded the boat and got the loading halled round the Falls — and run the boat up by the poles and cord — Ell — then loaded up and started again but did not go far, for we were ·much fatigued. We find it a laborious job to take a keel boat up over the falls of Ohio —

— 27th. In consequence of the rain we lay by all day at Jeffersonville — here we found a Perogue and some other property that we had left in store when moveing to busro in 1811 — we put some of the property on board of the Perogue — and left some yet in store. for which we took a receipt —

— 28th. We pushed off early and with the help of some wind we got up as far as the 18 mile Island — and encamted for the night — all in pritty good spirits — tho' midling tired —

OF THE WAGGONS.

place — and before dark another waggon, from Pleasant Hill came to our assistence — which was a great relief to some of the sick, and was thankfully received

— 29th. A number are very sick — the roads very bad — but considering all diffcultys we got along tolerable well — And arrived at Pleasant Hill about 2 o. clock. where our good friends received us very kindly. and treated us with much friendship during our stay —

— 30th. We stayed at Pleasant Hill all day rested and refreshed ourselves as far as circumstances would admit — the sick was carefully attended to — Some of our waggons was repared some of our horses shod — and a number of other repares and preparations for the remaining part of our journey were bestowed upon us by our strange friends at Pleasant Hill —

Also Louis Willhite with one of their waggons went on with us to Union Village for all of which we felt very thankful, more so than could be expressed by words.

— 31st. We hoisted our baggage and bid farewell with our kind friends at Pleasant Hill and started for Union Village — we crossed Kentucky river and encamped just on the top of the hill — which occupied us the most of the day — tho' the distance was but about 4 miles —

November 1st. We started early made a good days travel — no difficulty occurred —

OF THE BOATS.

— 29th. We had some wind by the help of which and the use of our poles we pushed on about 23 miles

— 30th. We had some wind and by hard pushing we got along 22 miles —

— 31st. With a fair wind we sailed up the river 27 miles and thought we were geting along quite fast and easy —

November 1st. Nathan Pegg and William Price were dispatched at the mouth of big-bone creek to go on foot to Union Village — we pushed on 21 miles, tho' we had some very strong water —

OF THE WAGGONS.

— 2d. We started early — — passed through Lexington soon in the day — here Daniel rankins took the road to Limestone[38] — and all his family (but the oldest son whose name was Daniel) followed him to the old place on Eagle Creek Ohio — The rest of the company moved on, passed through Georgetown — and turned off the road to a convenient place and encamped for the night — some rain

— 3d. Nothing material — we moved along slowly — the road quite hilly — &c.

— 4th. Was a wet day, the road muddy and slippery — walking dis agreeable — we encamped by small creek — the rain fell in copious showers almost the whole night — so that it was impossible to keep up the fires — this was surely a very disagreeable night — in consequence of all being so wet and geting so little rest —

— 5th. After making up our fires, drying and rubing off some of the mud — we took some breakfast — and moved on in pritty good spirits considering our circumstances — we traveled about 12 miles no material difficulty occurred. tho the day was rather wet. and the road very bad —

OF THE BOATS.

— 2d. We poled 18 miles and had a very wet disagreeable night—

— 3d. All wide awake and full of anxiety — 9 miles hard pushing brought us to Cincinnati which was our last landing — here we met Elder Issachar and Nathan Sharp.[30] which afforded us much comfort indeed —

— 4th. With the help of two waggons, we unloaded the boat — stored up the property and started for Union Village on foot — walked about 3 miles, and lodged in a large convenient house and was kindly treated by the owners

— 5th. Last night may be remarked for heavy rain. we thought it rather exceeded any that we had seen on any part of our journey before — The morning was wet — the road all afloat with water and mud. We started early and went on well all day. till night overtook us a few miles from Union Village — we then procured some hickory bark for torches — and after resting awhile we set them on fire and went on, so that we arrived safe in Union Village about 8. o. clock where our friends received us with

OF THE WAGGONS.

OF THE BOATS.

every possible manifestation of kindness and friendship.

After we had washed and cleaned up a little — they gave us some supper — and after awhile we lay down to rest and felt thankful that we had found an asylum of peace amidst the tumults of War —

And so ended the journey of the Boat company —

— 6th. This day we had to face a cold North west wind and rain all day — and after traveling till night we were obliged to ly in our wet cloths — because fire wood was so scarce — this was quite uncomfortable —

— 7th. The rain fell in abundance. the road was all aflote with water and mud — the branches and creeks were bankfull — and the traveling was bad beyond discription — however we got along somehow, about 12 miles and encamped at night, some 3 and some 6 miles from the river — so that we were better accomodated with wood than we had been the night before —

.— 8th. Sabath — This morning we met Elder Issachar, and John Wallace[34] just before we got to the river and they gave us much comfort and encouragement — All moved on with increased zeal to the Ohio — and the Ferry boats were soon in motion and kept a going till all were safely landed at Cincinnati — we then moved about five miles and encamped for the night — The weather still wet and disagreeable —

— 9th. We started early on a level but very wet and muddy road, and as all were anxious to

OF THE WAGGONS.

OF THE BOATS.

see the end of this tedious and fatigueing journey, we made a good days travel, and stoped for the night about 6½ miles from Union Village, and encamped for the last time — .

— 10th. Early this morning the trumpet was sounded for a general move. and all were soon in motion and on the road — and just . about 10 o. clock we arrived safe in Union Village where we were cordially received and kindly treated by our loving Brethren and Sisters —

This and the similar circumstances that took place at South Union and Pleasent Hill — has made a lasting impression of thankfulness on our minds which time or distance will never eradicate — The chief part of the people were entertained in the meeting house for a few days, till the different familyes were fitted out and moved to their respective places—The last moved on Satterday the 14th ot November — which comes within one day of two months since we started from home on the Big Prairy at Busro —

Thus we find that the Boat Company arrived at Union Village on the 5th and the waggons and foot company on the 10th of November 1812 — And so ended the tedious and tiresome journey —

MEMORANDUM.

After the people were all settled in the vicinity of Union Village and tolerably well situated for house room and provision, the fall and winter become quite sickly — and those who had been exposed to so much cold and wet. had to take the highest heats of scorching fevers — with all its distressing consequences — which caused much tribulation and sufferings throughout the Society — The common application of medical aid seemed to have but little affect for the better in any cases

20

— a fewe weeks passed on and the disease seemed to increase, but more particularly among the youth and children — So that many of them were almost hopeless of life being prolonged from morning till night, or from night till morning — And finally the sufferings of some were terminated in their disolution — For on the 20th of December Rody Rolly departed this life in the 12th year of her age —

December 24th Magia Edgington departed this life in the 10th year of her age — Daughter of John and Polly Edgington —

— 27th Nancy Worthington departed this life in the 14th year of her age —

The fever with all its malignant consequences went on almost unmolested notwithstanding every possible known preventative, was thrown in (we might say almost by gallons) to try if possible to stop the rage of the disease — but it eventually had to run its race — and great sufferings was the consequence —

And so ended the Remarkable Events of the year 1812

1813.

The beginning of this year may be remembered by the continuation of that distressing sickness which began last fall And tho' it would be tedious to note very particular circumstance that occurred dureing its existence, it may hereafter be a satisfaction to know some of the most particular which is all that can be expected in the present case —

January 4th. Charls Boyls Departed this life in the 13 year of his age —

— 30th. Polly Edgington Departed this life in the 36th year of her age — Mother of Magia that died 24th December 1812 —

· February 2nd. Amy Legier Departed this life in the 14th year of her age after having suffered extreemly —

Many of the Union Village people were also sick — and three Brethren and two Sisters died before the scene was closed —

The disease was very obstinate, and many of its unfortuneate subjects suffered extreemly — However it was mostly cleared off during the course of the winter —

Some of the Brethren were imployed in shop work — some in takeing care of the cattle and geting fire wood, and others were clearing ground and preparing for the Summers crop —

The Sisters were imployed at their house-work as usual &c. &c. —

When harvest came on some of the Brethren went out through the settlement and reap by the day for wheat —

June 25th. Elder Archabald set off for South Union, and returned on the 15th of July —

About these times the people began to contemplate on removing back to Busro again — As the danger from the war department appeared to be pritty well over —

August 26th. Noah Legier Departed this life aged something near 18 years — haveing a few week previous received the kick of a horse on his bowels, of which he suffered extreemly —

— During the summer some calculations were made in relation to moveing back to Busro — And on the 4th day of October — John Handcock set off for Busro by the way of South Union —

October 18th. John Edgington and Daniel Redmon[36] set off for Busro on horse back.

October 25th, four Brethren with a waggon and ox team set off for Busro — After which business went on much as usual —

Still makeing prepareations for removing back to Busro —

And just about so ended the year 1813.

1814.

The weather was somewhat changable during the winter, but generaly cold — Some few were quite sick for a time — bad colds were pritty common — but the disease was not so distressing nor so fatal as it had been in the winter of 1813 —

The greater part of the business was makeing prepareations for our journey to Busro —

On the 24th of January Adam Gallagher and Enoch Davis set off for Pittsburgh for the purpose of procureing materials for building such as Iron, nails, glass, Paint, Oil &c.—

February 3d. Six Brethren and four sisters set off for Busro — and as these were the first Sisters that went back in the beginning of this general removeal — And had almost every difficulty to encounter in the beginning of almost a new settlement on the frontier. It will be no more than just to incert their names — which are as follows — Betsy Worthington — Nancy Boyls — Sally McComb — Eunice Slover[37] —

The weather was cold and the waters high — and of cours plenty of mud, when the frost was not hard enough to hide it —

March 12th. There was thirty Brethren and Seven Sisters set off for Busro — some by water and some by land, with some horses

March 15th. William Douglass's family had their kitchen burnt with some of the furniture — however the loss was not very greate —

March 22nd. Adam Gallagher and Enoch Davis returned from Pittsburgh, and landed at Cincinnati — Also there was eight brethren set off from Union Village for Busro — and stayed at Cincinnati all night.

Of the journey, and arival at Busro — of the 30 brethren there was no account ever kept that I know of — neither is there anything to show of the procedure or journey of the main body of the Busro people from Union Village to Busro — more than their departure and arival — therefore the journal will now show the proceedings of this company that

started on the 22d of March, with A. Gallagher and E. Davis — from
Cincinnati to Busro —

— 23d. Loaded our boats and made ready for the river — and stayed
all night —

— 24th. We pushed off early — the river was low — we passed the
mouth of Big Miami about 8 o'clock in the eavening and sailed all night —

— 25th. Went on well — passed the mouth of Kentucky river about
sunset we had a pleasend day and sailed all night —

— 26th. The wind was strong against us — we were obliged to
land about dark and lay by all night —

— 27th. Went on to Jeffersonville and landed about 9 o'clock —
and after a short stay, went on to Louisville and delivered some frate
that we had for that place — then passed over the falls and landed for
the night.

— 28th. Pushed off early, had a pleasant day and sailed well —

— 29th. The river was quite low and the traveling tedious — we
therefore concluded to put as much on board of the keelboat as she
would carry safe, and leave the flat boat with two hands on board —
and so go on with the Keel boat as fast as we could — calculating for
those on the flat boat to store up their load at the Dimond Isleand —
we then parted the boats, took hold of the oars and pulled away in
hast — till we got out of sight of the flat boat — but was obliged to land
about midnight on account of a heavy storm of wind and rain —

— 30th. Our boats were close together again this morning we started
Early and went on well till about 9 o'clock when we had to land and
wait the passage of another gale of March wind — After which we left
the flat boat and saw her no more — And with 9 hands on board of a
large and heavy loaded Keelboat — we set down to the oars, and pulled
away for the mouth of Wabash — the wind was strong against us and
we were obliged to land about 4 o'clock in the afternoon, where we lay
till about 2 on the morning of the

— 31st. When we pushed off and went on well till about 4 o'clock
in the afternoon when the wind again proved too hard for us, and we
were obliged to land, and lay till after dark, when the wind ceased and
we pushed off and sailed all night.

April 1st. At a leven o'clock we landed at the old camping ground
just above the Redbanks, thence pushed on to the Dimond Island where
we were obliged to land and lay all night on account of the wind —

— 2nd. Pushed off early and kept the Oars a going all day, and
just at six o'clock in the eavening we Entered the mouth of Wabash
under the affliction of a pritty Sharp gale of wind and rain blowing
down the Wabash river — we soon landed and had a wet night —

— 3d. Sabath, the wind and rain continued very cold, and about 9
o'clock the snow began to fall quite heavy — we made out to get along
about one mile when we concluded to land, Strike up a fire and make
the best we could of the bad weather all day and night —

— 4th. A cold morning every thing covered with snow. We had to get along by halling brush and spikeing the trees for the river was so high that poleing was out of the question, and the current too strong to gain much by the oars — however we encamped at night just above Bone-bank, 9 miles from the mouth.

— 5th. By halling brush and spiking the trees we got along about 10 miles, the snow vanished and the weather was now pleasent —

— 6th. Went round the lower cut-off —

— 7th. Pushed on to the three Islands and encamped for the night.

— 8th. Went through the upper cut-off — all safe —

— 9th. Nothing material — we got along by hard work, and encamped for the night 3 miles above the half-way bend — all in good plight —

— 10th. Sabath — Last night we had quite a heavy thunder storm — had a wet day and a cold night —

— 11th. Landed at coffe Island about one o'clock and encamped for the night just above the mouth of White river —

— 12th. Passed the Grand rapids — and Little rock — and lay five miles above —

13th. The river had fallen so much that we found good poleing on the sand bars — we made a good days push and lay all night just above Vincennes — with out fire (for want of wood) and had a cold night —

14th. Early this morning the snow began to fall — we pushed on about five miles to a convenient place for wood and encamped for the balance of the day and night — This was a heavyer snow than any we had remembered of seeing in winter — tho the weather in general was not so very cold —

15th. We pushed off early, went on well and arrived at the mouth of Busro about 12 o'clock — then pushed up to the old landing place — where one stayed to take care of the boat and all the rest walked home —

16th. The boat was unloaded and the property was halled home — And so ended the second trip to Busro by water — the boat is ready for another trip —

The brethren that had been at Busro during the latter part of the winter, had been mostly imployed in the business of preparing the fields for the plow — Halling rails, makeing and repareing fences &c. — Also, we removed the old meeting house and some other log buildings from Robert Gills place, down to Robert Houstons and Joseph Worthingtons improvements — That place being close to the mills and the timber — all things considered, it was concluded to make our final settlement there — Business went on for a while with a considerable degree of vivacity and altho we had (as it were) to begin the world anew, we felt glad and thankful that we were landed safe on our own possessions once more where we expect and intend to remain through life the Lord willing —

William Davis went to Union Village, and returned with the cattle
on the 29th of May — And on the

31st of May — The Keel boat set sail for the mouth of Wabash to
meet another company of boats and people from Ohio —

June 4th. The day of the great whirlwinds on the Wabash — many
plantations and houses were distroyed, and some people badly wounded.
Truly the track of these tornadoes was cheerless and disolate —

— 12th. The Keel boat arived with the second load of property
from the mouth of Wabash — some of the brethren were sick — ·

July 12th. Elder Archabald started for Union Village —

August 1st. Issacher and George Legier arived at Busro —

August 2nd. Lucy McComb Departed this life at Union Village —
aged 7 years the youngest of John McCombs family —

— 4th. The main body of the Busro people started from Union
Village in company with Elder Archabald and Eldress Ruth —

— 15th. The waggons and boat started from Busro to meet the
people at the Red-banks — and help them along —

— 21st. The Elders arived safe on the Prairy in the carriages,
and we were all very glad to see them — Also the same day

— 21st. The school family arived with some waggons, and generally well with a few exceptions — after a fatigueing journey of 18
days, hot weather

— 22nd. The main body of the people arived safe, with all the
waggons and in pritty good health considering the heat of the weather
and the fatigue of the journey

· Notwithstanding the people were generally well when they landed
— their comfort in that particular was of but short duration, for the
fever began to make its appearance almost immediately, and many were
taken violently sick — which, together with the spirit of appostasy brought
on very extensive sufferings boath within and without — and on the

— 30th of August* Nathan Pegg Departed this life in the 44th year
of his age — he had hitherto been a stout harty man —

The fever went on, with increased rapidity — notwithstanding all
the medical applications that could be made —

September 1st. Israel Edgington Departed this life — in the 15th
year of his age — Also the same day the Keelboat arived with the last
load of property and people, After a very laborious trip of about 12
days and some sick, the river low and the weather very warm — and many
other difficultys too tedious to mention —

The fever still goes on with violence — The days of trouble are at
hand — In the course a few (of which) 7 of our promiseing young
brethren set the faces towards the world, and seemed determined to
go at the risk of all — This circumstance in addition to the great sickness then rageing, and our haveing just landed on the ground that had
promised us comfort, caused much labour and extreem sufferings — Indeed, we could not think it extravicant to say, that if the heart rending

sorrow sustained by the Ministry in those days — (and part of them sick too) could be written at all, it must be in some unknown language — for we can discribe none after this — (Eldress Ruth was then on her death-bed) — However they were baffled from starting on the 6th as they intended and all but one recanted their Ideas for the preaseasent —

— 8th. Esther Knox Departed this life in the 54th year of her age she had been a zelious believer from the time she first received the Gospel — The mistaken beauty of the world was not yet out of sight — reasoning with them, on the evil consequences of the practice, was of but little use — and on the 11th three of the remaining six went off — desolation and distress seemed to invade almost the whole Society &c. &c. —

— 18th. Just at 3. o. clock in the afternoon our much beloved Eldress Ruth Departed this life. Alas! alas! she is gone * * * Her funeral was attended with great lementation and much deep and heart-felt sorrow, the following hymn was composed by Elder Issacher and sung over her corps with great solemnity —

1   A mother in Israel, A mother indeed
     Has left her dear children her spiritual seed
     She is gone! She is gone! we shall see her no more
     While we remain pilgrims on this mortal shore.

2   O! pitty O! pitty may we not complain
     Why did our young Eldress no longer remain
     To teach us and lead us the way she has trod
     And by her example conduct us to God

3   Her spirit now answers this grievious complaint
     I've finish'd the labour for which I was sent
     In patience I've travel'd and suffer'd with you
     Till Heaven inform'd me my labours were through

4   What soul in their reason according to truth
     Can ask any more of kind Eldress Ruth
     Then while we're intering her loanly remains
     We'll thank her kind Spirit for her toil and pains

5   All her blessed council we'll ever retain
     And her pure example we'll ever maintain
     For she from an infant in virtue has run
     And who among woman her zeal has out-done

6   And now to kind heaven we make our request
     That with such another we yet may be bless'd
     Yet we will rejoice in the gift that remains
     Yet subject and thankful for their care and pains —
                                        Issachar Bates —

And she was buried on the 19th of September 1814 — In the 35th year of her age — on the Big Prairy at Busro —

The fever still goes on with all its desolateing consequences till it seemed as tho' Providence or good fortune had almost forsaken this people — and the messenger who, so lately had snatched Eldress Ruth from us, was again at the door in quest of another — which he soon found — for on the

— 23rd. Naoma Miller Departed this life — Aged about 40 years. This valuable and much respected woman, was a sister to John Dunlavy[39]

— 25th. Betsy McKeen Departed this life in the 17th year of her age — During the month of October the fever began to abate a little, and the distress was not quite so grate — tho many wer yet quite sick and weakly —

November 19th. The School family had their kitchen burned with some of the furniture — The business of building a new one was soon begun —

December 28th. Pegg Tann Departed this life — Age not accurately known but must have been near 50. This was the companion of Anthony Tann that died on the 17th of June 1811 — She was a real white woman —

This about closes the year 1814 —

1815.

The begining of this year brings with it the remains of the last fall's fever — the chief part of the sick are geting better — However there are a few that are still quite sick — and on the

30th of January Martha Johnston Departed this life, her age is not accurately known, but must have been near 60 —

The winter was very cold, the spring wet and the waters high —

May 20th. Nancy Knox Departed this life — quite a pale woman at the age of 50

June 4th. The upper dam broke — much labour and pains were spent in trying to repare it, but did not answer the purpose, for which reason we were obliged to build a new one in another place —

— 11th. William Davis and Joseph Lockwood arived from Union Village — And the new dam was begun in July under the direction of Joseph Lockwood —

August 10th. Joseph Edgington Departed this life — haveing been sick of a violent fever nearly three days — A speedy dispatch indeed at the age of 48 years

September 21st. John Martin Departed this life — his age is not properly known, but must have been something near 40. He was our first and best blacksmith and as cleaver a man as broke bread — But he was compeled to drop his hammer, and lay down his Iron to cool —

November 10th. John Knox departed this life Aged 60. He had

been in revolutionary service a number of years, and found in the Gospel that Liberty for which he had contended so long ago — he was a jelious believer last.

No more deaths occurred dureing the remainder of this year and business went on about as usual — The timber for the new Mill house was ruff hewn in the woods and halled to the frameing yard dureing the latter part of the summer and fall —

And so ended the year — 1815 —

1816.

The weather is changeable, and disagreeably cold — Some few still remain quite unwell, tho' the sickness is not very general at preasent —

No material circumstance that is worthy of note occurred in the Society previous to

January 21st, on which John Johnston Departed this life in the 66th year of his age — Another valiant revolutionist and a good cleaver old man —

— 22nd. James Evans Departed this life — haveing suffered very considerable for several days — Age not known — but was about middle aged —

February and March can be remembered by cold changeable weather and high waters — which always caused great difficulty in geting firewood —

April 10th we began to counter-hew — the timber for the new Mill house. The frameing also was carryed on under the direction of Joseph Lockwood —

May 2nd. Elizabeth Rubart departed this life of the pulmonary disease her age I know not but would suppose she was upwards of 30 or thereabouts

June 27th. We began to raise the frame of the Mill-house — and on the

29th finished the square up to the first rafter plates — for it was a high roof — and 40 feet square on the foundation and 72 feet high to the ridge beam —

July 1st. Harvest was begun — and on the 13th we finished cuting 95 acres of wheat — and 30 acres of rye —

— 14th. Polly Bennet Departed this life — leaving her husband and six small children to lement the loss of a kind Mother — Age unknown —

22nd. John Edgington jur departed this life in the 13th year of his age —

— 28th. Joseph Bennet Departed this life — age not known — the poor little fellow was close by his Mother when she died — and soon followed her to that state from whence no* traveler returns —

---

*A later hand has rubbed out "no" and inserted "there is"

August 16th. The roof of the Mill house was finished — shingled' and painted —

October 18th. Elder Archabald started to Union Village — from whence he returned on the 12th of November in company with Eldress Martha Sanford[30] —

November 14th. Rebecca Price Departed this life — Aged about 67 — a very cleaver old woman

December 9th. Samuel Johnston Departed this life in the 41st year of his age — after a severe tour of sufferings — He was one of the three that was appointed trustees for the Society — and a right cleaver fellow too —

This about closed the year 1816 —

1817.

No material event took place in January — but on the

20th of February Samuel McKeen, Departed this life in the 22nd year of his age — After a long and severe scene of suffering —

March 7th. The first run of stones was started to grinding in the new Mill house — their diameter was 3 feet 10 inches —

July 3d. The second run of stones was started — diameter 3 feet 2 inches boath reaction wheels —

July 8th. Father David,[40] Elder Solomon, James Hodge, with Mother Ruth[41] and Eldress Hortincy[42] — Arived safe in 8 days from U. V.ge

— 10th. Harvest was begun — and on the 19th we finished cutting 85 acres of wheat and 75 acres of oats — Large fields and fine crops —

— 24th. Father David with all the Elders started to Harmony[43] to visit the people, from whence they returned on the 28th all in good health —

August 10th. Ruth McComb Departed this life in the 18th year of her age after haveing suffered extreemly for a number of days, with fever and cramp

— 11th. Father and Mother[44] with all their company started home to Union Village — and Samuel McClelland went with them to Peola —

— 25th. We began to hew timber for a new saw mill — the old one about run down

— 29th. Little Pelly Bennet Deceased — Aged 13 months — the youngest child

November 16th. John McComb Departed this life in the 52nd year of his age — After haveing suffered extreemly from fever and weakness —

This brings us so near the end of the year that we have no further accounts of any more being dead or missing — Thus you see we have lost but four by the hand of Death during the whole year of 1817.

1818.

The winter was considerably wet, but not very cold — for January and February we have nothing more to say, than what is commonly said of moderate winter weather — But when March came onto the stage he soon whistled up a set of gales, breezes and winds — Blowing to and from almost every point of the compas — And from the appearence of their opperation on the anamel — An invisibl spectator might have thought they had been Excently manufactured in the highest — Promontory of Plots and Seditious — This was only the begining of trouble — However the storm at last passed over, but we lost 20 members of Society before the end of the year — Some carpenter tools, and many other articles — both good and bad — All was blown clear off to the world in the storm —

April 24th. Jesse McKeen Departed this life — aged near 40 — he had a few week previous fell on some timbers that lay at the end of the bridge and so hurt his side, that he never got over it — he was attending the Mill —

April. — Also the first Improvement was made at Ambrau — Illinoy state nearly 18 miles west from Busro —

May 19th. Elder Arcnabald and James Davis[45] with Eldress Martha· and Peggy Steward set off for Union Village — From whence they re-turned on the 14th of June —

July 1st. Harvest was begun — and finished on Saturday 18th.

August 10th. Under the influence of a spirit of prophecy James· Price exhibited a very strikeing Example of obedience and humiliation. the scene was truly strange and shocking — and would have made an, unprejudiced spectator feel very awful[46] —

August 18th. James Price Departed this life — aged about 39 years· — after haveing suffered extreemly for eight days — with a kind of hypothetical Insanity —

The fevers began just about these days, and went on with violence so that before the scene was closed, there was but 7 of the whole Society that escaped without takeing a pritty smart brushing[47] — so much so at eny rate that the aforsaid prophecy, was promptly fulfilled — before all was wiped off —

September 28th. Benjamin Gill a little boy departed this life — aged

November 9th. James Bounfield and Benjamin Miller started for Union Village with a waggon and teem — and James returned on the 27th —

December 30th. · Elder Issachar and Calvin Morrel started for Union· Village — And so ended the year 1818.

1819.

January 10th. John Maggs arived from South Union —
During the months of January and February the weather was remarkably warm — Lightning and thunder with showers of rain like those
of summer was quite common. So that on favorable situations the grass
grew, from two to three or four inches high — And had the season not
changed in March it would have been an early spring —

March 4th. Henry Miller moved to the North House to live —
and on the same day the wind shifted to the North west, and with
violence brought on a storm of snow which fell to the depth of eight
inches on fair ground — The frost was very hard and the wind more
than commonly cold and oppressive — so that from the 4th of March to
the 4th of April there was but four days that was tolerably comfortable
to work out of doors — A late spring after a warm winter —

April 7th. James Brounfield Departed this life, after a very tedious
illness of about seven weeks — most of the time severly afflicted with
very acute pains darting through different parts of his body and limbs,
he had but very little fever, and not one day of real sickness — his age
is not accurately known but must have been near forty —

May 7th. By the appearence of a black and fearfull looking cloud
that arose a little west of south, we were warned to witness the passage
of a tremendious hurrecane, which removed everything that his power
was master of — the fences were taken from the ground — trees taken
up by the roots — Indeed it seemed, for a few minutes at one time, as
tho all would be lost — And a new frame barn which had just been
raised and shingled (but not weatherboarded) was litterly toren to peices
— It was 65 feet long and 28 feet wide — large peices of the roof was
found 10 or 12 rods from the foundation — It was surely a frightful
storm — On the evening of the

— 8th. The wind and rain was repeated — but with less violence —
tho there was more hail with the last than the first —

— 15th. The new saw mill was started to sawing —

— 16th. Rain, hail, snow, and very cold disagreeable weather —
Some of the Brethren took hold of the broken barn — collected the
peices — got some new timber and rebuilt. And finished it off —

June 28th. Harvest was begun — And finished on the 9th of July —

August 2nd. 14 Brethren went to Ambrau, to help to rais the
frame of the Milldam and bridge — which was finished on the 12th —
and on the 14th they all returned home — On the night of the

— 15th. There was a dreadful scene of Lightning thunder and
rain — And the new barn, tho' just finished had well-nigh suffered a
second and total defeat — The lightning struck the south west corner,
tore off some of the boards and opened the post about half way down —
and so let go —

— 26th. Jane Martin Departed this life — After haveing suffered grievously of a kind of Pulmonary complaint — together with an In-flamation of the splene — She was the companion of John Martin that died on the 11th of October 1815 — Her age is not known — but she was near the middle stage of life — and a cleaver woman —

September 15th. Missoury France. A little girl departed this life. Age unknown —

October 1st. George Bush Departed this life — Aged 72. he had been a simple good believer for a few months —

Nothing very material took place after this to the end of the year 1819.

1820.

January 10th. The North family was broke up and moved to the other houses and the first order of young believers established at the North house under the immediate care of Henry Miller — the day can be remembered by a storm of snow —

— 31st. Samuel McClelland moved to the North house to live with Henry — During the month of January the weather was cold and frost hard —

February 9th. Robbery — in the night there was stolen — a rifle gun. Some Irons from the smiths shop — and 27 yards of linnen cut out of the loom —

— 11th. About 10 o. clock at night, there was fire found on the floor of the North house Kitchen — supposed to have been put there with the intention of burning the house —

April 17th. Elder Issachar and Mark Hinkly started for Union Vi' ge

May 23d. Elder Archabald, Daniel Rankin,[48] with Eldress Martha and Eldress Saloma started for Union Village in the carriage —

June 28th. The Elders — all come home with David Cory in place of Daniel Rankins — On the 29th Harvest was begun —

July 17th. Mary Hopkins[49] moved to the North house and was con-stituted Elder Sister in that family —

Some time previous the water had broke under the dam at Ambau which now had to be repaired — for which purpose Samuel McClelland and James Mead with some other brethren went out to Ambrau and stayed, from six weeks to two months, during which time they went through a pritty heavy job of repareing at the Mills — part of which was an addition to the forebay, and a new water wheel for the grist mill — faceing and dressing the stones — new cogs in the spur wheel — new bolting reel and chest — and a number of other fixings — Also made a new breast for the sawmill and sank the wheel 22 inches — made a new pitmon — and many of the repairs — after which the mills done good business for a short time — till the river raised very high and the water broke round the abutment at the grist mill and the river soon took its course there and left the grist mill standing near the middle of the river — after which it was 'rented to Alva Beacher — and again to Colonal Heath of Ohio — And finally the Society lost — or nearly the whole possession — However there was but very little ever paid for it — after 5 or six years. trouble and disappointment Dureing some part of the time we were at ambrau — the come a young man to West Union by the name of William Porter — he was sick when he stoped — so he opened his mind and — Left the world in peace — Age unknown —

October 3d. Joseph Johnston,[50] Betsy Murphy and Ruth Pegg[51] set for Union Village in carriage

October 11th. Isabella Gill Departed this life — Aged about 51 years

October 31st. Joseph Johnston and Betsy Murphy returned from Union Village, with Henry Valentine,[52] William Moor,[53] and Ruth Edie —

During the summer and fall the brick for the new house was made .and burnt — The foundation was also dug out 50 feet long and 44 feet wide — and the cellar wall partly built — quarrying stone halling. and makeing preparations for cuting the underpining, door and window caps .and sills — &. c. To the end of the year 1820 —

1821.

January and February was cold weather — and the chief part of the business was cutting stone for the house. two courses of foundation stone. door sill and caps. window sill and caps, mantle peices Door steps &. c. —

Early in the spring the building was commenced, and went on with a good degree of vivacity — but the precise time of the different stages of the work was not kept, that I know of —

The washing Mill was built — along about this time — and the first motion it made it broke the two fore fingers of Peggy stewarts left hand — and finally rendered them useless. after suffering greatly for seven or eight days the forefinger was cut off close to the hand, and the middle one grew crooked and was never of any use to her — Also the frameing timber for the house was got — and the carpenter worke carried ·on by James Mead —

July 6th. James Jinkins Departed this life — Aged nearly 19.

October 23d. Aged, William Knox Departed this life, haveing been sick of a kind of cholic. five or six days — Aged near 60 years —

November 18th. Rebecca Boyls — Departed this life — Her age is not accurately known — but according to the account of some of her children she must have been 60 or upwards —

December 22nd. William Knox Junr Departed this life in the 31st year of his age — haveing suffered greatly of the Inflamatory sore throat accompanied with rageing fever —

After this there were no more deaths occurred to the end of the year.

December 25th. On Christmas day the whole number of the people was 152 — 65 Males great and small — Old and young — 87 Females. great and small — old and young —

Thus the year 1821 was about closed — Without any great degree of sickness —

1822.

The principal business, was working at the house and finishing it off, for which purpose, Samuel Harris and James Voris came from Pleasent Hill — And Robert Johns came from South Union, and the work was kept a going all winter, tho' the weather was pritty cold sometimes.

January 28th. Adam Gallagher Departed this life in the 40th year of his age after suffering extreemly of fever and debility — He was the second one of the three first Trustees that died — and a cleaver fellow too —

Note. on the 23d of April. Elder Benjamin arrive from South Union in company with Eldress Molly,[54] Eldress Mercy,[55] and Nathaniel Rankin in a two horse carriage — Also Ely McLean on horse back — The waters are very high — they stayed 15 days at West Union and set off for home again on the 9th of May —

During the winter and spring the house was finished and on the May 23d the family moved into it, and Elder Archabald handed out the rules and regulations to be observed therein —

July 1st. Father David, Elder Solomon, Eldress Rachel and Sister Eunice Serin[56] arived from Union Village in the carriage

August 3d. William Douglas Departed this life. Aged 57 years. He was born in Iarland June 1765, and died on the Big Prairy at Busro of the Dropsy — he was the last one of the three first Trustees and as cleaver a soul as ever blood warmed —

The timber for the meeting house was got and framed and raised during the summer and fall — but of the precise days or months when it was begun, or finished I have no account in the original —

December 26th. William James Departed this life, being just 46 years and 4 days old — Father of nine children, six of whome he left with Betsy among the believers at West Union —

We have no further accounts in the original for this year 1822.

1823.

February 8th. Chester Fowler Departed this life — He was a young believer and had been confined to the room and bed about one year with Pulmonary Consumption before he died — his age is not accurately known, but supposed to be something about 22 or 24 —

May 5th. Eldress Martha, Polly Worthington, Daniel Boyd[57] and Samuel McClelland, started for Union Village in a carriage, and returned home on the 14th of July — Soon after which Eldress Martha began to be sick. She suffered much with the cancer on her breast — which togather with the Asthmetic affection of her lungs finally terminated her existence in this world — and on

September 19th. She Departed this life — Aged 54 years, the loss of this kind and Motherly woman was truly great, but like that of Eldress Ruth we are obliged to sustain it without redress —

The following is her Funeral Hymn composed, by Elder Issachar

1   Our dear beloved Elderess Martha's fled
     To worlds beyond the regions of the dead
     To join her order in the relms of light
     Where there's no sickness death or gloomy night

2   But everlasting day with her's begun
     She's closed her work, on earth, her race is run
     And with her kindred souls that's gone before
     She shares her just reward forever more

3   Methinks I hear the shout, come Mother come
     Your work is done on Earth you'r welcom home
     You've suffer'd just enough to try your soul
     Now fly to Mother's arms she'll make you whole

4   Her tortured body of material clay
     In which we've seen her suffer night and day
     She fully has discharged with its disease
     And left for us to treat just as we please

5   In honour now to her beloved Soul
     We'll sing a solem song and each condole
     Then lay this body safe beneath the ground
     But Eldress Martha's prais we'll ever sound.

                Issachar Bates September 20th 1823 —

No more deaths occurred during the remainder of this year — nor have we any more remarkable Events on record —

1824.

January 24th. Charles Boyls Departed this life — Aged 64. He came from Iarland — a soldier in the British Service at the time of the Revolutionary War. Was taken prisoner at Little York and never returned again to his own country — He had suffered extreemly with the Dropsy for about two years before he died.

Dureing the winter and spring business went on about as usual, and no particular accounts were kept — of every day, or every weeks procedure —

June 27th. Aley France Departed this life Aged 14 years She suffered much of that distressin complaint called Palpitation.

We have no further accounts for this year — but it is certain that there was but two died during the season —

Quite pleasent were the days of yore
In Eighteen hundred twenty four —

1825.

The winter was not very cold but rather open and moderate — the waters midling high — And on the 7th of February John Fredric Wissmon was drownded in the ditch of the Cross-way his Age is not accurately known, but supposed to have been something near 50 or upwards — He had been among believers a number of years but had left them a few months previous to his death — We took him from his watery grave, dressed him, made a coffin — and buried him with as much deacency and honour as the nature of the case demanded — he was a very industrious man — A dutch man and he said he was of the royal family too —

February 25th. Claricy France Departed this life in the 19th year of her age. After haveing suffered extreemly of Pulmonary Consumption and Palpitation —

— 26th. Doctor Robert Ford Departed this life — Aged near 30. he had suffered much for a number of years with the Pulmonary Consumption —

March 6th. Amelia Shermon Departed this life, in the 15th year of her age — The 7th she was buried, and the day was so wet, cold and snowey that the sisters could not go to the grave-yard —

May 7th. Fanny Price Departed this life — Age She had suffered much from weakness and disease — and had been afflicted with a breast complaint for some years — She was one cleaver kind hearted woman — in a general sence —

No deaths occurred dureing the months of June and July but on the 31st of August, a coloured man by the name of Oremsted Page Departed this life. Aged something about he had come from South Union K. y. some time in the winter —

The spring and fore part of the summer was quite seasonable till about the first of July, after which the drouth set in and continued till near the last of August, which Injured the crops very much — particularly the corn —

From the 8th of May to the 7th of September, there was 13 members left the Society and went to the world — eight men and five women — all young people —

November 15th. Samuel McClelland and James Mead started for Union Village and after staying ther about two weeks, they started for Pleasent. Hill on the 15th of December where they arived on the 22nd — And after a few days it was concluded on for James to stay all winter —

21

This year was closed with a considerable degree of general health —
Nor was there any more died after the 31 of August — And so ended
the year 1825 —

1826.

January 19th. John Dunlavy and Samuel McClelland arive from
Pleasent Hill, about 10 o. clock at night
— 22nd. Henry Miller set off for Eagle creek to gather some people
who were anxious to come and take up The Cross —
The winter was cold and dry. The spring quite irregular — by
which means we had heavy rains and high waters —
April 15th. James Mead and Robert Barnet arived from P. H.
— 17th. John Daily Departed this life. After haveing suffered
severly for the space of 17 days, with his old complaint (Pulmonary Consumption) which he said had afflicted him for about 8 years — his age
is not accurately known — but supposed to be near about 40.
— 24th. Henry Miller returned from his tour to Eagle Creek and
two sisters come home with him, leaveing the main company at Evansville
— 27th. John Dunlavy and Robert Barnet started for home to
Pleasent Hill — Three waggons started to Evansville to help the new
comers, that had come with Henry to move out to Busro —
May 6th and 7th. They all arived safe at West Union — Seven
familyes, consisting of 34 persons, great and small. Male and Female —
— 29th. A Keel Boat started to Evansville for their property —
June 3d. John Dunlavy Arived at Busro the second time —
— 5th. The Keel Boat was loaded at Evansville — and on the
— 6th it started for Wabash loaded down to the screws —
— 8th. Elder Archabald and John Hutcheson, with Eldress Salloma
and Rachel Dennis" started to Union Village — The sickness began
among the young believers pritty soon after they landed on the Prairy
— 21st. The Keel Boat landed at McCortyes landing with all safe,
after a tedious trip of allmost 16 days, the river was very low and the
weather very warm —
— 23d. Harvest finished —
Just about these days the newcomers began to get into deep tribulation — the fever fell on them like a monster — and before the scene
was closed they were all sick but two — and four of them died — before
all was over — Indeed the suffrings on both sides was very considerable
but the newcomers had the heavyest part of the sickness to bear —
July 21st. Nancy Hall Departed this life. She was the first of
them her age is not accurately known — but probably was between 50
and 60 —
August 1st. Sally Laycocks child died being just six weeks old —
4th. Elder Issachar and Joshua Worley,[59] with Elderess Salloma
and Eunice Bedle Arived in the carrige just from Union Village, and

Elder Issachar was quite unwell, and remained so (less or more) till he started away again —

— 19th. Elder Issachar and Joshua set off for Pleasent Hill, in the cariage — And we afterwards heared that he was quite sick the greater part of the way and several days after they arived at P, H,

— 27th. Martha Shreeves Departed this life, haveing been sick of the Billious fever only nine days — Her age is not propperly known, but must have been upwards of 50 — a New comer —

September. The New comers are now in the deep waters of tribulation — and many of them are suffering almost unto death —

— 8th. John Dunlavy began to get sick, and took the first portion of Tarter Emetic which opperated well —

— 10th. James Newlin Departed this life leaveing Polly with five children among believers — his age is not accurately known, but supposed to be something near 30 — a New comer —

The fever now rages with violence in almost every quarter of the Village — three of the New comers are already dead and a number more appear to be dangerously ill.

John Dunlavy was taken sick on friday the 8th and after the Opperation of the first portion of Tarter, he was closely attended with all the medical aid that he (being himself a Physition) or any of the nurses could think of — A great quantity of Billious looking matter evecuated his sistem almost every day — and still his external symptoms was not very alarming till near the last. He was able to set up and walk about the room every day but the very last — which was Satturday and even then he set up a Short time on a chair in the morning — His feelings appeared to be more than usually sunk tho' he spoke strong and desisive — but when going from the chair to the bed he was taken with a kind of fainting fit in which he exhibited very alarming symptoms. however it was over in a few minutes and he seemed to be quite composed — The warm bath was prepared as soon as possible and after he got into the water he seemed to revive and washed his hands and arms a little — but when going from the tub to the bed, he was taken with another fit, and the green billious looking liquid gushed out of his mouth in a stream — he came too again in a few minutes — And so it was every time he got up till towards the last he grew so weak that he could rise no more!! And about 3 o. clock in the afternoon he Departed this life on the

— 16th of September 1826. Much lemented by all who was acquainted with him

— 17th. David Price[60] started to Union Village for the express purpose of conveying the information of Johns death —

18th. William Redmond started to Pleasent Hill for the same purpose —

October 6th. Elder Elezar.[61] Henry Miller, and William Redmond all arived safe just from Pleasent Hill —

— 21st. David Price, James Mead, Eunice Slover, and Rebecca Brazelton, set off for Pleasent Hill, in the Deerburn —

November 5th. Peter Laycock (one of the New comers) started with his family to move back to the old place on red-oak — his father-in-law and brother had come after them with a waggon —

— 9th. David Price returned from his trip to Pleasent Hill and all that went with him found their home and stayed —

— 19th. Elder Elezar gathered all the people and after speaking a few sentences, he proceeded to read a letter that he had received from Elder Archabald, which contained the result of all his Labours and journey to the East, together with the conclusion of the Ministry at all the Societyes in the west, concerning all matters and things at Busro — The substance of which (In short order) was this — That it was universally thought and felt best, for all the people to rise once more and move away from Busro, and so abandon the place forever! —

— 21st. Robert Houston, and Robert Gill, Arived just from South Union

— 22d. Jesse Legier·and John Hutcheson, with Polly Newlin and her five children started for Union Village in a two horse waggon — Also Jonah Shreeves (her father) went along in a Deerburn —

— 22d. Also Henry Miller, and Lucinda Miller,[62] with John Fowler and Nancy (and their two children) started to Pleasent Hill — in a light waggon

Saturday 25th. The great removal took place — of which it would be useless to state the particulars — However a great part of the family in the Brick House was changed and exchanged from room to room — up stairs, and down stairs — The Elders moved up to the garret, and part of them were dismissed and others nominated in their stead —

December 5th. Robert Houston and Robert Gill started home to South Union — and Elder Elezar went with them as far as Harmony —

— 7th. Pheby Murphy Departed this life, in the 22nd year of her age of the Pulmonary Consumption — she had been under weakness, (more or less) for about five years — And endured her sufferings with remarkable fortitude (for a youth) She was set up with only two whole nights near the last — and she sat up on a chair and spoke senceable, not more than half an hour before Death chilled the last spark of life —

December 18th. Peggy Stewart Departed this life in the 42nd year of her Age after haveing suffered extreemly of a confirmed Pleuricy for the space of 26 days. On the 7th and 9th days of her sickness, her Pulse was not preceivable at the wrists her extrimityes were cold and every hour seemed as tho it would be the last — but life continued. and on the 10th and 11th the violence of the symptoms abated a little, and her sufferings was not so very extreem till on the 21st after which she grew weaker very fast till on Monday eavening she died — The 18th of the month and 26th of her illness —

19th. Henry Miller and Francis Vores arived from Pleasent Hill —

— 29th. Nathan Sharp arived from Union Village And so ended the year 1826 —

1827.

January 1st. The Society was gathered, in the brick house at one o. clock — and after Elder Elezar had made a few remarks. on times and circumstances — He proceeded to read an Instrument of writing, which the greater part of the Society signed. as a conveyance of all their Possessions to the care of Nathan Sharp and Frances Vores, as Trustees — &. c.

— 2nd. Anny Handcock Departed this life, Aged about 58 — haveing been afflicted less or more for about five years with the Breast complaint —

— 7th. Alija Hill, Arived just from Union Village —

— 8th. Jesse Legier, Returned from his trip with Jonah Shreeves and Polly Newlin —

— 10th. Henry Miller and Daniel Rankin started to Watervliete, Ohio

— 12th. Samuel G. Whyte and Jesse McComb arived just from South Union K. Y.

— 13th. Jonathan Douglass started to Watervliete, Ohio

— 25th. Jesse McComb and Samuel Whyte with Betsy McComb and Nancy McComb started home to South Union — Also the same day

— 25th. Elder Archabald and James Mead Arived just from Pleasent Hill — This was the first time that Elder Archabald returned from the journey that he had started on the 8th of June 1826 —

— 30th. Abija Hill started home to Union Village, with Brittanna France, Margary McKeen and Lovina Davis. In a two horse carriage. and George Legier on horseback —

February 1st. Daniel Rankins and Johnathan Douglass returned from Watervliete, Ohio —

— 10th. Benjamin Knox and Jesse Legier started for South Union on horse back —

— 16th. Samuel Whyte Arived from South Union the second time—

March 1st. Francis Vores and Daniel Rankin started for Pleasent Hill —

3d. Francis Whyte, George Waddle, Samuel Fisher, and a little boy arived with two waggons —

Packing up and makeing preparations for moveing is the principle business at preasant

— 10th. Four Waggons started for South Union[63]— with seven of the old believers and three familyes of young believers on board, In all makeing 24 in number besides the 4 that came with the two waggons from South Union — 28, In company —

As the society was now partially devided into three companies — viz — The first for Union Village, the second for Pleasent Hill, and the

third for South Union — The principle business from the 10th to 15th
was gathering up the plunder, devideing it out, makeing boxes and packing up — Every hand was busy and every mind full of anxiety —
    The weather is good and warm, and the waggons are in motion.
tho' the road is very disagreeable for boath teems and drivers —
    From the Mill to the little Prairy (nearly half a mile) the water
and mud is up to the waggon beds a good part of the way — and even
the balance of the road is much cut up .with the waggons and quite
muddy —
    The property was stored in McCartyes warehouse —
    — 16th.   James Guess, and Francis Vores arived from Pleasant Hill
— They had imployed the steamboat Lawrence Daniel F. Reeder — Master
— bound for Terrehote on the Wabash. and was to return as soon as
possible — Packing and halling is still going on Industriously, and every
preparation makeing to leave the ground when the boat returns —
    — 17th.   Packing and halling — &. c.
    — 18th.   Packing and halling through the water and mud, the
weather still good —
    — 19th.   Loading and halling with all speed — The boat waiting at
the landing
    — 20th.   The waggons were kept a going till about three O. clock
in the afternoon — When the last load of property and people were delivered at the landing — During the cours of the day the property had
nearly all been tumbled into the boat by the sailors, and altho each
partyes share was pilled by itself they mixed all together, which caused
a difficulty in unloading at different places — The Captain soon ordered
all to come on board as soon as possible — the steem was already up —
The lines were loosed — And just 35 minutes after 5 o. clock we pushed
off from McCartyes landing, and bid a final Adieu to all our hard
earned and dear-bought Possessions on Busro Prairy — The pen, even
of the learned, would fail should it undertake to discribe the ieelings of
this unfortunate people comment would therefore be useless, as every
one concerned can think of, or forget it, for themselves. just as you
please —
    The boat run well, and stoped at Vincennes a few minutes after 7
— seven o. clock and lay too for the night —
    Many of the citizens being acquainted with us, and sorry for our
departure gathered on the bank and strove to entertain us with music
boath Instrumental and vocal — with many good wishes for our welfare
— And one of them spoke aloud in the following words — Farewell to the
Shakers, a people whom we shall ever esteem, and ever wish well —
Smith — This sleepless night was mostly spent in solem meditation —
    — 21st.   The boat pushed off about 3 o. clock — stayed about an
hour, and then pushed off again — went through the lower cut-off and
got into the Ohio just about sunset — and began to stem the current but
the motion was not quite so rapid as it had been comeing down the

Wabash — However the boat was kept a going all night, and just about daylight on the morning of the

— 22. we passed Evansville, And landed at the Yellow Banks about one o. clock — Here we unloaded the property belonging to the South Union company, and left it in the care of Samuel McClelland and Washington Rice — After which the boat pushed on all evening and night without any difficulty

— 23d. Pushed on safe and easy all day — and just at six o clock we landed at shippings-port K. Y. and lay too for the night — we soon learned that the boat could not pass over the falls —

— 24th. We continued on board of the boat all day — Louis Willhite and Tilar Baldwin from Pleasent Hill came on board today and we were very glad to see them

Sabath 25th. The weather is fine and pleasant. The most that is worthy of remark for this day, Is the great number of people from Louisvil and Shippingsport that appeared on the bank. Intencely gazeing at — what they called a new and strange circumstance — viz — The Sabath strictly observed on board of A steem-boat — We however spent the day and night as comfortable as our situation would admit of —

26th. People and property were all unloaded and halled round the falls and those that were bound for Union Village, were shipped on board the steemboat Decatur bound for Cincinnati — And those that were bound for Pleasent Hill were shipped on board of a Keel boat, for Kentucky River, and lashed a longside

The opperation of this day has finished the long service of sepparating this small society into three campanyes — The South Union Devision was finished on the 22nd at the yellow banks — And the Pleasant Hill Devision is finished today — Each property with their property are now on board of their respective boats and the passage from one boat to the other was only a narrow plank, and of course our comimunications were lessened in a great degree — so much so, at any rate the Separation was almost complete — we lay all night in the port of Louisville —

27th. The Engine was early in motion this morning. And the Old Commodore set his face for Cincinnati — the day was pleasent, the wind high and the river very rough — However we sailed well all day — and till about two hours after dark, when we arrived at the mouth of Kentucky river.

The moment of our final parting had now ariven, and the narrow path between the boats prevented the vocal expression of many complimentary good wishes for each others well-fare — One of the brethren performed the chief part of the ceremony of biding farewell —

The Keel-boat was soon unlashed and put to shore for the balence of the night. and the Commodore bore away for Cincinnati —

28th. The poles and oars had now to be substituted for the steem Engine and through much difficulty, hard labour and fatigue we ascended the river very slow — Of which a minute account of every days procedure was not kept probably oweing to the sickness that was on board — As all had bad colds and felt more or less unwell and quite unfit for the preasent fatigue — On the 5th of April Wm. Redmon was taken with a severe chill and fever — And after spending two sleepless nights and days on the boat without eating anything — he was taken ashore and left at the house of a friendly man, where he lay all night and part of the next day — when Louis Willhite came to his assistance with a cariage and took him home — The rest of the boat company was still makeing the best of their way up the river — And so it come out that the whole company arived safe at Pleasent Hill on the 9th of April — where they met with many friends, and every possible attention that their situation required — And after resting and recruiting a few days they were all settled at their respective homes —

And so ended the tedious journey of the Pleasent Hill Company on the 9th of April 1827 —

On the night of the 27th of March the Decatur left the Keel boat at the mouth of Kentucky and went on about four miles and stoped for the night, because of darkness —

28th. The Decatur moved along unmolested until the steem boat Atalanta run afoul of one of his wheelhouses and rather like to have crippled the Old commodore a little, so that he had nearly been somewhat lamed on that side — This Circumstance created many unpleasent feelings among the brethren and sisters — And also many hard speaches among the boatmen and sailors for a few minutes — However it was soon all blown away like steem when the blast was over. — and the Old Commodore moved on with all the majesty and Independence he was master of — when we got to the mouth of the big Miami. Elder Archabald and some others landed at Lawrenceburgh. and the boat went on to cincinnati, where we all landed safe. and met our good friends from Union Village with cariages prepared to convey us to their Hospitable habitation — we remained all night in town —

29th. At eleven o.clock the whole company moved off from Cincinnati we proceded as far as Reading and stoped for the night —

30th. Early this morning the wheels were in motion, and we went on well till we arived safe in Union Village — where our friends uniformly bid us welcome — And treated us with all the kindness and respect that heart could wish —

This completes the second tour of moveing from Busro to Union Village — We spent several days in resting and Visiting from house to house — dureing which we were treated with every possible degree of kindness and friendship — After we had thus, recruited a few days we were conducted to our respective homes for the remaining part of this uncertain Life —

And so Ends, this short Memorandum of Remarkable Events, on the 30th of March, 1827.

South Union, September 17, 1832 — Kentucky.

Copyed by Samuel S. McClelland, for William N. Redmon of Union Village, Ohio —

NOTE:— William Redmon died at Union Village, Feb. 1, 1876, aged 76.

NOTES BY THE EDITOR.

1. I find no other record of this campmeeting, neither do I know of any instance where the Shakers held a campmeeting. At the time mentioned John Dunlavy and the major part of his congregation had become Shakers.

2. Elder Solomon King and Benjamin Seth Youngs. The former was born Jan. 22, 1760; arrived at Union Village June 29, 1805, and was second in the Ministry under David Darrow until 1825, when he became acting first; left Union Village in 1835 and died at Mount Lebanon, N. Y. in Aug. 1858. Youngs, one of the original triumvirate that introduced Shakerism in the West, was born Sept. 17, 1774; became first in the Ministry at South Union, Sept. 25, 1811, and so continued until he was ordered to Watervleit, N. Y., in 1835, and died there in 1855.

3. Now Pleasant Hill, Ky.

4. George Legier, born Nov. 1, 1767; joined Shakers in 1805, and died May 5, 1850; farm Deacon at Busro.

5. Of Samuel McClelland but little is known. He probably united at Union Village, and on the final abandonment of West Union, he was transferred to South Union, and there remained until 1839, when he left, married and then removed to Indiana.

6. Archibald Meacham continued first in the Ministry during the existence of the Society. He was born Jan. 12, 1774 and died in May, 1844.

7. Ruth Darrow was a daughter of David Darrow. She was born Nov. 29, 1780; arrived at Union Village May 31, 1806, and died at West Union, Sept. 18, 1814.

8. Saloma Dennis, second in the Ministry, was born Apr. 3, 1783; united with the Believers in 1805, and died Jan. 9, 1853. Her right name was Edith.

9. James Hodge, born June 9, 1781; joined Believers Dec. 6, 1807, and died Mar. 24, 1865.

10. Probably this was the same Robt. Gill who had entertained the missionaries on their early travels, and who then lived near Pleasant Hill, Ky.

11. This would indicate that the Prices, from Eagle Creek, lived together in their new home.

12. Peggy Knox was born Feb. 18, 1789; converted in 1805, and died May 31, 1855.

13. It was in May that Issachar Bates arrived at West Union, in company with old John Knox, "to help gather the people to Archibald." I have sketched Bates elsewhere *in extenso*.

14. The Shakers did not make special efforts to convert negroes, but occasionally admitted such to membership.

15. Joseph Allen, born Aug. 9, 1772, came to Union Village in 1808, and returned to Tyringham, Mass., in 1819 second in the Ministry at South Union in 1811.

16. William Davis, born Dec. 13, 1781; converted in 1805, and died Jan. 10, 1846.

17. Patience Naylor born June 18, 1794; converted 1807, and died July 16, 1861.

18-19. I have been favored by A. G. Hollister with a copy of the following letter from Issacher Bates written to Richard Spiers, and dated at Union Village, Ohio, Dec. 13, 1811. "Beloved Deacon Richard:

As I have a privilege in union with my Elders to send a short narration of sundry things that have taken place in course of my labors the season past, and feeling confident .that my Elders and brethren in the East will make suitable allowance for my infirmities, I shall carefully proceed to write. Having spent the winter in Ky. I returned in March to Turtle Creek. The 23d of April, I sat out for the Wabash. Arrived there the 29th. Found Archibald, James, Ruth and Saloma safely arrived in that country and in health, and enough to do. They received me thankfully, and opened the door for my gift. Surely said I, here is work enough for us all, and this witness was true. There were upwards of 200 professing faith, that were resident at Busero, and about 140 just arrived from Eagle Creek. The latter had neither house nor cabin to move into, nor any land of their own. And tho' some of them had money to purchase with, there was no Land Office opened, so our first labor was to get them settled to the best advantage, & to raise a crop, which we accomplished through the kindness of the Busero brethren, so that every family has raised plenty. And tho' there was almost a famine for bread in that part of the world, yet all the Believers had plenty through the summer, and some to sell and give to the world.

"This done, our next move was to prepare for building a mill, and through much tribulation on our part, all things went on in a measure of peace & order.

"But as Satan would have it, a rumor of an Indian war soon broke out, and report said Shakers were at the bottom of it. The country was all in an uproar. The Governor issued orders that every company in the Territory should muster every week, and be in readiness, for the Prophet was determined for war.

"The Believers were warned every week, and threatened by the whites, that if they would not fight, and the Indians did not kill them, they would. Still a number of the principal men were friendly. This work was kept up all summer, until a worse took place.

"About the middle of June, a number of the Prophets' party came to get their tools repaired. There were Shawnees, Kickapoos, Wyandots, Patawatomies, but mostly Winnebagoes. They left some of their hoes with other tools, and took the rest to be fixed at Vincennes, for they were much engaged in raising corn. But the Governor refused to allow them to be fixed, except particular ones, telling them that they were for war, which they denied. Then the Governor wrote us a letter with this injunction, 'Not to do any smith work for them, but we might feed them.' We had before informed the Governor that we had no such connection with them as people judged, and asked his counsel as to how we should treat them when they came in. He told us to be kind to them and feed them. We wrote to the Governor that we should punctually comply with his orders, and did so. The Indians returned very sorrowful and much grieved at the white people's jealousy, declaring that they had not so much as thought of war. Howbeit, the Governor sent messengers to the Prophet to come immediately down with his chiefs and attend a council, and answer for his conduct.

"Accordingly, about the middle of July, the Indians began to gather in from the different tribes, and as we were on the outmost bounds of the frontier, they encamped near us, waiting for the tribes to collect, which occupied about two weeks, when Tecumtha, then Chief, came on and led them to Vincennes.

"These were trying times with us. We had use for all the wisdom and patience we possessed. These hungry creatures were about us nearly three weeks, singing and dancing to the Great Spirit. Some of the time there were upwards of 200, all peaceable, showed no abuse to any one — would drink no whiskey, and never to our knowledge took to the value of one cucumber, without leave. Nor could we discover in them the least hostile symptoms,— still declaring their innocence, grieved that the people would not believe them — saying to the people, 'Look, see our squaws and children. We do not go to war so. We only come here because the Governor sent for us.' But notwithstanding all this, the people moved into forts, and into town, bag and baggage, all around us.

"Oh how often did my soul cry out within me, Lord God! What can ail this people? Surely the prophesy of Esdras is fulfilled upon them? 'Wit has hid itself from them, and understanding withdrawn itself into its secret chamber.'

"A number of leading men in the Territory were sorely tried with the manner in which things were conducted. The Governor had the light horse, and 3 or 400 footmen together for a week or ten days, to guard the town against this unprepared company of Indians, squaws and children. After all the parade was over, and every voice from the Indians was peace, and no foundation but jealousy, to build upon for war, the Governor sent them away with a party of men hard at their heels, to keep them from pilfering from the inhabitants. But this was like setting the dog to watch the butter — for they did more mischief in one night, than the Indians had done all summer.

"This is now about the 5th of August,— the matter is settled. War! War! War! The Governor receives liberty from the President to manage all these things according to his own wisdom. The militia are ·drafted, Believers with the rest — an army is raising, tribulation and vexation are our portion day and night.

"On the 19th, Joseph Allen arrived here, and all the brethren that could be spared off the plantation, turned in with him to build a grist and saw mill on Busero Creek. At this work, I must confess that a little more zeal than wisdom attended me. Travelling nearly every day 7 miles to and from my work, and sometimes in mud and water to my knees, the effect of which will appear hereafter.

The drafting was kept up, till every Believer on the muster roll was drafted, but the Believers paid no attention to it. At length the fever and ague began to draft, and that had to be attended to.

"Sept. 2. Archibald, James, Ruth and Saloma set out for Turtle Creek, heavy laden with the weight of those things which they left behind.

"But as the appointment was, they must go now, or not this season. The day after they started, I was taken down with the fever, and went out of my room no more for 13 days. Here the billows went over my head. Here I lay sick, with as much pain as I thought I could bear — And above 40 more of the Believers down sick at the same time — whole families. The attention of the brethren being all taken up at the mill, I felt that they would be neglected, and would murmur that we had brought them into the wilderness to perish. For it was the Eagle Creek people that were sick — The Governor expected on every day.

"O, my sorrow! my sorrow! I cried, but there were none to help me. And to mingle my bitter with gall; some of the wicked Pottowatomies came by night and stole our team from the mill ground, four of the best horses that were owned by Believers, that were given up for the work. The brethren were thrown into confusion, and came to me for counsel. Nothing would satisfy them but to follow the thieves. Accordingly two of the Believers and a world's man set off, which was a great grief to me. They followed them about 90 miles, overtook them, and took the horses from them without meeting resistance. The Indians soon persued, run them about 10 miles, retook the four, and the two they rode on, with the saddles, saddlebags and bridles, and escaped. In about six days, Capt. Robbins, who went with them, came in and said he saw an Indian shoot, and saw black Abraham fall, and that was the last he saw of the Brethren. A few hours after, James Bromfield came in and gave the same account of Abraham, the next morning Abraham came in well. By this time the loss of the horses felt very small to me, seeing the Brethren were alive, and had kept the counsel that was given them, not to fight. This loss, which was about $500, was gain on the ·other hand, for it cooled the prejudice of the world, concerning our friendship with the Indians.

"I will just note that this a trick these wicked Pottawatomies have carried on two or three years, to follow the Prophet's party and steal, that it might be fathered on them that did it not. This was about the 16th. I got about so that I could ride and visit the people. But there was so much confusion and sickness, that it was hard work to keep their spirit up. They had been warned and drafted so many times, they concluded it would take the chief they had to pay their fines.

"The 17th, the army began to come on — one company of light horse, and two companies of riflemen encamped by us. The contractor used our shop in the dooryard for a store house, and made a slaughter yard at the back of it. Here it was, drums and fifes, blood and whisky! Alas! alas! here they staid, waiting for the troops to come on. They had their washing, baking, some lodging, and all their forage for their horses, from us, though they paid for it, and behaved with civility toward the Believers. Yet, alas! alas! about the 26th the whole army came, with the Governor, and encamped at the same place. In their army were 500 regular troops from New England, commanded by Col. Boyd, from Boston.

"Here the kind hand of God, in His Providence, was stretched out a little to help us. These people testified that they were acquainted with the Shakers at the East, and they were a good people. Col. Boyd bore a public testimony in Vincennes and other places, that the Shakers at the East, were the best people on this earth. This blunted the edge of every weapon that was formed against us. He appeared to be as glad to see us, as tho' we were his natural kin.

"There was also Col. Davis from Kentucky, who commanded the troop of horse. He was acquainted with Believers there, and was very friendly. As he was a lawyer, and Joseph Allen was acquainted with him, he went to him for counsel. For at 12 o'clock all the brethren that were on the muster roll, were ordered to join the army.

"We went to the Governor, according to Col. Davis' counsel, and told him what we do, and what we could not. The Governor replied that he knew our faith, and the matter might rest until he returned, and that he would assist us in forming a petition to the Assembly, to be released. This settled, Believers continued their kindness to the army, and the army was very friendly, and much applauded us for our kindness. On the 28th, the army marched, and left their sick with us.

"They marched forty miles up the Wabash, to Tarhole, where they built a garrison. We had news and company, every day a plenty, such as it was. On the 30th, Archibald and others returned, and I was thankful, not only that they had come, but that the army had gone before they came, tho' there was confusion enough left behind them to distress us, day and night. We labored our best to dispel the darkness that was left among Believers, but it was deeply rooted. Sickness prevailed. Notwithstanding the mill and other business went on tolerably well.

"Joseph Allen staid till the 21st of Oct., and then returned to Ky.

The 24th, I set out for Turtle Creek; left Archibald, Ruth and Saloma, which were all that were sent for helps, for James was left at Turtle Creek. It felt very hard for me to leave them, altho' it was in union, and we still hoped that the tumult would end without fighting. I arrived at Turtle Creek on the 30th, and being somewhat impaired in body, it was thought best for me to stay awhile and recruit. So Matthew Houston, Calvin Morrell, and Peggy Stewart were sent down to help them."

20. The Valley of the Mississippi from New Madrid, Mo. to the mouth of the Ohio, in one direction, to the St. Francis, in another, was so convulsed as to create new lakes and islands. The shocks were also felt in South Carolina.

21. Several violent shocks were felt in Caraccas, March 26, 1812. The surface undulated like a boiling liquid, and underground there were terrific sounds. In an instant the whole city was a heap of ruins, under which 10,000 of the inhabitants were buried.

22. Rachel Johnson was born May 10, 1779; came to Union Village in 1807, and returned to the East in 1835.

23. Calvin Morrel born Apr. 29, 1765; converted in 1805, and died Sept. 3, 1833. He was a physician.

24. I find that Joseph Lockwood was a very active Shaker; birth unknown; united in 1805; started for Mt. Lebanon June 3, 1809, and early took an interest in West Union.

25. The precipitate flight of the Shakers from Busro is a sad commentary on their wisdom. The leaders had either lost control of the community, or else, what is more likely, shared in the common fears. Living so close to Vincennes, they should have known that city would be protected, and the Busro community was too serviceable to be left in jeopardy. Issachar Bates (MS. Autobiography) says "it was tumult upon tumult, war, war, war, all the people talking of armies coming among us till the greater part of our people were so filled with fear that they could not rest day nor night; so we held a council and concluded to move out of that place and go among our brethren in the other states where there was not so much danger." Elder Henry C. Blinn (The Manifesto, Jan. 1885) says that "Gov. Harrison very kindly offered to assist the Believers to a residence in Vincennes, and would provide all the tents that they would need, and then guard the place with his soldiers." There must be some mistake here, Gov. Harrison at that time had reached Piqua with the Kentucky troops, and sent a detachment to the relief of Ft. Wayne. He was nowhere in the vicinity of Vincennes at the time named. The attempt of the Indians against Ft. Harrison, on the Wabash, was foiled by Captain Taylor, afterwards President of the United States.

26. The following account of the journey is given by Calvin Morrel, in the MS. Record Book of the Whitewater Community: "Every team, waggon and carriage was put into requisition. What added much to the

affliction was that many of the people were sick of the fever. and some
very sick. Perhaps this number might have amounted to twenty or
more. However the sick were taken into wagons and accommodated as
well as the case would admit of. The best of the property having been
loaded up. And the flocks and herds gathered by the 15th day of September, 1812. This suffering company were ready to take their flight
& leave their peaceful home, to go they knew not whither. Having left
behind them 150 acres of corn, their whole stock of hogs, many of their
cattle, and much other valuable property. Also grain in the ground, and
stacks of different kinds. About two weeks previous to this move
Eldress Rachel Johnston & Calvin had been sent from Union Village
on a visit. This was a fortunate circumstance for the sick, as E. Rach-
ael's skill in nursing tended greatly to alleviate the suffering part of that
body. It is not our intention, neither would it be a pleasing task to
describe the tribulation and almost endless perplexities of moving a company of more than 300 Men, Women, and children through mud and mire.
and storms of rain, with old wagons, worn out gears and baiky horses,
upwards of 400 miles. Yet we cannot forbear having been an eye witness
of the whole scene. to bestow now and then a passing remark as we
jog along through mud and storms. You may consider the camp in
motion, with every now and then a wagon stuck in the mud. Some one
two or three of the cattle breaking off. And for the first day or two
returning home. After that lost in the woods. After a sore travel of
five or six days. Safely landed on the Kentucky side, and camped on
the lower end of an extensive cane break a little above what is called
the Red Bank. In the mean time be it remembered that about 6 of the
Brethren tarried on the ground to take care of what was left behind.
Among that number was William Davis, who was at time the principal
Deacon. Though William saved much, and after all that was done, the
loss of this move and waste of property by the army, has been computed
at ten thousand dollars. After waiting two or three weeks at the Red
Bank, word came on by one of the brethren from the Village to move
on as fast as possible, for that place. And the camp was soon in motion
being glad to get off from a place where we had been very inhospitably
treated by the surrounding inhabitants. Having had several valuable
horses stolen and a number of our cattle. Our intended rout was through
Kentucky, having in contemplation to pass by our brethren at South
Union and Pleasant Hill. From this place our Keel boat passed up the
river for Cincinnati. and the teams started for South Union. the roads
at this time were very dirty. and frequent rains was constantly increasing the mud. and some teams had heavy pulling to get along. We shall
only mention an afternoon's travel and fare at night as a specimen of
our journey to South Union. The rain began to come down about 3
o'clock at which time we were met by a number of brethren and horses.
8 or 10 were mounted, and set out for the village. Matthew Houston
was along, tarried all night. The rain increased till sunset when we

encamped near a Baptist meeting house made of logs. We immediately
set about building fires. in this matter but few succeeded. Only one
fire was kept burning all night.· The rain gradually increased till midnight, and the people drenched with one continuous pour, without a
shelter except a few of the Sisters who had crawled into the little cabin
of a meeting house. To get supper in this situation was out of the
question. So that both it and sleeping was laid aside for the night.

In the night while the rain was descending in floods someone came
and told Calvin that, the sisters had crowded into the house, and was
treading on the children every now and then, that they feared some of
their arms or legs would be broken and requested him to come and
entreat them to go out. This was a bitter pill for Calvin. But on
viewing the scene for awhile, there appeared no other ·way. And the
sisters kindly withdrew and took the storm again. About two oclock
the rain ceased suddenly. The fires were all kindled up. The people
all dryed and warmed themselves and appeared exceeding thankful. And
by day light the sisters had a fine warm breakfast which we all eat full
of gratitude. And in a short time the whole camp was on the road
But oh the mud! As soon as the daylight appeared Matthew Houston
made his escape for the Village ahead where he had been tarrying for
some. months. This day a team met us from our good brethren at South
Union loaded with provisions which was very acceptable. We soon
cleared the wagon and loaded it with about twenty children who were
wading through the mud. The next day we arrived at the Village of
South Union. Which seemed to be paved with love. The spirit of
love that was manifested and felt on this occasion cannot be expressed
by words, neither can any of this generation have any conception thereof.

The people had moved out of their good houses into cabins and
sheds to make room for us. The same was also done at the School to
make room for our children. * * * * We feel unwilling to discuss
the subject, without saying a thing or two in relation to General Hopkins and the army under his command, from the state of Kentucky,
which things we have a desire to record as an everlasting Stigma on the
spirit of War & Carnage. The army under the command of this noble
Kentuckian crossed the Ohio river at the Red Bank about the same
time we crossed four miles above. They encamped on the shore opposite
where we lay. From this place they sent over a party of armed men
and plundered our camp of about thirty Blankets and Coverlids. In
which act they discovered a savage cruelty which we believed, that they
were going to destroy us. Contrary to the law of humanity in an un-
feeling manner they violently forced the coverings from several of the
Sisters then laying in the fever and on the ground without shelter,
and what was still worse, from some they pulled away even the blanket
they were laying on and left them sick as‾they were to the naked ground.
After they had satisfied their desires, and accomplished their nefarious
purpose they returned to camp. The general rendezvous (for this army)

destined for the destruction of a peaceable people was at Shakerstown on the great P. Here they assembled and fared sumptuously. Yea even riotted on the spoils of an innocent industrious people. The beasts were turned into the cornfields. Cattle and hogs butchered. Bee hives stolen, and every waste that folly and envy could invent was made of property. the believers several times petitioning Congress, received no remuneration.

27. After plundering the Shaker camp, and making havoc of the Shaker plunder at Busro, the army of Hopkins marched to Ft. Harrison. but finding no Indians there, then for four days it marched through the great prairie, when falling short of provisions and suspecting treachery in the guides, and frightened by the fires which the Indians had kindled, this army of Kentucky horsemen, was seized with a sudden panic, turned about and retreated to Vincennes. Gov. Edwards had advanced up the Illinois River with 400 men to co-operate with Hopkins, and he succeeded in destroying several Indian towns above Peoria.

28. "Our hearts were saddened when we realized how we had been cast out from our beautiful home at Busro, from our fruitful fields and well tilled gardens, to make a weary pilgrimage of hundreds of miles, which could only be through great anxiety of spirit and severe toil of body." *Manifesto*, July. 1885.

29. The route from Busro to Union Village, as pursued by the pilgrims, covers a distance of 522 miles. Why they should have been sent out of their way to South Union, instead of going direct to Pleasant Hill, from Red Bank, does not appear on the records. The authorities at Union Village so willed it, and there was no questioning their "gift."

30. Matthew Houston was a prominent figure in the Kentucky revival; born Dec. 25, 1769; became a Shaker in Feb. 1806, and died Mar. 20, 1853. He lived at Union Village, and at the North Family his vest is still preserved. He was short and became corpulent.

31. Peter Pease, born June 12, 1767, arrived at Union Village from Mt. Lebanon, N. Y., May 31. 1806, and returned May 2, 1822. He lived at Union Village.

32. Those who took up their permanent homes at South Union were, "John Miller & family 8, John Slover Jr & family 3. Wm. Legier, John Johnson, Matthew N. Houston and Justis Davis 4. Benj. Price & family 3 white & 5 black 8. Leonard McReynolds & family 9. Adam Kirkindall & family 5. Robt. Houston & family 5. Joseph Shaw & family 5. Total souls remaining here 47." Leonard McReynolds finally became wormwood to the South Union Believers.

33. Now Maysville, Ky.

34. John Wallace, born in 1779; admitted in 1805; long a trustee at Union Village and well trusted; he decamped with $8,000, Feb. 14, 1818; went down the Ohio; built a mill, which was carried away by a flood; returned to Ohio, and made trouble for his former friends.

35. Nathan Sharp, born Oct. 20, 1786; admitted 1806, decamped

22

Sept. 9, 1835, with about $10,000. He was a trustee of the Society. Afterwards he kept an inn, called "The Green Tree," about a mile from the North Family of Union Village.

36. Daniel Redmon, born Feb. 20, 1779; admitted 1805, and died Dec. 26, 1846.

37. I judge these four Sisters were original members of the Busro Society.

Issachar Bates says he was sent "to provide some shelter for the people, because the property at Busro had been taken from us by fraud, while we were gone. I will mention in this place that five or six brethren were left on the ground, when the move took place, to protect all they could and in the time of war I was sent to Busro with other brethren to help them settle affairs and bring them home, which was in 1813."

38. John Dunlavy was one of the most prominent actors in the Kentucky revival, besides being an able theologian. He was the author of "The Manifesto," a theological work of 520 pp., first published in 1818. He was long the preacher at Pleasant Hill, and, as will be seen, died at West Union.

39. Eldress Martha Sanford, who died at West Union, was born May 15, 1769; arrived at Union Village May 31, 1806.

40. David Darrow was among the first Believers in America, and also suffered with the early Shakers, for opinions sake, and even incarcerated in the Albany, N. Y. jail without trial; was born June 21, 1750; an officer in the American Revolution; arrived at Union Village June 29, 1805, to take "the lead" in building up Shakerism in the West, and as such continued until his death, June 27, 1825.

41. Ruth Farrington born Apr. 27, 1763; arrived at Union Village May 31, 1806, to become first in the Ministry, in the Sisters' Lot, and so continued until her death, Oct. 26, 1821.

42. Hortense Goodrich arrived from Mt. Lebanon May 26, 1809, to stand second in the Sisters' Lot at Union Village. She died at Pleasant Hill, Ky. I have no farther particulars, save her devotedness to the cause she had espoused.

43. These people were Separatists from the established church of Germany; migrated to this country in 1803-4; removed to New Harmony, Ind. in 1814, having purchased 30,000 acres of land; in 1824, to avoid malaria and bad neighbors, sold their property to Robert Owen, and established themselves at Economy, Pa., on the Ohio, 20 miles north of Pittsburgh.

44. Father and Mother were terms of endearment bestowed upon David Darrow and Ruth Farrington. It was given first to Ann Lee and then Lucy Wright, but after the death of the latter, the then existing Ministry, abolished the custom.

45. James Davis, born Jan. 3, 1791; admitted 1805, died Nov. 19, 1833.

46. The early Shakers were much given to what they called "mor-

tifying the flesh." This is often referred to in the Church Records of Union Village, but no descriptions occur. I have conversed with the older members about them, and while the scenes were harmless, yet the later Shakers have very wisely discontinued the practice.

47. Calvin Morrell writes: "In the year 1818 word having been sent to Union Village that nearly all the people were laying with the fever. Calvin and William Davis was sent to render some assistance. in this trying time. When we arrived the sickness had began to abate, but it seemed as the visage of death had spread its gloomy mantle on every countenance. Such a set of ghostly looking skeletons, did not fail to excite in Calvin the strongest of sympathy. For the people here were his beloved friends. Few had died but nearly all had been sick. The report of Arsenath Edy, who was at that time the principal Nurse. that for several weeks she did not pretend to undress, or go to bed, being steadily employed by night and day. from house to house. and naping of it as necessity required. In this condition of affairs the regular business of the kitchen was set aside. Very few being able to attend their meals. And such was the affliction for awhile, that it was difficult to find as many that were able to move about to care for those confined. In many cases the sick suffered for want of suitable help. Elder Archibald was among the suffering throng, and barely escaped with his life. Elder Isachar kept on his feet through the whole scene. In about two months from this time health was in a great measure restored to the people." *Church Record of Whitewater.* As Calvin Morrel had been a physician, it was perhaps on this account he was sent to Busro.

I am favored with another letter of Issachar Bates, furnished by Elder Hollister. It is to the Mt. Lebanon Ministry, and dated Union Village, Ohio, Jan. 29, 1819. "I left West Union, Dec. 31st, in company with Bro. Calvin Morrell, who was sent to help us in an time of affliction. We arrived at Union Village, Jan. 8. The Elders, brethren & sisters there were in a comfortable state of health, with some exceptions. By this time ye have found out where I am, & how & when I came here. For some cause it has been our lot at West Union, to burden our beloved friends in the East with our calamities, either by the distress of war, or sickness, or some other work of the Devil, so that it becomes irksome to write. But from fears that this originates more from pride than good faith, I believe it as well to be honest and let our afflictions be known. We got along with our affairs the season past, tolerably well, and the Society was more healthy than it ever was in this place before, till about the middle of August, and then the fever came on us with fury. The first attack was on a number of our best members. Elder Archibald was also taken down. They were taken with such violence that in a few hours their breath would stop, and no medicine had any effect. Then we betook ourselves to pray, and obtained help from God, so that we made war with the Destroyer. When any were violently seized, we assembled in the meeting-house, and labored until they were released, which frequently took place, till finally we obtained a confident promise from God, that we should have our lives for a prey, although we should all be sick. After this, confidence was gained, and medicine operated well. Six or eight were taken in a day, till a hundred were down at once. Finally all who escaped the fury of this cruel enemy were as follows: James Bromfield, our first farmer Deacon; myself, who never got into bed for four weeks; Eldress Martha, who was a warrior indeed, and treated her bed much the same; Lucy Houston, who had the care of the children; and Ascenath Edie, our chief nurse, who acted a noble part through the sickness, and was blest in her labors. I do not think she had one regular nights sleep in 2 months.

"Elder Archibald lay 17 days, before alteration for the better, while prayers & labors were made for him without ceasing. He was the sickest person in the Society, but he was held fast, and hath recovered his health, although it is reported in the world that he is dead."

48. Daniel Rankin was born in 1798 and withdrew about 1829.

49. Mary Hopkins, born Sept. 29, 1784; admitted Mar. 1808, and died May 22, 1855.

50. Joseph Johnston, born Sept. 4, 1776; admitted 1805, and died Mar. 21, 1849.

51. Ruth Pegg, born Apr. 7, 1798; admitted 1812, and withdrew Oct. 28, 1836.

52. Henry Valentine, born Nov. 6. 1799; admitted 1805, and died Dec. 24, 1841.

53. William Moore, born Jan. 15, 1789; admitted 1805, and died June 6, 1867.

54. Eldress Molly Goodrich, born Dec. 14, 1779; arrived at Union Village Mar. 31, 1806; arrived at South Union, Oct. 6, 1811, as first in the Ministry, in Sister's Lot, and so continued until her death, Dec. 9, 1835. She was a strong character and firm in the rules of her faith.

55. Mercy Pickett arrived at Union Village, from Mt. Lebanon, May 26, 1809, and Oct. 6, 1811, stood second in the Ministry to Molly Goodrich. In 1834 she returned to Mt. Lebanon.

56. Eunice Sering, born July 11, 1795; admitted 1806; was in the Ministry order with Rachel Johnston at Union Village, and seceded Jan. 29, 1847.

57. Daniel Boyd, born Oct. 16, 1783; united in Feb. 1807, and died June 25, 1845.

58. Rachel Dennis, born Nov. 20, 1789; united 1805, and died Aug. 9, 1859.

59. Joshua Worley, once prominent at Union Village; born Aug. 12, 1800, and seceded May 24, 1839.

60. David Price, born Oct. 29, 1773; admitted 1808, died Jan. 24, 1855.

61. Richard McNemar was given the name of Eleazer Wright by Lucy Wright. He was one of the leaders of the great "Kentucky Revival," born Nov. 20, 1770; became a Shaker, Apr. 24, 1805, and died Sept. 15, 1839. Archibald Meacham was off on a junket, and John Dunlavy was in temporary charge, and on the death of Dunlavy, Richard McNemar acted as first head.

62. Lucinda Miller, born June 13, 1804; taken to Believers in 1805; died Dec. 29, 1869.

63. The following list gives the names of the West Union Believers that found their homes at South Union, with ages and the time, so far as known: Samuel S. McClelland, 41; Jesse Legier; Benjamin Knox, 35; John Hancock; Samuel Worthington; David Lathom, 35; William Roberts, 42; William Roberts, Jr., 16; Elijah Roberts, 4; John Ford, 11; Robert Ford, 8; Charles Ford, 5; Henry M. Ford, 3; Frederic W. Royce, 36; Joseph Roberts, 14; Elizabeth McComb, 65; Sally McComb, 32; Betsy McComb, 24; Nancy McComb, 20; Rebecca Boyles, 26; Ruth Edie, 24; Hortency Bedell, 31; Peggy Ford, 34; Mary Ann Ford, 6; Martha Roberts, 37; Peggy Roberts, 9; Salome Roberts, 1; Catharine Latham, 30; Julia Latham, 16; Betsy Jenkins, 26; Olive Jenkins, 5. Soon after (Aug. 5) Jessie Legier went to Pleasant Hill; Benjamin Knox seceded Dec. 20, 1835; William Roberts withdrew Jan. 30, 1836; his son William had previously left. There appears to be no record at Pleasant Hill of the Believers that went there. The older and those in authority went to Union Village, but no record is now there. The recent converts (called by Shakers "Young Believers") went to Whitewater. There is no record there of their names, but Eldress Adaline Wells recalled the following for me, who settled with the North Family: Ezra Sherman, Jr., Ezra Sherman, Sr., Manly and Anna Sherman, Rachel and Ann Hall, Louisiana, Indiana, Betsy and Reece Stroud.

At the time of the dissolution of the West Union Society it numbered about 100, most of whom were females. Nearly all the older members had succumbed to malaria.

In Richard McNemar's "Selection of Hymns and Poems for the Use of Believers," in the appendix he has a caustic poem on some of the Believers at West Union, written in 1827. He also furnishes the following:

"The dissolution of this once flourishing Society, may serve as a warning and as a ground serious examination to all concerned, as to the real and radical causes which produced such a lamentable effect: and to pass over such things with a covering spirit, is giving the enemy great advantage to keep the same causes in operation, for like causes will produce like effects. Sed verbum sapientibus sufficet.

"A LAMENTATION FOR WEST UNION.

"TUNE — THE DEAD MARCH.

"What language shall we borro, to paint the grief & sorro
　　That ev'ry cheek might furro, with tears of pious grief,
When West Union's whole foundation, her beautiful plantation,
　　Is doomed to desolation without relief.

"This pleasant situation was view'd with admiration,
　　And with much animation, we lived at Busro,
Till the bugs and the river, brought on the chill & fever,
　　To ev'ry good Believer, the first grand foe.

"When war and desolation invaded our plantation,
　　And we had found relation, where we could be at rest,
When by troubles so repeated, our hopes had been defeated
　　We're sorry we retreated back to the west.

"When we were reinstated, and troubles new created,
　　What numbers really hated upon the ground to stay;
We cannot but be pained, to think we were detained,
　　Until so few remained, to move away.

"When order must be gained, and faithfully maintained,
　　What burdens those sustained, who stood as first in care;
When by manifold transgression, & little true confession,
　　More evil got possession than they could bear.

"With sorrowful sensation we view their situation,
　　When their best ministration could but create distress —
Disorders still increasing and faithful ones deceasing
　　The number still decreasing, and growing less.

"The rising generation, deserting from their station,
　　Was truly a vexation — the sorest grief of all,
This dreadful complication, of death and desolation,
　　For some grand alteration, did loudly call.

"When matters were preparing, to get a final hearing —
　　Our minister preparing for counsel from the east,
Our lack of resignation has been the sad occasion,
　　By which our tribulation has been increas'd.

"When father Jno.* appeared, our spirits were so cheered,
  We thought him well prepared to man the steering oar
But our very souls are grieved to think we were deceived
  And of this gift bereaved, we ask no more.

"To part with such a brother, our grief we cannot smother
  And to accuse each other, can but augment our wo,
Yea truly we are pained, to think he was detained,
  And such a loss sustained from the grand foe.

"But now the scene is closed, our souls are now composed,
  And since it is proposed to seek a better place,
We accept the invitation, and 'tis a consolation,
  That our past tribulation is no disgrace.

"THE RESPONSE — TO THE QUEEN OF HEARTS.

"Arise! Arise ye valiant band!
Prepare to quit this wretched land,
For here the gospel cannot stand,
  The trial is completed;
Surrounded by a savage brood,
Oppos'd to ev'ry thing that's good,
Believers here too long have stood,
  "To be despis'd and hated, *Reliqua caret.*"

A hymn of welcome of forty-eight lines was composed, inscribed "to the West Union Believers in the year 1827." Where and by whom it was composed I know not. I find it in McNemar's "Selection of Hymns and Poems." I judge, however, from the first verse, herewith inserted, it was the product of a member at Watervleit:

"Come Mount-Zion's lovely children!
  Come and welcome to these plains!
Welcome to each spread pavilion!
  Rest from all your toil and pains.
We do feel a tender spirit
  To our kindred from the west,
And their tried faith does merit
  Love and Union of the best."

ADDITIONAL NOTES.

Eldress Jane Cowan, of South Union has furnished me the additional particulars concerning certain individuals mentioned in the text:

---

* John Dunlavy.

Samuel G. Whyte was trustee at South Union; born in Maryland in 1774, and died in 1833. Francis Whyte was born in Maryland in 1768; was an elder in the Gasper church at the time of the Kentucky revival; died in 1830. Samuel Whyte was a nephew of the trustee, but left South Union when young. Robert Gray was a Believer a number of years, but afterwards left South Union. Eli McLean, a trustee, was born in N. C. in 1793 and died in 1870. George Waddle left South Union in 1849. Both the Redmons died at Union Village. Nathaniel Rankin, born in N. C., in 1794; was minister many years at South Union; died in 1890. Benjamin Price, born in 1771; came from Busro in 1812, and became the most successful business manager ever at South Union; died in 1833. William and David were brothers of Benjamin Price, both went to Union Village and died there. Luanna Slover, who went to South Union in 1812, died there in 1864. Eldress Hortency, was a sister of Eldress Molly Goodrich. She died at Pleasant Hill.

All other persons, whose deaths are recorded in these notes, unless otherwise specified, died at Union Village.

Of the orders we get but a slight glimpse in the McClelland MS. Of the Ministry, Archibald Meacham stood first, with Ruth Darrow first and Martha Sanford second, in the Sisters' Lot. After the death of these two Eldresses, Saloma Dennis and Patience Naylor were sent to take their places, from Union Village. No trustees are mentioned except Samuel Johnston, Adam Gallagher and William Douglas, all of whom died in office. James Hopkins was a trustee at the time preparations were made for dissolving the Society. Only Henry Miller and Mary Hopkins, both at the North Family, are mentioned as family elders or eldresses. George Legier was the farmer, or land deacon.

All the land at West Union was bought by John Grider, who also purchased the lands on the Kankakee, owned by the Shakers of Union Village,— but purchasing price not stated. The Church Record of Union Village has this memorandum: "1832. June. The West Union premises are sold to a Virginian, by Nathan Sharp."

On May 23, 1827, Samuel McClelland, Benjamin Knox and Samuel Fisher left South Union for Yellow Banks for the West Union property and returned on 31.

Oct. 31, 1831, Ezra Sherman and Edward Burnham left Whitewater with a wagon and yoke of oxen for the Wabash for a pair of mill-stones left there by the Busro people. They were gone a month.

So ends the records of the Eagle and Straight Creek and West Union Shakers as separate bodies.

FRAKNLIN, OHIO, June 18, 1903.

More recently the following facts have come to hand:

Aug. 27, 1903, I found at Union Village an interesting document relating to West Union. It contains the Covenant of Feb. 25, 1815, and to this document are appended the following names:

NAMES OF BRETHREN.

Henry Miller,
Joseph Johnston,
John Johnston,
Benjamin Knox,
William Douglas,
William McComb,
James Brownfield,
Geo. Legier,
William Boyls,
Samuel McClelland,

Robert McGill,
John McComb,
John Martin,
John Youngman,
Frederick Wisman,
David Bornan,
Jesse McKeehan,
Adam Galagar,
James Price,
Abraham Jones,

James Hodge,
John Knox,
Alexander McKeehan,
John Hancock,
Wm. Price,
Samuel Johnson,
Wm. Price, Jr.,
Wm. Knox,
David Price,
Benjamin Miller.

NAMES OF SISTERS.

Sarah Jenkins,
Prudence Redmon,
Betsey Mayall,
Elizabeth Gallagar,
Betsy Worthington,
Hannah Davis,
Rebecah Price,
Isabell Gill,
Rebekah Brasilton,
Poly Tann,
Any Hancock,
Nancy McReynolds,
Jeney Galagar,
Rebecca Gill,
Fanny Price,

Peggy Steward,
Elizabeth Legier,
Elizabeth Martin,
Rebecca Boyle,
Olive Green,
Elizabeth Jenkins,
Peggy Knox,
Saly Houston,
Elizabeth McComb,
Nansy Knox,
Catey Boyle,
Poly Edie,
Poly Price,
Jiney Slover,
Nancy Boyls,

Jeney Martin,
Peggy Boyls,
Mary Hopkins,
Peggy Knox,
Aney Brownfield,
Susannah Lanill,
Sally Johns,
Peggy Naylor,
Betsy Murphy,
Nansy Jenkins,
Saly McComb,
Barbary Evins,
Nansy Galagar,
Tinsey Bedle.

The leading characters who first received the gospel were Robert Houston, Robert Gill and William Brazilton. In the spring of 1809, John McComb, John Hancock, Joseph Worthington, &c., moved from Kentucky with their families and joined the society. The principal men from Eagle Creek were Henry Miller, John Knox, John Johnson, Joseph Johnson, Daniel Redmon, Wm. Douglas, Alex McCechen, Geo. Legier, Wm. Gallagher, David Edie, John Edgington, John Martin, James Brownfield, Wm. Knox. At first the Believers numbered about 300, distributed into three localities, — one at Price's settlement, one at Robert Gill's, and the other at Robert Houston's. Geo. Legier founded the Center Family which consisted of 72 members. James Hodge stood second to Archibald Meacham.

Under date of Sept. 5, 1903, Elder Henry C. Blinn, East Canterbury, N. H., writes me that Issachar Bates made the statement that at the time the people decamped from West Union, during the War of

1812, "Gov. Harrison told Robert Gill and myself that he was going to move right out of his house, in Vincennes, to Cincinnati, and we might move into it, and if that would not hold us all, he would provide tents for the rest, and set six hundred to guard us, and it should not cost us one cent."

There were two John Slovers — father and son — both of whom joined the West Union Shakers. The elder died at South Union, Ky., in 1813, aged 80. He was one of the guides to the ill-fated expedition of Colonel Crawford against the Sandusky Indians in 1782. He was captured and had a remarkable escape. See Butterfield's "Crawford's Campaign"; also "Memoir of John Slover," first published in Pittsburgh in 1782; again at Nashville in 1843, and finally, in Cincinnati, in 1867. The younger John also died South Union, in 1858, aged 74. Of him Eldress Jane Cowan writes (Nov. 10, 1903): "I have spent many hours interested by listening to his tales regarding their escapades, hunting and trying to avoid being captured by the Indians." He owned Daniel Boone's pocket pen-knife, — a small hornlike instrument — which he presented to Elder John Perryman, of South Union, who still owns it.

In "A Declaration of the Society of People commonly called Shakers," published in 1815 by the officers of the Mt. Lebanon and Watervliet, N. Y., Shakers, referring to the sufferings of the West Union Society is the following statement: "A large society of our people in the Indian Territory has suffered much. In the time of General Harrison's campaign against the Indians, several divisions of his army, at different times, encamped in that Society; in consequence of which they suffered the loss of nearly all their living, and the whole Society, which consisted of nearly 400 people, were obliged to perform a journey of several hundred miles through the wilderness, under great sufferings and difficulty to seek a shelter among the Brethren of their own Society, in the states of Ohio and Kentucky. Their damage and loss consisted mostly in grain, cattle and other articles of provisions, consumed and taken away by the army, exclusive of what was paid for, was supposed to exceed 10,000 dollars; the whole of which was borne without assistance from any other source than the people of our denomination."

The celebrated Indian Chief, Tecumseh, was so favorably impressed with William Redmon that he informed him that so long as he remained at West Union the Shakers would not be harmed by any of his tribe.

In a memorandum of the Western Shaker lands, David Darrow, under date of August 13, 1814, says: "The Believers at Busserow own 2,110 acres."

SHAKER MISSION TO THE SHAWNEE INDIANS.

INTRODUCTION.

It is but a slight exaggeration to state that the aborigines of this country have been made the objects of conversion from all the religious sects that have found a domicile within our borders. Under the civilizing influence of the dominant exotic race the American savage has constantly gone down. It is not the fault of Christianity, nor of the civilization of the nineteenth century, but in the application. The missionary in his zeal has mistaken both ethnology and his calling. It required Christianity five hundred years to civilize the Norsemen. Wandering tribes neither jump into civilization nor Christianity. Both require generations of constant instruction. It is exceedingly difficult to overcome that hereditary disposition to revert to an original savage condition. The Jesuits, who had a peculiar faculty of adapting themselves to the manners, conditions, and habits of thought of the American savages, made but a slight impression on their dusky subjects. Whatever failure made by one sect, has been of little result to another. The same old methods constantly applied which previous failures experienced. It may be affirmed that the methods applied have been more in the nature of a persecution than in an elevation. The study of ethnology would have been of greater benefit and the chagrin of disappointment might have been avoided by utilizing this science.

The history of the various types of mankind demonstrates that the various conditions operate differently. The Esquimo has discovered that the kyack is the proper boat for his pursuit of food and raiment. The conditions force out that which is necessary to maintain the struggle for existence. The habits of life more or less govern mental acquirements. These and other considerations must enter into the conclusions that form intelligent conception of advancing the status of any tribe or type.

The American savage is a debased creature, prone to take up the vices of the white man, and, in his original condition, incapable of penetrating the exalted conception of life as expounded by Jesus Christ. He is a being requiring many generations of culture before fully comprehending the ethical qualities propounded in the New Testament.

If the large or powerful sects spend a part of their energy in missions to degraded tribes, it is not to be wondered at that the weaker denominations should imitate the example. That the Shakers, always noted for the paucity of their number, should waste their energy in such a fruitless enterprise as a mission to the savages, commands a different view than that necessarily accorded to other isms. Shaker theology and sociology radically differ from all other types of Christinaity. It may be affirmed that Shakerism contains no phase but may be elsewhere found among Christians; yet it must be noticed that it combines more peculiar features than can elsewhere be discovered. The Shakers have more perfectly approached the teachings of Jesus and his Apostles than any other of the organized bodies of believers. On the other hand the nature of the Indian is largely animal. He is where the ancestors of the white man were many thousands of years ago. To expect an Indian to lay aside his brutal nature and take upon himself the life of a Shaker, requires a credulity too vast even to contemplate.

Shakerism in 1807 was practically in its infancy. In the west it was only in the third year of its existence. It was five years later before it was organized into church relationship. The people, for the most part, lived at Union Village, in log houses. The first frame dwelling-house was not completed until October, 1806, and that was built for the Elders. However, the leaders of Shakerism at Union Village were alive to what they apprehended were the needs of humanity, and were ever ready to drop seed on whatever appeared to be good soil. They were not far removed from the Indians, and any religious commotion among the latter would necessarily attract their attention. In the simplicity of their hearts they believed that the subtle, treacherous, ferocious and diabolical savage could be transformed into a gentle, non-resistent, God-fearing and man-loving celibate.

KENTUCKY REVIVAL AND INDIANS.

During the "Great Kentucky Revival" of 1800 and 1801, the Indians received the attention of the awakened and zealous. Fervent prayers were offered up that the Indians might also share in the blessed hope and joyful anticipation of the future state; and missionaries were repeatedly sent out from among the subjects of the revival, to convert them to the Christian faith, but with little success. In the fall of the year 1804, a great number of savages, belonging to different tribes, assembled together and held a feast of love and union, and during their conclave danced and rejoiced before the Great Spirit, with the purpose of reviving the religion of their ancestors. The fame of the meeting was wafted to the whites, among whom were those who queried whether God would convert them in some way different from what had hitherto been employed.

During the year 1805 fresh reports broke out concerning the Indians, which affirmed that a large body of them was moving down the western border of Ohio, and were about to form a settlement. The rumors caused much agitation concerning them. Some proclaimed that the movement presaged war, while others affirmed that they were in pursuit of religion and the means of an honest livelihood; that they intended to labor, and in their present circumstances the neighboring whites were supporting them by charitable donations.

SHAKER PROPAGANDA.

The continuance of the various reports, concerning the movements and condition of the Indians, created much anxiety among the Shakers at Union Village (then called Turtle Creek). It was determined to direct a missionary body to proceed to the Shawnee Indians, then living at Greenville, in order to find out the real situation, both in respect to things temporal and spiritual. The persons selected were David Darrow, Benjamin Seth Youngs and Richard McNemar.

David Darrow, who was born June 21, 1750, and died June 27, 1825, has been sketched in my article on the Shakers of Union Village in the QUARTERLY for June, 1902, and need not here be repeated.

Benjamin Seth Youngs was born September 17, 1774. He was a member of the propaganda that set out from New Lebanon, N. Y., on January 1, 1805, and was one of the first three Shakers in the west, and the ablest of the trio, and, in all probability, the most indefatigable missionary ever belonging to the sect. So far as I have been able to learn no account of his life or missionary labors has been preserved. His itinerary, as preserved in the church record, was as follows: On January 16, 1809, accompanied by two of the brethren, he set out on foot for Buserow (West Union, Ind. A society was here established, but after many vicissitudes was abandoned), and returned on March 29; April 25, accompanied by Elder Matthew Houston, he set out for Gasper (now South Union), Kentucky, by way of Eagle Creek, Caneridge and Shawnee Run; he was present and took a very active part in resisting the mob at Union Village on August 27, 1810, although the record is silent, but for September 13, records that in company with two others, he started on that day for Buserow, on the Wabash, in Indiana, and returned on December 4th; February 20, 1811, accompanied by Ruth Darrow, Edith Dennis and Peter Pease, he set out for Buserow (West Union), and at Cincinnati, on the 22nd, met the boats containing the believers from Eagle Creek, who were destined for the same place; he must soon after have returned for on April 9th he set out for Kentucky and returned on August 2d; September 25 he went to Kentucky and returned on September 11, 1812, and on the 29th· started for Gasper, where he probably staid until September 30, 1814, at which date he arrived at Union Village; on July 16, 1818, he passed through Union Village on his return from New Lebanon to Gasper; March 27, 1820, he was again in Union Village and returned to Gasper on April 1st; November 8, 1829, he was on a visit to Union Village, but departed from there on the 24th; May 27, 1833, he arrived in Union Village but after ten days set out for home; on May 14, 1835, he was on his way to New Lebanon, and on September 22, arrived at Union Village on his return, and on the

30th set out for Gasper. The last record of him is for October 16, 1836, and is as follows: "Elder Benjamin S. Youngs arrives here from South Union," and "is now leaving the west to return no more. He goes to his old home at Watervleit, New York, after a residence of more than thirty years in the west. He gave us his valedictory address in meeting today. We bless him and pray that heaven may. He proceeds on the 20, same." During his long stay at Gasper he was an elder, but whether in the ministry — which he probably was —the record is silent.

Richard McNemar, born November 20, 1770, was a Presbyterian clergyman, who had a commanding influence during the Great Kentucky Revival. He was one of the six witnesses that met at Caneridge, Bourbon county, Kentucky, June 28, 1804, and on that day dissolved the Springfield Presbytery. While in charge of the church at Turtle Creek, he was converted to Shakerism, and united with that sect on April 24, 1805, followed by his entire family. During the rest of his life he was an elder in the order. In the Church Record his name occurs but sixteen times. April 22, 1807, he set out for Gasper, and returned December 4; January 16, 1809, he set out for Buserow on foot, and returned March 29, accompanied by Youngs and Issacher Bates; with the latter and John Hancock, on the 5th December, 1809, he again set out for Buserow, but failing to reach his destiny, on account of the high waters, he returned on the 10th; March 27, 1810, with Archibald Meacham, he set out for Buserow and returned May 1st; in company with David Moseley, Ruth Darrow and Peggy Houston, on October 15, he set out on a visit to Eagle Creek to visit the colony of believers at that place, returning on the 27th; April 9, 1811, he "set out for Kentucky" and returned August 2; June 1st, 1812, he started for Dayton to see the Governor respecting military matters which concerned believers; March 8, 1813, he went to Watervleit (near Dayton), where he was taken sick, and Nathan Sharp, on the 15th, started to bring him home; September 5, 1817, he was indicted at Lebanon, for assault and battery, on a false oath given by John Davis; February 14, 1830, he was released from his eldership at the Centre House, *pro tempore;* December 28, 1835, he was "released from his care as an Elder at Watervleit; but does not remove from Watervleit till 13th January,

1836." The last record is made for September 15, 1839: "This evening, Richard McNemar, Sen., deceased; after a protracted illness of chronic bowel complaint. He was among the first who received the gospel in the west, — being previously a Presbyterian minister in this place. One of the most zealous and loyal believers who ever embraced the gospel in this western land. Altogether more than ordinary intelligent."

Issacher Bates, born January 29, 1758, was one of the original propaganda that set out from New Lebanon, on January 1st, 1805. He is mentioned thirty-four times in the Church Record. April 22, 1807, he set out for Gasper and returned December 4; May 2, 1808, he "set out on a visit to Kentucky" and returned home June 12 following; July 27, he returned from a tour to the Wabash; he started for the Wabash September 18 and returned November 7; January 16, 1809, he set out for Buserow on foot and returned March 29; August 29, he set out on a visit to Buserow and arrived home on Sunday, September 24; December 5, he started for the Wabash, but returned the 10th, on account of high waters; on the 14th, he again set out for the Wabash and returned February 19, 1810, via Caneridge, Kentucky; March 15 he started for Shawnee Run (now Pleasant Hill), Kentucky, and arrived home March 28, 1811; November 11, he arrived from Buserow, and returned there December 19; he arrived from Buserow September 10, 1812; June 1, 1814, with Solomon King, he set out to visit the Harmony Society of Dutch people, returning the 21st; December 14, 1816, he arrived from West Union (Buserow), Ind., and returned the 17th; January 7, 1819, he arrived from West Union; April 21, 1820, he again came from West Union, and on June 22 returned; January 24, 1822, he arrived from, and on the 29th returned to West Union; January 8, 1823, he went to Darby Plains, Ohio, and returned the 24th; January 29, 1824, he removed from West Union to Union Village; March 30, he started for Zoar, a communistic society of Dutch people, where he was taken very sick, and on May 10, Calvin Morrell and Charles D. Hampton (both formerly physicians) started for Zoar to take care of him, and returned with him on the 27th; September 2, he set off to visit the Society at North Union, near Cleveland, and returned October 9, and on the 21st, removed to Watervleit; June 27, 1825, he came to Union Village in order to attend the funeral of Elder David Darrow; July 29, 1826, he set out for West Union, and returned home, via Pleasant Hill, Kentucky, on September 16; June 1, 1830, he started for New Lebanon and returned September 2; May 27, 1833, he arrives at Union Village, and "expects to take a long visiting tour in Kentucky." The last record is for April 16, and 30, and May 14: "It is now concluded for our good old veteran pioneer, Elder Issachar, who has done so much, and spent all his latter days, nearly, in planting and building up the gospel in the West, to return to the East, and retire from these labors. He will visit among us till the 30th inst., when he will return to Watervleit." April 30: "Elder Issachar returns to Watervleit (Ohio) to-day, preparatory to starting to New Lebanon; we therefore have taken our final change of salutations and farewell, with many well wishes for each others welfare." May 14: Elder Issachar starts from Watervleit to join his company at Circleville to go East to return no more."

NARRATIVE OF THE MISSION TO THE INDIANS.

For a full account of the Shaker mission to the Shawnee Indians we are indebted to the report given by Richard McNemar, who based his narrative upon the Journal kept by the missionaries. On March 17, 1807, the three brethren, David Darrow, Richard McNemar and Benjamin S. Youngs set out in search of the Indians, and on the 23rd arrived at their village, now Greenville, Ohio. "When we came in sight of the village, the first object that attracted our view was a large frame house, about 150 by 34 feet in size, surrounded with 50 or 60 smoking cottages. We rode up and saluted some men who were standing before the door of a tent, and by a motion of the hand were directed to another wigwam where we found one who could talk English. We asked him if their feelings were friendly.

A. O yes, we are all brothers.

Q. Where are your chiefs — we wish to have a talk with them?

23

A. They are about 4 miles off making sugar.

Q. What are their names?

A. Lal-lu-e-tsee-ka, and Te-kum-tha.*

Q. Can any of them talk English?

A. No; but there is a good interpreter there, George Blue-Jacket. He has gone to school, and can read and talk well.

Q. What is that big house for?

A. To worship the Great Spirit.

Q. How do you worship?

A. Mostly in speaking.

Q. Who is your chief speaker?

A. Our prophet, Lal-lu-e-tsee-ka. He converses with the Great Spirit, and tells us how to be good.

Q. Do all that live here, believe in him?

A. Yes; we all believe — he can dream to God.

Conducted by a pilot, we repaired to the sugar-camp, where 30 or 40 were assembled with the prophet, who was very sick and confined to his tent. We expressed our desire of having a talk with him. But George informed us that he could not talk to us, that ministers of the white people would not believe what he said, but counted it foolish and laughed at it, therefore he could not talk; besides, he had a pain in his head, and was very sick. After informing him we were not such ministers, he asked:

Do you believe a person can have true knowledge of the Great Spirit, in the heart, without going to school and learning to read?

A. We believe they can; and that is the best kind of knowledge.

After some talk of this kind with George, he went into the prophet's tent, where several chiefs were collected, and after continuing their council there about an hour, Lal-lu-e-tsee-ka came out and took his seat in a circle of about 30 persons who sat round the fire. All were silent — every countenance grave and solemn, when he began to speak. His discourse continued about half an hour, in which the most pungent eloquence expressed his

---

* Where Tecumseh lived at Greenville is still called Tecumseh's Point. It is now owned by Herschel Morningstar.

deep and heart-felt sense of what he spoke, but in language which George said, he could not correctly translate into English. However, the general sense he occasionally communicated during our stay.

In the first place, that he (the prophet) had formerly lived on White river; had been a doctor and a very wicked man. About two years ago, while attending on sick people at Attawa, in a time of general sickness, he was struck with a deep and awful sense of his sins — cried mightily to the Good Spirit to show him some way of escape, and in his great distress, fell into a vision, in which he appeared to be travelling along a road, and came to where it forked — the right hand way he was informed led to happiness and the left to misery.

This fork in the road, he was told, represented that stage of life in which people were convicted of sin; and those who took the right hand way quit everything that was wicked and became good. But the left hand road was for such as would go on and be bad, after they were shown the right way. They all move slow, till they come here, but when they pass the fork to the left, then they go swift. On the left hand way he saw three houses — from the first and second were pathways that led into the right hand road, but no way leading from the third. This, said he, is eternity. He saw vast crowds going swift along the left hand road, and great multitudes in each of the houses, under different degrees of judgment and misery. He mentioned particularly the punishment of the drunkard. One presented him a cup of liquor resembling melted lead; if he refused to drink it he would urge him, saying: Come, drink — you used to love whiskey. And upon drinking it, his bowels were seized with an exquisite burning. This draught he had often to repeat. At the last house their torment appeared inexpressible; under which he heard them scream, cry pitiful, and roar like the falls of a river. He was afterwards (said the interpreter) taken along the right hand way, which was all interspersed with flowers of delicious smell, and showed a house at the end of it where was everything beautiful, sweet and pleasant; and still went on learning more and more; but in his first vision he saw nothing but the state of the wicked; from which the Great Spirit told him to go and warn his people of their danger, and call upon them to put away their sins, and be good. Whereupon he began to speak to them in great distress, and would weep and tremble, while addressing them. Some believed — were greatly alarmed — began to confess their sins — forsake them, and set out to be good. This spread the alarm, and brought many others from different tribes to see and hear, who were affected in like manner. But some of the chiefs who were very wicked, would not believe, and tried to keep the people from believing, and encouraged them on in their former wicked ways. Whereupon the Great Spirit told him to separate from these wicked chiefs and their people, and showed him particularly where to come, towards the big ford where the peace was concluded with the Americans; and there make provision to receive and instruct all from the different tribes that were willing to be good.

Accordingly all that believed had come and settled there, and a great many Indians had come to hear, and many more were expected. That some white people were afraid, but they were foolish; for they would not hurt any one.

We asked a number of questions:

Q. Do you believe that all mankind are going away from the Good Spirit by wicked works?

A. Yes; that is what we believe. And the prophet feels great pity for all.

Q. Do you believe that the Great Spirit once made himself known to the world, by a man that was called Christ?

A. Yes, we believe it, and the Good Spirit has showed our prophet what has been in many generations, and he says he wants to talk with some white people about these things.

Q. What sins does your prophet speak now against?

A. Witchcraft, poisoning people, fighting, murdering, drinking whisky, and beating their wives because they will not have children. All such as will not leave off there, go to Eternity —he knows all bad people that commit fornication, and can tell it all from seven years old.

Q. What do those do who have been wicked, when they believe the prophet?

A. They confess all.

Q. To whom do they confess?

A. To the prophet and four chiefs.

Q. Do they confess all the bad things they ever did?

A. All from seven years old. And cry and tremble when they come to confess.

Q. How did you learn this? The Roman Catholics confess their sins.

A. Some Wyandots joined the Roman Catholics at Detroit, who now believe in our prophet. Roman Catholics confess their sins, but go and do bad again. Our people forsake their bad way when they have confessed.

They asked us several questions concerning our people, and particularly whether they drank whisky; and appeared not a little rejoiced, to learn that there were some among the whites, so far reclaimed, as to lay aside the use of that pernicious liquor. We inquired how they made out for provisions. They answered they had none. So many people came there—eat up all they had raised.

The only meal we saw them eat was a turkey divided among thirty or forty. And the only relief we could afford them, was ten dollars for the purpose of buying corn.

After the evening conversation closed we concluded to return to the village, with George and several others; and mounted our horses. It was now in the dusk of the evening, and the full moon just rising above the horizon, when one of their speakers stood up in an alley, between the camps, and spoke for about fifteen minutes, with great solemnity, which was heightened at every pause, with a loud *Seguoy* from the surrounding assembly. . On this occasion our feelings were like Jacob's when he cried out, "How dreadful is this place! Surely the Lord is in this place!" And the world knew it not. With these impressions we returned to the village, and spent the night.

Next morning, as soon as it was day, one of their speakers mounted a log, near the southeast corner of the village, and began the morning service with a loud voice, in thanksgiving to the Great Spirit. He continued his address for near an hour. The people were all in their tents, some at the distance of fifteen or twenty rods; yet they could all distinctly hear, and gave a solemn and loud assent, which sounded from tent to tent, at every pause. While we stood in his view, at the end of the meeting-house, on rising ground, from which we had a prospect of the surrounding wigwams, and the vast open plain or prairie, to the south and east, and which looks over the big fort, toward the north, for the distance of two miles, we felt as if we were among the tribes of Israel, on their march to Canaan. Their simplicity and unaffected zeal for the increase of the work of the Good Spirit—their ardent desires for the salvation of their unbelieving kindred, with that of all mankind—their willingness to undergo hunger, fatigue, hard labor and sufferings, for the sake of those who came to learn the way of righteousness— and the high expectations they had, of multitudes flocking down to hear the prophet the ensuing summer, etc., were considerations truly affecting;—while Ske-law-wa hailed the opening day with loud aspirations of gratitude to the Good Spirit; and encouraged the obedient followers of Divine light to persevere.

They showed us several letters of friendship from the Governor of Ohio, Gen. Whiteman and others, from which they appeared that the Americans believed their dispositions to be peaceable and brotherly. Their marks of industry were considerable, not only in preparing ground for cultivation, but also in hewing and preparing timber for more commodious buildings. From all we could gather, from their account of the work, and of their faith and practice — what we heard and felt in their evening and morning worship — their peaceable dispositions, and attention to industry, we were induced to believe that God, in very deed, was mightily at work among them. And under this impression, we invited three or four of them to come down and see us, as soon as they found it convenient."

The stay of the deputation was short, for on March 27 they returned. The time actually at Greenville is no where stated, but in all probability it was not more than five days.

To the foregoing account Mr. McNemar adds the following:

"Near the middle of June upwards of twenty appeared at Turtle Creek, encamped in the woods at a small distance from the church, and tarried four days. They had worship every evening at the encampment; and several on the Sabbath attended the

meeting of the Believers, and behaved with order and decorum. During their stay they conducted with peace and civility,
and received no contrary treatment from any in the place. And
to relieve, in some degree, the pressing wants of hungry fama-
lies at home, 27 horses were loaded each with provisions, from
among the Believers. Yet this act of charity, however small,
did not long escape the censorious reflections of some hard-
hearted mortals; but even furnished a pretext for implications the
most monstrous and unreasonable. However, in this, as in all
other cases of the kind, those who busied themselves about what
did not concern them, were much divided in their opinion. Some
had it, that a number of the Indians had joined the Shakers, and
many more were coming on. Others, that an Indian had offered
to confess his sins, but that the Shakers could not understand
him; and therefore the Indians were convinced too, that the
Shakers were deceivers. Others tried to make believe that the
Shakers were encouraging them to war — or at least to contend
for the land on which they had settled. And some were foolish
enough to go all the way to the village, and put on a mask of
hypocrisy, to find out whether this was not the case. Of all
this trouble, both of mind and body, such might have been saved,
had they accustomed themselves, at an earlier period, to believe
those who tell the truth and nothing but the truth.

About the 12th of August (1807) they were visited again
by two of the brethren from Turtle Creek, who found them in
possession of the same peaceable and brotherly spirit. They had
but little conversation with them, yet obtained abundant satisfaction by attending their meeting, which continued from a little
after dark till the sun was an hour high the next morning.

The meeting was opened with a lengthy discourse, delivered
by the prophet; after which they assembled in a close crowd, and
continued their worship by singing and shouting, that might have
been heard at least to the distance of two miles.

Their various songs, and perfect harmony in singing, shouting, etc., rendered the meeting very solemn. But all this appeared
far inferior to that solemn fear of God, hatred of sin, and that
peace, love and harmony which they manifested among each other.
They needed no invitation to pay another visit to Turtle Creek;

nor were they forbidden. Therefore, pursuant to their own choice, a number of them appeared again at the church, August 29th, and were received with usual kindness and charity. On this occasion, some in the neighborhood expressed their uneasiness lest there was some mischievous plot carrying on. But amidst the threats of the ignorant or misinformed, the Shawnees testified that they were wholly for peace, and abundantly proved it by their meekness, gentleness and forbearance. The only expression like resentment that I heard from them on the occasion, was from Nancy, the interpreter, while a bold advocate for the New Christian doctrine, was boasting how the white people could cut them off. She said they were for nothing but peace; but if white people would go to war, they would be destroyed by a day of judgment, that not one soul would be left on the face of the earth.

Although these poor Shawnees have had no particular instruction but what they received by the outpouring of the Spirit, yet in point of real light and understanding, as well as behavior, they shame the Christian world. Therefore, of that Spirit which hath wrought so great a change, the believers at Turtle Creek are not ashamed; yet they are far from wishing them to turn to the right hand or to the left, to form an external union with them or any other people. But they are willing that God should carry on His work among them without interruption, as He thinks proper."

CHURCH RECORD AND THE INDIANS.

The Church Record book, on the Shakers' relation to the Indians, is brief and unsatisfactory, as upon almost every other point. A fair illustration is afforded in the fact that the manuscript record book extending from January 1, 1805, to April 30, 1861, contains but 480 pages. None of it is closely written and innumerable lines are skipped.

Such records as the Church Book gives are here reproduced:

1807. Mar. 17. "Elder David D. — B. S. Youngs and Richard McNemar set out for Greenville, to pay a visit to the Shawnee Indians, and witness the Reported revival of religion among them: (for an account of which see pamphlet entitled Ky. Revival) They return home on 27 of same."

May 30. "James Patterson and wife arrive here from Beaulah,

:and in company with them were 21 Indians and 2 squaws, being a party of the aforesaid religious Indians."

"Sab. 31. Part of the Indians attend meeting, and also a great multitude of spectators. Indians set out for their homes June 4." "Aug. 10. Issachar Bates and Richard McNemar set out this morning to visit the religious Shawnee Indians."

"29. About 50 Indians arrive here last evening; we are threatened with being put to the sword's point, for showing charity to the poor Indians. This threat is from one Saml. Trousdale, a militia officer."

"Sep. 3. Indians return to Greenville."

CONCLUSION.

The records show that the Shakers desisted from any real efforts to promulgate their doctrines among the Indians. While they were well received, the evidence conveys the idea that the missionaries saw no opening for instructions after their manner. On the other hand, all things considered, they made encouraging strides among the civilized. Besides Union Village, permanent lodgment was effected at North Union, Watervleit, and Whitewater, in Ohio; South Union and Pleasant Hill, in Kentucky, and West Union in Indiana. Many additions and much encouragement were received at Beaver, Eagle Creek, Straight Creek and Darby Plains, all of which were in Ohio. If the same persistency had been continued by the later Shakers as was manifested by the original leaders of this sect would not have been on the wane as so clearly demonstrated at this time. Shakerism depends on no large church for its moral support and increase. It receives from the world and is its own magnetic center. At this day it is wholly wanting in missionary enterprise. At Union Village there are but two men under fifty years of age. The Society has all the appearance of being doomed to extinction when the present members pass away. Still, we do not know. No man knoweth what another hour may bring forth.

Franklin, Ohio, February 23, 1902.

MOBBING THE SHAKERS OF UNION VILLAGE.

It may be affirmed that of all the Christian sects of America, not one is less aggressive or lives more within itself than that known as The Shakers, or more properly speaking The Millennial Church. It is true that in its early history it possessed a little missionary zeal, but this was not of the offensive kind. In common with all the sects it placed its own doctrines to the front, proclaiming them to be the true representative ideas of Jesus Christ. It cannot be denied that the Shakers indulged in extravagant expressions of religious emotions, and were excessively strict in their discipline; but this was all within themselves, for they did not encroach upon their neighbors. Towards the strangers and co-religionists they were harmless, kind and considerate.

It is worthy of remark in this age of endowments or special benefactions, the Shakers have never received any donations or gifts save those which have come from within their own communion. In proportion to the number and wealth, no sect has been so generous. In all probability no sect has lived so closely to the Christ ideal as that under consideration.

When it is considered that a sect free from trespass, given to good works, benevolent and devout, refraining from the turmoils of political strife and the carnage and inhumanity of war, should be subject to the passions of a mob, it behooves one, having optimistic views, to inquire into the source or controlling motive that led to the public violence. It is the history of every Shaker community to experience rough treatment even at the hands of those who should have been respecters of law and order.

ORIGIN OF THE MOB OF 1810.

Religious hate and rancor have been the source of untold misery. Even in the light and discoveries of this age, only a small portion of the enlightened have been brought to the realizing sense that every man must be supreme within himself respecting his tenets. It does not require wide observation to note the fact that even those claiming to be most liberal, and really having broad views, are too often the most illiberal. Numerous instances can be produced to prove that many liberals are even more illiberal than the dogmatist and the bigot. Such may be shown to be the case in the persecution of the Shakers of Union Village, Ohio.

The origin of the various communities of Shakers of Ohio and Kentucky may be directly traced to the "Great Kentucky Revival" of 1800, 1801. This was the greatest religious upheaval ever known in America; and the conditions were such as to make it impossible to have the same ever repeated. The causes that led to the commotion and insured its success were manifold. The cry for a broader basis, or more toleration, was not among the least. While the exictement lasted there was a display of emotions, an extravagance of expression or manners, that beggars all description. Among the leaders there were really able men; who during the revel were unfortunately overcome by the pressure and gave countenance to transactions that, in their cooler moments, would meet with their condemnation. The outbreak began in Logan and Christian counties, Kentucky, on the waters of the Gasper and Red Rivers. The first camp meeting was held at Cabin Creek, May 22, 1800, and continued four days and three nights. "The scene was awful beyond description; the falling, crying out, praying, exhorting, singing, shouting, etc., exhibited such new, and striking evidences of a supernatural power, that few, if any, could escape without being affected. Such as tried to run from it were frequently struck on the way, or impelled, by some alarming signal to return." Among the prime movers were such men as Malcolm Worley, John Dunlavy, Richard McNemar, Robert Marshall, John Thompson, David Purviance, Barton W. Stone, etc. Before the year 1805 the Schismatics had regular societies in Ohio at Turtle Creek, Eagle Creek, Springfield, Orangedale, Salem, Beaver Creek, Clear Creek, etc. In Kentucky at Cabin Creek, Flemingsburgh, Concord, Caneridge, Indian Creek, Bethel, Paint Creek, Shawny Run, etc., besides an innumerable multitude scattered throughout Tennessee, North Carolina, Virginia, and the western parts of Pennsylvania. These Schismatics were known then, and are still called by the name of New Lights, but among themselves they take the name of Christians. Their recognized leader was Barton W. Stone.

The news of the Revival spread all over the country and in due time aroused the interest of the Shaker Ministry at New Lebanon, New York, who dispatched John Meacham, Issachar Bates and Benjamin Seth Youngs to the scene of the commotion. These missionaries set out on foot on January 1st, 1805, and arrived at Turtle Creek Church (Union Village) on March 22nd, as a propaganda. The first convert from the Turtle Creek Church was Malcolm Worley, on March 27, a wealthy and influential man, but somewhat eccentric. The next was Anna Middleton (colored), March 29, and on the 31st, Cornelius Campbell. Richard McNemar and his wife Jenny joined on April 24. In the year 1805, or soon after, the families or heads of families that joined the Shakers, besides those already mentioned, were Francis Bedle, Samuel Sering, Samuel Holloway, Elijah Davis, Jonathan Davis, Stephen Spining, David Spining, John Dennis, Abner Bonnell, Stephen Williams, Benjamin Howard, Amos Valentine, John Miller, Joseph Stout, James Bedell, David Hill, Calvin Morrell, Joseph Patterson, John Wallace, John Able, Samuel Rollins, Thomas Hunt, Charles West, Allen Woodruff, Moses Easton, David Corey, Daniel Boyd, Lorenzo Belcher, John Gee, David Johnson, John Sharp, Matthew Houston, Andrew Brown, John Naylor, John Carson, Belteshazzar Draggoo, John Houston, Robert Baxter, James Dickson, Joseph Irwin, Nathan Pegg, John Woods, James Smith, Garner McNemar, William Davis, Sr., Abigail Kitchell, Malinda Watts, Jenny Byrne, Rachel Seward, Betsy Anderson, Reuben Morris, Jacob Holloway, Caleb Pegg, John Slater, Jonathan Gaudy, Joseph Lockwood, Thomas N. Naylor, William Runyon, and some others. To these there must be added about thirty unmarried.

It is safe to assume that the greater percentage of these, as well as those who soon after followed (numbering in all prior to 1812, 370 souls) was converted from the New Lights.

Add to this the fact that Shaker missionaries were sent among the New Light Churches, and, in the vicinity of some, Shaker communities were being established, it may easily be seen that all the venom of religious hate would be stirred up among the New Lights, however much they may have called for more freedom. The heart of Barton Stone was stirred within him, and he with some of his coadjutors set about to put down Shakerism.

It is not intended here to have it inferred that Barton Stone desired violent means against the Shakers. His intentions may have been of the more peaceful order. However that may be he certainly paved the way that the thoughtless and violent might pass over.

The leaders of the Schismatics must be judged in the light in which they taught. Revolting against dogmatism they became dogmatists; proclaiming religious liberty they became persecutors, and decrying a written creed they became advocates of "a system of theology." The first words against the Shakers did not come from any of the members of the Turtle Creek Church, but from Springfield, and under date of April 5, 1805: "It matters not to me who they are, who are devil's tools, whether men or angels, good men or bad. In the strength of God I mean not to spare. I used lenity once to the devil, because he came in a good man (Worley). But my God respects no man's person. I would they were even cut off who trouble you. I mean in the name and strength of God to lift his rod of Almighty truth against the viper," etc. Thompson followed the Shakers to a campmeeting held at Turtle Creek, and in a loud voice proclaimed, "They are liars! They are liars! They are liars! According to the fable, 'A liar is not to be believed, even when he speaks the truth.'" Another Christian followed Issachar Bates, crying out, "Go to hell," and another pursued John Meacham from place to place, spitting in his face, and crying aloud to make a great fire, and burn these false prophets, while others laughed and encouraged him. Stone having invited McNemar to attend a general meeting at Concord in August, 1805, forbade him to speak or even come in the house. At the same time silence was imposed on John Dunlavy, Benjamin Youngs and Malcolm Worley, while John Thompson, Robert Marshall, Barton W. Stone, David Purviance, J. Stockwell and A. Brannon, alternately delivered addresses against the Shakers, in which some of them were named out, pronounced liars, defamed by many slanderous reports, which they could have proven false if opportunity had been given. The only reply given was, "I am sorry to see you abusing your own light." In the introduction to his "Letters on Atonement" Stone observes that the arguments used by his opponents are "Bold, inscriptural assertions — hard names — delusion — error — doctrines of devils — Arminianism — Socinianism — Deism, etc. Such arguments have no effect on a candid mind, but they powerfully influence dupes and bigots. The candid look for truth and plain, unequivocal arguments." In the postscript of his reply to Campbell's strictures, he says: "You have heard no doubt before this time, of the lamentable departure of two of our preachers, and a few of their hearers from the true gospel, into wild enthusiasm, or Shakerism. They have made shipwreck of faith, and turned aside to an old woman's fables, who broached them in New England, about twenty-five years ago. These wolves in sheep's clothing, have smelt us from afar, and have come to tear, rend and devour," etc. It was currently reported among the New Lights "that the Shakers castrated all their males, and consequently exposed their necks to the gallows; or divested of all modesty, stripped and danced naked in their night meetings, blew out the candles, and went into a promiscuous debauch. And what was still more shocking — the fruits of their unlawful embraces they concealed by the horrid crime of murder." It was charged that "these men say that each one of them is a Christ, and we must throw our Bibles away and follow them; they forbid to marry, and attach criminality to that for which we have the express command of God; they encourage men to beat and abuse their wives, and turn them away; they are a set of worldly-minded, cunning deceivers, whose religion is earthly, sensual, and devilish (see Stone's Letter, July 1806); these men have testified they would never die." Even the grave was robbed of its sanctity, and the word went forth that Prudence Farrington had recanted Shakerism on her death bed. She arrived at Union Village May 31, 1806, and died April 11, 1807, in the 31st year of her age, a loving sister, a blessed virgin, a holy woman. Among her last words she uttered: "Strengthen the brethren."

> "Her holy examples of infinite price:
> Brought up in the gospel, a stranger to vice;
> Her cross from the first she did faithfully bear,
> And finish'd her course in her thirty–first year:
> Her heaven–born spirit, to angels akin,
> (Not stain'd with the flesh nor polluted with sin)
> Has now got releas'd from the sorrows of earth,
> And shares the full joys of her heavenly birth."

There is another factor too important to overlook. Every community has a few restless spirits ever ready to take up with the latest fad or· doctrine. Such an upheavel as the Kentucky Revival would throw all sorts of humanity to the surface, many of whom would be left stranded on the shoals of uncertainty. Many of these would be taken with Shakerism, but only to leave and then vilify those who had trusted them. They would circulate reports having no foundation, but tending to excite the lawless or vicious. Taking all things into consideration, it is not surprising that a mob might be incited.

NARRATIVE OF THE MOB OF 1810.

The first mob that assembled at Union Village was on Monday, August 27, 1810. The mob consisted of a body of five hundred armed men, led by officers in military array, preceded and followed by a large concourse of spectators of all descriptions of people, estimated at nearly two thousand in number, whose object was to witness a conflict between the military and a few harmless and defenceless Shakers. Among this great concourse were many who were friendly to the Society, and whose only wish was to prevent mischief and preserve peace; but the far greater number was either entire strangers or decided enemies, who came to support the military in case of necessity. Many of these were armed in mob array, some with guns and swords, some with bayonets fixed on poles or sticks of various lengths, and other with staves, hatchets, knives and clubs. These formed a motley multitude of every description, from ragged boys to hoary-headed men, exhibiting altogether a hideous and grotesque appearance. This ruthless assemblage, gathered for the purpose of infringing on the rights of conscience, and in the public press of the day was called "An expedition against the Shakers."

This extraordinary proceeding first began to be agitated principally through the instrumentality of one John Davis, John and Robert Wilson and John Bedle, apostates, who had become bold in wickedness and false accusations against their former co-religionists, whereby those who had long waited for false witnesses to accuse the Shakers of something criminal seized the opportunity to accomplish their purpose.

Accordingly, about the 'first of June, Col. James Smith inserted in the public press a declaration that he had been informed by the aforesaid apostates that the education of children among the Shakers was chiefly a pretense; that they whip their underlings severely, and also their children; that they count it no sin to have carnal knowledge of their own women; that all surplus money and property are given up to Elder David Darrow; that he keeps the whole treasury of the Society in his own hands; that he, like the pope, exercises unlimited authority over all under his control; and that he, with his council, live sumptuously on the labors of others; with many other things of a like nature, all of which were made to exasperate the public mind with indignation against the Believers.

What seemed intended to be the weightiest charges in the publication were certain things therein alleged against James Smith, Jr., who was a Believer, and for which there was a plausible pretense. James' wife, Polly, having deserted him on account of his faith, and he refusing to give up his children to her, furnished the old man with many charges of oppression.

The advertisement of Col. Smith did not go unchallenged, but was answered publicly in a spirited manner by Richard McNemar, who not only exposed its falsity, but also cited its author to prove what he had alleged, or else bear the character of a slanderer. The answer was little regarded, and it appears that Smith and his associates had no intention of prosecuting the matter in a lawful manner.

During the month of July the Shakers were secretly informed that a subscription was being circulated for the purpose of raising a mob and that John Davis and the two Wilsons were active agents. Having been publicly accused of the matter they denied that there was any such thing in agitation. On August 23, an intimation was given that Col. Smith, with a number of men from Kentucky, were over and engaged in collecting others to assist in carrying off his grandchildren. On the next day, Friday, it was learned from credible authority that five hundred men were to assemble on the following Monday at Capt. Kilbreath's, distant about three miles, and intended to come as a mob and take off the Smith children and enact other outrages. The next day the news became more definite, and in the afternoon Wade Loofbourrow, a young man living near Hamilton, informed them that he had seen the written instrument which the designing party had signed, but did not read it; that it was in the hands of Major J. Potter at Hamilton Court the day before; that the mob was a subject of common conversation on that occasion; that he heard Major Potter say that five hundred were subscribed; also, that Rev. Matthew G. Wallace was forward and active in the business; that Major Potter would be second in command; that the Springfield Light-Horse would be on the ground and many more of the baser sort from Springfield, the Big Hill, from around Hamilton and from the vicinity northwest of the village; that the party would appear on Monday; and that he came purposely to inform them and desired to tarry that he might witness the result. The same evening information came in from every quarter of their preparations and threats of abuse; that they meant to tar and feather Richard McNemar and drive the old Shakers out of the country and restore the rest to their former faith and method of living.

The following Sunday. (August 26) some of the party attended the religious services, especially Captain Robinson, who avowed that they would be on the ground the next day for the purpose of violence.

24

The State's Attorney, J. Collet, and the Sheriff of the county, T. McCray, both of Lebanon, went to the place of rendezvous and warned the party of the unlawfulness of their intentions. Attending the Sunday services were Dr. Budd and Dr. Bladgley, of New Jersey; Colonel Stanley, from Cincinnati, and D. Corneal; a noted young man from Kentucky. They determined to return the next day and witness the event.

Early Monday morning, August 27, all the Shakers of Union Village might have been seen at their usual avocations, just as though no note of warning had been received. About 8 o'clock strangers began to come in from different quarters. Early on the ground was Francis Dunlavy, first Circuit Judge of the State, intending that the peace and dignity of the law should be upheld. Dr. Bladgley, with some company who had rode out to meet the mob, returned at noon with the information that the troops would arrive in less than an hour. About 1 o'clock the troops appeared, entering by the Dayton road from the north, marching in order and finally halted in front of the Meeting House. A number of the officers were in uniform and the troops armed and generally equipped in regimental order.

The peace-loving men were active with the troops and the undisciplined multitude. It is more than probable that through their intercession the expedient was reached of choosing a committee to state to the Shakers their proposals and to receive and return answers. A committee came forward and faced the dwelling house of the old Believers. They requested three of the original men (meaning John Meacham, Benjamin S. Youngs and Issachar Bates) to come forward in order to confer with them on the occasion of the people's assembling, observing that a committee was chosen for that purpose, consisting of twelve men then present, among whom was one chief speaker. As only Benjamin S. Youngs of the three called was present, assent was given that two others might be called. Standing in the yard at that time were Judge Dunlavy, General William Schenck and J. Corwin. As the mob's committee contained twelve persons the Shakers desired that these three gentlemen might be permitted to act with them, but this request was denied. Judge Dunlavy then asked, "Have you any objections to by-standers?"

They answered, "Yes." It was insisted that the three Shakers should go alone with them to the woods. Unreasonable as the demands were the Shakers consented. Benjamin S. Youngs, Peter Pease and Matthew Houston withdrew with the committee to a woodland lying about sixty rods south of the dwelling house and half a mile south of the Meeting House.

The leading characters of the committee were Matthew G. Wallace, a noted Presbyterian preacher, chief speaker; Doctor Squire Little, a Newlight; Captain John Clark, and John Fisher. The names of the others have not been preserved. Wallace began in the name of the people to state their grievances, observing that the Shaker principles and practices had caused great disturbances in the minds of the people and led to the extinction of civil and religious society, which they are determined to uphold; that their system was a pecuniary one and led mankind into bondage and oppression; and that the people were determined to bear it no longer. The committee insinuated that they were in a capacity to prevent evil being done and perhaps prevent much blood being shed, because as the people were fully resolved on a redress, provided the terms were complied with, that were proposed. After speaking *in extenso*, in this matter for some time, the following conditions were the only ones that would be accepted, and which would prevent forcing a compliance by violent measures:

1. The children of the late James Watts should be given up to their grandfather; it being alleged that the said James Watts, at his decease, gave his children to his father. It was hoped that the propriety of this would readily be seen.

To this the Shakers answered: "We had not seen the propriety hitherto, as we supposed the mother, under whose care the children now were, had the greatest right to them; and asked them if it was recorded, that the said James gave his children to their grandfather? They answered that it was not. We told them that we could not give up that which was not in our possession. The children were with their mother, and under her care, and we exercised no authority over them. We were sure that the mother and children might be seen by any two or three civil men, and if the parent was willing, and the children wished to go, it was not our wish to have them retained; nor if any demanded them, and chose to force them away, would any violence be used to prevent them."

2. That old William Bedle be permitted to see his grandchild, a son of Elijah Davis, alleging that the said child came away (from his father) and was forcibly brought back contrary to his inclination.

To this it was replied: "That the child was under the care of his own parents; that we had not any control over him; that we did not usurp the parents' rights over their children, but we doubted not that the child might be seen," etc., etc.

3. That the children of James Smith should be given up. To this the observation was offered that the Shakers were doubtless well acquainted with the circumstances relative to these children.

To this the information was offered: "That the children were under the care of their father; that they were now in the hands of the authority, and that a suit in court had commenced respecting them."

4. In presenting the next demand the speaker observed that it probably might seem hard, and then declared that the weightiest proposition was, that the Shakers must cease publicly to inculcate their principles, and their practices must cease; that no dancing on the Sabbath or any other day should be permitted; or else all should depart from the country by the first Monday in December next.

This demand was tantamount to a renunciation of faith and practice, mode of worship, preaching and manner of living.

These terms were a declaration that if acceded to all would be well; and if not they should be enforced by violence. It was requested that these propositions should be reduced to writing, but Wallace stated that what had been proposed was short and could easily be remembered without writing. The reply was made that as the proposals were short they could readily be committed to writing, but the point was abruptly refused.

It is worthy of mention that although the committee had solemnly agreed not to admit or suffer any of the party near them while they conferred together, yet during the conference there was present a number of false witnesses and accusers standing by, particularly the apostate John Davis, who brought false accusations.   Again and again the Shakers asked the committee if their replies were understood, and every time the answer came in the affirmative; but still the Shakers were urged to comply, for it was impossible for them to resist a thousand men.

At 2 o'clock the conference adjourned for one hour, that the Shakers might in that time give a positive answer.   All the elder brethren and sisters there present were assembled together in an upper room of the residence near the Meeting House. Judge Dunlavy, General Schenck and Squire Corwin were invited to take part in the consultation.   In their presence the committee of Shakers stated the proposals and demands and the answers agreed upon, with the observation that the requirements were unreasonable and unjust, particularly because no person was allowed to be present at the conference who might serve as a witness against the unlawfulness or injustice of their demands; and also of the unreasonableness of grandfathers demanding to be given up to them their grandchildren who were under the care of their own parents.   The three invited guests took no part in the meeting, but appeared to be much affected and feelingly interested in the cause of justice.   When the meeting ended Judge Dunlavy and General Schenck went out and found Dr. Little, one of the committee, in the yard before the house, and talked to him in an affecting manner on the illegality and consequences of the concourse of people.

The hour having expired Benjamin S. Youngs informed Dr. Little that they were ready to meet them, and accordingly both committees retired to the same place in the woods, and there delivered the following answer:

"1.   Respecting the children demanded to be given up, we observed, that we had already stated what we had to say on that subject; adding, that all adults among us were free, and that it was contrary to our principles and our practice to oppress any, or hold them in bondage.

2.   Respecting our faith which we held in the gospel, we esteemed it dearer than our lives, and therefore meant to maintain it, whatever we might suffer as the consequence.   And as

to our leaving the country, we were on our own possessions which we had purchased with money obtained by our own honest industry. It was our endeavor not to owe any man anything; we had not a cent of any man's money; we enjoyed our own peaceable possessions in a free country, and were entitled to those liberties (including the liberty of our consciences) which the laws of our country granted us."

In the course of the first sitting of the committee the Shakers observed that things were misrepresented and wrongly reported concerning them; that there was no evidence of the existence of those things of which they were accused, and that the reports came from prejudiced persons; that there was no need of all this concourse of people; if wrong had been done in any matter the laws of the country made ample provision for a redress of grievances. To all this Wallace replied that the means required too lengthy a process, and that the people would not wait the issue of such measures. It was necessary to rehearse some of these facts during the sitting of the second conference.

While these proceedings were transpiring, about the Meeting House, the school house, the children's family, and the first family of young Believers, there was a vast and promiscuous concourse of armed men and spectators, some disputing, some inquiring, others railing out against and endeavoring to scatter falsehood, and urging the propriety of banishing the Shakers out of the country by violence. Women of the baser sort, who were in fellowship with the riot, had placed themselves within sight of the buildings, on the edge of the woods, waiting to see the Shakers destroyed; others, of the same cast, were taking an active part in urging on parties of the mob to take away, by force, children of their connections, and other such like acts of violence. In the meantime there were men of talents and good principles who engaged in contesting those violent measures agitated by the mob party, urging the Shakers' right of citizenship from their peaceable deportment, and the unconstitutionality of infringing upon their right, which had never been forfeited by any misconduct.

About three o'clock, a public speaker of the party, standing in the street before the door of the Meeting House, proclaimed liberty, that all who had any charges against the Shakers might come forward and enter them. A number of charges were produced; but none however that was regularly entered and taken up, except a charge of murder against Amos Valentine, upon the assertion of John and Robert Wilson, two of the before mentioned apostates, who deposed, that when they 'lived among the Shakers, the said Amos had a boy afflicted with fits; that he whipped said boy unmercifully; also, that the said boy was whipped by Daniel Moseley, and that the said Amos and Daniel both wished that he was dead; that the boy for some time past had been missing, and the said witnesses believed that the said boy was murdered, and put out of the way. A habeas corpus was immediately served on Amos and he was put under arrest until the said boy should be produced. The boy was immediately sent for, being at Moses Easton's, about two miles off. About this period of the transaction, the committee was holding its second session, with the three Shakers before mentioned. Judge Dunlavy, who understood the proceedings of the committee before, followed them to the edge of the woods, and there sat down upon a log, about five rods distant from where the committee was sitting, and there waited to see the issue. Immediately after the Shakers withdrew from the committee, he mounted his horse, in the midst of the assembly, and, with a loud voice, delivered a solemn injunction, that no one violate the laws of Ohio, and required all civil officers present to take cognizance of the conduct of any who should violate them. Soon after this, the aforesaid boy arrived, very corpulent and hearty. This was about four o'clock. Judge Dunlavy, understanding the case, gave public information of the boy's arrival, and the satisfaction which was given of the innocence of the party accused, ordered the prisoner to be released, and the people to disperse, as nothing remained for investigation. Nevertheless Capt. Kilbreath refused to comply with the judge's order to release the prisoner, alledging that he was just as high an officer as Dunlavy. Upon this Judge Dunlavy ordered him to be apprehended, and put in prison; but Kilbreath being armed with a sword and pistol, and refusing to be taken, the matter there rested. The prisoner, however, was released; but some of the mob treated the judge with great contempt, and uttered the most bitter invectives against him for his interference. At this stage of the proceedings, the committee having returned and mingled among the multitude; Judge Dunlavy having given his orders, the mob was thus irritated and thrown into confusion. But the word of command being given, and the party mounted, they moved down the street in a violent career, amid clouds of dust, and halted in a vast crowd facing the dwelling house of the Elders; and after a little pause, Major Robinson, with a loud voice, demanded of those in the house whether they would comply with the proposals of the committee, Yea, or Nay. This was repeated a number of times, crying aloud, "Give us an answer, Yea, or Nay!" but no one answered a word. Then all the people in the house, men and women, young and old, were commanded to come out of the house, and place themselves in a circle on the green before them. But none offered to move.

Then Major Robinson continued his harangue to the following effect: that the Shakers must comply immediately with the proposals of the committee, and accede to remove out of the country by the first of December next, to suffer the consequences; and then cried, "Is not this the voice of the people?" which was immediately answered by the mob with uplifted hands, and a general loud and hideous yell, in the most exasperated manner. But as none appeared or answered, they ordered the gates to be thrown open, which, after considerable hesitation, some of the concourse ventured to perform. The doors of the house were now instantly shut and fastened, as hitherto they had been left open. After the gates were thrown open, the house was immediately surrounded by a promiscuous multitude of armed men and spectators, but the main body of the corps remained on their horses in the street. After some consultation among the mob, they proposed a committee from among them, whom they wished to enter and search every apartment of the house, to see whether there were not some held in bondage, and such other like instances of cruelty and injustice as were reported. This committee consisted of Major William Robinson, Captain John Robinson, Captain John Clark, Captain Cornelius Thomas, and one or two others. They entered upon conditions of behaving civilly, and began their search and examination with the young sisters, and asked them, one by one, if they desired to leave the Shakers.

To the question of the mob committee Betsey Seward replied, that she was satisfied with the people, and her present place of abode; that she liked it better than among her natural relations; because they treated her more kindly than ever her own relations had done, and that she did not wish to see any of them again, while they remained so wicked. The committee then said, "Let her stay." Prudence Morrell being interrogated, replied, that all the world would be no inducement to her to leave; that she preferred to place her head on the floor and be decapitated than to be taken away from the Believers. Caty Rubart also made a firm reply, in substance as above; and so did Jenny McNemar, and all the rest,—all declaring that they were free to go away, if they chose, at any time, and that nothing bound them but their faith and love. All others, whether brethren or sisters, made the similar replies.

After searching every apartment of the house the committee expressed their satisfaction. Captain Thomas, more upright than the others, said he saw a "decent house with decent people in it." Then they drank copiously of cold coffee, went out, and reported themselves as "well satisfied." After this, they returned to their former ground at the Meeting House, and the same committee proceeded to examine the family of the young Believers. All who were interrogated, made firm replies, that they were free, and might go away whenever they chose, but would not; some said they would rather die, than abandon their faith, or forsake the people of God. By this time the committee was under great mortification, and their zeal began to abate, having been disappointed in all their researches, and some persuasion had to be used in order to get them into the school house. Matthew Houston being present at their examinations, desired them to go, especially, as they had it reported that the Shakers would not suffer their children and youth to read the Bible. When they went into the school they found Testaments in abundance. Elder Houston observed they might see at least one lie had been told them. They looked at the children's penmanship, which they acknowledged surpassed their expectations. Houston next requested them to ask the children questions, whether they had enough to eat, etc., observing, that he had children among them, and had long been absent, and knew not at present how it might be with them. When they asked, First: "Have you enough to eat?" they answered, "Yea! yea! yea! as much as we want," which ran all through the school. Second: "Are you punished more than you deserve?" They answered, "Nay! nay! nay," and some replied, "We are never whipped." Third: "Do you want to leave these people? If you do, fear not, we will protect you." "Nay! nay! nay! sounded through the school. Next the committee was invited to hear the children read, but this was declined, declaring they were fully satisfied. Next they were requested to go to John Wood's, in order to find that enslaved woman, of whom they had spoken, and about whom there was so much agitation (for it was reported that a certain woman was enslaved by the Shakers; those in search had not yet found her, for another select party had searched the Meeting House for her a little while before, and the Children's Order at John Wood's had also been searched and examined.) But the committee refused to investigate farther, declaring that all of them were fully satisfied.

No ground of accusation being found or reported to the party, and the generality being wearied and perplexed with the same, and under a mortifying disappointment, were dismissed; the last of them disappeared as the darkness of night began to creep over the horizon, without leaving behind them any visible marks of cruelty.

Through this whole transaction no visible disturbance or confusion appeared among the Shakers. The greater number kept busy at their usual employments; took dinner in the usual manner, and entertained such as they could with convenience. They answered those mildly who spoke to them, whether peaceably or in a taunt. Such as wished to enter the rooms from the noise and clamor, did so, and spent their time in conversation.

That no evil or cruelty was transacted after such formidable preparations of design, can only be accounted for by the stand taken by Judge Dunlavy, assisted by the persuasive powers, of those who came with good intentions, and their love of justice and right.

The foregoing account of the transactions of the mob is taken from the narrative of Benjamin Seth Youngs, written August 31, 1810. When I visited Union Village May 10, 1901, Miss Susan Liddell was sent for. She is among the oldest Shakers, in point of service, in the village, and the best acquainted with its history. She gave me the additional information which she received from Shakers who were living at the time of the mob; Judge Dunlavy was a cousin of Richard McNemar; George Harlan had a sister who was then a Believer and came to assist and protect the Shakers; Richard McNemar found it necessary to go among the younger members and insist on nonresistance, for there was an indication among them to act in self-defence, and some of the Shakers were struck with whips and knocked down. This was particularly true in the instance of Calvin Morrell, a physician, who had become a convert.

Book A, of the Records, for Dec. 29, 1810, notes that again the Shakers were threatened by mob violence, which would indicate that nothing was done with the ringleaders of the mob of August 27.

MOBS OF 1813.

The records of the mobs of 1813 are exceedingly brief. They must have been of small moment or else an interested chronicler would have preserved the details. The first was on May 12, and the following is the sole entry: "Mob at the West Section; trying to take a woman away against her will."

For December 16th we have the following minute: "A violent mob came to the Center House today, in the employ of James Bedle, who had previously left the Society and bound his children to Peter Pease. His present aim is to take the children away by force. The house doors being closed and barred, they took a battering ram and broke a door in two; they then rushed in and committed considerable violence and abuse; but failed in getting the children. After a shameful day's riot, they dispersed for the night."

For December 29th the subject is continued. . "Another mob appears to be collecting at Bedell's; meanwhile they are trying to prove before referees that the children have been abused by the Society; in this Bedle failed. The referees then recommended to Peter Pease to give up the Indentures, for the sake of peace, which was accordingly agreed upon; and the mob dispersed." The next day James Bedle came in the "morning and dragged off his 2 youngest children, much against their wills. They went off screaming and hollowing. The mother and the 2 oldest children have fled to some other quarter to avoid violence and enjoy their own faith."

MOB OF 1817.

The year 1817 was fruitful in disturbances at Union Village. The Church Record is very brief,on this subject, although naming some of the parties participating in the riots. The Hampton MS. is more complete, and in the main, will here be followed.

The riotous proceedings commenced as early as January 12, when Patty Rude, an apostate woman, came to church, with a party of ruffians, to take her daughter Sarah (a young woman) away, by force.

On July 31, under pretence of law, a scene of mobbing and rioting was perpetrated. The object was to get a youth (Jonathan Davis, Jr.) away, who had left the society some time previously. Being under age his father authorized some of the brethren to go and bring him home, which was done. John Davis, an outsider and cousin, by whom he was harbored, raised a company in Lebanon, who came out in great indignation and threatened to burn the village to ashes, if the youth was not given over to them. Thirty or forty men came with a constable and arrested the brethren who brought the boy home; and had them bound over to court. They were indicted before the grand jury, but nothing came of it.

On December 3rd, Richard McNemar and Calvin Morrell went to Columbus to present a remonstrance to the Legislature against Van Vleet and Cameron, editors of the Western Star, and others on account of persecutions. These persecutions gradually died away, and in a few years ceased altogether.

As there was some little after-litigation on account of the John Davis affair, and as at the time of these troubles, the prosecutors had their say in the Western Star, added to which there was placed in circulation a book derogatory to the Shakers, it may be well here to note the facts as they occurred. The following is a narrative of William Davis, a near relative of the said John and Jonathan Davis: "This is to certify that I, William Davis, of the County of Warren, and State of Ohio, being one of the party included in the deposition of John Davis for committing a riot etc., on the bodies of the said John Davis and Jonathan Davis, which deposition hath been published to the world: in consequence of all being indicted who were present at the transaction, we have never had a suitable opportunity to open the matter as it really was. I now feel it my duty to give the public a statement of the facts which were as follows:

Some time in the month of July 1817 my youngest brother Jonathan Davis ran away from the school where my father Elijah had placed him and went to the town of Lebanon, to the said John Davis, his cousin. My Father and I went after the boy, but John Davis, Eli Truitt, and others forbade us to have anything to do with the boy; stating that they would protect him from his father, to the shedding of the last drop of their blood. — I went several times, to see if by any means I could get them to give him up to his father; but to no effect. My Father and Mother went, but could effect nothing. Some time after, John Wallace was informed by a friend, where John Davis and the boy were at work, some distance from the town. My father, anxious to obtain the boy, and insisting on having him brought home, myself and four others went to the place where they were at work; I went forward and took my brother by the arm and told him he must go home with me; John Davis rose up with a large drawing-knife in his hand and told me if I did not let him go, he would cut off my arm; — at this time John Wallace came forward and said to John Davis, 'Be civil we want nothing to do with you; — we only wish to take Jonathan to his father;' — the said Davis then left me and turned to Wallace with his knife drawn, in a position to strike. At this time, it is said, that Wallace showed a spear to Davis and bade him stand off. — I then took the boy some distance, when John Davis called to the boy and said, 'You have got my hat.' We then threw the hat back to Davis. When we had gotten about 50 yards with the boy, John Davis passed us with the knife in one hand and a club in the other, stating that he would soon have help, and take the boy from us. After passing us a little, he turned back and came to where we were, and drew the knife as if to strike; one of us then stopped the knife with a stick — he drew it again and it was stopped in like manner, which ended the attempts at striking. We frequently requested him to withdraw peaceably, for we wanted nothing to do with him; nevertheless he continued to follow us for sixty or seventy rods, threatening us with violence. — He then returned to the town of Lebanon, and made oath that violence was committed by us and obtained a warrant for us all; which was executed without resistance. — He also, on the same day, collected a mob who came to take the boy; — they surrounded the house where the boy was, with clubs, loaded whips etc. — but the boy made his escape through the midst of the crowd, and went to the woods and secreted himself from them. — I do further testify, that we had no intentions of injuring the said John Davis, nor any other person or persons; — our only object was to bring the boy to his father and mother. This I am willing to testify to, when legally called upon.

WILLIAM DAVIS."

MOB OF 1819.

On the 7th of August, while the Shakers were quietly attending to their respective duties, suddenly a mob of horsemen, from about Middletown, between thirty and forty in number, entered the village from the North, passed the Meeting-House, and moved on swiftly, till they reached the South House; where they stopped, hitched their horses, and with great agility entered the yard, rushed to the door, but finding it barred, commenced striking it with their feet, to burst it open. There being none but women in the house at their arrival, a number of the Brethren collected to see the cause of the uproar, and their business was demanded. The reply was that they had heard that one Phoebe Johnson, a member of the Society, wanted to leave, but was forcibly restrained. Miss Johnson, at that time, was in the orchard, and could have kept out of the way, but refrained from so doing. It was agreed that members of the mob should converse with her, conditioned however that she should not be abused in any manner whatsoever. The young woman then came to the opposite door and conversed with them through the window, and informed them that she had no desire to leave the Society, and if she had there was no one to hinder her from going whenever she chose; that she was of lawful age to choose and act for herself, and especially would scorn to go in such company as those men assembled. They persisted however, as if they meant to force her away, surrounded the house to prevent her from escaping, and grew insolent and daringly wicked with railing and cursing. Attempts were made to enter the house, which were successfully frustrated, and the intruders were ordered off the premises, but without effect. They mocked at the mention of the law, and answered every suggestion of reason with curses. In this manner they went on until late in the afternoon, when they withdrew after being convinced that the lady had effected her escape from the house.

On the Monday (August 9th) following, early in the day, the mob again appeared with a formidable reinforcement of horse and foot, amounting in all to about two hundred. They passed through the village in the same manner as before, and towards the same place, but with greater fury and less appearance of order or government. Their abuse was perpetrated on all such as they could sieze on the road till they reached the South House, where they hitched their horses and then paraded towards the gate, where they were met by the Deacons, and by the authority of the laws of the State, were forbidden to enter the yard· but with savage shrieks they leaped the fence in swarms, bearing down all who stood in their way. Calvin Morrell was knocked down and beaten almost to death, though he had uttered no word nor made any interruption. They rushed on towards the house — the Shakers standing in crowds to obstruct the passage; but with fists, clubs and loaded whips, the mob forced its way to the door which they commenced beating. Captain Spencer, who had some authority over the mob, now commanded the rioters to desist; but on every side the outrage continued, crying out in false terms, and seeking every occasion to vent their lawless fury with hard blows on both men and women, for no distinction was made. Thus, in one continued uproar of violence, they continued until 2 o'clock in the afternoon, when Squire Welton appeared, and by the laws of the State commanded them to disperse; that, if there was any duty to be performed, it belonged to the civil officers; that only resistence to the constituted authority could the military be called out, etc. To this some mocked, and others stated the magistrate should be tarred and feathered. However, the civil authorities were strong enough to disperse the mob.

This mob had been incited by the "Western Star," published at Lebanon, under the pretence of liberating the children of David and Anna Johnson, who had been with the Shakers for thirteen years, and that with the consent of the parents. Their mother, who had there deceased, a member of the Society, left it as her last and special request, that her children might be brought up under the care of the Shakers. The father, who was not a member had given his consent that they should remain. Indeed he appeared in the midst of the mob and disapproved of their proceedings, but they heeded him not. The Shakers did not prohibit the mob from taking the children, provided they could be found, because their lawful protection was in their father; and they would not be justified in giving them up, contrary to their own feelings, and the will of both parents. Some of the children fled and hid themselves. Ithamar, who was nearly of age, was overpowered and dragged off to Lebanon and there put under keepers, under a pretence of a precept for debt; but obtaining his dismission, he returned home the next morning. David, the father, collected his children and encouraged them to persevere, promising to protect them to the utmost of his ability. The good offices of the Shakers supplemented the efforts of the father.

MOB OF 1824.

The last recorded acts of a mob I have been able to find in the Journal is that of September 7, 1824. It is mentioned as follows: "This evening at 8 o'clock, a small mob of about 16 men, came to the East house with one Francis Drake, to take away his daughter, Harriet R. D., a young woman, who did not choose to go. After making some disturbance in the family; the chh. heard the alarm. The Brethren immediately repaired thither and took 10 of them prisoners without any harsh means, and brought them to the office — fed and lodged them comfortably till morning.—Sept. 8. This morning we discharged our prisoners, on their giving us their '*Word and honor!!*' that they would do better hereafter."

SOME SHAKER METHODS.

From the statements already made it may be assumed that the Shakers did not rest quietly under persecutions. At times they were compelled to take a bold stand. The attitude of the "Western Star" was so flagrant and bitter towards the Shakers as to cause hatred towards the Society by the people of the village of Lebanon. Just why this hostility was displayed mention is not given. In order to resent the bitter course of the denizens of Lebanon the Shakers employed drastic measures. Under date of June 15, 1818, the Journal state that, "Elder Peter (Pease?) and Nathan S. (Sharp) went to Lebanon and settled all accounts, intending to trade no more with them at present, in consequence of their inveterate prejudice and persecuting spirit." When trade was again resumed the Journal does not state. In all probability this condition did not last long, for the people of Lebanon could not afford to suffer the stand thus taken, and concluded to mend their manners.

For Sunday, August 5, 1829, the following notice occurs: "The execrable John Wallace dared to come here today, and set his feet within our Meeting House door." Nothing more is added. This is too frequently the case throughout the entire Journal. The Shakers had every reason to feel resentment towards John Wallace. My Mother, then a girl of thirteen, was present on the occasion above referred to. I have often heard her tell the story. On that day a large crowd attended the Shaker meeting. John Wallace entered and quietly took a seat and behaved with decorum. One of the Shakers arose and said: "The children of God cannot worship so long as the devil was in their midst," and then commanded Wallace to leave the Sanc-

25

tuary. Wallace made no disposition to comply with the demand. For a few moments the silence was oppressive, whilst all eyes were turned on Wallace. The same elder again arose and informed the spectators that unless they ejected Wallace the religious services would not be performed. Of course such a demand could not be complied with. It was no concern of the audience, but a matter that rested with the offended. Silence again reigned supreme for a few moments. All at once, without any preconcerted signal the Shakers suddenly arose, and like a person driving geese, began to "shoo" the people out. The visitors made a rush for the doors, most of whom were laughing, and in the struggle at the door my Mother was thrown violently from the steps to the ground and hurt. For this she never bore them any ill-will, and always told the incident in a good-natured way."

The Shakers have always been subjected to petty annoyances, even down to the present time. My Mother stated that she knew, in her younger days, of a party of young men and women from Franklin, who went to Shakertown, evidently bent on a lark. They rudely entered the dwelling house, took possession of the bedrooms, emptied vessels in the middle of the beds, and from thence to the yard and garden, plucking such flowers as they fancied, besides committing other depredations. And all this by persons who considered themselves to be the *elite* of Franklin.

Elder Joseph R. Slingerland informed me that the public services were dispensed with owing to the conduct of the students from the Lebanon Normal School. Not long since he was forced to reprimand a stranger, then on their premises. For his pains he received the reply, "I have as much right here as you."

CONCLUSION.

The foregoing relation of persecution and mob law inflicted on the Shakers covers nearly the entire amount of serious attacks and troubles which they were called upon to suffer. This, however, was as nothing compared to what their Eastern coadjutors were forced to endure. A gradual change was taking place all the time. People who attended their public services became better acquainted with their principles and manner of life. These public meetings long continued to arrest the attention of large crowds. As many as a hundred sleighs have been counted at one time hitched about the Meeting House. I remember while I was yet a boy large crowds were attracted to "Shaker meeting." On one occasion, the crowd was so great that I sat on the floor within two feet of the speaker, who had scarcely room to stand. But at that time all ill-feeling had long before died out. There never was a good motive for afflicting the Shakers. Misrepresentation, falsehood, malice and officious persons caused wrong and fear. The order never was strong enough, nor sufficiently aggressive to arouse religious rancor and hatred, although such was displayed. They should have been accorded the same right as their tormentors had demanded for themselves. Their persecutors were not savages or barbarians, but those professing to be civilized and believers in Christianity, yet refusing to practice the Golden Rule.

Note.—It is a matter of justice to state that in the preparation of the foregoing article I have consulted only Shaker documents. I made efforts to secure the writings of Barton Stone but failed. Besides the documents referred to, I have used McNemar's "Account of Shakerism among the subjects of the late revival in Ohio and Kentucky." The Church Journal or Record, I have used is volume A, covering the period from March 27, 1805, to April 30, 1861. This Record was not in my possession when I wrote the history of the Shakers of Union Village. From the year 1805 to 1842 the Record is in the hand writing of Peter Pease, which is neat and plain. From the beginning to Dec. 19, 1811, it is made up of extracts from a journal kept by Peter Pease. Besides this series there is another called B which contains copy of covenant, declarations, deeds, etc.; C contains a list of members and minors, admissions, ages, nativity, etc.; D is devoted to necrology, and E of withdrawals. These I have not examined. The Shaker authorities have been very polite and pleasant to me in my researches, granting every request that has been made.

Franklin, O., January 6, 1902.

SPIRITUALISM AMONG THE SHAKERS OF UNION VILLAGE, OHIO.

INTRODUCTION.

What is known as modern spiritualism may be said to represent an entirely different phase from that outbreak that occurred among the Shakers three-quarters of a century ago. The former dates its origin from the Rochester rappings of 1847-48, when the house of John D. Fox was disturbed by noises, which replied to the raps of his daughter Kate, then a child nine years old. Such noises had haunted houses before, but it remained for the Fox family to interpret the same by the construction of a mode of signals. If modern spiritualism arose from one of the commonest superstititions in the world—a belief in haunted houses—the same cannot be asserted of the manifestation among the Shakers, for the type partook purely of the Biblical form—that of visions and inspiration. There were no rappings, table-turnings and other phenomena so common among spiritualists. The agents through which the revelations were given were called "instruments," "seers" and "inspired ones." The name "medium" or "sensitive" nowhere occurs in such records as have been placed at my disposal. Neither are the two phases of the same common origin. That of the Shakers preceded the one at Rochester by a period of ten years, and reached its decline and practical extinction before the latter had been inaugurated. It was even prophesied among the Shakers that the revelations should cease in 1847, after which the world should take up the phenomena. The first notice of the Rochester rappings by the Shakers of Union Village occurs in their "Church Records" for February 9, 1850, in the following note:

"A curious account appears in the N. York Tribune and other public prints, giving out that there are now and have been for some time, strange and mysterious Knockings and sounds, heard in the neighborhood

Rochester, Auburn and many other places in the state of New York—And that no investigation hitherto made, could ascribe them to any other than a spiritual agency, as a cause — Many speculations, and contrary opinions are prevalent in relation to them, and much mockery and derision offer'd by those who admit nothing as true, only that which is made known to them thro' the medium of other external senses—The more rational and consistent part of the community, forming no positive opinion, are waiting to see what time will develop on the interesting subject."

ORIGIN OF SPIRITUALISM AMONG THE SHAKERS.

From the very inception of spiritualism the Shaker leaders appear to have been determined and anxious to accept it even in its most extravagant forms. It was received without question or investigation. It is not to be inferred that every member of the order throughout Shakerdom was carried away by the new belief, for the records indirectly indicate that a small minority held aloof. The belief then inculcated is the prevalent opinion down to the present time. As nearly all the members of the various communities accepted the revelations of the seers, it becomes a very interesting question in sociology whether this circumstance is due to the mode of life as practiced, or to the fact that the class drawn into this kind of organization is more susceptible to the supernatural. In all probability both are more or less responsible. It has been noticed by all visitors to Union Village that the women have peculiarly spiritual and resigned faces, with a sweetness of expression that cannot be described. It must be specially noticed that all the leaders and influential members of the various communities were ardent believers in the revelations given during the period of excitement that swept over the various communities.

During the month of November, 1837, a religious revival broke out among the Shakers at Watervleit, Albany County, New York, and soon after a member of that society, a girl named Ann Mariah Goff, began to receive revelations, which were reported to the various communities, soon followed by the notice that all would within a short time be visited by heavenly messengers.

For a period of ten years the Shakers bestowed more time and thought on these visions than on any other question. Nor did they attempt to hide their light under a bushel. In 1843 they published "The Sacred Roll and Book," given by "the Lord God of Heaven to the inhabitants of the earth," 500 copies of which were distributed among the rulers of the earth. This book was affirmed to have been given through a holy man of God, who wrote and spoke as he was moved by the Holy Spirit. This work contains 402 pages, divided into two parts, the first of which (222 pages) consists of the revelations, while the second (180 pages) is an appendix embracing the testimonies of ancient prophets, holy angels and living witnesses. The author was Philemon Stewart. The book is now rejected by the people of Union Village, and copies are becoming scarce. In 1849 appeared "The Divine Book of Holy and Eternal Wisdom," in seven parts, by Paulina Bates, constituting a series of revelations commencing December 3, 1841, and ending December 5, 1843. The book contains 696 pages. The work did not receive the same welcome as the former, probably because the enthusiasm had spent its force.

The first published record of which I have any knowledge is the "Youth's Guide in Zion and Holy Mother's Promises," said to have been given by inspiration at Mount Lebanon, New York, on January 5, 1842, and printed at Canterbury, New Hampshire, the same year. It is a pamphlet of 36 pages, and purports to be a communication from "Holy Mother Wisdom" (the Holy Spirit) to the elders of the first order, to be given to the youth among believers. Following this there was published at the same place in 1843 "The Closing Roll" and "Sacred Covenant," the first revealed January 8, 1842, and the second December 31, 1841. The book containing these is a small quarto of 40 pages. I have never seen but two copies. In 1843 appeared "The Gospel Monitor," purporting to have been revealed by Ann Lee, and for the benefit of those placed in the care of children, and revealed at Mount Lebanon, New York, March 1, 1841. It embraces 48 pages. It is divided into four parts, the first containing an interview between the writer and Ann Lee; the second, Ann Lee's word to the children care-takers; the third, to the children, and the last to the elders. In all probability neither of these two small works were ever intended for public inspection. I never have been able to find either in any of the Shaker communities. I secured some copies among the archives of North Union, which fell into my possession. They had been preserved by James S. Prescott.

"The Sacred Roll and Book" was introduced at Union Village September 11, 1843, and read in part on that day. On November 19 following, Elder John Martin read a long epistle from Canterbury, N. H., concerning it, and also an order for distributing it to the various states, nations, etc. The books, after 40 days' travel, arrived at Union Village on December 23, and on January 6, 1844, two copies were sent to Governor Shannon of Ohio. I find no reference to the "Divine Book of Holy Wisdom," although a large consignment was received.

SOURCES OF INFORMATION.

Very early in the history of the spiritual revelations an order came to Union Village from Mount Lebanon, New York, that whatsoever was made known by the spirit should be recorded. This was carefully done, but all the books devoted to that purpose have disappeared, save part 2 of volume J of the Spiritual Journal, beginning July 6, 1845, and continuing to the end. As Oliver C. Hampton declares in his manuscript History of the Society that "the veil of oblivion" should be drawn over some of the extravagances of that time, and they should "rest in eternal sleep," added to which the fact that some two or three years ago a lot of manuscripts were purposely destroyed, it is presumable that the holocaust contained the missing documents. Volume J, Spiritual Journal, now in my temporary possession, is in the handwriting of Charles D. Hampton, father of Oliver. It is the most legible of any manuscript I ever saw. In short all the Shaker manuscripts are very legible. The Church Records from July 2, 1843, to August 1, 1856, is also the manuscript of Dr. Hampton. From 1815 to 1843 the same book was kept by Andrew C. Houston. The main source of our information is derived from this record. Oliver C. Hampton's manuscript is derived both from memory and the records kept during the passing of the events. I have received valuable reminiscences from Sister Susannah C. Liddell, who was born near Union Village, June 4, 1824, and joined the society in 1835, and has continued her membership ever since: For many years she was a teacher. She possesses an intelligent, spiritual, sweet face, and is held in the greatest respect by her co-religionists. Her honesty goes unquestioned in the community.

The soil for the advent of spiritualism was in part prepared by the most remarkable revival of religion that ever occurred in Union Village. This "season of refreshing" began Sunday, February 5, 1837, and was due to the reading of an old sermon once delivered in the East by Eldress Lucy Wright. Freegift Wells, then first in the lot of the ministry, read the sermon in a very solemn and impressive manner, and followed it up by strongly urging upon his hearers the necessity of gaining the gift of repentance, humility and a deeper inward work. On the following Sunday (February 12) the church meeting "was the most extraordinary of the kind that we ever witnessed in this place, attended with mortifying and humiliating gifts, calculated to unfetter and free souls and enable them to serve God in spirit and in truth. Surely the Spirit of the Lord is striving wonderfully with this people." On March 27 the "meeting was overwhelming in point of spiritual gifts and sensations. The heartfelt humility and contrition, together with the many melting expressions of thankfulness and love to the way of God, caused the tears to flow." Thus inaugurated, the revival continued for many weeks without cessation, growing more intense with every succeeding meeting. The Ministry from the other societies came and attended these meetings and, partaking of the same spirit, carried the influence to their respective communities. Before the enthusiasm of this revival had died out, the outbreak of spiritualism at Watervleit, N. Y., had taken place. The first notice of this phenomenon occurs in the Church Journal for January 15, 1838: "Two letters read from the East, giving extraordinary accounts of a great work of God commencing among them of late, attended with many bodily operations of the power of God, and many supernatural gifts, among which visions and trances are very common, as well as other supernatural and apostolic gifts."

OUTBREAK AT UNION VILLAGE.

The ten years' revel of spiritualism was first directed by Freegift Wells and then by John Martin, both of whom were deeply imbued with its influence. The first named guided the movement until July 9, 1843. He was a short, corpulent man, rather jolly in his temperament, but intellectually weak. The ministry of nearly all the Shaker societies from 1835 to 1850 appear to have been decidedly weak. The extravagances noted at Union Village during this period prove that the Ministry had lost all control and allowed matters to drift. The polity of Shakerism must of necessity bring weak men to the front. The Mount Lebanon Ministry appoints its own successors, and the sub-Ministry is selected with a view to carrying out the edict of the head man. This would not necessarily happen in every instance. It would be safe to affirm that Shakerism at Union Village reached its zenith under David Darrow. Besides being a man of intelligence, strong will and a good heart, he had the thorough drill given him as an officer in the American Revolution, which he applied wisely to those over whom he had charge. The weakness—some would call it shrewdness—of the presiding elder was too often exhibited in the directing of the visionist to accomplish his purpose.

Reports from various committees had reached Union Village of the wonderful transactions there takingplace. The people wondered why they were denied the phenomenon, and looked anxiously for the spirit to descend upon them. South Union and Pleasant Hill, in Kentucky, were aglow with visions. The first intelligent outbreak at Union Village occurred on August 26, 1838. On that day "Elder Freegift read a letter from the Ministry at Pleasant Hill, and after reading he spoke some concerning this marvelous work of God that was going on in other societies of believers, and said confidently that we should be visited in like manner without doubt. After he had concluded a song was pitched up and shaking commenced, and it appeared almost like electricity; the power of God seemed to shower upon the assembly, and to a number it appeared to be irresistible. It affected a large proportion of the assembly more or less." About this time involuntary exercises, such as jerks, occurred in a few instances. During the latter part of October "several individuals heard heavenly sounds of trumpets, instrumental music, singing," etc. For November 18 we have the record that "the supernatural work of God (called "Mother's* Work") in its new increase, has now broken out into an open flame in the young order of believers at the West Section. The powerful bodily operations and heart-searching conviction that accompanies it baffles all attempts at description." For November 20 the record states that "sometimes the visionist will lie for hours abstracted from things of time."

With two exceptions the Church Journal is silent as to the names of those through whom the revelations came. Elizabeth Wait was "taken under supernatural operations and power of extraordinary character" on November 26, 1838, and Vincy Mc-Nemar "was taken under operations, such as turning, falling into trance and singing new songs some time previous to this date; but there is as yet comparatively little of this work in the chh. to what prevails in the young order."

From Miss Liddell I learn that the first manifestation at Union Village was through Amittie Ann Miller, then five years of age. She came into a room where some of the sisters were at work, and looking up she exclaimed, "Oh, how pretty! Oh, how pretty!" and at once commenced to spin around, which was continued for an hour, repeating all the time the above exclamation. This influence did not leave her until two days after. When of age Miss Miller left the society. Among the very first visionists were Eliza Hampton, aged 10, left the society; Harriet Collins went away; Margaret O'Brian, left, returned and then left again; Mary Ellen Grover and Mary Ann Jennings. The last named had the greatest gifts of all. In 1840 the spiritual work took on an extraordinary form, which was called "Holy Wisdom's Visit," and was felt throughout all the societies. While this lasted every family at Union Village assembled in meeting one hour every day, and all received Mother Wisdom's mark on the forehead. And

---

* Reference is here made to Holy Spirit.

the same questions* were asked of each one separately. The sole medium in this work was Mary Ann Jennings. She kneeled in the aisle of the meeting-house, and as Mother Wisdom called the name the owner thereof came forth, and with closed eyes kneeled

---

* The questions asked were as follows:

"Do you sense and feel that you have come to kneel down before the judgment seat of your Eternal Mother Wisdom?

Are you thankful that I have come?

Do you believe that I am sent by the Lord Jehovah in union with my anointed?

Have you confessed and righted every wrong and prepared your soul to meet me?

Do you love and respect the gift I have sent?

Do you believe in the wonderful work of God that has commenced in my Zion?

Are you willing to receive whatever mark I have brought to set. upon you?

Do you honor and respect my chosen and beloved?

Do you believe my gift is placed in them?

Will you be subject to them in all things?

Are you willing to drink of the cup of deep tribulation which I have prepared?

Do you desire above all things to receive the mark of my name?

Are you willing to sacrifice and give up all to be owned and acepted of me?

Are you willing to receive the mark of name from your beloved elders?

Will you receive in thankfulness?

Are you willing to bow your soul in low humiliation and thankfulness for the mark that is sealed upon you?

Will you ever walk worthy of the mark that is sealed upon you?

Will you be faithful and never, never forsake the way of God?

Are you thankful for the gifts I have given you?

Will you keep them pure and holy?

Will you remember and keep the words I have spoken to you in this my solemn day of judgment?

Do you believe I am your Mother?

Do you believe I have come to comfort the poor and needy and the afflicted?"

These questions I have in the handwriting of Eldress Malinda Watts. She was a sister of Elder Ashbel Kitchell, and was reputed to have been a woman of great intellectual power and devoted to the cause she had espoused. There is nothing in the questions, but evidently framed to suit the caprice of Freegift Wells.

before the medium and answered the several questions as propounded. The medium remained kneeling during the entire hour
on the successive days, while the visitation lasted. Though the
seer's eyes remained closed while kneeling in the aisle, yet she
knew the one who approached, no matter how quiet the step.
Nor in her arduous task was she ever known to be in the least
exhausted. She was sent to South Union, Kentucky, there to
continue her work, as none could be found in that society equal to
the labor. When she returned to Union Village she felt that her
gift had spent its force. Still she would speak in the assembly
and relate messages of encouragement, love, hope and blessing.
She was a gentle and kind girl and well-beloved at the West Brick
family, where she resided. At the age of 15 she abandoned the
society. Among the boys were John Ross, aged 7, who lay in a
trance $37\frac{1}{2}$ hours, and Reason Nace, aged 9. Elizabeth Wait died
a Shaker, September 26, 1839. The power that exercised the
sensitive was called a "gift." The gifts consisted in visions,
music, angelic songs, and repeating such revelations as had been
given them. The greater number of these individuals were not
reliable, and most of them soon withdrew from the order. When
the person would be seized with "a gift," that moment the body
would fall to the floor and become perfectly rigid.

During the early stages of these manifestations the phenomena consisted of bodily operations, visions, new and heavenly
songs, and powerful testimonies "against sin, hypocrisy and in-
sincerity." But about the beginning of April, 1839, the work
took on a phase which was pushed to an extreme, in several
directions, which the leaders appeared unwilling to interfere with
or prevent.

EXTRAVAGANT ACTIONS.

In all probability the most extravagant actions reached their
culmination during the year 1839. Just what these actions were
may never be known. Oliver C. Hampton, in his MS. history,
speaks of them as "indiscretions" which were "finally corrected,
condoned and reconciled among all parties." He further states,
in viewing the whole period of the prevalence of Spiritualism, "in
looking back over the whole ground covered by it, we are able
to see many things which happened during its advent that were

the consequences of a want of wisdom in the Leaders of the Society; yet when these untoward features are allowed their full weight and measure, there still remains a precious residuum, vastly outweighing all the more eccentric, and, in some cases, unfortunate features of this work amongst us."

There were phenomena difficult to account for. As an example take the case of Elder William Reynolds, who became first in the ministry in 1875. During a portion of the time mentioned he lived with the West Family, and for a period of three years, every Sunday he would turn over and over like a cart wheel from the residence to the church. On leaving the church he would be seized with the same impulse, which at times would take him to "Jehovah's Chosen Square," notwithstanding all his power to prevent the same. At this unusual and unseemly practice he was intensely mortified. The power controlling him was so great that at times he would turn over fences, just as though they were naught.

Miss Liddell informs me of a strange gift possessed by herself. In due course of time the spirits would write letters in an unknown tongue. One of these letters was communicated at Mount Lebanon, where it was translated, and the interpretation written out in full. The spirit letter was sent to Freegift Wells, who placed it within his vest pocket, buttoned his coat over it and then went to the school-room. Arriving there he said, "What do you see?" Miss Liddell, still in her teens, replied, "I see a letter in your vest pocket." "Read it," commanded the elder. She read it and wrote it out in full. This was forwarded to Mount Lebanon, and on comparing it with the translation there, both agreed exactly in every particular. It was then that Elder Wells determined on a quick method of communicating with Mount Lebanon. He wrote a letter, pinned it near the left shoulder of Miss Liddell's dress, and commanded her to take it to Mount Lebanon. She was not only nonplussed, but greatly grieved, and bursting into tears, went to her eldress, and stated the case. The eldress kindly told her to go to her room and remain quiet. She obeyed, threw herself on her cot and after having composed herself, she felt her body lifted up and then passed out of the window, and rapidly glided over the earth, passing rivers, cities and forests, until she came to the community at Mount Lebanon. When she arrived there no one noticed her. She passed on until she came to a very large house and entered the doorway. Here she saw two young Sisters who recognized and spoke to her. One of them unpinned the message, when Miss Liddell immediately glided back to Union Village. In due course of mail Elder Wells received an answer to the message. So delighted was he with the success of his enterprise that he sent Miss Liddell on a second errand. On her way back she became greatly frightend by being pursued by an immense animal in shape like a hog. She then absolutely refused ever to go on a similar errand.

The operations appear to have been manifold. For Dec. 6, 1838, it is rcorded that "public meeting to-day presented a scene hitherto unparalleled for involuntary operations, especially among the Sisters; a large number came into the meeting house shaking, bowing and jerking, and continued at it throughout meeting with additional power and velocity and returned home under similar operations; there was no attempt to form into ranks till near the close of meeting, and even then, many went whithersoever they were carried by this miraculous impulse."

On January 13, 1839, a number of boys, 6, 8, 10 and 12 "year old, were carried out of time, and many times be in the company of departed friends who were well known to us; they would bring and take love from and to the spiritual world, and learn songs from good spirits and angels, and sing them unconsciously (to all appearance) until those of us in time would learn them and unite in the strain. They would sometimes see beautiful spacious mansions, and see the angelic hosts in their beautiful worship." On March 3rd, there were about 20 in the trance state in public meeting, and on the 10th nearly 60 messages were received from the world of spirits. The following notice taken from the Record for July 18, 1839, exhibits some of the extreme measures to which the Believers were subjected:

"The exercises in our meetings are mostly very simple and mortifying. These gifts are often prescribed to us by revelation. We are numberless times required by messages of inspiration to stoop down and eat simplicity off of the floor. and a vast many other little requisitions that have no kind of agreement with what the wise of this world call even common sense:—Nay, they are revolting to the wisdom and pride of man : and to this end are they given, no doubt, to mortify and subdue the haughty pride of man."

EXTRAORDINARY CREDULITY.

That the great majority were exceedingly credulous is given over and over again in the MS. records. The following extract from the Church Journal for July 1, 1840, may be used in evidence :

"This evening the Church met at the meeting house, in pursuance of a message from Mother Ann—requesting us to meet and labor, in particular, for a further increase in the power and gifts of God. There was a general attendance of the chh. and it was thought, that in some respects, the meeting exceeded any one we ever saw. There was one gift which presented a solemn scene: viz., a young visionist girl about 15.—being inspired, received, and administered a gift to the people from mother: namely: that there was a large spring in the midst of the meeting house, that the Eldership were to form in a circle around the spring: and mother's children that were justified might come forward (2 or 3 at a time) and kneel down in the spring, and the elders were to mark them: this was attended to by the whole assembly." Another visionist had the Society drinking at a fountain near the corner of the church building. Credulity will farther be illustrated under proper selections.

PUBLIC EXCLUDED.

It is probable that many of these strange transactions had been witnessed by the public, and finally, some of the cooler heads, realizing that Believers were making themselves objects of derision to the outside world, deemed it necessary to make certain absolute restrictions. Hence, in the "Western Star," published at Lebanon, for July 22, 1842, a notice was given to the public, which is here transcribed :

"TO THE PUBLIC."

It becomes our duty, as acting Trustees of the United Society at Union Village (commonly called Shakers), to give information that the Public Meetings will be discontinued in this Society thro'out the season and probably for one year or more to come. The Society feel it to be their duty to God, in a special manner at the present time, to

spend the Sacred Day of His appointment in solemn prayer and supplication that we may be enabled to walk more closely with our God
and thereby merit His blessing and protection to preserve us from all
sin and its consequent condemnation. And we are called and required
by His Holy Angels to spend every day of our lives in the solemn fear
of God, and in a special manner His Holy Sabbath in walking softly
and humbly before Him; and to enable us to offer acceptable Offerings
of prayer and thanksgiving to a pure and Holy God. But we regret to
say, that for some years past many have thronged our Meetings, with
no higher motives, than to pass time away, and satisfy and amuse a vain
curiosity at the expense of the peace and repose of those who assembled
with sincere and honest hearts, to devote themselves to the solemn worship of God, and in sacred reverence to His Holy Son, the Savior of
fallen Man;—before whom we are called, in a special manner to walk
softly and humbly, and to watch and pray without ceasing.

"We are the friends and well-wishers of all mankind, and deeply de-
plore the unhappy condition of lost Man, and we shall, and do pray to
God without ceasing, for their and our redemption and restoration. But
it is thro' the revealed will of God only, that all the inhabitants of
the Earth can be protected; and in disobedience to the same, shall we
with all the rest of the human Family be left to drink deeply of his
rolling judgments, which slumber not, but are even now at the door
—sent forth from Him in whose Hands we all are, and whose mercy
every soul will yet most humbly implore, who finds a mansion in His
Kingdom of peace. Under these considerations, we think it more consistent with our present duty, to hold our meetings retired from the
world of mankind, that we may feel more perfectly devoted and given
up to prayer and supplication to seek the mercy and favor of God, than
to be thronged and disturbed by a giddy multitude, who, in general, resort here for no good purpose.—But all such as desire information respecting the religious faith and principles of the Society, will be duly
attended to when they apply.—To prevent disappointing sincere and well
disposed persons who might come from a distance to attend our meetings,
together with a short statement of our reasons, is the object of the
present notice.

"DANIEL BOYD,
"ITHAMAR JOHNSON,
"DAVID PARKHURST."

"Union Village, July 18, 1842."

The Church Journal for Aug. 7, 1842, contains the following:

"This morning the two following Commandments, received from the
Savior, were set up in the form of Public Notices, in little frames cov-

ered with glass. One was set up near the paling in front of the meeting house, and the other was similarly situated in front of the office.

'A COMMANDMENT FROM THE HOLY SAVIOR, REVEALED BY DIVINE IN-
SPIRATION, JULY 21, 1842.

"Thus saith the Holy Savior: Enter not into this holy sanctuary, nor open the gates of the enclosure: for I have taken up my abode in this place. And for the purification of Zion, I have caused her doors to be shut, and her gates closed, that none but my chosen people may enter in. Many who have come to this holy place, have come with unclean hands and defiled hearts, to make sport of the work of God! Therefore I have caused the doors of this Holy Sanctuary to be closed against all strangers And now as an evidence to the children of men that I have taken up my abode in this place; I have caused Sign to be erected here, with my Commandment written upon it. Enter not into this holy Sanctuary, to disturb the peace of my chosen people; but go your way and the gospel will be preached to you in due season. No one that will obey my counsel, and go their way in peace, shall ever suffer loss for the same; for I will reward them, and call them to my feast when the time has come. But on them that break over the bounds wh a I have set, and fear not to disobey my words, there shall come sore affliction and distress."

'A COMMANDMENT FROM THE HOLY SAVIOR, REVEALED BY DIVINE IN-
SPIRATION, JULY 21, 1842.

"Thus saith the Holy Savior: There is a place of trade and public business. But enter it not on the holy Sabbath. For this day is set apart for my people to worship the living God, undisturbed by the cares and burdens of earthly things. Yea, this day I require my peculiar people in this Holy Zion, to be entirely excluded from the world: Therefore enter not upon this consecrated ground on the holy Sabbath. Yea, fear ye to break my commandments, or to make light of everything that is here done in my name, lest there be sore and heavy judgments sent on you for the same. Yea I say, let all be careful how they speak concerning this Holy Zion; for the time may yet come, when you will humbly seek for a home in this retired mansion, to escape the judgments and afflictions that are rolling on the wicked. When you enter into this holy ground (between Sabbaths) to do business with my people; be quiet and still; do your duty and go away peaceably and you shall find favor in my sight. But if you come merely to make sport and run over order, then you shall not prosper: but all that you do, will prove a curse on your own hands. Now I say, let all believe, and regard the words that I have spoken; for Zion shall flourish, while the lofty towers of Babel shall be broken to pieces."

These signs were taken down on Christmas following.

*26

As might be inferred, the most frequent visitor from the world of spirits was Ann Lee, the founder of the sect. Following closely in her visitations was William Lee, the brother of Ann. The manifestations assigned their origin and close to Ann. The visionists were not united concerning Mother Ann's visits. On March 13, 1842, it was announced that "Mother Ann was present, and paid the Church her last visit before she returns to her heavenly abode. She gave us her parting blessing and instructions, in two or three pretty lengthy addresses through her inspired Instrument. The scene was truly sublime, solemn and deeply affecting; insomuch that the assembly shed tears freely. There were several of the Inspired ones who saw, and bore witness to Mother's presence on this occasion." Nevertheless she was the most frequent of all the visitants long after the above period. Among the spiritual visitors were Jesus Christ and all his Apostles, the prophets Nathan and Isaiah, the angels Muculan and Urias, Angel of Mercy, Angel of Judgment, Angel of Peace, Angel of Strength, Holy Angel of Love, Holy Angel of Wisdom, Holy Message Bearing Angel, Washington, Bonaparte's Army, Indians, Laplanders, etc., etc. Generally the Church was filled with whole troops of angels, and frequently an angel would stand in the center of the floor of the Church.

The Indians, who cut such a common figure among mediums, first appeared at Union Village May 9, 1839. "They brought us presents, love, etc. These Indians are often seen by those who are under inspiration: They have embraced Mother's gospel in the spiritual world and they appear in color, singing, dancing, dress, etc., just as they did in time. This evening Pocahontas, the Indian princess, was seen in our meeting. She touched an inspired one (among the sisters) on the head, who forthwith began to speak in the Indian tongue; and could not then, and for some time afterwards, speak only in the Indian tongue. The presents we receive from the Indians are highly characteristic of their peculiar manners and customs." The Indians again appeared on the 11th, but dropped out until Sept. 24, 1843, when they came in force with other nationalities.

On Dec. 13, 1843, the meeting was "attended by a rough savage and hollowing Indian, untractable and boisterous, but finally calmed down, told the bad, and became much more reasonable." The Indians appear to have been frequent visitors down to 1845. As the Message Book is missing the character of these revelations is sunk in oblivion.

Washington, with David Darrow and a large company of poor people, visited the Society on Sunday, Oct. 4, 1846. Washington and David Darrow simply wanted to know if the Shakers were willing to receive the poor of their company into their Society.

VISITS OF JESUS CHRIST.

The Savior of Man appears to have been a frequent visitor at Union Village, but through whom we are left in entire ignorance. His first visitation was on July 18, 1842. I here subjoin the account in the words of the Hampton MS: "We received a gift from the Holy Savior, through an Inspired messenger; — that at 6:30 p. m. He would come and view us all in our respective places and callings. And that at 7 o'clock p. m. He required all to be in their rooms, sitting upright in two straight rows facing east and west; — and that two Brethren should be selected to accompany Him to every room, to visit and notice every one in silence. — This solemn duty was delegated to Brethren Ashbel Kitchell and Lewis Valentine, who went round to every room in the First Order, walking softly as was required. After this, the Family proceeded to the meeting room, and after a short meeting, the solemn requisition closed. At this meeting we were informed what manner of gifts the Savior had bestowed upon us; —viz., Faith, Charity and Wisdom. This same solemn gift was ministered to the Second Order and Second Family on this same evening."

Jesus frequently visited the Community in company with Mother Ann, made speeches and composed songs. During His first visit He went also to the North Family and there taught a young sister "a very beautiful little anthem," running thus:

"O hearken to me my dear little ones, who have faithfully kept my precepts and laws, and have walked in low san ra va through sorrow and tribulation. For you I have brought a treasure of love, and a crown, and a crown, and a shining crown, and a ro-o-o-o-be of righteousness and beauty."

On January 25, 1846, Jesus is reported to have said in church meeting: "The younger class and rising generation were very much lacking in the true spirit of thankfulness for the many blessings by which they were surrounded. They could not conceive of the misery and wretchedness that the children of this world, thousands and thousands of them suffer'd daily, in privations of food and clothing and all manner of Comforts, which they enjoyed all the time here in a luxury of abundance. Much less could they realize the infinite blessing of the Gospel of Mother with which they were surrounded, and made able by Obedience to keep a sound justification. I say the young and rising generation in the Zion of God in this place, cannot draw a just comparison between their situation and others in the world, and for this reason there is a great lack of the true spirit of thankfulness, but it is desirable that on this subject there should be an increase. Moreover there was a lamentable deficiency of an interested feeling among the people in general, and particularly among the rising generation and younger part, insomuch that often they would pass by a fence down, or a gate open, and not put up the one or shut the other, because it was not their special duty, nor even would they take the trouble to inform a deacon, saying it was not their business. But this is not the way for believers to do; but true Children of their Mother consider'd they had an interest in everything pertaining to the gospel, as well in temporals as in spirituals, and in all cases woud learn to act and do, as people would who had an interest."

A SPIRIT MEETING.

The record of Part 2, Vol. J, of the meetings from July 6, 1845, to Oct. 31, 1847 (which practically closes the Record), shows that every meeting was virtually a counterpart of others that had been held. As an example of all I herewith transcribe the first recorded session of Vol. J, Part 2:

"July 6, 1845. Church Meeting. Being assembled, the meeting was opened in the usual manner. After the first anthem was sung, the seats were brought forward.—We sat down and Elder John Martin read an inspired book which was given at Holy Mount, New Lebanon, concerning the true order of the Godhead — The existence of Original Evil — and the conception and birth of the Two Anointed Ones — The Holy Savior and Blessed Mother Ann the head of the new Creation of God.— This communication was the most satisfactory of anything I ever heard on the subject.—

"After laboring a few songs we were visited by a large company

of Holy Angels one of whom addressed us thro an instrument to the
following effect,—

"'Behold, O my people, what I now say is that which you have
heard from time to time—It is nevertheless the word of the most high
God, and it shall be given you in a way in which ye shall be able to
understand the meaning—Let every soul be engaged, there is no time to
sleep and slumber in this day of light, but every soul should be awake
and able to sense the goodness of their Heavenly Father, by daily keeping his holy fear and putting their hands to work and their hearts to
God in the line and way as directed by His visible Order.—Hear ye my
words at this time—What I mean by putting your hands to work and
your hearts to God, is not merely to do what you are requested by those
who direct in temporal things, but to improve all your hours in doing good
and let no time pass idly by — Ye know not all the plans of the enemy,
neither do ye know what is cloaked in the wisdom of God—but these
words are as unchangeable as the living God, and may be relied on with
safety: 'hands to work and hearts to God'—The Enemy only wants to
lead you one step at a time, for if he should aim at more he would
open your eyes and hazard being detected and his designs frustrated, but
if he can lead you one step and lull you to sleep making you feel secure he will be encouraged to lead you on and on till your soul is
lost—It hath not entered into the heart of man the good things that
God has laid up for those who faithfully serve him; but remember,
one half hour spent in idleness and the pleasures of time will do you
great harm — put ye on the fear of God and in obedience to his word
ye shall from this time be blest in your undertakings.' The instrument
then bore witness to the mighty power of God as a burning fire that
was now poured out upon the Assembly—which was also witnessed by a
number.

"After more exercise the same Instrument said he could testify that
he saw in this meeting that the heavens and earth had drawn nigh together (a short pause under agitation) exclaimed in the form of a query:
Who knows, who can tell what God will yet do in this branch of his
Zion? What means this pulling one this way and one that—one building up and one pulling down—One saying I'll be obedient, thus and so,
but will take liberty to judge of what I please—You may say so and so
and I will think so and so, etc.—The day is at hand and is even now
come when, if we do not stand united and purge out the evil and discordant spirits we will all perish together—There is here at this time a
mighty Angel from the East, he is covered with beauty—he is clothed
with power to do the will of God—The day is come when the separation will be made between the precious and the vile, and that line
will be drawn over which if they pass destruction will be their fate—
Yea the day is come when the wicked will see that the work of God
is one work and all shall be made able to feel it—(a short pause under
heavy labor of mind) he resumed—I feel poor and needy—I feel utterly

unable to portray the spirit of inspiration that is given me at this time
—there is a great flow of it at this time poured upon the body—I feel
mean in the sight of God — It· is I who am possessed of evil — It is I
who have a fleshly nature that stands opposed to good — I can find plenty
in myself without looking to others — I do want the prayers of all my
good Brethren and Sisters, and I will covenant that I will come into the
work of God more thoroughly than ever I have done — I will crucify
the flesh in myself, and not look to other souls to find something to
purge out — It is me that feels now to supplicate my good Ministry,
Elders, Brethren and Sisters to help me to do the work in my own
soul that the increasing work of God demands — And now saith a Holy
Angel, — 'The light of heaven is poured upon you more abundantly than
Ever and all that will receive it shall be able to see more clearly every
thing that stands opposed to the work of God.' — Another Instrument
spake saying:

"The bright heralds of God are flying over our heads saying: 'Know
ye O Zion, we visit every branch of Zion and behold we wing our way
over the Earth from the East to the West and from the North to the
South, to waken up souls and prepare them for the gospel — O Zion!
O Zion prepare, prepare to receive the souls that will be sent unto you:
for Lo! sorrow, yea sorrow doth mark their steps. 70 is the number now
present in this mission.'

"An inspired Anthem was then sung as follows by (name in pho-
nography) — 'Hear, Hear ye O Zion, for lo the day of the Lord Almighty
is at hand, and his precious word is not yet ended with you. — Behold
O Zion the beautiful gifts of Heaven, hear the sweet sounds that come
from the mansion above — Heaven and earth shall join the sweet
chorus with the holy Angels of light who goeth to them that cry for
help — O sound ye, sound ye your trumpets with the power of God.
Yea with the Angels that go forth to do the work of the Lord — Prepare,
prepare O Zion to receive the lost Nations of the earth; for behold they
come to find a place of rest for their souls, so prepare ye, for they shall
be upheld by the strength, by the light and by the power of the Lord God
in his Zion in this place.'

"Another Instrument spoke thus: 'Mark ye well the day of this
date, says the Holy Angel — from this day shall Zion's light increase
— mark ye well the day — I will kindle the flame that will purify the
courts — Yea from this day shall the work of Inspiration increase, and
all who will may receive the mighty power of God' — One of the 70
holy Angels has planted the tree of charity by the fountain, that all may
receive charity therefrom if they desire it; — We all then partook of the
fruit of this tree.—

"Another holy Angel desired to speak, if in union — 'I am a holy
Angel that is sent at this time from the holy throne of God to effect
his most holy will — I am the holy Angel of decision that will effect
a separation between the servants of God and the servants of evil, for

this purpose have I come at this time to do his will — It is not, saith the Angel, in the power of mortals to know what is in the future, nor what will be the work of the Angels in this place — I saw this Zion afar off. I examined her Watchmen and found that they slept not, but were watchful at their posts. But I looked again among the flock and found that some slept, and behold now my work is of God and who may hinder? My command is from Him and who shall disannual it? The light of God has gone forth and is given unto you and shall prove a savor of life unto life, or of death unto death to every soul — I will do the work for which I am sent, it shall not be the work of another — I will dig and evil shall be cast out till there shall be nothing left to annoy in all God's holy mountain — Nothing shall remain to oppress — When this day shall come Zion shall be as a flowered garden — Yea, the time shall come when all shall flourish, when virtuous beauty shall spring up as the tender grass in the vernal season—but before this time shall come to pass, heavy tribulation shall roll on, and the cup ye shall drink will be tinged with crimson — Ye cannot escape it — ye cannot cart it way — yet ye shall be able to drink it, and it is not to be drank 100 years hence. but it is now prepared for you — Nothing can stand that corrupts in the Zion of God on earth — Who are ye that tremble at this moment, lest the light of God expose you to his Zion? — And who are ye that think to hide from his searching light? But ye that stand in the light, take courage and ye shall in the end be crowned with everlasting joy.'

"Elder John then spoke a few words which the writer (Elder Harvey L. Eads) could not distinctly hear — At the close of the meeting the Bros. and Sisters blessed the Ministry and Elders."

SESSIONS AT JEHOVAH'S CHOSEN SQUARE.

It was early revealed that twice a year, for ten years, the members of all the communities should worship on the highest point of land, within the boundaries of said communities. This land was "Jehovah's Chosen Square." Every Society received, at the same time, a spiritual name, viz., Union Village — Wisdom's Paradise; Mt. Lebanon — Holy Mount; Watervliet, N. Y. — Wisdom's Valley; Whitewater — Lonely Plain of Tribulation; North Union — Valley of God's Pleasure; Groveland — Union Branch; Tyringham — City of Union; Hancock — City of Peace; Enfield, Ct. — City of Love; Enfield, N. H. — Chosen Vale; Harvard — Lovely Vineyard; Shirley — Pleasant Garden; Canterbury— Holy Ground; Alfred — Holy Land; Sabbathday Lake—Chosen Land. Who gave these names, and who indicated

"Jehovah's Chosen Square." although I have persistently inquired, I have been unable to ascertain.

Jehovah's Chosen Square was located about two-thirds of a mile northeast of Union Village Meeting House, and consisted of an enclosure of about half an acre. This was the spot dedicated to the great outpouring of the Spirit. It was also a proper place for the manifestations from the world of spirits. The following is an account of a meeting held on this spot, on May 24, 1846:

"This morning the whole Society met with the intention of visiting the chosen square. Elder John open'd meeting by stating that he consider'd our privilege great, that we were kindly noticed of God, in being taught the way of God, and being instructed in the doctrine and practice of self-denial. He wished all to be engag'd and be alive in their spirits, and labor for the quickening power of God, to bless and strengthen us through the coming day. After dancing a lively song and gaining some freedom we were inform'd that the holy Savior and Mother Ann was with us and would accompany us to the chosen square.

"As usual we march'd to the square to the sound of music; stopping once on our way to sound on our trumpets; on arriving at the gate we were met by a large company of holy Angels from the S. West. They said if we would turn to the South and blow with our trumpets they would unite with us tro' the day. They now march'd in with us, and recommended to us be simple and labor for the precious gifts of God, promising to the faithful and devoted that they should experience the blessing of God. They declared that as the kingdom of heaven could only be obtained by those who were willing to become as little children, so neither can the gifts of God be truly realis'd, without becoming as a little child, but all that will humble themselves shall feel a fullness of the goodness of God in the present instance.

"Moreover they testified that the Love of God, and the power of God would be manifest here to day in an exceeding degree, that all might feel their freedom, bear the word of testimony to one another, and enjoy a fullness of the blessing and goodness of God. And indeed as the meeting progressed, the truth of the Angel's word was particularly fulffilled. The power of God fell on the assembly in a wonderful manner, many powerful and awakening testimonies were deliver'd, and many and diverse were the gifts of God which were receiv'd by the people, some spake with tongues, and others prophesied, and spake of the wonderful works of God. Many under the gift of inspiration spake much to the edification of the people. There was also a general expression of thankfulness for the privileges which this pure and holy Gospel affords. Mother pours her love on the multitude, it is flowing all

around and the company feel its invigorating influence; the blessing
flows in a full stream, and the baptism becomes universal tro' the body.

"In the midst of this outpuoring of the spirit, there came a large
company of departed spirits and asked permission to unite with us, and
liberty was granted them, and immediately 500 Angels desired admittance. They came cloth'd with Love and blessing from the heavens for
the children assembled in the chosen square to worship God. Father
Joseph* now arrives, and requests six of his class to go to the tree
of victory which is standing in the S. East corner of the square, and
take their baskets and fill them, then bring them forward and give the
Contents of them to the people. — An Angel entered the Square with us
that has a word to the people, if it is in Union; Granted and he proceeds, 'Hear all ye people, the day of God is at hand, and a great and
mighty work shall be manifest amongst the people of the world; such as
was never known before. Remember what You have come here for, Remember that all who have come here have a sacrifice to make, which will
take all that is selfish. This sacrifice cannot be made without the help
of God. No one will pretend to be stronger than Jesus, and he said
of himself he could do nothing. We have come here to make the sacrifice, and to strive to gain the favor of God, to enable us to do the
will of God. And now to day is strength offer'd to all. Yea this is a day
for all to come forward and drink freely of the waters of Life, and I
am now ready to pour out the blessing, the power and strength into
every soul, that is hungering and thirsting after righteousness. It
may be received by bowing. And the Angel cries aloud. 'He that soweth
to the flesh shall of the flesh reap corruption, but he that soweth to
the spirit shall of the spirit reap life everlasting.'

"Father William,* Father James† and Father David‡ say 'Liberate
Your Spirits, and gather now of the treasures of heaven, for God will yet
send thousands to this place to worship him on this ground, and for
that reason You should be wide awake and alive in the work that Ye be
not found in the way of them that are Yet to come. And mind Ye,
the work of God from this time will be quick and powerfull and Ye
have no time to spare in idleness or indifference if You intend to make
the living substance of the gospel Your only treasure. O dear Children, the fruits of heaven are flowing all around You, do gather them
now while You have opportunity, strengthen Your souls in good, and
learn to possess Your vessels in honor. Many express'd thankfulness for
the freedom of the day, and thanked Mother for the pure and holy

---

* I know not who is here referred to. Doubtless the spirit of a departed Shaker, perhaps Joseph Meacham.

* William, brother of Ann Lee.

† James Whitaker.

‡ David Darrow, first bishop of Union Village.

gospel, which enabled them to secure the blessings which flow from it. Thankful for deliverance from the bondage which the Devil casts round the Soul; deliverance from sin, from Evil, and error, and made free to worship God in the beauty of holiness in spirit and in truth as simple innocent children. The people seem full to overflowing, they break out in such Language as the folowing: 'I know this to be the power of God, and am not mistaken; I am thankful for it, for the Gospel is the power of God unto salvation in deed and in truth, and I know it, and feel it this moment. O it is a pretty way; it is the best thing I ever knew and I will be thankful for it; Let the flesh go, I will not be subject to it; I am thankful to God, he has made me able to hate the flesh, and keep it under subjection. The angels have the heavenly fruits and blessings from heaven and have ministered them' to us and we feel the divine impulse in the stimulous of Love in our souls, Glory.—An inspir'd one cried out. 'I know and feel by the inspiration of the holy Spirit, that the day is nigh at hand that God will separate the wicked from the good; Yea bow low and be wise, and see that Ye hurt not the oil and the wine, for all shall be accountable for the use they make of their privilege in the gospel. The Love I feel extends to all souls, and the Love of our heavenly Parents and all the good Spirits which are here are commingling with ours. A holy Angel has just gone to the N. West with a proclamation that God is about to bring all mankind into judgment immediately. And O let Zion be prepared for the souls of men for the time is at hand that God will require You to open Your hearts wide, and that you feel nothing but Love towards all nations, and keep not back Your stores, nor Your Love and Your sincere desires for the Children of men. It is the desire of the holy Savior for us to sound a shout to the four quarters of the Earth. And then kneel down and pray for the nations and kingdoms of this world, that they may feel the arrows of conviction, and be brought where the power of God may be found to their salvation. — An intermission of half an hour, previous to which there was read to the attending Spectators a small essay of Counsel to the world entitled 'The word of the Lord to all People that shall follow his chosen ones to the Holy feast upon this consecrated ground,' extracted from a Communication given at the East on an occasion somewhat similar — After the intermission we again assembled and the power again for a time ran through the congregation, filling every Vessel full of joy and delight; until our bodies were wearied, and our souls replenished and it was thought reasonable to adjourn for the present, Elder Jno. seriously recommending to all to open their hearts wide, to receive any and all souls which the goodness of God might see fit to prepare as subjects of the Gospel, and in doing this we might reasonably expect a continuation of blessing.— As usual we march'd home, closing the service of the day, having been together about 5 hours."

SPIRIT PERSECUTION.

It is an unfortunate fact that power is a dangerous weapon. in the hands of most men. The weaker the man the less considerate is he with the weapon. While the leaders at Union Village were imbued with the principles of Shakerism and were not•liable to be too arbitrary, yet they were of a class that would thoroughly entrench themselves in their positions. That they used this spiritualism to further their own aggrandizement there can be no question, even if evidence was wanting outside the MSS. still preserved. The alleged revelations show that the sensitives catered to the leaders. During the whole period of ten years there was a constant flow of gifts from the spirit world,. consisting of boxes of jewels, baskets of fruits, rare fruit trees, etc., etc., most of which came from Mother Ann Lee, — the precious ones almost invariably bestowed upon the Ministry. The sensitives were emboldened even to use the authority of Jesus Christ, for, on April 12, 1846, the following words were brazenly attributed to this the greatest of all Teachers: "The Ministry and Elders were impressed from a divine source, and thus enabled to give such advice as your general conditions demanded, that it originated from a spirit of Love and tenderness and would do you good." On Aug. 24 the following "six testifying Angels" appealed "with great earnestness to the Church in behalf of supporting the visible Lead and head of the body, and also communicated fearful denunciations against the opposite spirit and its adherents." During the same session, John Martin, then first in the Ministry, "spoke with vehement energy and living power,. denouncing those who were the cause of the obstruction with terrible and withering effect, and warning them in the most feeling and searching manner to come to the light before it was too late."

During the reign of design and credulity there were Shakers. who were not swept into this maelstrom of fanaticism. They came in for their share of reproof and upbraiding, as may be witnesed by the public reprimand given Jan. 20, 1847:

"Our heavenly Parents are weeping over us, there are some who still continue to sit in the judgment seat from day to day and to insult the living God in his holy Order. The church must become a pure receptacle for honest souls to gather to, and her members must be holy and exemplary. Ephraim must be joined to his Idols if he will have it so; all have been warned again and again, and that which will not have the gospel must and will be separated from that which will obey it, and keep its precepts, for all opposition to the gospel shall assuredly be put down forever. The truths and precepts and laws of the gospel are not all to be explained away, but they must be believ'd and obey'd in simplicity and truth. Believers in Zion must live the faith of the gospel, and if a young believer comes in amongst us, he must see, yea and feel that here is the holy gospel of salvation. The armies of God surrounded the house, and blazing light shone round about, and all thro' it, and a stream of the burning shone in a piercing ray on the heart of each individual, showing to the Angels his true state and shutting up all hope of ever turning again from the light of God. While the armies of God were moving swiftly along, the instruments with streaming eyes and convulsive struggles, of extreme pain and suffering cried and pray'd, saying Awake! Awake! O dear brethren and sisters, Awake! O Ephraim, awake, for the day of judgment in Zion is now here, and yet will you try to reason every thing away. Will you still attempt to account for everything with your Philosophy. How can you sleep and slumber a moment. O proclaim it on the house tops, Proclaim it in the high way. Destruction cometh as a whirlwind, O brethren and sisters tremble and fear exceedingly. O repent, repent: for the hour of God is come: we must be broken to pieces, and find a contrite spirit.

"Through the whole meeting the excitement was intense. It was testified that the Zion of God was seen as a large wheel turning swiftly round, and there was three Cogs broken. And also it was seen as a large tree, vigorous and stately; but as having three limbs wither'd and dead and dropping to the earth. The instruments suffer'd in an astonishing manner very uncommonly so, and almost everything they did or said was indicative of extreme distress and pain."

EXPULSION OF RICHARD M'NEMAR.

Among the extreme actions was the expulsion of Richard McNemar, Malcolm Worly and Garner McNemar, by order of Freegift Wells. This unfortunate circumstance I have entered into at length in my "Life of Richard McNemar," and need not be here repeated. Since that book was published I have learned from the Mount Lebanon Shakers that Freegift created trouble at Watervliet, New York, and also in the North Family at Mount Lebanon.

SPIRIT BOOKS.

The Records make frequent reference to the spirits presenting books in the meetings, but as to their nature nothing was said.
I have already enumerated four of these spirit books which were
published. For Jan. 7, 1840, the Church Journal states: "We
continue to have an inexhaustible supply of Books, letters and
messages from the spiritual world, accompanied by verses, songs,
and anthems, many of which are in unknown tongues." There
are two references (Mar. 1 and Dec. 25, 1840) to the "Holy
Laws of Zion," without any definite description of the contents
of the same; and the only clew given is that it "is a sacred instrument," and required most of a day to read it. It exists only in
MS. form, — "Written by the Angel Vikalen. Appointed and
recommended by the Ministry and Elders of the Church at New
Lebanon." It was the handiwork of Philemon Stewart, and contains 128 quarto MS. pages. The following are the "Particulars
to be observed in reading The Holy Laws of Zion:"

"Commence reading at half past eight A. M. to all the Family
that can attend that are 14 years old and over. See page 60.

"Continue reading till you have finished the 61st page, then make
8 low bows, — then repeat the following words with 3 bows: 'I will
keep — thy holy Laws — O Zion.' Then let the assembly again take their
seats, and read to the end of the 64th page. This completes the fore-
noon reading.

"Commence reading in the afternoon at half past one (see page
103) at the 65th page, and after reading the 15th part, have all under
18 years old leave the room; then read the Note at page 110, and part
16; — then let those who went out return, and continue the reading until
you finish part 20th, page 105.

"Then let all the people bow three times; then with 3 more bows
repeat the following words; 'Even so Lord, — let it be, — Amen.' Then
repeat the words of the roll, at page 104, with 4 bows, viz, 'Love! Love!
— from God — your heavenly — Father.' Then kneel and pray, as directed at page 108, near the bottom.

"Again commence reading at the Communication, page 103, skip page
110, and go through the supplement; which completes the reading. Those
who read should have three hours notice to gain a proper gift. See
page 60th."

I judge the most popular of all the MSS. of this period was the "Harvard Book." which contained the life and sufferings of Jesus and Ann Lee, "Given by inspiration in the Church at Harvard, Oct., 1841," by William Leonard. It is a quarto of 172 pages.

ANGELIC SONGS.

References frequently occur to the songs of the angels, and some wonderful effects of the same. An instance of this kind is recorded for Oct. 4, 1846:

A sister lying "on the floor, was heard learning a little song from the Angels, and soon she sang it loud enough to be caught by the singers, and when it was started up fresh from the heavens, in the very gift of divine inspiration, and sung by the singers in the same spirit, the effect on the assembly was almost like Electricity. All sprang for the floor, and as the Music made the heavens ring, so the dancing shook the immense house we were collected in, as tho' an earthquake was moving it; again and again was the sacred music called for, and again and again was the house shaken from end to end, by the exact and simultaneous movement in keeping time with the soul stirring song beginning

"Hail the day of Jubilee
Hail the day of Liberty."

The remainder I know not.

The following is a song of an angel delivered Nov. 1, 1846 in "a most sublime and moving time:"

"Now is the day, Call my children, O Yea call my Children from afar, and my little ones from the ends of the earth, call my children from afar, and my little ones from the ends of the earth, Lift up the trumpet in Zion, yea sound aloud the trumpet of God, and call the needy souls from the four quarters of the earth, for behold I have sheep that do not belong to this fold, they know not thy word, nor have they heard my call, but they are mine saith the Lord, and with my right arm will I bring them, from among the nations, and in my strength will I protect them. And for this cause have I sent forth my mighty Angels, and my flaming spirits over the earth. Therefore come, O ye Sons of affliction, and ye daughters of sorrow, make haste to obey my call, and learn to obey the voice of mine Anointed, for consolation yea sweet consolation is flowing from the heavens. Come O come ye desolate and afflicted from the North and from the South, from the East and from the West, for behold the gulph is opened, and will not more be clos'd, untill it swallow up the wicked, and destroy the ungodly from among the righteous seed, and they shall be separated forever. Behold the day is come when I will call home my lost sheep. O Ye holy saints of God, pray for them, lift up the voice and cry aloud for the lost sheep of the fold, for to the fold shall they come, and within my enclosures of safety shall they flock, as doves to the windows shall they come. Blow ye aloud the trumpet, O ye children of Zion, and behold my chosen ones shall come. O who will raise up the voice in mercy, and sweetly call my wanderers home they shall sound the blessed sound of salvation, and O my Lovely Children, ye who are own'd by the most high, and blessed by the God of heaven, let your souls flow out in Love to the poor lost children of this world, and pray ye O my little ones, that my scattered flock may find the fold, and praise to God, and glory to his holy name, shall sound and sound, Yea sweetly sound, because redemption and salvation shall reach the honest soul. Therefore call my wandering Lambs, and erring children home. Yea to the fold of safety call them home and securely in the everlasting gospel shall they find a lasting home, and they shall skip and play before the Lord, and rejoice in thankfulness and holy praise before the God of their salvation, forever and forever more — Amen."

DECLINE OF SPIRITUALISM.

Near the close of the year 1847 the reign of Spiritualism practically came to an end. The people of Union Village had simply tired of it, although elsewhere foretold of a cessation by revelation. There was a gradual decline nevertheless, and as late as June, 1853, some of the young people were exercised by spiritual influence. Even to this day the spirits of departed Shakers are occasionally seen at Union Village, but no special account is made of it.

NOTE — For the MS. records used by me in the preparation of this paper my acknowledgments are due to Mr. James H. Fennessey, trustee of the Society at Union Village. I am also under obligations to Mr. Moore S. Mason, Secretary of the Society, for searching through the archives for such MSS. as would be of value in this investigation.

Franklin, Ohio, July 28, 1902.

ImTheStory.com

Personalized Classic Books in many genre's

Unique gift for kids, partners, friends, colleagues

Customize:

- Character Names
- Upload your own front/back cover images (optional)
- Inscribe a personal message/dedication on the
  inside page (optional)

Customize many titles Including

- Alice in Wonderland
- Romeo and Juliet
- The Wizard of Oz
- A Christmas Carol
- Dracula
- Dr. Jekyll & Mr. Hyde
- And more...

CPSIA information can be obtained
at www.ICGtesting.com
Printed in the USA
BVHW05s1223300718
523021BV00016B/287/P

9 781314 384758